Lecture Notes in Computer Science

Lecture Notes in Computer Science

Edited by G. Goos and J. Hartmanis

252

VDM '87
VDM – A Formal Method at Work

VDM-Europe Symposium 1987
Brussels, Belgium, March 23–26, 1987
Proceedings

Edited by D. Bjørner, C.B. Jones,
M. Mac an Airchinnigh and E.J. Neuhold

Springer-Verlag

Berlin Heidelberg New York London Paris Tokyo

Editors

Dines Bjørner
Department of Computing Science, Technical University of Denmark
DK-2800 Lyngby, Denmark

Cliff B. Jones
Department of Computer Science, University of Manchester
Manchester M13 9PL, United Kingdom

Mícheál Mac an Airchinnigh
Department of Computer Science, University of Dublin
Trinity College, Dublin, Ireland

Erich J. Neuhold
Gesellschaft für Mathematik und Datenverarbeitung mbH
Braunshardter Weg 11, D-6100 Darmstadt, FRG

CR Subject Classification (1987): D.2.2, D.3.1, F.3.2

ISBN 3-540-17654-3 Springer-Verlag Berlin Heidelberg New York
ISBN 0-387-17654-3 Springer-Verlag New York Berlin Heidelberg

Foreword

VDM-Europe is a technical advisory group to the *Commission of the European Communities* (CEC) in the general domain of *Information Technology*. As such, VDM-Europe is responsible to the CEC with respect to all issues concerning the specific formal software development method VDM[1]. In particular, it holds the brief to bring about more widespread awareness, use, development and standardisation of VDM in the *European Economic Community* (EEC).

The CEC recognises the important role that standards play in the harmonisation and development of the European software industry. Whereas the CEC does not itself devise such standards, it does use its good offices to promote such standards whenever and wherever they exist with the expressed intent to support the development of an open market within the EEC. A standardised use of VDM will give a strong competitive edge to the European software industry with respect to one formal software development method.

VDM is a formal method for the description and development of computer systems. Its formal descriptions (or "specifications") use mathematical notation to provide a precise statement of the intended function of a system. Such descriptions are built in terms of *models* of an underlying state with a collection of operations which are specified by pre- and post-conditions. VDM's design approach is guided by a number of *proof obligations* whose discharge establishes the correctness of design by either data reification or operation decomposition.

Thus it can be seen that VDM is a complete development method which addresses all of the stages of development from specification through to code. It has now reached such a stage of maturity that (commercially available) support tools are reported on in this Symposium.

The origins of the IBM Laboratory in Vienna go back to a group which Heinz Zemanek brought from the *Technische Hochschule* (now the "Technical University of Vienna"). The group initially worked on hardware projects. A compiler for ALGOL 60 followed. The recognition that language definition was a crucial issue for the future safe application of computers was emphasized by IBM's creation of the PL/I language. The Vienna group built on ideas of Elgot, Landin and McCarthy to create an *operational semantics* approach capable of defining the whole of PL/I including its TASKING features which involved parallelism. These massive reports were known as the "Universal Language Document 3" and appeared in three more or less complete versions. The meta-language used was dubbed by outsiders the "Vienna Definition Language" or VDL. As well as such people as Kurt Bandat, Hans Bekič, Peter Lucas and Kurt Walk, one member of the current Programming

---

[1] The "Vienna Development Method"

Committee (EN) was involved in these descriptions and another (CBJ) in the attempt to use them as the basis for compiler design in 1968/70.

The attempts to use the VDL definitions in design were in one sense successful; but they also showed clearly how the operational semantics approach could complicate formal reasoning in an unnecessary way. The Scott/Strachey /Landin work on *denotational semantics* was taking shape in Oxford, Hans Bekič had long been pressing the Vienna group to adopt a more mathematical approach, and CJ had shown a "functional semantics" for ALGOL 60 in a Hursley Technical Report. The challenge, starting in late 1972, to design a compiler which translated the evolving ECMA/ANSI standard PL/I language into the order code of a completely novel machine presented the ideal opportunity to try out the denotational semantics approach.

Another member of the PC (DB) joined the Vienna group in 1973 and CBJ also returned. The project was fraught with difficulties and did not result in a finished compiler because of IBM's decision to abandon the machine architecture. But it did create VDM.

The formal description of PL/I in a denotational style is contained in a 1974 Technical Report which was authored by Hans Bekič, Dines Bjørner, Wolfgang Henhapl, Cliff Jones and Peter Lucas. The notation used became known as "Meta-IV" (both this awful pun and the name "VDM" are due to DB).

The diversion of the IBM group to handle more practical problems led to its dissolution. Among others to leave, Wolfgang Henhapl became a Professor in Darmstadt, Peter Lucas moved to IBM Research in the US, and DB took a visiting chair at Copenhagen and then a permanent one at the Technical University of Denmark. Of the key people only Hans Bekič remained pursuing — in his spare time — important research on parallelism until his untimely death in 1982 (see Springer LNCS 177).

Like other dispersions of scientists, this one did not kill the ideas but led to a larger community. The first step was to publish what had been done and DB/CJ edited Springer's LNCS 61 to this end. DB pursued the language description and compiler development work with Danish colleagues. This led to descriptions of both Ada (see Springer's LNCS 98) and CHILL and the first validated European compiler for the Ada language. CJ picked up the work he had been doing on formal development methods for non-compiler problems. Between them, DB and CJ have published three books with Prentice Hall International on VDM. There are also numerous papers tackling problems such as parallelism.

Peter Lucas has applied formal methods to application problems and Wolfgang Henhapl has worked on a support system (PSG) for VDM specifications.

In fulfilment of the responsibilities set out by its brief, VDM-Europe has identified five specific areas of endeavour:

1. **Technology Transfer** awareness and use of VDM shall be promoted by means of education and training.

2. **Application** strategies and tactics adopted, and experience in the use of VDM, shall be recorded and analysed.

3. **Support Environments** issues such as the portability and reusability of specifications written in the VDM meta-language shall be addressed. In particular, the development of tools which support VDM will be of special interest.

4. **Foundations** as with all formal methods, VDM's mathematical foundations must be sound and complete. By its very nature, which is essentially mathematical, VDM will continue to evolve. There are open areas of research which need to be addressed. There are explicit relationships with other branches of mathematics that need to be elaborated.

5. **Standardisation** whilst VDM is continuously evolving, stable concentric kernels must be established for standardisation.

To ensure a coherent programme which addresses each of the areas of endeavour of VDM-Europe and to bring state-of-the-art research and practice in VDM to a wider audience, the Programme Committee has adopted a symposium[2] format for this meeting. Of the originators[3], Dines Bjørner, Cliff Jones, and Peter Lucas will present key papers. The other papers have been solicited from the respective VDM experts in their field.

VDM is a formal software development method that is practised in the software industry. Such is its state of maturity that the Programme Committee are pleased to announce that a significant number of the speakers come from industry. There is a major upheaval taking place in the whole philosophy of software development. The coining of the phrase "software engineering" has forced a comparison with traditional engineering disciplines where an end-product results from a very specific engineering process that may be partitioned into distinct phases. The experience in the use of VDM in the software industry will be of major significance in fuelling the revolution that is currently taking place in software development methods.

In VDM, as in mathematics in general, one notes the continuous tension that exists between researchers and practitioners. On the one hand, new ground is being broken, frontiers are being extended. On the other hand, that which was once novel and revolutionary is now stable. The stability of a VDM kernel is essential for the construction of tools and the associated

---

[2]Interestingly, among its definitions, the Oxford English Dictionary gives the following: "symposium: 1. Drinking party, esp. of ancient Greeks with conversation etc. after banquet; 2. Philosophical or other friendly discussion; ...".

[3]The "ancient Greeks"?

VDM Support Environments. It is just such a kernel that is the basis of the standardisation process. However, life at the frontier looks very different. The VDM novice is confronted immediately by a diversity of notations, all of which purport to express specifications in VDM. Such diversity is healthy and may be ascribed to several historical factors:

- Printing Technology - originally being a "pencil and paper" method, the VDM meta-language notation was bounded only by the ingenuity of those who used it. However, VDM material in published form gave rise to notational variants dictated by the available printing technology.

- Application Domains - the uses to which VDM was put differed to such an extent that methodological as well as notational variants sprang into existence. The most obvious of these differences is between the use of VDM in the description of programming languages and in other applications.

- Pedagogy - without wishing to be dogmatic, one may identify two extreme variants of the VDM meta-language notation. There is the one which most resembles mathematical notation, which is succinct, expressive and terse. At the other extreme—and this is the one most likely to appeal to conventional software practitioners—there is a verbose, programming-like notation. Pedagogical concerns tend to force a particular form of notation that is most likely to be accepted and adopted by students of VDM who share a particular culture.

The papers in this Symposium reflect that reality. It is imperative to realise that, irrespective of the particular notational variant used in a given paper, the underlying formal development method is VDM. The sessions on Standardisation Issues and the Panel Discussion will clarify the position of the VDM kernel and that body of notation for which tools are and will be made available.

It has been noted above that VDM is but one formal software development method in use in the European software industry. However, its position is unique. A glance at the Symposium programme indicates the wide range of European users. It is now the only formal software development method for which there is a technological advisory group of the CEC and this Symposium will surely mark a new era in the development and use of VDM in Europe.

D. Bjørner
C.B. Jones
M. Mac an Airchinnigh
E. Neuhold

TABLE OF CONTENTS

VDM Environments

Foundations I

Specifications

Foundations II

Standardisation Issues

A Case Study

Tutorial Papers

* Ada is a registered trademark of the U.S. Government
    (Ada Joint Program Office)

VDM: Origins, Hopes, and Achievements

Peter Lucas
IBM Almaden Research Center
650 Harry Road, San Jose, CA 95120-6099

1. Introduction

In this talk I want to trace the history of VDM by highlighting the important ideas that contributed to its present form and status. The emphasis of this paper is on ideas more than on events, persons, or institutions. Accounts of the history of the subject have been given elsewhere, for example in [Lucas78,Lucas81]. Historical details can also be found in [Bekic84]. A few remarks on history are, however, in order, together with a clarification of acronyms. VDM is short for Vienna Development Method, an allusion to the IBM Vienna Laboratory, which started relevant work in the early 1960's under the direction of Heinz Zemanek.

The Vienna Laboratory elaborated the subject for more than 15 years. Later the work was carried forward mostly by Dines Bjorner and his group at the Technical University of Denmark and the DDC, and by C.B. Jones and his group at the University of Manchester.

Initially, the focus was narrowly set on language definition and compiler design. Probably the most visible and best known result of the early period was a formal definition of PL/1 produced by the Vienna Laboratory in cooperation with the IBM UK Laboratories in Hursley. The Metalanguage in which the definition was written is known as VDL (short for Vienna Definition Language). However, much more was accomplished during the early period, including the first examples of rigorous proofs of certain compiler algorithms.

Later, the objective broadened to program development in general, including aspects of project management and programming in the large.

VDM in its present form is a method for designing software systems. VDM is equipped with a suitable notation (known as META-IV) for documenting designs. The result of a VDM design process is a series of specifications, starting with an abstract specification of the functions the desired system is intended to perform. Each specification in this series is more concrete and closer to the implementation than the previous one. Each level is linked to the previous one by an argument of correctness. Of course, the initial functional specification can only be linked by an informal argument to (informal) requirements.

Besides imposing an orderly process, there are two major advantages to documenting each level of the design. The documentation represents a tangible state of a project and is therefore a management tool for assessing the progress of a project. Secondly, it makes the design reusable. Since the levels of the design differ by the degree of abstraction, a redesign or reimplementation may only need to backtrack to an intermediate level.

The development of VDM was not an isolated effort but was influenced by related work in the scientific community.

2. Language Definition

The advent of high level languages in the late 50's and early 60's posed new problems. The stated purpose of high level languages was to make programs portable between different machines and between different implementations. Also, high level languages were meant to be problem oriented rather than designed to reflect the architecture of the implementing machine. Therefore the definition of these programming languages had to be independent of hardware and independent of particular implementations.

The Vienna Laboratory produced an early compiler for ALGOL 60. The experience was painful. The language definition, although done with great care, had hidden ambiguities, and some surprising consequences. Furthermore, even after the definitional problems were understood and fixed, the implementation design remained a non-trivial problem. This is mainly due to the fact that there is no simple correspondence between the methods used in the definition and efficient methods of implementation. For example, ALGOL 60 procedure calls and parameter passing was defined in terms of the so called copy rules. By definition a procedure call is equivalent to replacing the call by a copy of the body of the called procedure, and replacing parameter references (in case of call by name) by the corresponding argument (enclosed in parenthesis whenever syntactically possible). To avoid name conflicts caused by these textual replacements certain systematic name changes were also prescribed. In the implementation, on the other hand, one certainly would not want to copy a procedure body for every call, nor would one want to copy argument expressions. What has to be found is a more efficient, possibly more complex way of accomplishing the same effect. The gap between the definition of a desired effect and the actual implementation needs to be bridged by a proof of correctness. For the example mentioned above this proof is non-trivial.

The gap between definition and implementation is inherent and not avoidable. In the definition we seek the simplest language constructs most suitable for the human user, defined in terms most easily comprehended. In the implementation we seek efficient and effective algorithms for a particular hardware architecture.

These problems with language definition and implementation motivated our initial effort. *We hoped to find a systematic design process that would lead from a rigorous definition of a given programming language to its implementation.*

Our initial effort was encouraged by the success of BNF (Backus Naur Form), the formalism used in the definition of the ALGOL 60 syntax. ALGOL 60 was the first programming language with a rigorous and formal definition of its syntax. The formalism gave rise to the systematic design of parsers and parser generators.

3. Definitional Interpreters

The first important idea in the present context is the idea that the semantics (meaning) of a high level language can be defined by a machine, albeit a hypothetical machine, analogous to machine languages.

There are two basic avenues open for defining a language. One can specify a translation of the language to be defined into a language whose semantics is already known. The second possibility is to specify an interpretation or model. Initially we followed both avenues and eventually settled for the second one. A definition by translation is documented in [Bekic65].

Before elaborating on the winning method, let me explain why translation did not work so well. First of all the translation approach leaves some core language which must be defined by a direct interpretation. It would be a sound language design strategy to start by defining a small core language and then introduce convenient notations as "syntactic sugar" of the core language. Variants of the lambda calculus have been used as a core language.

But, we were initially concerned with the formalization of existing languages, trying to capture their intended semantics. A language not designed from a core language to begin with, it is very unlikely to have a small subset in terms of which the rest of the language can be defined.

To understand the second alternative, i.e. definition by direct interpretation, one has to consider the nature of algorithmic languages. The main sentence type in languages like ALGOL and PL/I are imperative sentences whose actual execution changes the state of the machine. Thus, a direct interpretation of an imperative sentence is a state transition, i.e. a function from states to states. The definitional framework of such a definition is therefore a set of possible states. What these states are, and what structure they should be given depends entirely on the language and the objects it can refer to. We will come back to the subject of structuring states later.

A system consisting of a set of possible states and commands denoting state transitions is called an abstract machine.

On a very general level the semantics of a programming language is specified by defining a set of states Σ, a set of end states Σ_e, and two function *init* and *step*. A given program p and some input data d define a computation:

$$\sigma_0, \sigma_1, \dots, \sigma_i, \sigma_{i+1}, \dots$$

where: $\sigma_0 = init(p, d)$ and $\sigma_{i+1} = step(\sigma_i)$

Thus the initial state contains the program; the step function elaborates the program. If an end state is encountered the process terminates and the computation is finite, otherwise the computation is infinite. Usually, the step function is only a partial function. If so, a computation may be undefined.

The idea of using abstract machines for the definition of programming languages was first described by John McCarthy [McCarthy62]. In [McCarthy66] the method is illustrated by the definition of a language called Micro Algol containing simple variables, assignment, and conditional goto's.

Programs in Micro Algol are finite sequences of assignments and conditional goto's. States for the abstract machine defining Micro Algol would be triples:

$$<stg, c, p>$$

where $stg : ID \xrightarrow{m} R$ models storage as a finite map from identifiers to real numbers, $c : N$ models a statement counter pointing to the next statement to be executed and p is the program. The step function is easy to define. Assignment statements change the stg part of the state and increment the statement counter, goto's change the statement counter. Since the program cannot change, it need not be part of the state, as is the case in the original presentation in [McCarthy 66].

Micro Algol left out all the difficult parts of ALGOL (J. McCarthy in [McCarthy66]). During the mid and late 60's the Vienna Laboratory produced definitions of ALGOL 60 and PL/I modelling all aspects these languages (see e.g. [Lucas69,Lucas81] for references).

In Micro Algol the storage model is a simple map from identifiers to values. With the inclusion of scopes of names and sharing patterns that can occur among variables, one (ALGOL) or more (PL/I) steps of indirection between variable names and their values have to be introduced. As a consequence the structure of the state becomes more complex. In [Lucas71] I have shown how the structure of the state has to change with each additional language concept.

For languages like ALGOL it is necessary to introduce the concept of locations (an abstraction of storage locations). Storage is modelled as an association of locations and values, but cannot be viewed as a simple map. This is because locations holding composite values, such as arrays and structures, have sublocations. The subject of appropriate storage models for the various languages is a complicated one and has been studied in depth in [Bekic71] including the storage concepts for PL/I and ALGOL 68.

With the inclusion of nested phrase structures, procedures and recursion, the statement counter has to be replaced by a more elaborate control component (see e.g. [Lucas69]). The issue is complicated by the fact that some non-determinism has to be included which leads to a step function that maps states into sets of states (the potential results of the next execution step). VDL definitions modelled non-determinism in just that way.

4. Abstract Syntax

Abstract Syntax is born of the idea that one can describe the essential structure of sentences without specifying a linear notation.

This is an important idea because it separates two rather complicated problems: associating meaning with abstract forms of sentences, and mapping abstract sentences into linear character strings.

Sentences have phrase structure; they are composed of parts which may again be composed of parts, etc., until we reach a level of atomic parts. Sentences are represented by linear strings of characters. The syntax of a languages (e.g. specified in BNF) defines a set of character strings: the syntactically valid strings. This set is chosen to contain the meaningful sentences as tightly as possible. For each valid string, the syntax defines a structure, the meaningful parts of a sentence. Such structures can be encoded as linear string in various ways, mainly by using special symbols such as parentheses, punctuation marks, such as comma and semi colon, etc. Once we have parsed a sentence and made the structure explicit (as a parse tree) these special symbols are no longer necessary.

The concept of abstract syntax was first described by John McCarthy in [McCarthy62] and further illustrated in [McCarthy66]. An abstract syntax is a system of functions for constructing and decomposing composite objects. McCarthy used a property oriented approach for the definition of these function, defining their relationship by means of axioms. We used a model oriented approach in both VDL and Meta-IV definitions. The example below shows the abstract syntax of assignment statements using Meta-IV notation.

> *assignment* :: *variable expression*

An assignment statement has two parts, a variable and an expression. The object can be visualized as a tree whose root node is labelled *assignment*, with two immediate subtrees one for each part.

For manipulating such objects one needs predicates for testing the type, and functions for constructing and decomposing objects. There is a convention which provides these functions automatically. For example, the definition of assignment statements provides a function for constructing assignment statements, and a predicate for testing whether an object is an assignment statement.

> *is_assignment(a)*

is true if *a* is an assignment, otherwise false.

> *mk_assignment(v, e) = a*

constructs an assignment *a*, given a variable *v* and an expression *e*.

For decomposing a given assignment statement, we most often use an implicit pattern matching form:

> *let mk_assignment(v, e) = a*

defines *v* and *e* to be the variable and expression part of *a*.

Explicit selector functions can also be defined:

> *assignment* :: *s_v* : *variable s_e* : *expression*

where *s_v* and *s_e* are the two functions selecting the two respective parts from a given assignment statement.

5. Single Metalanguage

The realization that abstract forms of sentences and states of abstract machines can both be formalized within the same framework was a milestone, at least in my own understanding of the subject.

In VDL, the object domains used for both purposes consisted of several types of elementary objects, such as identifiers, integers, etc., and a single type of composite objects. Composite objects were finite trees with labelled branches. There was a single operator on composite objects, called μ, for constructing composite objects and for adding deleting and changing components of composite objects.

For example, an assignment statement consisting of a variable *v* and an expression *e* is constructed as follows (using VDL):

$$\mu(\Omega; < s\_v : v >, < s\_e : e >)$$

starting with the empty object we add the two components. The result is a tree with two immediate subtrees. In contrast to Meta-IV trees , nodes are not labelled, but branches are lablled with the name of their respective selector functions, s_v and s_e in the example.

In general, an expression of the form:

$$\mu(O; < s : C >)$$

would result in O where the s component is replaced by C if it exists, otherwise an s component is added to the object. Deletion of the s component is achieved by making C the empty object.

An example for the use of trees for the abstract machine state is the representation of the memory or storage component, *stg*, for the language Micro Algol. The storage component can be defined as a tree whose branches are labelled with the names of variable and whose subtrees are the respective values of these variables. The semantics of an assignment, assigning the value *val* to a variable x can then be formalized as:

$$\mu(stg; < x : val >)$$

This is a very elegant, simple basis for formalizing both abstract forms of sentences and states of abstract machines. The advantages and disadvantages of of the composite object domain described above are similar to those of LISP, or any other untyped language. Every function is applicable to every object. But of course most functions only make sense when applied to certain subsets of objects. Intended restrictions could be expressed as pre- and post-conditions, i.e. conditions that constrain the domain and range of a function, to indicate the intended argument and result types. However certain kinds of conditions are so common that it turns out to be more economic to express these conditions as types.

For this reason, following suggestions mainly from Hans Bekic, we changed (in Meta-IV) to a more orderly world of typed objects. For example, as pointed out above, trees have labelled nodes, indicating the type of objects.

However, there are still only a few "built in" types in Meta-IV. Since there exist variants of Meta-IV, the following summary should not be taken as absolute.

The scalar data types are: *boolean*, *integer*, *number*, and *token*.

The composite types of Meta-IV are:

• *Sets*

• *Sequences*

• *Maps*

• *Trees*

Sets and *sequences* are what one expects. *Maps* are finite mappings. *Maps* are a particularly useful domain because many of the concepts in programming languages are most naturally modelled as finite mappings, for example, declaration parts, environments, dictionaries, etc.,.

There is an open ended collection of tree shaped composite object types, but all of these behave uniformly. Trees in Meta-IV have labelled edges (for selectors) and labelled nodes (for type tags). The abstract assignment statement, as defined earlier in this section, is an example.

The community using Meta-IV has always resisted standardization of the notation, and kept it open to extension. However, in practice the notation is very stable, and the variations seem to be relatively small. The emergence of automated tools may make standardization more desirable.

6. Constraints

I don't know whether this one should be called an idea or just a lucky decision.

In both VDL and Meta-IV we have always used context free grammars for the definition of composite objects types. Context dependent constraints are expressed as conditions, using suitable VDL or Meta-IV functions, narrowing the domains as appropriate.

Thus, the decision was, to stick to context free grammar rules rather than attempt to use context dependent grammars (e.g. two level grammars as in ALGOL 68).

Grammars defined in BNF are context free grammars. In practice most syntax definitions are given by context free grammars. However, the domains of syntactically valid sentences (or states) are usually much to wide, containing sentences that have no sensible interpretation (or states that cannot arise).

For example, in languages like ALGOL or PASCAL, identifiers must be declared, and the use of an identifier must be compatible with its declared attributes.

These are context conditions, that cannot be expressed by context free grammars. Similarly, the states of an abstract machine defined by a context free grammar, will very likely contain states that can never arise in an actual execution.

In the first case (meaningless sentences) the definitional interpreter could contain appropriate checks marking these cases as invalid. However, it is much more useful to factor these checks out and collect them as a part of the definition called context conditions. Context conditions can be viewed as preconditions for the meaning function. The definition of the meaning function becomes less complicated as it need not be bothered with meaningless programs that can be eliminated by a static check. This structure is also useful for the compiler writer who finds the statically checkable context conditions together in one place.

In the second case (states that cannot arise) one could simply leave it to the user of a specification to find out which states arise and which ones don't by exploring the definitional interpreter. Context conditions in this case are actually statements about the interpreter.

Nevertheless, it is important to specify the context conditions on states explicitly. It is our experience that these conditions add much to the understanding of a definition.

7. Denotational Semantics

The methods of denotational semantics constitute a major advance in the formalization of programming languages and its theoretical foundations. Denotational semantics has its roots in the early work of P. Landin [Landin65] and C.Strachey [Strachey66] with the lambda calculus as the formal basis. Fundamental mathematical results due to D.Scott [Scott70] rendered a firm basis upon which the plan of denotational semantics can be carried out.

As much as possible, VDM makes use of the principles of denotational semantics. Ther are two major principles.

First, denotational semantics strictly separates syntactic domains (phrase structures) and semantic domains (mathematical objects). Each phrase (element of a syntactic domain) is given a meaning (element of a semantic domain)

Elements of semantic domains are suitable mathematical objects, e.g. a numbers, or functions. In fact the major problem in establishing a denotational semantics of a given language is to find such suitable mathematical objects to model the intended meaning.

To associate meaning with phrases, one uses a meaning function mapping syntactic objects into semantic objects,

M: *syntactic objects* → *semantic objects.*

Second, The meaning of each composite phrase is defined as a function of the meaning of the immediate subphrases.

For example, the meaning of numeric expression consisting of numerals and operator symbols such as ' + ' and ' − ' can be defined by a mapping from the syntactic domain of expressions to the semantic domain of numbers. Then, simple arithmetic expressions are defined by a meaning function mapping numerals to numbers: $M('1') = 1, M('2') = 2, ...$ The meaning of composite expression is defined in terms of the meaning of immediate subexpressions: $M('e_1 + e_2') = M('e_1') + M('e_2')$. The functionality of M in this simple case is

$M('e')$: *Number.*

Quotes in the above formuli are used to indicate that the meaning function M applies to syntactic objects.

When expressions involve not just numerals but also variables, one has to modify the semantic domain, i.e. the range of the meaning function. We introduce an auxiliary domain, called environments:

Env: $Id \xrightarrow{m} Number,$

mapping identifiers to numbers. Then functionality of M becomes:

$M('e')$: $Env → Number.$

For example let $env = [x → 2, y → 3]$ then: $M('x + y')env = 5$. In general:

$M('e_1 + e_2')env = M('e_1')env + M('e_2')env$

The principle of denotational semantics forces a strict correspondence between the syntactic and the semantic structure of a language. This correspondence can be made precise in algebraic terms by considering operators like ' + ' in dual role. They can be viewed on the syntactic side as constructors of expressions. On the semantic side they are viewed as functions on numbers.

The following examples are intended to illustrate the semantic domains used for the definition of programming languages, considering such concepts as simple statements, goto, block structure and procedures.

Simple Statements

We start with Micro Algol without goto's, i.e. programs are sequences of assignment statements. As in the operational definition we need an auxiliary domain of storage objects, $Stg = Id \xrightarrow{m} R$ (in this simple language storage and environment are the same). The meaning of a single statement is a change in storage, i.e. a map from storage to storage.

$$M('stmt'): Stg \to Stg$$

putting two statements together amounts to functional composition of the meanings:

$$M('stmt_1; stmt_2') = M('stmt_2') \bullet M('stmt_1')$$

where: $(f \bullet g)(x) = f(g(x))$.

Goto

Denotational semantics works well for programming languages as long as the control flow follows the phrase structure. Go to statements reach across the phrase structure and are therefore difficult to model. One widely used model for goto's are so called continuations. The idea is that labels denote the state transition that is to take place starting with the labelled statement all the way to the end of the program. A statement, in this generalized setting denotes a state transition given the state transition from the point after the statement in question to the end of the program (the continuation of the statement). The functionality for the meaning of statements then becomes:

$$M('stmt'): (Stg \to Stg) \to (Stg \to Stg).$$

This formulation of jumps has the advantage that it works for very general cases situations. However the semantic domain is not very intuitive.

Meta-IV has a predefined mechanism, called exits, which permits the definition of gotos, among other concepts, in a more intuitive fashion. Cliff Jones has investigated the relation of exits and continuation in [Jones78a]. The subsequent discussion excludes goto's for simplicity.

Block Structure

Block structured languages require more complex semantic domains. Block structure, i.e. nested scopes of names, require some mechanism for distinguishing different uses of the same identifier.

The possibility of sharing patterns among variables forces the introduction of some (abstract) concept of location.

Here is a typical example for semantic domains including block structure and procedures.

$$Env = Id \xrightarrow{m} (Loc|Proc), \quad Stg = Loc \xrightarrow{m} Val$$

Environment and storage would also be used as state components in a definition by an abstract machine. Because each state only depends on its predecessor state, states have to contain some more information, for example a stack of environments and a control component.

Procedures

The more important difference between abstract machines and denotational semantics should however be seen in the formalization of procedures. In the VDL style definitional interpreters, we associated procedure names with a pair (*body*, *env*), where body is the procedure *body*, and *env* is the environment in which the procedure was declared. This pair is a mixture of syntactic (body) and semantic (environment) elements. Denotational semantics chooses a cleaner solution by associating the state transformation affected by the procedure when called. More precisely a procedure denotes a function from the argument domains of the procedure and states into states. This leads however to complications, mainly because in ALGOL like languages, procedures can take themselves as arguments. This leads to the rather complicated construction of so called reflexive domains due to D. Scott.

To avoid this mathematical complication, it may be better to modify the procedure concept so as to eliminate the cause of the complication. The issue has been investigated by A.Blikle and A.Tarlecki in [Blikle83]

8. Modularization

Programming languages and their implementations are usually very large and complex objects. The same is true for the design of software systems in general. To make this complexity manageable, one has to structure their specification in some modular fashion.

There is one very obvious idea for structuring language definitions namely to follow the syntactic structure. For example, following this principle, there will be a separate part of the definition (a meaning function) for each type of statement, one for assignment statements, one for if statements, one for while statements, etc. All formal language definitions I have seen follow this principle, earlier definitions done in VDL as well as more recent ones using Meta-IV.

There is another structuring principle which is somewhat subtle and different. It is difficult to express this principle in precise terms at least for the time being. The following exposition is therefore somewhat pragmatic.

For economic and aesthetic reasons one wants to build a language or system from a set of orthogonal concepts. Orthogonal in this context means that none of the concepts can be left out without loss of expressiveness or function.

Here is a list of concepts found in many programming languages:

- value types, e.g. integer, boolean, etc.,

- storage, i.e. locations with assignment and retrieval operations,

- the block concept

Value types are algebras. There is no concept of state or computation in the sense of change affected in time, no concept of action. Thus domains of numbers, such as integers, with their operations, and functions on these domains are exactly what we learned in mathematics. It is important to separate these conventional mathematical concepts from such ideas as storage locations, which complicate matters. As long as we talk about value types, all the reasoning we have learned to use in mathematics is applicable. As soon as we add the concept of storage this is no longer true. For example, with the concept of storage included we may have functions with side effects and simple laws like: $f(a) + f(a) = 2 \times f(a)$ are no longer true.

The concept of storage is the idea of containers. A container has a contents and an address. Assignment is the operation of putting something into a container and retrieval is the operation of taking something out of a container. Both operations refer to containers by address. Storage cells are such containers. However, in an abstract machine underlying a high level language, storage may take more structures and more abstract forms than a linear space of storage cells of equal size.

The block concept is concerned with names, their scope and the relation of definition and use. In properly designed languages, this is an orthogonal concept: scope rules and the relation of definition and use of a names are independent of what names denote.

What one would like to achieve is that these concepts can be defined in isolation and these separate definitions can then be put together to form a complete language definition.

I believe that we were moderately successful with our languages definitions, the definitions done in VDL (including PL/I) as well as the later definitions done in Meta-VI. The separation of concepts is achieved mainly by an appropriate choice for the structure of the state (in the case of a definitional interpreter) and by a suitable choice of the semantic domains (in case of a denotational specifications).

Each of the concepts referred to above is formalized by a particular semantic domain. Each of the value types has its own domains and operations. Actually the value types form a system of domains because of some interaction between these.

Storage, in its simplest form is usually formalized as a map from locations to values (the content function). However, most higher level languages would require a more elaborate semantic domains for its storage component.

The block concept is usually reflected in a domain called environments. An environment is a map from identifiers to a set that includes all objects that names can possibly denote in the given language. Typically name can denote values, locations, procedures, and. other objects depending upon the language.

However, although some isolation of concepts has been achieved, proper compositionality has not been accomplished. To appreciate the problem consider a series of languages, each having all the concepts of the previous language plus some more. For example consider MicroAlgol, Alogol 60 (without gotos), Algol 60 (with goto's), and PL/I. The first one has just a global name space and no sharing patterns (two names bound to the same location), restricted Algol

60 adds the block concept and sharing patterns (because of call by reference), next we add goto's, and finally we add tasking, new storage classes among other features.

To go from one language to the next one would like to be able to compose the given definition with a definition of the additional concepts, thus preserving what exists so far.

However, in reality, one has to modify all definitions because the functionality of the basic building blocks (for example assignments) changes for each language level. This is equally true for operational and denotational definitions. Peter Mosses has made progress towards a solution of this problem, using an algebraic framework [Mosses82].

9. Indirect Definitions

Many of the definitions used in the definitions of PL/I and ALGOL 60, both VDL and Meta-IV style, are model oriented and direct. Both, syntactic and semantic domains are modelled using some elementary types such as numbers, truth values, etc. and some composite types such as sets, sequences, and trees. The functions that need to be defined on the syntactic and semantic domains are defined directly in terms of the predefined primitive functions of the above mentioned types.

However, there were certain concepts that proved to be difficult to capture, without over-specifying, i.e. without defining properties that were not intended to be defined.

The storage concept in PL/I is a case in point. On the one hand it would be too specific to define a precise mapping of PL/I structures onto a linear array of storage cells. On the other hand, based variables permit the access to the same piece of storage by means of different templates, a features which constrains which mappings one can have. There are also other features which influence the storage model.

In cases like these, we used an axiomatic definition. An axiomatic definition postulates the existence of certain domains and functions on these domains. The functions are not defined directly but only by a set of conditions, called axioms, that must be satisfied.

Here is an example from the definition of the PL/I storage concept. The postulated domains are storage (Stg), locations (P), and value representations (Vr). Locations are viewed as functions which can be applied to storage to retrieve their content. There is a predicate that tests whether two locations are independent, i.e. non-overlapping:

$$is\_indep:P \times P \rightarrow Bool.$$

There is an elementary assignment function,

$$el\_ass:P \times Vr \times Stg \rightarrow Stg.$$

The set of axioms needed to specify the storage concept is rather large, here are two examples of such axioms.

$$is\_indep(p_1, p_2) \supset is\_indep(p_2, p_1)$$

$$is\_indep(p_1, p_2) \supset p_1(stg) = p_1(el\_ass(p_2, vr, stg))$$

The first axiom says that relation of being independent is symmetric. The second axiom says that the assignment to a given location does not change the content of any location that is independent of the given location.

Such definitions are much like algebraic data types, although these are usually restricted to equations as axioms. Axiomatic definitions are very difficult to use in practice, and great care and mathematical background is needed.

It is sometimes believed that axiomatic definitions are necessarily more abstract than model oriented definitions. This is not the case. C.B.Jones has shown in [Jones86] that it is possible to define precise notions of models being *sufficiently abstract* or being *implementation biased*.

The following definition is quoted from [Jones86] A model-oriented specification is based on an underlying set of states. The model is biased with respect to a given set of operations if there exist different elements in the set of states which cannot be distinguished by any sequence of operations. A model that is not biased is sufficiently abstract.

For example the concept of a stack can be defined axiomatically by defining axioms which relate the standard operations on stacks (*push*, *pop*, and *top*). Without loss of abstraction, the same concept of stack can also be defined using sequences and defining the stack operation directly in terms of the sequence operations (head, tail, etc.).

There is a second form of indirect definition, called *implicit definition*, which is very useful and much easier to handle. Implicit definitions are used to define properties of functions, by so called pre- and post-conditions, replacing direct definitions in the model-oriented specifications.

Here is an example of an implicit definition of the square root function, using the style and notation proposed in [Jones86]

sqrt(*p:Real*) *r:Real*
pre $p \geq 0$
post $p = r^2 \pm \varepsilon$ & $r \geq 0$

where *p* is the parameter and *r* is the result.

10. Systematic Development

As stated in the introduction, the major objective was, from the start, to find a systematic way of developing compilers, and later programming systems in general. A precise specification is only a necessary prerequisite.

The VDM methodology is a stepwise process that leads from a given specification to the final implementation. each step leads to another specification that is linked to the previous level by a formal or informal argument of correctness.

As explained before, a specification involves semantic domains and operation on these domains.

One important kind of design step is the choice of a representation for the semantic domains and the design of the required operations in terms of operations available in the representation domain.

Ultimately, all that is available for representation are the data types of the implementation language. For complex systems it is better to go through some intermediate steps, to make these smaller and more manageable, and also to preserve some of the design on a more abstract level. A standard example for such a design step is the representation of sets by ordered lists and the definition of the set operations in terms of list operations.

There are some early papers on the subject, for example [Lucas73]. However, it took quite some time to clarify the issue. A thorough and formal treatment has been achieved by C.B.Jones in [Jones86] in chapter 8 on data reification.

This is a summary of data reification as described in [Jones86]. The key to relating an abstract semantic domain to its representation is a retrieve function. Let A be the abstract domain and R the domain chosen to represent the elements of A. A retrieve function is a function *retr*: $R \rightarrow A$ that maps R into A. The function is give the direction from R to A because it is frequently the case that an element of A has more than one representation. For example in representing sets as lists one may permit the elements in arbitrary order and not necessarily remove duplicates. On the other hand, if A is sufficiently abstract relative to the particular design level, there should by only one abstract object for each element of the representation domain.

For a retrieve function to be *adequate*, it has to be total and each abstract object has to have at least one representation.

Next, one has to find for each basic function f_a in the abstract domain a corresponding function f_r in the representation domain. Of course f_r has to mirror the function it represents. For the simplified case were *retr* is one-one and f_a is total the correctness condition is:

$$\forall a \in A.\ retr(f_r(abs(a))) = f_a(a)$$

were *abs* is the inverse if *retr*.

If the retrieve function is many-one, one can consider the equivalence classes of elements of R that map to one and the same element of A.

The situation maybe further complicated by operation which may be partial (precondition) and/or non-deterministic (post-condition). The conditions, given in [Jones86], that must be satisfied are:

$$\forall r \in R.\ pre\_A(retr(r)) \supset pre\_R(r)$$

$$\forall \bar{r}, r \in R.\ pre\_A(retr(\bar{r}))\ \&\ post\_R(\bar{r}, r) \supset post\_A(retr(\bar{r}), retr(r))$$

11. Achievements and Discussion

In this last section I would like to mention some highlights as they occurred during the evolution of the VDM methodology. It is a somewhat historic perspective and I am eager to learn more recent experiences with VDM from this conference.

The first result of practical significance was the formal definition of PL/I (see [Lucas81] for references). The formalization was done in parallel while the detailed design of the language was still in progress. The effort had a tangible positive influences on the language.

The ANSI PL/I Standard is based on the VDL methodology, though not identical to the earlier VDL formalization. The ANSI standard uses an abstract machine whose state is formally defined and whose shape is somewhat different from the Vienna definition. The state transitions are defined in a semi formal way, using a stylized English (called Basis).

The methodology was applied to a number of other languages.

As mentioned in the introduction, our objective was to find a systematic way of designing compilers (and later programs in general). For a long period we investigated examples; during this period a significant improvement was achieved by switching to Meta-IV and adopting some of the principles of denotational semantics. The first stumbling attempts to use VDL for the purpose is found in [Lucas68] Some further trace of the activity is found in [Henhapl70,Henhapl 71,Jones71,Lucas73,Jones75,Jones78a]. The most rewarding examples were those around a cluster of concepts including blocks, procedures, recursion and parameter passing, a combination of concepts that leads to some complexity in the implementation. The examples not only revealed some shortcomings in actual implementations but also made visible alternatives that we had not seen before.

D.Bjorner and his group were first to apply in the large a systematic design of an implementation based on a formal language definition; the language was ADA [Bjorner80]. Some of the experience and the implementation process are discussed in [Bjorner85]. The same group also produced a formalization of the language CHILL.

More information on the VDM and institutions involved with VDM can be found in the ESPRIT preparatory study on formal methods [Cohen83] and its companion volume [Prehn83].

One key to further progress are tools. Actually tools were used right from the start, for example we produced and used a syntax directed formatter for the first formal definition of PL/I (!). Such tools seem to emerge for VDM, see for example [Hansen85]. Eventually these tools will have to go much beyond editing, formatting and type checking and include suitable operation for transformations of designs and programs that can be used interactively.

As indicated on an earlier section, we do not yet sufficiently understand how to modularize designs and specifications. When we do, we will be able to design and implement systems using predefined building block to a larger extent than is possible today.

Bibliography

[ANSI 76]   ANSI X3.53, *Programming Language PL/I*, Institute/ (New York/American National Standards, .

[Bekic 65]   H.Bekic, *Mechanical Transformation Rules for the Reduction of ALGOL to a Primitive Language M and their Use in defining the Compiler Function*, IBM Laboratory Vienna, TR 25.051 (1965).

[Bekic 71]   H.Bekic & K.Walk, *Formalization of Storage Properties*, in: [Engeler71] (1971).

[Bekic 84]   H.Bekic, *Programming Languages and Their Definition*, LNCS, Springer-Verlag **177** (1984).

[Bjorner 78] D.Bjorner & C.B.Jones (Eds.), *The Vienna Development Method: The Meta-Language*, LNCS, Springer-Verlag **61** (1978).

[Bjorner 80] D.Bjorner (Ed.), *Towards a Formal Description of ADA*, Springer Verlag **98** (New York, 1980).

[Bjorner 82] D.Bjorner (Ed.), *Formal Description of Programming Concepts (II)*, IFIP TC-2 Work.Conf., Garmisch-Partenkirchen, North-Holland (1982).

[Bjorner 85] D.Bjorner, T.Denvir, E.Meiling, J.S.Pedersen, *The RAISE Project Fundamental Issues and Requirements*, RAISE/DDC/EM/1/V6 Dansk Datamatik Center (1985).

[Blikle 83]   A.Blikle & A.Tarlecki, *Naive Denotational Semantics*, IFIP'83 (1983).

[CCITT 80]   C.C.I.T.T., *The Specification of CHILL*, International Telegraph and Telephone Consultative Committee), Recommendation Z200, Geneva, Switzerland (1980).

[Cohen 83]   B.Cohen and M.I.Jackson, *A Critical Appraisal of Formal Software Development Theories, Methods, and Tools*, ESPRIT preparatory study,Standard Telecommunication Laboratory, Harlow, Essex, England (1983).

[Engeler 71] E.Engeler (Ed.), *Symposium on Semantics of Algorithmic Languages*, Lecture Notes in Mathematics Springer Verlag **188** (1971).

[Hansen 85]   I.O.Hansen & N.Bleech, *Meta-IV Tool-set, Functional Specification*, DDC 165/RPT/2, Dansk Datamatik Center, Lyngby Denmark (1985).

[Henhapl 70] W.Henhapl & C.B.Jones, *The Block Structure and some Possible Implementations with Proofs of Equivalence*, TR25.104, IBM Laborator Vienna (1970).

[Henhapl 71]   W.Henhapl & C.B.Jones, *A Runtime Mechanism for Referencing Variables*, Info. Process.Lett. **1** (1971) pp. 14-16.

[Jones 71]   C.B.Jones & P.Lucas, *Proving Correctness of Implementation Techniques*, in: [Engeler71] (1971) pp. 178-201.

[Jones 75]   C.B.Jones, *Yet Another Proof of the Block Concept'*, LN25.3.075, IBM Laboratory Vienna (1975).

[Jones 78a]   C.B.Jones, *Denotational Semantics of GOTO: an Exit Formulation and its Relation to Continuations*, in: [Bjorner78] (1978) pp. 278-304.

[Jones 78b]   C.B.Jones, *The Vienna Development Method: Examples of Compiler Development*, in: Le Point sur la Compilation, M.Amirchaby & D.Neel, Eds., Institut de Recherche d'Informatique et d'Automatique, 1978 (1978).

[Jones 86]   C.B.Jones, *Systematic Software Development Using VDM*, Prentice/Hall (1986).

[Landin 65]   P.J.Landin, *Correspondence between ALGOL 60 and Church's Lambda Notation, (two parts)*, Commun. ACM **8** (1965) pp. 89-101 and.

[Lucas 68]   P.Lucas, *Two Constructive Realizations of the Block Concept and their Equivalence*, IBM Vienna Lab. TR25.085 (1968).

[Lucas 69]   P.Lucas & K.Walk, *On the Formal Description of PL/I*, Ann.Rev.Aut.Progr. **6** (1969).

[Lucas 70]   P.Lucas, *On the Semantics of Programming Languages and Software Devices*, in: [Rustin72] (1972).

[Lucas 71]   P.Lucas, *Formal Definition of Programming Languages and Systems*, IFIP'71 (1971).

[Lucas 73]   P.Lucas, *On Program Correctness and the Stepwise Development of Implementations*, in: Proceedings 'Convegno di Informatica Teorica', Univ. of Pisa Italy, March 1973 (1973) pp. 219-251.

[Lucas 78]   P.Lucas, *On the Formalization of Programming Languages: Early History and Main Approaches*, in: [Bjorner78] (1978).

[Lucas 81]   P.Lucas, *Formal Semantics of Programming Languages: VDL*, IBM Journal of Res. & Dev. **25** (1981) pp. 549-561.

[McCarthy 62]   J.McCarthy, *Towards a Mathematical Science of Computation*, IFIP'62 (ed. C.M.Popplewell) (1963) pp. 21-28.

[McCarthy 66]   J.McCarthy, *A Formal Description of a Subset of Algol*, in: Steel 66a.

[Mosses 82]   P.D.Mosses, *Abstract Semantic Algebras*, in: [Bjorner82] (1982).

[Prehn 83]   S. Prehn, I.O.Hansen, S.U.Palm, P.Gobel, *Formal Methods Appraisal, Final Report*, year = '1983'/DDC 86/1983-06-24, Dansk Datamatik Center, Lyngby, Denmark.

[Rustin 72]   R.Rustin (Ed.), *Formal Semantics of Programming Languages,* Prentice-Hall (1972).

[Scott 70]   D.Scott, *Outline of a Mathematical Theory of Computation,* PRG-2, Oxford University Programming Research Group, Oxford, England, 1970. (1970).

[Steel 66]   T.B.Steel (Ed.), *Formal Language Description Languages,* IFIP TC-2 Work.Conf., Baden, North-Holland (1966).

[Strachey 66]   C.Strachey, *Towards a Formal Semantics,* in: [Steel66] (1966) pp. 198-220.

EXPERIENCE USING VDM IN STC

R.J. Crispin
Software Technology Division, STL
HARLOW, Essex CM17 9NA, UK

ABSTRACT

Introducing any new technology involves organisational, skill, method and tool
changes, which require a commitment from the industry concerned. The introduction
of formal methods into system and software design is no exception. Before the
widespread use of formal methods can be achieved, it will be necessary for the IT
industry to convince itself that the methods are genuinely usable in an industrial
context, can be made to fit within the market and technical environment, and yield
significant improvements over conventional methods. This paper describes some of
the ways in which STC has used VDM to develop real systems and the benefits which
we feel have been achieved. At the same time, some limitations of the existing
methods have been noted, giving pointers for further development of the technology.

1.   Background

The value of formalising the process of developing systems and software has long
been recognised in the major centres concerned with IT research. At STL Harlow
there has been active interest since the late 70's, which coincided with the
publication of "Software Development: A Rigorous Approach" [1]. Naturally there
was considerable interest in an approach which promised to be industrially
applicable, and a considerable amount of work has been done by STL in exploring and
understanding how to use VDM.

To begin to use the ideas in VDM for industrial developments, another part of STC
developed a specification and design language, commonly called 'Green' within the
company [2]. Green provides a means of writing specifications either in the style
of VDM pre- and post- conditions, or in the imperative style of a pseudo-code.
Choice of style is left to the user, within their project standards. The language
has a well-defined syntax and grammar for which checking software exists.

Further elaboration of the specification language associated with VDM led STC to define its own form of language, called the STC Reference Language (STC-RL) [3,4].

This essentially added basic facilities for structuring large specifications which the language in [1] lacked.

By contributing to the Esprit RAISE project [5], STC aims to provide a formal specification and design language with supporting tools which will provide the basis for future wider-scale use of formal methods. This represents one of the main threads of STC's ongoing research work in formal methods.

2.   Introduction

Three projects will now be described where VDM has provided the basis for a formal specification and design language. They are

(a)   The development of a toolset for VDM users
(b)   The development of control software for a monitoring station
(c)   The development of an electronic mail system for telex users.

These projects were studied initially to gain some insight into the software project management issues which arise when formal methods are being used [6]. Here, we are more concerned with broader issues of the usability of the formal methods technology in an industrial context.

The full VDM 'method', as described in [1], consists of starting with the most abstract specification, carrying out successive refinements and rigorously justifying the development steps. None of the projects considered set out to achieve this. Instead they chose to use 'VDM' as a means of expressing specifications and designs. The main reason was that none of the projects started with an abstract requirement specification, but each was developed with the possible implementations having an impact on the requirements. This involved an iteractive process rather than a sequence of refinements. Nevertheless, in each project considerable benefits have been achieved just from specifying in VDM.

3. "VDM Toolset" project:

3.1 Background

A team within STC has been developing a limited set of tools for use by people developing programs with specifications written in VDM. (This is a project sponsored by the UK Alvey Directorate and is undertaken in collaboration with Manchester University).

The facilities to be provided include

a) a library mechanism for storing and retrieving design components (in this case documents such as requirement statements, VDM specifications, etcetera)
b) a browse tool
c) a structure editor with an understanding of abstract syntax trees, and an "unparsing" capability for displaying.
d) checking tools - e.g. for type checking
e) a cross-reference tool

The toolset is being developed for use under the UNIX (R) operating system, and has versions for both BSD4.2 and System V.

3.2. Architectural Design

Not surprisingly, from the outset of the project the team intended to use VDM to specify the toolset. The STC Reference Language [3.4] was used, and indeed was created with the project in mind.

Specification at the most abstract level proved to be the most difficult stage of the project, and the least successful in terms of using VDM. Several abortive attempts were made to capture the specification, and progress was slow until there was a project decision to adopt an 'object-oriented' design. Object-orientation is known to provide a number of benefits in system design [7], and in the rest of the project it is somewhat difficult to distinguish between the benefits deriving from object-orientation versus those deriving from VDM specification. The most that can be said is that the two approaches worked extremely well together.

The breakthrough was to create a data-abstraction based division of the system into high-level objects. Each object was specified in STC-RL as an abstract data type (ADT) interfacing to a common man-machine interface environment (MMI). Some of the objects were mutually recursive.

Though the specifications for most objects were clear, a few objects required the notion of <u>sequencing</u>, which is awkward to express in the STC-RL version of VDM. The 'object coordinator' which had to invoke a sequence of other objects depending on 'if' conditions was extremely difficult to specify using this formalism. Additional English-language comments were used to express these aspects, rather than have unwieldy VDM-style conditions. In addition, and not surprisingly, aspects of specification such as modifiability, structure and portability could not be expressed formally.

The object specifications were subjected to a formal review, in accord with contemporary software development practice. Overall, the formal specifications of the objects enabled the team to recognise some interfaces that were inconsistent and some that were not needed at all.

3.3 Design and Implementation

Design proceeded by producing specifications of lower-level objects and eventually coding these in the 'C' programming language. A problem was encountered with interfacing the objects, however, which can be described as follows.

The design of the objects was distributed among the team members, so refinement of specifications was taking place in parallel. If one designer wished to refine an <u>interface</u> the others using that interface would have to be 'ready' to agree the details of the refinements. Therefore the team found it necessary to design the main interfaces at a concrete level (practically the code level) to avoid the problem of synchronising their activities. This made it difficult to link specifications written at an abstract level with the actual interfaces. It was therefore necessary to set aside the detailed interface definitions when dealing with the abstract specifications and use more abstract 'views' instead.

3.4 Application Limitations

The VDM Toolset provides the facilities of a small integrated project support environment. In particular there is a library mechanism and objects in the library are under version control. The team found they were unable to specify the version control mechanism in the STC-RL, because of the limitations on sequencing, and had to resort to informal specification methods. As a result it took considerable time to arrive at a satisfactory scheme.

3.5   Metrics

During the course of the project, the number of, and reasons for, modification of the components of the system have been recorded automatically by the development environment. In 1987 it is hoped that this data along with the specifications, formal review results and final code will be used to derive some quantitive measures of the effectiveness of using VDM on this project.

3.6   Experience from using VDM/STC-RL

Parts of the system with good informational abstractions available were easy to model in VDM. Some other parts were found to be as hard to specify and understand in VDM as they would have been to code directly ! Overall, the specifier's judgement is required about being "sufficiently abstract".

At the time of writing the project is nearing completion with most of the system now in operation. The later stages of the project have proved to be remarkably trouble free. VDM has proved to be a good method tool for abstraction, compartmentalisation and decomposition. Though VDM proved to be less than ideal when it came to dividing the design task between members of the team, the formalism provided a good way of expressing and stimulating thought.

4.   "TAT-8" project:

4.1   Background

A team within STC has been developing software to monitor the line performance of part of an optical fibre transatlantic telephone cable system.

The TAT-8 cable will connect telecommunication administrations in England, France and the United States, providing the highest capacity non-satellite transatlantic link to date.

The team's contribution is the control software for the UK shorebased monitoring station – the Home Support Unit (HSU) which will monitor the integrity of operation of the link between the UK and an underwater 'wet-connection' point on the continental shelf, and ensure virtually zero downtime. This will be achieved by checking the health of the laser repeaters including the received light level, and initiating real-time laser switch-over in the presence of fault conditions.

The software has been developed using STC's VDM-derived specification language 'Green' and the 'C' implementation language, for a microprocessor system running a proprietary operating system.

The development team has been using a DEC VAX-11/780 running under UNIX 4.2 BSD.

4.2. Project Lifecycle

The lifecycle model used was conventional:

1.   Product requirements (Hardware and Software)
2.   Top level design (Software)
3.   Detailed design
4.   Coding
5.   Unit testing
6.   Integration

Product requirements and a partial system design were supplied by the customer. The customer was uncommitted about details of the requirements and it was left very much to the development team to fill in details as they judged fit.

4.3   Top Level Design

The Home Support Unit (HSU), as the monitoring system was called, started with a partial system design, so this stage started well. It was decided to implement the functional specification as an object oriented design. An "object" was to be a grouping of data and code which minimised the interfacing. An object could be at any level, not necessarily just a high level of abstraction.

The architectural design (selecting the objects and their modes of interaction) was not supported by a recognised 'method' at all. The team of 5-6 people had separate objects to define and there was a great deal of iteration back to the functional specification. Eventually about 12 major objects were identified to meet the specification.

At the top level, the major object level split was described in one document. For each top level a top level version was specified using the Green language (reference [2]). This consisted of the data structures, operations and pre and post conditions for each object.

It was difficult to specify post-conditions of operations because of timing elements, hardware switches and multiple dependencies. (One requirement that was hard to capture was the need for the HSU to send a message to the other two HSU's every second, plus or minus a small tolerance).

About 200 operations were defined, which the developers did not find too complicated, but some of the post-conditions ran to three pages of listing and proved very difficult to comprehend because of their sheer size. It was felt that English comments or psuedo-code would have been easier to understand - but most of the team, even those with minimal background, picked up Green fairly quickly.

The Program Development Language (PDL) checker for Green (reference [8]) was used to check the syntax and to cross-reference each object for self-consistency. Despite the number of bugs in this tool when they started to use it, the developers found it invaluable. In all about 20K lines of Green were written and checked in this way.

4.4.   Detailed Design

The team could either have added pseudo code for each major object or have generated a second set of Green specifications for the detailed design. The later course was chosen and 'low level' Green created. The larger proprietary operating system constructs were built-in at this point.

Each object was to be an operating system job, so an operating system shell was also defined in Green, to enable the specifications to be checked for consistency with the PDL checker.

At this level there was a certain amount of built-in concurrency with the use of mail-boxes, semaphores etc. In retrospect the developers think it would have been better to have had a more abstract design of the objects so that it would not have been necessary to know full details of all the interfaces between them.

This need to coordinate interface development caused difficulties for the project manager in scheduling the development, because software engineers whose modules shared an interface had to be ready to agree its design at the same moment. (This was also observed in the VDM Toolset project). At this stage there were 16-18 people on the team; some top level objects needed to be split to allow independent working.

Some feedback was also being obtained on the accuracy of the original project time estimates : where the requirement specification was detailed, estimates were accurate, where it was weak, the estimates were wildly optimistic.

The operating system mapping was now becoming very significant in steering the design. Generally, an exported operation was to have a message associated with it and a mailbox, and it became an operating system task. Implementation therefore relied upon a multi-tasking operating system. Some operations were purely non-concurrent functions (did not change state) but most were concurrent tasks.

Deciding which operations had to be tasks is the point at which real time considerations had to be introduced.

Performance aspects of timing could not be captured in Green; the problems that emerged in this area are described later.

The mapping onto the operating system via mail boxes gave the developers considerable confidence that the functional design would work.

4.5   Coding

Coding was extremely easy and quick. In most cases code was created by manually editing the Green. In retrospect the Green descriptions should have been kept at a more abstract level, slightly lengthening the time for coding but reducing the design stage more.

Coding resulted in about 20k lines of 'C'.

4.6   Unit Testing

The unit testing stage proved to be very frustrating for the developers, for a combination of reasons. A prototype unit test harness was supplied as part of the 'IMPE' tool set (which included the PDL checker [8]). This was used on the VAX host for testing and cross-debugging. The test harness took so long to learn how to use, and the turnaround of results from a heavily-loaded VAX was so slow, that some felt it marred the advantages of using Green in the first place. (The two were associated in the minds of the developers because they were supplied as a package).

However very few bugs were found at the unit testing stage. Since code was not "registered" for configuration management until module testing had been done, no statistics were gathered. At the time this project was visited integration testing was underway.

4.7   Experience from Using VDM/Green

4.7.1 General

The developers were generally pleased they had used Green and a number of sceptics were converted. The small number of errors showing up during testing had confirmed the validity of the approach.

4.7.2 Expression

Some requirements were hard to express in Green but no formalism exists which will capture all the requirements (e.g. timing).

4.7.3 Comprehensibility

Green was hard to read quickly to get a feel for what it was doing. English language functional specifications had to be produced at each level. These were needed to allow new staff to be introduced to the project, and they were also found useful during integration when designers needed to be able to understand one another's modules.

Reviews and inspections were used at every stage of development.

4.7.4 Efficiency

Because of the inability of the formalism to model real time constraints, it was not until integration that the performance (throughput) could be confirmed. In fact the requirements to send regular 'health' messages every second was not met by the initial implementation: too much processing was going on to allow this event to happen on time. The solution in this case was not to optimise the design or re-do the mapping of objects onto the operating system, but simply to plan to change the hardware to use a compatible microprocessor four times faster. This increased the hardware cost of the HSU, but since it is a one-off, this solution is more economical than putting further software engineering effort into optimisation.

A strong feeling that the software design was well thought out and should have its integrity preserved contributed to this decision.

5.   "Mailman" project:

5.1   Background

'Mailman' is an electronic mail system for telex users being developed by the same unit. It extends the facilities of telex by allowing users to deposit into and collect from a mailbox, with all the usual attendent electronic mail facilities such as browsing, editing, filing and maintaining address files.

The system is hardware fault tolerant, with replicated processors, and therefore there is emphasis on low-defect software development methods. The main PNBC project work is to create the software running the mailbox system.

5.2   Project Lifecycle

An 'object oriented' approach was adopted from the outset (q.v TAT-8 project). Elementary system tasks were specified in 'Green' with the aim of implementing these as individual tasks on the operating system.

In addition, objects were specified, each of which correspond to a 'thread of functionality' from the user's point of view. 'Logging-on' would be such a 'thread of functionality', which would typically invoke several elementary objects during execution. The user-oriented objects generally contain no state, just being a sequence of object invocations. (Q.v. the 'sequencing' problem encountered by the VDM Toolset project).

The STC specification language 'Green' was used without any supporting tools being available, because the stand-alone type and consistency checker did not run on the target system where it had been decided to carry out the development. (The alternative would have been to host it on the DEC VAX, as was done with TAT-8).

There was experience already with 'Green' and the specifications were able to be reviewed for correctness and consistency.

The specifications were implemented by coding directly from 'Green' rather than being refined into more detail. (Although this was not investigated, the implication here is that, as with TAT-8, the specifications must have been at a very detailed level).

5.3   Experience from Using VDM/Green

With thoroughly reviewed specifications of objects, implemented directly as tasks on the operating system, the overall functionality of the system more than satisfied the customer's expectation. (Figures were not collected by the investigators on faults found during unit testing and integration, but these were not flagged as a problem).

There was, however, a serious problem with the throughput (performance) of the initial implementation. When elementary objects (which could be very 'small') were treated as tasks by the operating system, very poor processing rates were experienced (e.g. 10% of requirement specification). In retrospect, the designers realised that they did not know which features of the operating system to use to get the best performance and that treating objects as tasks was 'correct' but too naive.

Investigation by the designers revealed that during some 'thread of functionality' object invokations, such as logging on, many elementary objects were using operating system facilities in a way the makers never intended. For example, an object could open a file, read a record and close the file, only to be immediately followed by another object opening the same file and updating the same record etc.

This problem was tackled by combining objects into clusters. A cluster would correspond to an operating system task and would exploit the fact that, within a cluster, objects need not all behave as self-contained entities in the operating system sense. This approach achieved dramatic improvements in performance.

With this method of development, where specifications of objects are to be implemented as tasks on an operating system, it must be recognised that there is a mapping stage which depends as much on the properties of the target operating system as the properties of the application.

Initially poor performance of an implementation may be improved or corrected totally by changing the mapping. In this development, the designers have not had to change the abstract design, only the mapping.

The existance of a solid formal specification gave the 'Mailman' designers the confidence to try different mappings without worrying about damaging the functional integrity of the system.

6.   Conclusions

i)   The developments examined here all adopted VDM as a specification language rather than a full development method. This may have been due to the lack of suitable tools to support use of a rigorous approach, but it is an open question whether tools would have been sufficient.

ii)   VDM in the forms described here proved to be of no significant help during the architectural design stage. This may have been due to the lack of experience of the developers but it is more likely that it is not a very suitable vehicle for this stage. One suspects that the whole issue of architectural design has yet to be formalised and that all formal specification languages suffer from the same drawback.

iii)   An 'object-oriented' design strategy was followed in every case, despite the different application areas, and the two different groups of developers involved. This seems to have fitted particularly well with the use of VDM as a specification language. When looking at the satisfactory results the developers obtained, part of the success must be attributed to this strategy.

iv)   Eventual implementation of objects involves mapping onto a host environment, typically an operating system.

       When the implementors were not sufficiently familiar with the capabilities and limitations of the host system, the mapping stage caused problems. In the Mailman case, at least the VDM specification allowed optimisation with respect to the environment to be carried out with confidence and effectiveness, and without destroying the structure of the system.

v)   The inherent interdependencies between objects in a system often meant that problems arose from the need to define interfaces. To some extent this problem can be reduced by better design of the structuring aspects of future specification languages. Meanwhile it is a point to bear in mind when using existing variants of VDM.

vi)   In all cases the tool support was very limited. The perseverance of the developers is hence all the more commendable. Support tools in the shape of the VDM Toolset will shortly be available, and will hopefully deal smoothly with the more clerical aspects of the specification task. As a note of caution though, some users felt that simplistic tools could, however, 'get in the way' of the early stages of design, when the developer does not want to stop to make every detail consistent.

To sum up, these cases illustrate how the STC group is beginning to come to grips with VDM and to make effective use of VDM technology. More work clearly needs to be done to provide effective <u>tools</u>, better specification <u>languages</u> with facilities for structuring design and dealing with concurrency, and development <u>methods</u> which support the 'rigorous' paradigm in a practical way. There is also a serious need for more quantitive studies to be carried out on projects using formal methods, as there is for other aspects of software engineering. Meanwhile, I hope these success stories give sufficient impetus to other groups to begin to introduce VDM technology and reap the benefits in productivity and quality which formal methods promise.

Acknowledgements

I would like to thank Martin Ash, the co-author of [6] for permission to include many of the project details in this paper. I would also like to acknowledge the generous donation of time on the part of those project members and other colleagues who have provided source information and helpful comments on this paper.

Much of the material was originally collected for the RAISE Project 315, which is a collaboration between DDC, NBB and member companies of the STC Plc Group. RAISE is partly supported under the CEC Esprit scheme.

References

[1]   C.B. Jones 'Software Development : A Rigourous Approach' 1980
       Prentice-Hall, 1980

[2]   P. Jackson, 'Green Language Reference Manual',
       STC-IDEC 714-96410-UV, 30th March, 1985

[3]   R. Shaw & A. Walshe, 'Concrete Syntax for the STC VDM
       Reference Language', 725 05305, October, 1985

[4]   B. Monahan & A. Walshe, 'Context Conditions for the STC VDM
       Reference Language', 725 05308, February 1986

[5]   D. Bjorner, B.T. Denvir, E. Meiling, J.S. Pedersen, 'The RAISE Project -
       Fundamental Issues and Requirements', RAISE/DDC/EM/1/v6, 10th December, 1985

[6]   J.M.D. Ash & R.J. Crispin, 'Management Issues',
       RAISE/STC/JMDA/6/v3, 29th August, 1986

[7]   A. Goldberg & D. Robson, 'SMALLTALK-80 The Language and its Implementation',
       1983

[8]   P. Jackson, 'PDL Checker User Guide', STC-IDEC 714-96411-UW, 29th March, 1985

UNIX is a registered trade mark.

VDM in Three Generations of Ada[1] Formal Descriptions

Jan Storbank Pedersen

Dansk Datamatik Center

Lundtoftevej 1 C

DK-2800 Lyngby

Denmark

Abstract

Since 1980, three different formal descriptions of the Ada programming language have been developed, based on the principles of the Vienna Development Method (VDM). This paper characterizes each of the three descriptions and explains some of the differences.

1 Introduction.

Formally describing the semantics of programming languages has since the very first years of the Vienna Development Method (VDM) been one of the major application areas for this method; examples are [Bekić et al 74] for PL/I, [Bjørner et al 78] for Algol 60, and [Haff et al 80] for CHILL. For the programming language Ada ([Ada 79], [Ada 80], [Ada 83]), the situation is unique in the sense that at this point in time VDM has been used in three different formal descriptions of Ada. This paper presents an overview of the three descriptions and elaborates on some of the similarities and differences.

The reader is assumed to be familiar with the general concepts of VDM as described in [Bjørner et al 78].

The first VDM description of Ada ([Ada 79] and partly [Ada 80]) is documented in [Bjørner et al 80] and was developed by master thesis students at the Department of Computer Science at the Technical University of Denmark (TUD). It will in the following be referred to as the TUD 80 description.

---

[1]Ada is a registered trademark of the U.S. Government, Ada Joint Program Office.

The second VDM description of Ada ([Ada 80]) is documented in [Bruun et al 82], [Jørgensen 81], [Storbank et al 82], [Clemmensen et al 81], [Gøbel 81], and was developed as part of the DDC Ada compiler project ([Bjørner et al 80a]) at Dansk Datamatik Center. It will in the following be referred to as the DDC 82 description.

The third VDM-based description of Ada ([Ada 83]) is documented in [Botta et al 87] and [Astesiano et al 87] and was developed as part of the CEC Multi-Annual Programme project, "The Draft Formal Definition of ANSI/MIL-STD 1815A Ada" that was carried out by Dansk Datamatik Center, CRAI and I.E.I.-C.N.R. (sub-constractor to CRAI), and with significant contributions from consultants at the universities of Genoa and Pisa, and the Technical University of Denmark. It will in the following be referred to as the AdaFD definition.

Prior to presenting the three formal descriptions, some general remarks on Ada and formally describing Ada will be made.

2 Formally Describing Ada.

Ada is a fairly recent programming language developed during the late seventies and early eighties. It belongs to the class of procedural languages such as Algol and Pascal, but it has a number of additional features that make the language as large and complex as for example CHILL, see [Haff et al 87] in these proceedings. Some of the parts of Ada that make it "more than just Pascal" are:

- Separate compilation, which means that a program can be made up by units that have been compiled separately and reside in a so-called program library. These units may refer to each other, and the rules for how this can be utilized by the programmer are defined by the language, and the adherence must be checked by all compilation systems.

- Tasking, which allows the programmer to define that certain activities can take place concurrently, and means are provided for defining such processes (called tasks) and communication between tasks in the form of entries that can be called (by one task) and whose effects are defined by so-called accept statements (of another task). Apart from this form of communication (hand-shaking), tasks are also allowed to share variables.

- Packages. They are a kind of modules that allow types, variables, subprograms and other entities to be grouped together, and they allow certain details to be hidden from users of the package. The latter is obtained by dividing the information of a package into two parts:

  - the specification that describes the interface, e.g. the formal parameters of a procedure, and

  - the body that describes the implementation, like the statements of an exported procedure.

- A type and a subtype concept. The former allows user definition of simple as well as composite types (as arrays and records). The subtype concept allows the user to place, possibly dynamic, constraints on the values of a type; thereby requiring a run-time test to determine whether a given value belongs to a subtype (knowing at compile-time that the type of the value is correct).

- Input-output. The whole concept of using a file system from within an Ada program is defined by the language. This implies that an Ada program has a standardized interface to the native file system on all implementations.

The above features and many others make the development of a formal definition of Ada a non-trivial job.

It is not within the scope of this paper to describe all the activities related to formally describing smaller or larger parts of Ada that have taken place around the world. Only the first major attempt is briefly mentioned in the following. This very first attempt at making a formal definition of Ada was carried out by INRIA and it resulted in a number of definitions ([DoD 80], [INRIA 82]) of subsets of different versions of Ada, for example the dynamic aspects of tasking was never addressed. The style was denotational, using continuations, and it was expressed using a meta-language that syntactically looked like Ada itself. The latter in a few cases caused readers to wonder as to what was actually being defined. The major revision of Ada that resulted in [Ada 83] has not been followed up by a revision of the INRIA definition.

In the VDM-tradition of programming language semantics, a formal semantics consists of:

- An abstract syntax called AS1.

- A static semantics (well-formedness) definition based on AS1.

- An abstract syntax called AS2.

- A dynamic semantics definition based on AS2.

The abstract syntax AS1 describes, using a number of domain equations, the input to the static semantics. It reflects the structure of the BNF-grammar defining the concrete syntax of the language, but syntactic items, like keywords, that are present in the BNF-grammar to help parsing the program text are not present in AS1, similarly information on operator precedence has been used to represent expressions in AS1 in a tree-like fashion.

The static semantics defines the context sensitive conditions that a given AS1 construct must satisfy. These conditions can also be characterized as those expressable without reference to execution. Violation of any of these rules must in Ada be detected by a compiler. In language reference manuals, such conditions are expressed in natural language, typically using words such as "must", "allowed", "legal" or "illegal". The conditions comprise rules related to:

- Strong typing; meaning that an expression must have a type that is in complete agreement with the context in which it appears.

- Scope and visibility rules, defining the scope of declarations, the names that may occur at any given place in the program text, and what they denote.

- Overloading and resolution of overloading. In Ada, subprograms (and similar entities) may overload, meaning that a given name may denote several such subprograms and that the context of the occurrence of such a name must determine the correct subprogram. The static semantics must define the conditions under which overloading can be resolved (a unique denotation can be determined) and what the unique denotation is.

In the VDM-style, the static semantics is expressed by a set of, typically applicative, formulas in a denotational syntax-directed way so that to each syntactic construct there is a formula expressing the well-formedness thereof using some kind of context information. This latter context information can have several forms, more about this can be found in the following sections.

The abstract syntax AS2 is chosen so as to be suited for expressing the dynamic semantics (run-time behaviour) of a program. For simple languages, AS2 may be the same as AS1. But for complex languages like Ada it would be very cumbersome to use AS1 as a basis for describing the dynamic semantics. Just one aspect to illustrate the problems in using AS1:

- In AS1 an identifier may denote several entities due to overloading. But if a construct is statically correct, all such identifiers must have a unique meaning (determined by the static semantics), and since finding that meaning (given by the corresponding declaration of the identifier) does not depend on any fact not known statically, it would be confusing to the reader to redo the overload resolution as part of the dynamic semantics. For this reason unique names are introduced in AS2. The extent to which other transformations should be made is discussed in the subsequent sections on each of the three descriptions.

Introducing an abstract syntax different from AS1 requires that the relation between AS1 and AS2 is given. This is done in the form of a set of transformation formulæ mapping AS1 constructs into AS2 constructs. These formulæ of cource utilize the formulæ defined in the static semantics for resolving overloading etc.

The dynamic semantics describes the run-time behaviour of statically correct programs. In language reference manuals, this behaviour is expressed in natural language and the activities involved are described using terms as "evaluation" (of expressions), "elaboration" (of declarations) and "execution" (of statements). The existence of tasks in Ada has important impact on the dynamic semantics of Ada. Roughly speaking, the dynamic semantics can be divided into a pseudo-sequential part and a tasking or parallel part, where the former resembles the dynamic semantics of a traditional sequential language like Pascal. The division between sequential and parallel semantics is not the same in the three formal descriptions and the topic is further discussed in the sections to follow.

3   The TUD 80 Description.

The formal description of Ada contained in [Bjørner et al 80] deals with the earliest versions of Ada. Originally the papers that are part of [Bjørner et al 80], i.e. [Bundgaard et al 80] (static semantics), [Storbank 80] (dynamic sequential semantics), [Løvengreen 80] (dynamic parallel semantics) and [Dommergaard 80] (the design of a virtual machine for Ada; not discussed in this paper), described Ada as specified in [Ada 79] and then later minor ajustments were made to come closer to [Ada 80].

The formal descriptions were individual master theses and were a such primarily aimed at investigating and hopefully demonstrating the feasibility of using the VDM-approach in defining interesting aspects of Ada. Knowing at the time that CHILL (a language of similar complexity and size) could be defined using VDM ([Haff et al 80]), the activities undertaken in the Ada definition work can be described as somewhere between engineering and research. The formal descriptions did, due to resource-limitations, not cover all of Ada, but covered enough to demonstrate the feasibility of the approaches involved.

The following subsections give the overall characteristics of the different parts.

3.1   The TUD 80 Static Semantics Description.

The description of the static semantics of Ada is a very complex issue since a large number of more or less interrelated concepts are involved. As a means of dealing with this complexity, a number of subsets of Ada, having increasing levels of complexity, were identified. This approach was chosen based on an ideas of Dr. Hans Bruun from the Technical University of Denmark. The subsets were called A0, A1, ... through A6, the latter being the subset presented in [Bundgaard et al 80]. The other subsets were used for experiments carried out in order to come up with syntactic and semantic structures suitable for describing the difficult parts of Ada.

In AS1, it was for the sake of simplicity decided to assume that certain syntactic constructs that in Ada cannot be distinguished based purely on a syntactic analysis were distinguished in AS1. For example one cannot in all cases syntactically distinguish an indexed component, a function call, a slice (a sub-array) and a type conversion, since they may all have the form: F(A). So a (not defined) 'disambiguator' was assumed to be involved in yielding the AS1 representation of an Ada construct.

The main problem investigated during the analysis of the subsets was how to represent the context information needed when expressing the well-formedness of a syntactic construct. This context information was termed "the surroundings" and it corresponds to what others may call a "static environment". The most important part of the surroundings is the one describing the visibility of names. It is discussed in some detail later.

The formulæ follow the structure of AS1 and they are expressed using the applicative parts of Meta-IV (the meta-language associated with VDM, see [Bjørner et al 78]). A minor technical detail that had some stylistic impact on the formula was that the *exit* mechanism of Meta-IV was used to describe error situations related to the generation and extraction of descriptors. These *exits* were then trapped by an 'enclosing' (or 'calling') well-formedness formula.

The following is a short example of a static semantics aspect and how it was described in the static semantics.

Visibility

An important part of the static semantics of a programming language is the visibility rules. In Ada, a declared entity may sometimes be referred to by several different names. This is illustrated by the following short example:

```
package P1 is
    package P2 is
        V: INTEGER;
        - - V, P2.V and P1.P2.V are here all legal names
        - - for the above V (Point 1)
    end P2;
    - - P2.V and P1.P2.V are all legal names for V
    - - here, whereas V itself is not
end P1;

V: INTEGER; - - another V!
- - The only legal name for the inner V here is P1.P2.V
```

Figure 3.1

The visibility at a given point in AS1 (and hence in the original Ada text) is described in a component of the surroundings called the dictionary. It contains the associations between identifiers and their descriptors. In order to reflect the visibility at Point 1 in Figure 3.1, it seems natural to consider a dictionary something like Figure 3.2.

$$\left[\begin{array}{l} P1 \rightarrow \left[\begin{array}{l} P2 \rightarrow \left[\begin{array}{l} V \rightarrow \text{'descriptor for V'} \\ * \end{array} \right] \end{array} \right] \\ \\ P2 \rightarrow \left[\begin{array}{l} V \rightarrow \text{'descriptor for V'} \\ * \end{array} \right] \\ V \rightarrow \text{'descriptor for V'} \\ * \end{array} \right]$$

Figure 3.2

Figure 3.2 mimics the hierarchical structure of the program text and immediately constains all three possible paths to the inner V's descriptor at Point 1. However, it is easy to see that updating such a structure; for example, declaring an additional variable just after V would mean updating at three different places in the structure (indicated by * in the figure). In order to avoid cumbersome updating and the duplication of information (V's descriptor occurs three times), a so-called "high dictionary" shown in Figure 3.3 is introduced.

$$\left[P1 \rightarrow \left[P2 \rightarrow [V \rightarrow \text{'descriptor for V'}] \right] \right]$$

Figure 3.3

If one in addition to this 'high dictionary' at all times during the static analysis keeps track of "where one is" (in this case, Point 1 of Figure 3.1 could be identified by the tuple $<P1,P2>$) updating will be easy, and before trying to find the meaning of a name (like P2.V), one can in a simple way, knowing for example that one is in $<P1.P2>$, "expand" this dictionary to be exactly as the one in Figure 3.2 (if you are within P1, extract the contents of its descriptor, if your are within P2 ...). This latter dictionary is more convenient when analyzing names such as V and P2.V. In this way, both updating the (high) dictionary which is part of the surroundings and using it in its (temporarily) expanded version is easy.

3.2 The TUD 80 Dynamic Semantics Description.

First, let us consider the abstract syntax AS2. As described in section 2, AS2 differs from AS1 at least by having unique names (and overloading resolved). Still, one needs to decide which other differences to introduce, if any. In TUD 80, we took the approach of making AS2 as abstract as possible, by for example using sets and mappings where possible to indicate that the order among certain constructs have no importance (like the identifiers in the identifier list of a variable declaration and the alternatives in a case statement, since the latter are known to contain disjoint choices). Introducing all these differences, made writing the dynamic semantics easier but put an extra burden on the AS1 to AS2 transformation (not part of [Bjørner et al 80]) and increased the "distance" from the original Ada program.

The dynamic semantics itself is divided into two parts: one deals solely with the pseudo-sequential parts of the language and the other with parts involving tasking. This division was made based on the CHILL experience [Haff et al 80], and following that approach Meta-IV was extended by a meta-process concept taken from Hoare's CSP as described in [Hoare 78]. A semantics of the combined language is presented in [Folkjær et al 79]. It meant that the sequential parts of Ada were described using the imperative parts of Meta-IV and that the meta-state in a sense became the combined states of all meta-processes (more about those processes later). One important impact that the tasking parts had on the non-tasking parts was that since tasks (processes) in Ada can share variables and meta-processes (following Hoare) cannot, a special meta-process had to be defined to model the store of an Ada program. However, by defining a special set of formulæ to handle the communication with this storage process, the tasking influence was hidden from most of the sequential semantics.

The sequential dynamic semantics is described in [Storbank 80] and is expressed using a denotational, syntax directed style following the structure of AS2. The direct semantics *trap exit* mechanism has been used to model transfer of control, like goto, Ada exits out of loops, and exceptions (dynamic errors that are propagated and for which a handling routine may be specified). The dynamic semantics still uses the concept of an environment and a store as for other block-structured languages.

The following briefly describes the environment and storage structures chosen.

Storage and Environment

Ada allows the definition of composite types which implies the existence of composite values. The question to answered when modelling the store is whether one wants to use structured locations, as in the CHILL definition [Haff et al 80]. In Ada, they are not needed due to the controlled way in which record structures are allowed to vary (as opposed to the situation in CHILL). Hence, the storage is modelled as a mapping from non-structured locations to possibly structured values (structured for composite types). However, due to the possibility of renaming a subcomponent and also of accessing a subcomponent by reference if it is an actual subprogram parameter, the concept of sub-locations is needed. But this is easily handled by using the non-structured location of the composite object and a 'path' into the value. The latter is a list of record field identifiers or index-tuples corresponding to field selection in records and indexing in arrays.

When looking at the dictionary structures described in section 3.1, one might expect the (dynamic) environment to be hierarchical as well. But due to the unique names introduced in AS2, there is no need to use 'expanded names' like P1.P2.V when accessing the inner V in Figure 3.1.

Therefore, a 'flat' environment has been chosen. It then, of course, does not reflect the true visibility rules of Ada (too many entities may be accessible). This is however only a minor disadvantage since the static semantics guarantees that these entities are never accesssed anyway, since it would have violated the visibility rules.

The tasking aspects of the Ada are described in [Løvengreen 80]. As mentioned earlier, it required an extension to the Meta-IV language. The process concept introduced can be briefly characterized as processes whose only means of interaction are a high-level, value-passing, hand-shaking mechanism. Each process has a local state. Process types can be defined and instances thereof can be created possibly with parameters. Using this process concept gives the tasking description an operational flavor. But we felt that it corresponded fairly well to a reader's notion of processes that often tend to be operational.

The execution of an Ada program is modelled by the following processes:

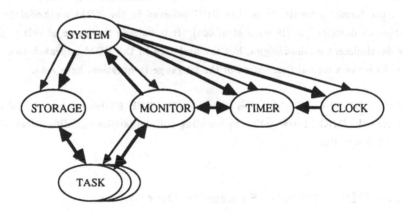

Figure 3.4

The thin lines indicate creation. Bold lines indicate communication. Only one copy exists of each of the processes SYSTEM, STORAGE, MONITOR, TIMER and CLOCK; whereas the number of TASK processes may vary depending on the number of tasks currently existing for a given Ada program. The SYSTEM process is used to start up the system and close it down when the outermost task terminates. The TIMER and CLOCK attempts to model the passing of time and expiration of delays (a special Ada feature that allows a task to ask to be delayed at least D seconds). The MONITOR keeps track of the status e.g. of all tasks.

This model is more restrictive than actually required by Ada. For example, it implies mutually exclusive access to all of the storage (administered by the STORAGE process) which is not required and probably not even intended, in Ada. Another problem that was not fully solved was to determine and describe the level of 'granularity' at which a task can be interrupted either because some other task aborts it or raises an exception (FAILURE) in it, the latter is particularly troublesome. Such interrupts are said to be able to occur "anywhere" in the meta-language 'program' except where it is explicitly precluded by using a special symbol in the formulæ (in a very few places).

4   The DDC 82 Description.

The DDC 82 description is a further development of the TUD 80 description. But this time the context was different.

First of all, the definition activity was now part of a CEC Multi-Annual Programme Project called "The Portable Ada Programming System Project" (or the PAPS project for short), where DDC was to develop an Ada compiler. The reason for making a more complete and up-to-date version of the formal semantics was that DDC believed in the VDM methodology for compiler construction as described in [Bjørner et al 80a]. It is outside the scope of this paper to discuss compiler development methodologies, but the first step in the VDM approach to compiler development is to make a formal description of the langauge in question, here Ada.

Since the DDC 82 description relies heavily on the TUD 80 description, the following subsections describe the DDC 82 description by pointing out similarities and differences with respect to the TUD 80 description.

4.1   The DDC 82 Static Semantics Description.

The static semantics well-formedness formulas of the DDC 82 definition are found in [Bruun et al 82]. AS1 was pretty close to the TUD 80 one, meaning that some disambiguation was still assumed, but of course AS1 was extended to (almost) full Ada (from the subset A6). A few things like pragmas and representation clauses were not included.

In the static semantics, the formulæ were still written using the applicative Meta-IV. But the usage of *exits* was avoided since it had a bad influence on the readability of the formulæ; moreover, the alternative: to construct error descriptors and use those, was more useful in the later development of a compiler front end.

The dictionary was in a sense made more abstract than the TUD 80 one described in section 3.1. This was done by observing that the structured dictionary of Figure 3.2 could be obtained more elegantly than by having to update sub-parts of sub-parts of a high dictionary such as the one shown in Figure 3.3, and then later to expand it (at the point of usage) to one like Figure 3.2. The solution chosen is to introduce a so-called "dictionary constructor function" that given the description of locally declared entities produces a dictionary as the one in Figure 3.2. Figure 4.1 shows the dictionary constructor corresponding to Point 1 in Figure 3.1.

$$\lambda\text{local-dict.}\left(\begin{bmatrix} \text{P1} & \rightarrow & [\text{P2} \rightarrow \text{local-dict}] \\ \text{P2} & \rightarrow & \text{local-dict} \end{bmatrix} + \text{local-dict}\right)$$

Figure 4.1

Having built such a function, all one needs to have is the local-dict that is always a flat dictionary (here $[V \rightarrow$ 'descriptor of V']) where inserting the descriptor of a new entity is very easy: no extra information on "where one is in the program text" is needed. When the total dictionary is required, the constructor is just applied to the local dictionary. Finally, new dictionary constructors are only built when entering composite units like packages, subprogram bodies, etc.

Since both AS1 and AS2 were going to correspond to intermediate program representations within the compiler to be build, the relation between the two needed to be documented. This is done in the AS1 → AS2 transformation document ([Jørgensen 81]), and as expected the transformation formulæ make extensive use of the static semantics formulæ, and they are syntax directed as well, following the structure of AS1.

4.2 The DDC 82 Dynamic Semantics Description.

Except for minor updates due to differences between [Ada 79] and [Ada 80] and the completion of certain parts that were left out in the TUD 80 description, the only change to the dynamic semantics is the addition of a formal definition of the input-output system for Ada [Gøbel 81]. The updated definition of the sequential semantics if found in [Storbank et al 82] and the corresponding tasking description in [Clemmensen et al 81].

The definition of the input-output system deserves a few remarks. Ada describes input-output based on the concepts of "external files" and "file objects" (or internal files). An external file is something existing outside the Ada program, whereas the internal files are objects of special file types provided in Ada. The latter means that internal file variables (variables declared to be of a file type) behave like other variables and in particular they may be shared among several tasks. When an internal file is open, it is associated with an external file (where values are read or written). One such external file may be used via several internal files.

In [Gøbel 81] the above features were described in the following way: It was decided not to involve the STORAGE process (see section 3.2) in keeping the internal file values. But since they may be shared among tasks, no single task meta-process can "own" an internal file, and the solution was therefore to let internal files be meta-processes on their own. Similarly, and maybe more naturally, external files are also modelled as meta-processes. In addition, a single file system process is introduced to keep track of the external files. Declaring a file object involves the creation of a new internal file process; opening a file makes an internal file process "aware" of an existing external file process; and reading from a file involves transferring the value in question from the external file process via the internal file process to a task process while updating administrative information local to the processes, like the current reading position of the file.

5 The AdaFD Definition.

The usefulness of formal descriptions of programming languages is beginning to be recognized outside the academic world. One of the signs is that the CEC has sponsored a project whose main result is a formal definition of Ada in its latest version ([Ada 83]). This section describes the main results of that project.

First of all, the formal definition had to describe what is defined in [Ada 83], no more and no less. It meant that "implementation bias" was unacceptable. In cases where [Ada 83] leaves a choice open to an implementation, for example the evaluation order of some sub-expressions, all choices had to be defined. Similar obligations were not always adhered to in the DDC 82 definition, since it was to form the basis for just one implementation.

One thing that had to be changed in the AdaFD definition with respect to the TUD 80 and DDC 82 descriptions was the description of tasking and the way tasking influences the overall dynamic semantics. Some of the reasons for that were explained in section 3.2. The main ideas of the new approach are presented in section 5.2.

It was foreseen from the start that the new formal description would contain a large number of formulæ, especially in the parts related to the semantic information structures used in the static as well as the dynamic semantics. This called for a structuring mechanism, and since Meta-IV definitions are (formally) "flat", new features had to be introduced. The solution chosen was to define a meta-language that allows the definition of algebraic specifications. Moreover, so-called modules are introduced that consist of a number of algebraic specifications, types that are particular algebras based on the algebraic specifications, and applicative formulæ with parameters of those types. Traditionally, the property-oriented specification techniques, to which algebraic approaches apply, are seen as "competitors" to the model-oriented approach, to which VDM belongs. But we felt that a useful result could be obtained by combining the two approaches, thereby allowing the user to use the algebraic parts when a property-oriented, axioms-based definition is felt appropriate, and use the model-oriented parts in other cases. The way this is achieved is by first recognizing that the Meta-IV domain constructors are useful and essential facilities when constructing a model, and then define parameterized algebraic specifications for all of the domain constructors, so that when the parameters are supplied, a new algebraic specification is generated containing all the traditional operations on values of the sort of this new specification. For example, the parameterized algebraic specification SET will when provided with the element specification, yield an algebraic specification with operations like $\cup$, $\in$, etc. The meta-language is documented in [Reggio et al 86].

5.1   The AdaFD Static Semantics Description.

In both the TUD 80 and the DDC 82 descriptions, a "disambiguation" was supposed to take place before the AS1 representation of a piece of Ada text could be constructed. Such a disambiguation would, however, sometimes require a deep semantic analysis involving overload resolution, evaluation of static expressions, etc.; activities that are complex and cannot be left undefined. Instead of defining this complex disambiguator, AS1 was made just as ambiguous as the Ada syntax (but still tree-structured). This places the disambiguation as an integral part of the static semantics.

The static semantics uses algebraic specifications to describe the semantic structures. These algebraic specifications define the operations available on the structures. Based on the specifications, types (i.e. initial algebras) are defined, and those are used in the applicative well-formedness and other formulæ. The applicative formulæ, for example the well-formedness formulæ, are still structured in a syntax directed way as in the two earlier definitions.

For the part of the semantic structures describing visibility, the idea of using a dictionary constructor (first used in the DDC 82 definition) was still found to be very useful in the AdaFD static semantics.

The static semantics is defined in [Botta et al 87].

5.2   The AdaFD Dynamic Semantics Description

The AS2 used by the dynamic semantics is closer to AS1 and thereby to Ada than those used i the TUD 80 and the DDC 82 definitions. This was the result of a trade-off between having an AS2 that made it easy to see the relation between [Ada 83] and the dynamic semantics, and having one that made the dynamic semantics formulæ more elegant. AS2 still has unique names and overloading resolved, and some unnecessary information has been removed, e.g. package renamings (for giving a new name to a package).

The two previous formal definitions were not satisfactory in modelling shared storage and in defining the right activity levels of interruptability of tasks. So instead of having meta-processes "executing" more or less sequential pieces of meta-language text (as in the older definitions), it was decided to do something else.

The new approach taken is described in [Astesiano et al 86]. It is based on the principles of SMoLCS (Structured Monitored Linear Concurrent Systems) developed by Prof. E. Astesiano at the University of Genoa.

Following the principles of [Astesiano et al 86] the dynamic semantics is divided into two steps:

- the first step, called the denotational clauses, associates to AS2 constructs terms in a language suitable for representing processes,

- the second step gives semantics to terms in the above langauge by an algebraic specification of a so-called "concurrent algebra" that represents a concurrent system.

A concurrent system is here seeen as a labelled transition system, that may be built hierarchically from a number of sub-systems. The state of a system consists of the states of the sub-systems and some global information. The global information contains a model of the Ada storage and other information needed by more than one sub-system. The transitions of a system are described based on the transitions of its sub-systems in three steps:

- Synchronization, which defines the transitions representing synchronized actions of sets of sub-systems, and their effect on the global information.

- Parallelism, which defines the transitions representing the allowed parallel executions of sets of synchronized actions and the compound transformations of the global transformation (mutual exclusion problems, for example, are handled here).

- Monitoring, which defines the transitions of the overall system respecting some global constraints (e.g. interleaving, free parallelism, priorities, etc.).

At the bottom of this hierarchy, are the so-called "atomic actions". They describe indivisible semantic effects of parts of Ada constructs. This means that when the set of all different atomic actions of the dynamic semantics were chosen they had to respect the granularity level of interruptability defined in [Ada 83].

The first step makes use of some semantic information termed "local information". This contains parts of what is normally known as the environment (here "local environment"). The global information (used in the second step) contains a "global environment". One of the reasons for dividing the environment in two is that in [Ada 83] as opposed to [Ada 79] and [Ada 80], it must for example be checked whether a subprogram body has been elaborated when the subprogram is called. One task may be responsible for elaborating the subprogram body and another, inner, task may be created with an environment in which the subprogram body is not (yet) elaborated, but this status of the subprogram will change when the outer task reaches (and elaborates) the body.

Such environment changes in other tasks are contrary to the well-established principles for how environments may be used. Hence, in order to reflect this change in all inner tasks' environments, the environment is split so that a local "fixed" part (here mapping the subprogram identifier to a unique name, an "entity global name") can be given to the inner task, and another more dynamic part (the global environment) associating the unique name with a subprogram denotation that may change (when the body is elaborated) can be made part of the global information.

All of the above information structures like local and global information and denotations are defined using algebraic specifications. All of step 2 is also algebraically defined but a special syntax has been used to express the axioms. Step 1 consists mainly of applicative formulæ that in a syntax directed way follow AS2 and "provides input" to step 2. Since suggestive names have been chosen for the atomic actions and the operators of the concurrent algebra (part of the semantics associated to AS2 constructs by step 1), the first step can be read and intuitively understood by a reader, without the reader having to get troubled by the underlying semantics.

The dynamic semantics is documented in [Astesiano et al 87].

References

[Ada 79]   "Preliminary Ada Reference Manual", ACM Sigplan Notices, Vol. 14, No. 6 (Part A), June 1979.

[Ada 80]   U.S. Department of Defense: "Reference Manual for the Ada Programming Language", Proposed Standard Document, U.S. Department of Defense, July 1980.

[Ada 83]   U.S. Department of Defense: "Reference Manual for the Ada Programming Language", ANSI/MIL-STD 1815A, U.S. Department of Defense, January 1983.

[Astesiano et al 86]   E. Astesiano, A. Giovini, F. Mazzanti, G. Reggio, E. Zucca: "The Draft Formal Definition of Ada, Generalities on the Underlying Model", CRAI/University of Genoa, December 1986.

[Astesiano et al 87]   E. Astesiano, C. Bendix Nielsen, A. Fantechi, A. Giovini, E.W. Karlsen, F. Mazzanti, G. Reggio, E. Zucca: "The Draft Formal Definition of Ada, The Dynamic Semantics Definition", Dansk Datamatik Center/CRAI/IEI/University of Genoa, January 1987.

[Bekić et al 74]   H. Bekić, D. Bjørner, W. Henhapl, C.B. Jones and P. Lucas: "A Formal Definition of a PL/I Subset", Parts I and II, Technical Reports TR25.139, IBM Vienna Laboratory, December 1974.

[Bjørner et al 78] D. Bjørner, C.B. Jones (eds.): "The Vienna Development Method: The Meta-Language", Springer Verlag, Lecture Notes in Computer Science, Vol. 61, 1978.

[Bjørner et al 80] D. Bjørner, O.N. Oest (eds.): "Towards a Formal Description of Ada", Springer Verlag Lecture Notes in Computer Science, Vol. 98, 1980.

[Bjørner et al 80a] D. Bjørner, O.N. Oest: "The DDC Ada Compiler Project", in [Bjørner et al 80].

[Botta et al 87]   N. Botta, J. Storbank Pedersen: "The Draft Formal Definition of Ada, The Static Semantics Definition", Dansk Datamatik Center, January 1987.

[Bruun et al 82]   H. Bruun, J. Bundgaard, J. Jørgensen: "Portable Ada Programming System, Ada Static Semantics, Well-formedness Criteria", Dansk Datamatik Center, March 1982.

[Bundgaard et al 80]   J. Bundgaard, L. Schultz: "A (Denotational) Semantics Method for Defining Ada Context Conditions", in [Bjørner et al 80].

[Clemmensen et al 81]   G.B. Clemmensen, H.H. Løvengreen: "Portable Ada Programming System, Dynamic Semantics, Description of Ada Tasking", Dansk Datamatik Center, November 1981.

[Dommergaard 80]   O. Dommergaard: "The Design of a Virtual Machine for Ada", in [Bjørner et al 80].

[DoD 80]   U.S. Department of Defense: "Formal Definition of the Ada Programming Language", Preliminary Version for Public Review, U.S. Department of Defense.

[Folkjær et al 79]   P. Folkjær, D. Bjørner: "A Formal Model of A Generalized CSP-like Language", ID 879, Department of Computer Science, Technical University of Denmark, 1979.

[Gøbel 81]   P. Gøbel: "Portable Ada Programming System, Dynamic Semantics, Input-Output Model", Dansk Datamatik Center, October 1981.

[Haff et al 80]   P. Haff, D. Bjørner (eds.): "A Formal Definition of CHILL. A Supplement to the CCITT Recommendation Z.200", Dansk Datamatik Center, 1980.

[Haff et al 87]   P. Haff, A. Olsen: "Use of VDM within the CCITT", (these proceedings), 1987.

[Hoare 78]   C.A.R. Hoare: "Communicating Sequential Processes", Comm. of the ACM, Vol. 21, No. 8, August 1978.

[INRIA 82]   INRIA: "Formal Definition of the Ada Programming Language", Honeywell Inc., CII Honeywell Bull, 1982.

[Jørgensen 81]   J. Jørgensen: "Portable Ada Programming System, Ada Static Semantics, AS1 → AS2 Transformation", Dansk Datamatik Center, November 1981.

[Løvengreen 80]   H.H. Løvengreen: "Parallelism in Ada", in [Bjørner et al 80].

[Reggio et al 1986]   G. Reggio, P. Inverardi, E. Astesiano, A. Giovini, F. Mazzanti, E. Zucca: "The Draft Formal Definition of Ada, The User Manual of the Meta-Language", CRAI/IEI/University of Genoa, September 1986.

[Storbank 80]   J. Storbank Pedersen: "A Formal Semantics Definition of Sequential Ada", in [Bjørner et al 80].

[Storbank et al 82]   J. Storbank Pedersen, P. Folkjær, I.Ø. Hansen: "Portable Ada Programming System, Dynamic Semantics, Description of Sequential Ada", Dansk Datamatik Center, March 1982.

EXPERIENCE WITH VDM IN NORSK DATA

Uwe Schmidt   Reinhard Völler

Norsk Data GmbH

Holzkoppelweg 5, D-2300 Kiel 1

Abstract:

Since 1982 NORSK DATA and the University of Kiel, Germany, have been cooperating in the area of compiler development. During this time a multilanguage multi-target compiler system has been developed using the Vienna Development Method (**VDM**) and its specification language, **META IV** A common intermediate language has been derived from the denotational semantic specifications of the source languages and the compiling algorithms have been developed. The formal specifications of the target machines are transformed automatically into executable **Pascal** programs to implement the code generators.

The paper describes the development of the system and the experience gained when using **VDM** and **META IV** in an industrial environment. Some ideas for future development of **META IV** tools are outlined.

1 The CAT Project

1.1 Project Overview

Since 1982 NORSK DATA and the University of Kiel, Germany, have been cooperating in the development of a machine independent compiler system for several source languages. This system may be viewed as a specialization of the classical UNCOL problem [Con58]. The main goal of the project was to lower the maintenance costs of the compilers and to allow easy portation to future computer systems.

The entire system is specified using the Vienna Development Method and its specification language **META IV**. Initially the languages **Pascal**, **FORTRAN**, **COBOL** and a **BASIC** dialect were taken into account. Today, compilers for **Pascal**, **C-BASIC** and C have been implemented on several mini- and micro-computers.

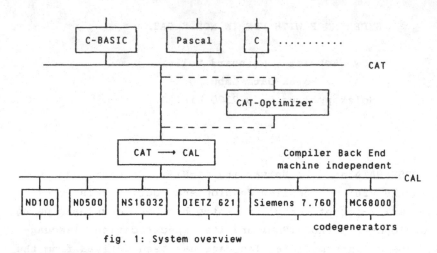

fig. 1: System overview

The source languages are compiled into the common intermediate language **CAT** (Common Abstract Tree Language) [ScV83,Völ83]. In this language programs are explicit abstract trees. **CAT** has approximately the level of **Pascal** and does not imply any specific machine model.

Compiler backends which are automatically generated from formal machine descriptions in **META IV** then compile the **CAT** programs into executable code [ScV84, Sch83].

1.2 The Compiler Front Ends

In order to build the compiler system upon an unambiguous and mathematically sound basis, formal denotational specifications have been derived from the language standards and/or language manuals. **VDM** ensures that these descriptions are complete, consistent and mathematically sound [Sto82]. Correctness arguments can now be carried out relative to these formal descriptions. A further advantage of this approach is that the comparison of different languages is considerably simplified. The formalization of the semantics helps to detect constructs with differing syntax but equivalent semantics, as well as constructs with similar syntax but different semantics. The **META IV** specifications of the compiler front ends are systematically transformed into executable programs in an implementation language. For the codegenerators this step has been automated.

The main idea of designing **CAT** was to derive the language from a comparison of the dynamic semantics of the respective source languages [ScV81]. An important precondition for this comparison is that the interpretation functions for the syntactic constructs of the different source languages act on the same semantic domains. This means that a common storage model had to be defined.

The syntactic objects of the intermediate language were chosen from the union of all syntactic objects of the respective source languages according to the following criteria:

- From language elements which have the same semantics in several source languages only one is chosen for the intermediate language.

- If a syntactic object of one language is the general case of one or more objects of other languages, then only this element is included in the intermediate language.

- Any complex object which can be broken down into a sequence of simple objects already available in the intermediate language is omitted.

- Finally new objects are defined, which implement several other constructs of the source languages.

Any time a source language object is not itself included in **CAT** but implemented by a combination of other syntactic objects in the intermediate language, the necessary transformation functions are specified in **META IV**, giving a formal specification of the actions to be performed by a front end. The abstract syntax, static semantics and interpretation functions associated with the syntactic objects of the intermediate language yield a formal specification of **CAT**.

The compiler front ends are mainly automatically generated. NORSK DATA implemented a scanner generator which works similar to LEX and generates a scanner from a specification of the lexical tokens of a language.

The parser is generated using a LR(1)-parser generator. This parser performs the syntactical analysis and produces a concrete syntax tree (not stored).

This concrete tree is transformed by a transformer into the abstract syntax tree which can be handled by the compiling algorithm. The transformer is also automatically generated from specifications.

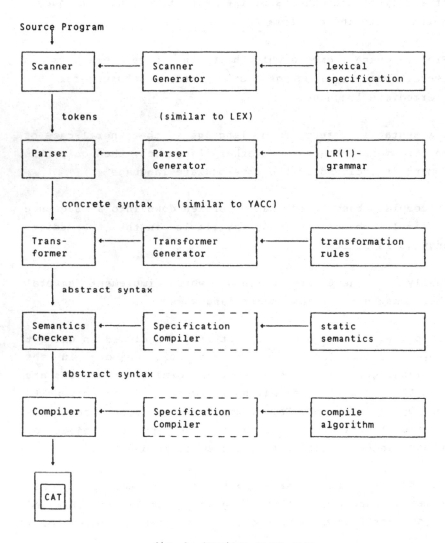

fig. 2: Compiler front ends

The static semantics and the compiling algorithm written in **META IV** are at present manually transformed into **Pascal** programs. We are quite confident that in the future this last step can also be automated using the experience we have made with the **META IV** compiler developed at the University of Kiel [Haß87].

Fig. 2 gives an overview of the construction process of the compiler front ends.

1.3 The Compiler Back Ends

The translation from **CAT** into a concrete target language is done in three steps. In this process we use a low level intermediate language **CAL** (**CAT** Assembly Language) which is still machine independent. Fig. 3 shows the structure of the compilers.

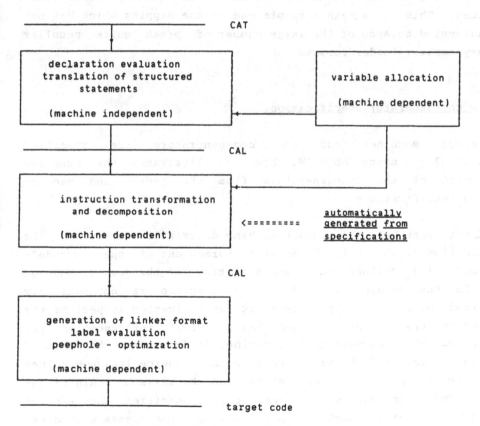

fig. 3: Compilation of CAT into target code

Firstly all **CAT** constructs are mapped into the **CAL** instructions of an "ideal" **CAT** machine, i. e. a machine realizing all required functions and operators. This step includes the decomposition of complex control structures, the declaration evaluation and the variable allocation. The generated **CAL** instructions mainly consist of assignments and conditional and unconditional jumps. The expressions contained in these instructions may still be arbitrarily complex.

A second step, which is the most important phase, performs a semantics preserving mapping of the general **CAT** operators into operators implemented on the given target machine. Complex instructions are decomposed into sequences of simpler instructions. The quality of the generated code is primarily determined in this phase.

In a last step the concrete bit patterns of the loader format are generated. This is a rather simple one to one mapping which has not been automated because of the large number of often quite peculiar and unsystematic loader formats.

1.4 The Codegenerator Specifications

The target machines and the codegenerators are specified denotationally using **META IV**. Fig. 4 illustrates the stepwise development of the codegenerators from the source and machine language specifications.

The first part of the target machine description consists of the specification of the available machine storage and of the "encode"-function which defines the representation of the source language values in the machine (box 1). This function is not uniquely determined by the target processor. Its specification is part of the compiler construction process and has a great influence on the quality of the language implementation. It determines the usage of the machine store and the set of representable source language values (e.g. the range of integer values and the maximum domain of set values). The second part of the description specifies the set of available elementary machine operations and associates with every operator a semantic function (box 3). This step is similar to the semantic definition of the **CAT** language operators (box 2). Important

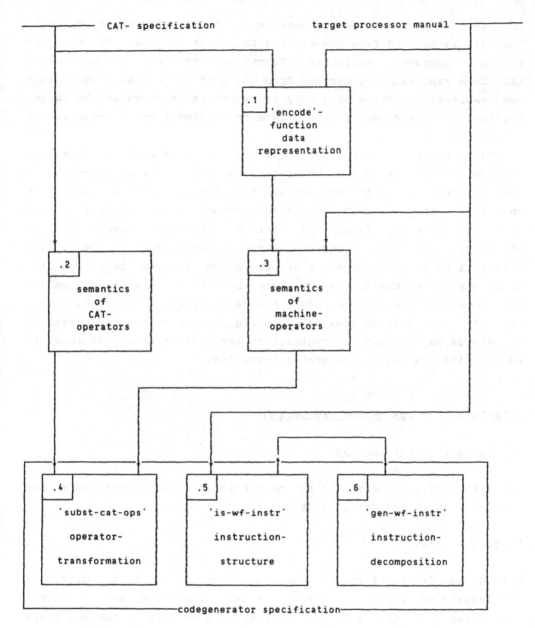

fig. 4: Codegenerator specification

for a comparison of the source and target language operators are the domains of definition of the semantic functions. The meaning of the machine operators is usually defined only for bit patterns. Therefore the domain of definition is extended to the source language values by means of the "encode"- function.

The first module of the codegenerator, the function "subst-cat-ops" (box 4), is derived from the meaning functions of the **CAT** and the machine language operators. Transformations are defined which transform expressions generated from **CAT** into semantically equivalent new expressions containing only operators implemented on the target machine. The selection of appropriate transformations is essentially controlled by the attribute values of the expressions. The instruction set of a processor is viewed as a subset of the **CAL** language. This is done by means of a Boolean Function "is-wf-instr" (box 5). This predicate contains all restrictions for the structure and the complexity of the machine instructions. No separation into syntactic (context free) and context sensitive conditions is necessary. This part of the codegenerator corresponds to the machine descriptions of the codegenerator generation systems based on the methods used by [Cat78, Glan78]. From the "is-wf-instr"- function the last module of the codegenerator, the decomposition algorithm "gen-wf-instr", is derived (box 6). This algorithm controls the breakdown of complex expressions. In contrast to the systems mentioned above it is not fixed in the codegenerator generator.

2 Influence of VDM on the CAT-System

2.1 Support of Correctness

The mathematical description strongly supports the correctness and completeness of the designed system.

Language Design

During the design of the **CAT** language it turned out that a difficult and lengthy description of a new language construct was a strong indication for the fact that the intuitive meaning of the construct was not clear yet. The size of a semantics description helped to decide whether a language element fitted into the language or should be rejected in favor of a less complicated solution.

Front end Generation

The front end development shows that a formal description of the
source languages in question is absolutely necessary in order to
cover all error situations and boundary conditions. This was true not
only for the implementation of the C-BASIC front end - the semantics
definition consisted of a set of examples and an interpreter - but
also for C. Even though the informal language definition in [KeR78]
is better than the C-BASIC definition, it is still necessary to have
a formal description to get a complete semantic definition also for
language constructs where the semantics are not obvious.

The Pascal programs which were derived by manually transforming the
META IV specifications of the front ends were free of index, subrange
or pointer errors from the very first day. Almost no implementation
errors were detected.

Back End Generation

The main goal in back end generation is the generation of efficient
object code. For complex machines like the ND500 this requires a
sophisticated search for the optimal code sequence. This results in
relatively long codegenerator specifications (4000 - 5000 lines).

The back ends which are generated from these specifications do not
contain the usual programming errors like index or subrange
violations. The remaining errors result mainly from incompletely
defined transformation functions. In general these errors do not lead
to the generation of wrong code but to a compiler crash.

To recognize these errors in an early stage an automatic prover - as
it is currently under development at the University of Kiel - would
be a useful tool. This prover will be based on a term rewrite system.

2.2 Productivity Aspects

The effort necessary for the generation of a front end is distributed
as follows:

≈ 6 weeks   specification of lexical and syntactical analysis
            and transform rules for the conversion of the
            syntax tree into the abstract program tree.
            The main difficulty is the concrete LR(1) syntax.

≈ 5 months META IV specification of static semantics and
            compile algorithms for the generation of CAT

≈ 1 month   manual transformation of META IV specification
            into Pascal

The implementation of the runtime systems for **C-BASIC** and **C** respectively consisted of an effort of approximately two person years. Thus with the **VDM** based approach and the **CAT** system the main effort for the implementation of a new language lies in the development of the runtime system.

For the back end construction the following figures hold:

≈ 6 months specification of the code generator. This
            depends very much on the complexity of the
            target machine and the desired quality of
            the generated code.

≈ 2 weeks   for the variable allocation module

≈ 3 months for the final coding module. This effort
            depends very much on the requested linkage
            loader format.

≈ 3 months test and final tuning of generated code and
            the compiler itself

It is important to note that the compilers developed with **VDM** turned out to reach a stable state in a much shorter time than comparable products which were built without the application of a formal design method.

2.3 Extendability

The system changes necessary to add or generalize functions can be detected by analysis of the formal specification. This helps to decide whether a feature can be integrated into the existing system or not. It also allows to estimate the effort required for the implementation.

Two examples in the **CAT** system are the extensions of **CAT** for certain C features and the generation of information for the symbolic debugger:

to provide the symbolic debuger with information about enumerated types in **Pascal** enumerated types were introduced in the **CAT** language. Until then enumerated types in **Pascal** had been mapped to subrange types in **CAT**. It took only two weeks to change the compile algorithm for the front ends and the **CAT** compiler.

To simplify the C front end and to allow for the generation of efficient code for expressions containing assignments, expressions on statement position and the pre/post decrement/increment operators the **CAT** language was generalized and the codegenerator extended. Again only two weeks were needed for the change.

3 Weaknesses of VDM

3.1 Acceptance Problems

Some difficulties were experienced trying to convince other groups in NORSK DATA that **VDM** improves software productivity. This is mainly due to the fact that a certain mathematical background is required by the method. The amount of mathematical symbols causes programmers with little mathematical education to back away thus preventing easy access to the method. To get out of this situation a readable introduction to **VDM** would be of great help.

It was also noticed that during a long specification phase the management tends to "panic" due to the fact that no real lines of executable code are produced. Until quite recently **VDM** was a pure paper and pencil method. Computer support for the development of a specification (editor, syntax and semantics checker etc.) would undoubtedly better the acceptance of the method because these tools would help to write the specifications in a shorter period of time. Furthermore the management could be provided a "checked" specification representing a measurable milestone.

Another criticism mentioned by sceptics is that there is no **META IV** specification written in **META IV** available - as it exists for **LISP** or **SMALLTALK**.

Another problem is that many of the required symbols cannot easily be displayed on average terminals.

Our experience is that the executability of at least a sublanguage of **META IV** is the most important aspect regarding the acceptance of the method. Regardless whether one likes the idea of executing specifications or not, the executability would greatly help to spread the use of **VDM** in industry. Only when we could compile the specifications of the codegenerators in the system other members in the language group of NORSK DATA turned to use **VDM**.

It should be noted that the programs derived (manually) in a straightforward manner from specifications had a performance which was initially not acceptable. But after a careful "tuning phase" satisfactory performance was achieved.

3.2 Desirable Tools and Language Features

To develop correct and <u>complete</u> specifications tools like syntax and semantic checkers as they are currently under development are of great importance.

Desirable would also be language constructs to support the modularization and parametrization of specifications. This is even more important in connection with the "reuse of software". Apart from that the parametrization of specifications would enhance the flexibility when changing or extending a specification. And maybe another disadvantage could be overcome with this approach. We noticed that the size of a specification grows unproportionally with the complexity of a problem.

4 Future Work

Based upon the experiences with the **META IV** compiler [Haß87] a system for rapid prototyping and generation of compiler front ends is planned. An application area for this development is the translation of special languages, e.g. languages for forms generation, query languages or 4. generation languages.

The implementation of the mathematical objects (sets, tuples, maps) using data structures of the target language (arrays, records, pointers) plays a central part in the generation of _efficient_ machine code. We intend to provide a library of standard implementations for the different **META IV** data types. This will not only be of great advantage for the manual transformation of specifications but also for the compilation process.

References

[BjJ82]   Bjørner. D., Jones, C.B.:
          Formal Specification and Software Development,
          Prentice-Hall, 1982

[Cat78]   Cattell, R.G.G.:
          Formalization and Automatic Derivation
          of Code Generators, CMU-CS-78-115,
          Carnegie Mellon University, Pittsburg, 1978

[Con58]   Conway, M.E.:
          Proposal for an UNCOL, CACM 1, 10 (Oct. 1958)

[Gla78]   Glanville, R.S.:
          A Machine Independent Algorithm for Code Generation
          and its Use in Retargetable Compilers, PhD Thesis,
          University of California, Berkley, 1978

[Haß87]   Haß, M.:
          Development and Application of a META IV Compiler,
          these proceedings

[KeR78]   Kernighan, B.W., Ritchie, D.M.:
          The C Programming Language, Prentice-Hall, 1978

[Sch83]   Schmidt, U.:
          Ein neuartiger, auf VDM basierender

Codegenerator-Generator, PhD Thesis,
Christian-Albrechts-Universität, Kiel, 1983

[ScV81]   Schmidt, U., Völler, R.:
Die formale Entwicklung der maschinenunabhängigen
Zwischensprache CAT, in: GI - 11. Jahrestagung,
Informatik-Fachberichte 50, Springer, Berlin, 1981

[ScV83]   Schmidt, U., Völler, R.:
The Development of a Machine Independent
Multi Language Compiler System Applying the
Vienna Development Method, in:
Proc. IFIP Working Conference on Software Specification
Methodologies, North- Holland, Amsterdam, 1985

[ScV84]   Schmidt, U., Völler, R.:
A Multi Language Compiler System with Automatically
Generated Codegenerators, in:
ACM SIGPLAN Notices Vol. 19, No. 6, June 1984

[Sto82]   Stoy, J.:
Formal Specification Meta-Language:
Mathematical Foundations, in: [BjJ82]

[Völ83]   Völler, R.:
Entwicklung einer maschinenunabhängigen
Zwischensprache und zugehöriger Übersetzeroberteile
für ein Mehrsprachübersetzersystem mit Hilfe von VDM,
PhD Thesis, Christian-Albrechts-Universität, Kiel, 1983

Using VDM in an Object-Oriented Development Method for Ada™ Software†

Chris Chedgey
Seamus Kearney
Hans-Jürgen Kugler

Generics (Software) Limited
7 Leopardstown Office Park
Foxrock, Dublin 18
Ireland

Abstract

In this paper the Vienna Development Method (VDM) is related to the various phases of activities throughout the process of software development. Several shortcomings of VDM are discussed and the combination of Object-Oriented Design (OOD) techniques, enriched by guidelines from the Jackson System Design method (JSD), with VDM is examined. The use of VDM to derive Ada package software is discussed.

Introduction

This paper describes the use of the Vienna Development Method (VDM) in the context of the development of software to be targeted at the Ada programming language [Ada 83]. Part of the objective of the work described here is to produce a method for constructing Ada software - a method which follows sound engineering principles in order to improve software quality as well as improving productivity on the part of the developers. Some aspects of this framework of techniques, called AdaM [Kugler 87], are discussed here.

Increasing productivity means introducing a certain amount of reusability, be it in the components built, or the tools and techniques used. The word *method* does in itself carry this meaning: a *method* is an orderly set of techniques and guidelines, designed for repeated use in developing products of similar properties. The authors are involved in examining the suitability of VDM in this context. ESPRIT project 510 *ToolUse* [Horgen 86] focusses on the relationship of VDM to the typical software life cycle. The use of VDM to derive Ada packages as directly as possible is addressed within ESPRIT project 496 *Papillon* [Chedgey 86].

™ Ada is a trademark of the U.S. Government, AJPO.

† Part of the work reported here is funded by the Commission of the European Communities under the ESPRIT programme.

This paper discusses some of the observations made about VDM especially in the earlier and later phases of software development, its shortcomings and some possible solutions. The experiences of the authors stem from applying VDM to a number of case studies [Ryan 86] and are therefore more applicable to a software engineering user of VDM, rather than a theoretician. Consequently the well-established mathematical aspects of the meta-language and the proof techniques are not discussed in this paper. It might be useful to note that the authors mainly use the "traditional" or "Bjørner"-brand of VDM [Bjørner 78] [Prehn 83] (specifically its metalanguage), rather than newer notations like those developed by Jones [Jones 86] or in Z [Abrial 80]. This has, however, mainly historic reasons rather than being based on an evaluation of the different styles.

Software Development

Software Development covers a large number of activities, commonly grouped into phases which comprise the software life cycle [SLC 80]. Without going into too much detail, the phases usually include:

* requirements specification and analysis
* system specification
* design (various levels of)
* code
* unit test
* integration
* acceptance test
* use & maintenance.

The overall view of the development process, on which experimentation with methods is based, is depicted in figure 1 [Biomatik 85].

VDM is often criticised about its limitations. One major bone of contention is the differing levels of support offered to the phases of the above cycle. VDM provides the user with strong guidance during the design phase recommending how the design should progress. The same level of support is not maintained during the requirements and system specification phases where the developer is fully responsible for formulating the problem description. The usefulness of VDM from the coding phase onwards is also questionable but its deficiencies are of a different nature [Lemaitre 85] [Kearney 86].

VDM and Requirements Specification

In this phase the software developer is concerned with identifying the important features the (software) system is to exhibit, its functions and its (nonfunctional) properties. The meta-language of VDM can be used to some extent here, although a stylised form of English and/or graphical expression will probably improve the communication between developer and customer [Alford 80].

VDM offers potential for formalising part of a requirements specification document, especially some of the functional features. By using *pre-* and *post-conditions* essential properties of functions to be provided can be defined in terms of the semantic level of the customer. *Invariants* can be used to describe both global properties, and non-functional properties. However, there is only a limited amount of detail available to describe the system state at this level, and relationships between certain components and their sub-structure still have to be discovered as part of the design process.

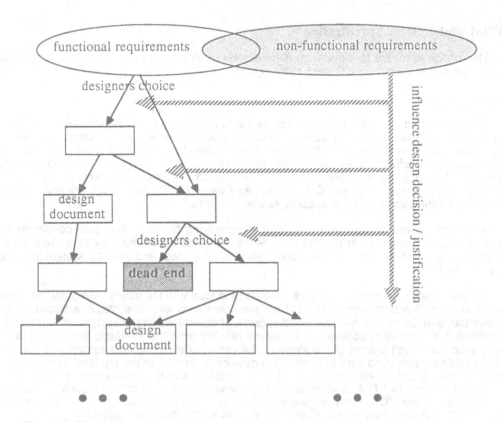

Figure 1: The Software Development Process - A Series of Tranformations

This problem may lead to often inconsequential and trivial looking formalisations of requirements given in English style. Examples of these are:

inv-SYSTEM(time(Elab(cmd)(σ)) < 0.5)

inv-MailSystem(s-MailReceived(ms)^s-MailInTransit(ms) = s-MailSent(ms))

The notion of treating functional requirements as a specification of the sort of services to be provided, and treating non-functional requirements as hypotheses about measurable constraints on how these services are to be provided (e.g. time and space behaviour, reliability etc.) may prove useful in relating later design documents to the original, contractual requirements specification document [Biomatik 85] [O'Neill 87]. In this way the requirements, especially the non-functional ones (see figure 1), influence design decisions in the development process just like sub-goals, in mathematical proofs, can influence the overall proof strategy. The difficulties in this area are inherent in formalising conceptual notions and their relationships rather than imposed by the limits of VDM. For this reason questions about consistency and plausibility of requirements specified (in whatever way) shall not be discussed further, except for hinting at the possibility of using mock-ups or executable specifications based on rapid prototyping.

VDM and System Specification

This phase is meant to move from a (relatively) unstructured requirements specification document to an overall specification of the system. It identifies the important components of the software to be developed, their properties and relationships in terms of data structures and control structures.

First and foremost, this phase is concerned with identifying those entities which will form part of the software system to be built, and those entities which exist outside the system boundary, but with which the software will have to interface. VDM as a method offers no assistance to a software developer at this stage; only the notation of the meta-language may be used to describe identified parts of the system. Jackson System Design (JSD) [Cameron 83] [Jackson 83] and Object-Oriented Design (OOD) [Booch 83] are examples of methods offering some decision support, however informal.

VDM can, however, be effectively used in specifying the pre- and post-conditions for operations, the attributes of objects and the values these attributes may take. This allows properties given in the requirements specification to be refined and the new system model to be checked.

In most cases of interactive systems it is helpful to start with the user's view of the interface: what are the objects manipulated, what are the commands available etc. At a second stage these can then be related and described in terms of objects within the system. In terms of the traditional denotational approach this means moving from the syntactic (i.e. outer) to the semantic (i.e. inner) entities of the system. The notion of syntactic and semantic domains in VDM could be employed here to support the developer. Entities in the top level system model can be introduced as elements of syntactic domains, actions correspond to (potentially partial) functions in VDM. Both data- and process oriented modelling techniques can be supported by the VDM meta-language. A JSD entity structure as given in figure 2 (see [Cameron 83]) can easily be translated into the following syntactic domains:

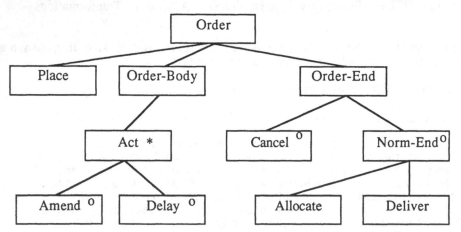

Figure 2: An example JSD Entity Structure

```
Order ::      Place
              Order-Body
              Order-End

Place = ...

Order-Body = Act*

Act = Amend | Delay

Amend = ...

Delay = ...

Order-End = Cancel | Norm-End

Cancel = ...

Norm-End = Allocate | Deliver

Allocate = ...

Deliver = ...
```

with elaboration functions like

```
elab-Order(mk-Order(p,ob,oe)) ≡
( elab-Place(p);
  elab-Order-Body(ob);
  elab-Order-End(oe))
type: Order ⇒
```

and so on. The translation from JSD model specifications to VDM's meta-language is straightforward. Mapping these onto process networks as prescribed by JSD is considerably more difficult, since VDM supports no concurrency concepts.

The data-oriented approach will be discussed later in the section on relating VDM and OOD.

VDM and Design

This is the stage where the system model has been completed and the process of refining specifications can begin. This is the phase where VDM provides most support to the user. The meta-language combined with the *reification* technique illustrated in detail in [Bjørner 82a], [Cohen 86] and [Jones 86] directly supports stepwise refinement of specification documents by functional decomposition or data abstraction. Proof obligations [Jones 85] generated to show that invariants or other properties are still maintained make this phase fit the underlying development model (figure 1).

The only major criticism here is that, at a phase where VDM is most understood and effective, there is no tool support available. This inhibits experimentation with the design and feedback through mock-up and prototyping. The authors are aware, however, that this criticism is only true at the time of writing the paper and that it will soon be overcome.

VDM and Coding

The meta-language of VDM is independent of any particular target language, which means that VDM specifications can be translated into a variety of languages. By using specifications given in functional style a transition to functional languages can be easily achieved. Moving from VDM functional style through relational notation to logic programming has been discussed in [Mac an Airchinnigh 86]. Many examples exist for moving to "conventional" programming languages (see [Jones 80] for PL/I). The examples in [Bjørner 82b] are particularly illustrative of the use of the state and meta-variable notation to achieve transition from functional style to imperative and non-recursive form.

There are, however, problems with the notation of the meta-language when considering languages supporting data encapsulation, such as Ada. The basic concept in Ada is the *package*, encapsulating data and operational abstraction. The particular discipline of writing Ada software advocated by AdaM requires a tight coupling of operational abstraction to data abstraction, a notion which is not directly supported in the VDM meta-language. The "traditional" version of VDM does not allow for grouping of domain definitions and operations into modules, nor does it support expression of information hiding other than through structuring of the specification document and careful choice of reification levels.

Realisation of this drawback led to some modification in the style of writing VDM specifications used by AdaM, and will be discussed later.

VDM and Unit Testing

The obligation to construct retrieve-functions and prove the adequacy of the chosen data representation at each design refinement helps to identify typical and important test cases and may, in many cases, make it unnecessary to test some units at all. This does, however, require that all proof obligations be satisfied, a notion which the authors would only accept if supported by a validation system such as provided in Affirm [AFFIRM 81] or B [Lemoine 86]. Verifying the code generated does need an annotation language for the target programming language, such as those given in Affirm for a variant of Pascal and in Anna [Krieg-Brückner 83] for Ada. Here proof obligations, constructed based on notions similar to Dijkstra's weakest preconditions [Dijkstra 76], can be used to extend the reification technique to include the last step of translating the VDM specification to a programming language.

VDM and Acceptance Test

Large parts of the customer acceptance test may also be replaced by analysing the formal design and the various proofs. Unfortunately, this lies even further in the future than the acceptance of rigorous development techniques by the software developer, although other engineering disciplines communicate (to some extent) with their customers through blueprints describing designs in a very rigorous mathematical notation.

The use of executable specifications and design models which can be simulated may help to push part of the activites of this phase into the design stage. Once again the possibility of using a combined verification and testing technique is a distinct advantage.

VDM and Use & Maintenance

More often than not software, once in use, needs to be maintained in order to remove flaws or to adjust it to changing requirements. A rigorous specification of the various levels of design gives the maintainer, who is often not the original developer, a better understanding of the software architecture and the interaction of various components.

Of particular interests are proofs, which establish the connection between requirements (what) and code (how). Unfortunately, VDM leaves proof obligations and justification of design decisions to the discipline of the software engineer. Tools which would record the history of a development, together with its individual specification "snapshots", are needed.

Modifications of VDM

Experiences with VDM caused the authors to attempt to combine VDM with a variety of other techniques and disciplines. OOD enhanced by some techniques adapted from JSD has been used to provide an underlying framework for guiding the user of VDM. A particular style of writing VDM specifications has been designed to facilitate the transition to Ada packages.

OOD and VDM

Object-Oriented Design (OOD) [Booch 83] is a technique widely used to construct Ada software. It is an iterative design technique which gives some support in the early phases of development, especially the system specification step. The process of OOD consists of:

OOD :: Problem-Definition
(Informal-Strategy Formalise-Strategy)*

Note that the leaves of this tree are elaborated in that order.

Problem-Definition = (Problem-Statement Analysis)*

The *problem definition and analysis* can be supported by other techniques and tools, or be performed as part of OOD itself. Within OOD the aim is to achieve a concise English-language description of the problem. This step is obviously the weakest one within the method. Generally the process of requirements acquisition and analysis is subject to substantial research and development [Greenspan 85] [Ryan 86], and is beyond the scope of this paper. The authors are currently experimenting with iterations of parts of JSD and SARS [Koch 83] to improve the guidelines which can be offered to the designer. This can then be used as the basis for a VDM style specification of proof obligations representing requirements.

The *informal strategy* step of OOD provides more guidance for the designer and can be linked more closely to VDM. This step aims at identifying the relevant entities and actions, thus forming the basis of the model for the system specification. In traditional OOD the informal strategy relies entirely on a natural language description of the problem, with an emphasis on highlighting

- the *objects* which are subjected to actions or which initiate actions,

- the *operations* which can be performed on objects, and

- *constraints* which apply to objects and operations.

There are various refinements and detailed guidelines for writing such structured text. The relationship to the *entity/action* and *entity structure steps* of JSD is obvious and can be exploited, since a more concise set of guiding rules exist [Connolly 86].

OOD leaves much of the analysis about the objects and their relevant operations to the *formalisation step*. The substructure of the formalisation step can be described as

Formalise-Strategy ::   Identify-Objects
                         Identify-Operations
                         Define-Interfaces
                         Implement

Identify-Objects :: Find-Objects-or-Types
                     Associate-Attributes

Identify-Operations ::   Find-Operations
                         Associate-Attributes
                         Group-Operations-and-Objects

Define-Interfaces :: ...

Implement :: ...
                         OOD

Many of the detailed guidelines given in the OOD literature, such as highlighting nouns, pronouns and noun clauses in the text, are very reminiscent of the entity/action and entity structure steps of JSD. More importantly, however, they are directly translatable to guidelines for using VDM.

Formalising the strategy progresses from the informal problem and strategy statements to identifying domains of relevant objects, moving from the syntactic domains in the initial iterations to the semantic ones, in terms of which the behaviour of the syntactic ones will be defined.

In VDM each object is an element of some domain, i.e. there is a type associated with it. This means that the notion of a single object, which exists in OOD, and the activity of grouping related objects into types needs to be modified. For each potential entity there is automatically a domain, even though there may only be one instance.

Note that, in general, OOD may involve the notion of types being objects themselves, to define either generic characteristics or inheritance relationships. Such properties have to be described separately through the use of invariants and well-formedness conditions.

Attributes of objects can lead to a substructure of the domain of interest, especially a tree form, and the definition of invariants and well-formedness conditions. This step may also lead to several domains being grouped together based on similarities in their attributes - disjoint union or tree constructions being amongst the most likely.

Identifying operations follows a similar pattern of examining verbs, verb phrases and predicates in the text produced in the previous steps. The emphasis on producing the objects of interest first before specifying the operations is very close to the usual ("traditional" or "Bjørner) style of VDM, i.e. specify the domains of interest and then the operations. Being a model based technique, however, VDM describes many operations implicitly by specifying an abstract model for the domain of interest. If the previous steps of object identification used this approach, then it is important to consider those operations here as well. OOD attempts to make all design steps and decisions explicit. It is quite clear that the two steps of identifying objects and operations are clearly interrelated and that the use of abstract models and implicitly defined operations will have major impact on the grouping of object and operations, possibly causing iteration over a number of sub-steps.

Associating *attributes with operations* is a step which is close to the similarly named step in OOD, but it cannot be enhanced by using additional rules from JSD, since JSD treats actions as atomic. However, attributes for operations will eventually contribute to the full definition of the interfaces of the operations. Therefore, this step will provide the material necessary for constructing argument and result domains of the operations although this can only be completed after the grouping step. It will help ascertain whether the operation is a complete or partial function, or a state changing operation, what the pre- and post-conditions are, and what conditions generally are to be fulfilled by the implementation of the operation (proof obligations). This information will also include sequencing and concurrency considerations, which will later facilitate the decision between subprogram and tasking implementations.

object	Bill_of_Materials
types	Bill_of_Materials = Part_No $_m\to$ Part_Record
	Part_Record = Part_No $_m\to$ N1
	Part_No = N0
needs types	N0, N1
interfaces	New_Bill_of_Materials : $\to$ Bill_of_Materials
	Enter : Bill_of_Materials Part_No $\to$ Bill_of_Materials
	Delete : Bill_of_Materials Part_No $\to$ Bill_of_Materials
	Add : Bill_of_Materials Part_No Part_Record
	$\to$ Bill_of_Materials
	Erase : Bill_of_Materials Part_No Part_No
	$\to$ Bill_of_Materials
functions	is-wf-Bill_of_Materials(b) $\equiv$ ...
	-- annotations: ...
	New_Bill_of_Materials $\equiv$ []
	type: $\to$ Bill_of_Materials
	...
end	Bill_of_Materials

Figure 3: An example Object Specification

The *Grouping of operations and objects* has already been discussed to some extent. The VDM meta-language does not offer (at least not in the "Bjørner" style) any linguistic means to express these associations. The meta-language has therefore been extended to support Ada, as the target language, by introducing a piece of notation [Chedgey 86] which is a generalisation of the type definition of Affirm [AFFIRM 81] and its VDM style described by Beech in [Beech 86] (see figure 3). This form is continuously refined for each of the relevant objects, and also indicates the distinction between objects and types mentioned earlier, something which is of specific relevance to the development of Ada packages.

The *definition of the interfaces* aims at completing the form as shown in figure 3, although the formulation of pre- and post-conditions should also be considered in VDM, based on material gathered earlier.

Implementing the model reached so far is the recursive step of reapplying OOD, just one level of design further down. This corresponds closely to the combined data refinement and operation modelling of VDM, leading to a new specification using the reified domains. From here on VDM is definitely superior to OOD, especially by making the corresponding proof obligations explicit. The remaining problems in the combination of techniques are discussed in the next section.

VDM and Ada

The schema shown in figure 3 already reflects much of Ada's package structure. The allocation of domains to be modelled into modules to form packages is not necessarily an easy task. Generally only one package would be needed to declare all types, but this would give code which lacks syntactic sub-structure just like "traditional" VDM specifications. Increasing the modularity also increases potential reuse. Therefore the schema shown in figure 3 is meant to be reduced to the special case of having only one type per object module, except in the rare cases where the definiton of one type depends on that of another.

The schema of an Ada package specification as prescribed in AdaM [Kugler 87] is given in figure 4.

```
with     N0_Model, N1_Model;
package Bill_of_Materials_Model is
   type Bill_of_Materials is limited private;
   function New_Bill_of_Materials return Bill_of_Materials;
   ...
private
   type Bill_of_Materials_IMP;
   type Bill_of_Materials is access Bill_of_Materials_IMP;
end Bill_of_Materials_Model;
```

Figure 4: An example Package Specification

Ada packages to model the VDM standard domains as given in the reference manual appendix of [Bjørner 80] are provided in AdaM to allow easy construction of the appropriate package bodies - which can later be refined and replaced (often without recompiling the specification part). This allows early simulation of the package behaviour.

The distinction between subprogram and tasking implementation is not handled in VDM, except by additions to the meta-language (e.g. CSP in [Bjørner 80]). Experimentation, based on combining VDM with SCCS, process models and net models, is continuing and early results (from the software engineering user's point of view) are encouraging. It might be worth pointing out that the AdaM schema recommended for Ada packages uses limited private types wherever possible, thus allowing objects to be implemented as tasks, with operations modelling concurrency.

Conclusions

In former years the use of design methodologies was restricted mainly to academics and theoreticians. This was due to the formal nature of many of the approaches, the lack of user-related documentation and the fact that most methods had to be applied using pen and paper. With the emergence of support tools, the trend has changed and nowadays the same techniques are being successfully applied in industry. These tools ease the user's task of learning and applying the relevant methods and, at the same time, constrain the user to adhere to the recommended approach. The tools were generally well received and helped to popularise the use of the relevant methods.

To date no tool support has been available for defining or developing VDM specifications. This coupled with the fact that VDM required a distinctly mathematically oriented approach has prevented its widespread use in large-scale industrial developments. If VDM is to have any chance of being adopted by the software engineering community these problems must be overcome. An adequate set of tools must be provided to support not only the clerical tasks of the method but some of the more technical tasks as well (e.g editors, consistency checkers).

A suitable set of experimental tools are under development to suport the application of the various techniques extracted from VDM, OOD and JSD which together comprise the approach proposed here. We envisage the definition of the following tools:

method advisor: advise the set of actions that are permissible at any point during the design

requirements acquisition and analysis tool

transformation tool: support the reification of specifications

theorem proving facility

history recording: maintain a trace on requirements through successive levels of specifications.

Our case studies have shown that the recommended guidelines provide a systematic approach for developing Ada software. Furthermore, users were able to control the complexity of the software by the provision of design documents at intermediate stages of the development. With support tools available we anticipate that the design steps will be easier to apply, the design sessions will be easier to monitor and the designer will have more confidence in the reliability of the eventual code.

Acknowledgements

The authors wish to thank all those working on projects ToolUse and Papillon, and their reviewers, for many interesting discussions.

References

[Abrial 80]   Abrial, J.R., *The Specification Language Z: Basic Library*, Oxford University Programming Research Group, Specification Group Working Paper, 1980

[Ada 83]   *Ada Language Reference Manual*
                   ANSI/Mil.Std 1815A, Alsys, Jan 1983

[AFFIRM 81]   AFFIRM Reference Library, 5 Volumes:
                   Lee, S. and Gerhart, S.L. (eds.), *AFFIRM User's Guide*
                   Erickson, R.W. (ed.), *AFFIRM Collected Papers*
                   Thompson, D.H. and Erickson, R.W. (eds.), *AFFIRM Reference Manual*
                   Bates, R.L. and Gerhart, S.L. (eds.), *AFFIRM Annotated Transcripts*
                   Gerhart, S.L. (ed.), *AFFIRM Type Library*
                   USC Information Science Institute, Marina Del Rey, California, Version 2.0, Feb.1981

[Alford 80]   Alford, M.W. et al.,*Software Requirements Engineering Methodology (SREM) at the age of Four*, in: Proceedings of COMSAC 4, Chicago, 1980

[Beech 86]   Beech, D. (ed.), Gram, C., Kugler, H.-J., Newman, I., Stiegler, H., Unger, C., *Concepts in User Interfaces: A Reference Model for Command and Response Languages*, Lecture Notes in Computer Science **234**, Springer-Verlag, 1986

[Biomatik 85]   Koch, G. (ed.) et al, *Final Report of Task 5.1: Selection of Case Studies,* Project ToolUse, November 1985.

[Bjørner 78]   Bjørner, D. and Jones, C.B. (eds.), *The Vienna Development Method: The MetaLanguage*, Lecture Notes in Computer Science 61, Springer-Verlag, 1978

[Bjørner 80]   Bjørner, D. and Oest, O.N. (eds.), *Towards a Formal Specification of Ada*, Springer-Verlag, Lecture Notes in Computer Scicence **98**, 1980

[Bjørner 82a]   Bjørner, D. and Jones, C.B., *Formal Specification and Software Development*, Prentice-Hall, 1982

[Bjørner 82b]   Bjørner, D. and Prehn, S., *Software Engineering Aspects of VDM*, in: Proceedings of the International Seminar on Software Factory Experiences, North-Holland, 1982

[Booch 83]   Booch, G., *Software Engineering with Ada*, Benjamin/Cummings, 1983

[Cameron 83]   Cameron, J.R., *JSP & JSD: The Jackson Approach to Software Development*, IEEE Computer Society, 1983

[Chedgey 86]   Chedgey, C. et al., *Technical Annex to 4th Interim Report of ESPRIT 496*, Generics (Software) Ltd., Dublin, Nov. 1986

[Cohen 86]   Cohen, B., Harwood, W.T. and Jackson, M.I., *The Specification of Complex Systems*, Addison-Wesley, 1986

[Connolly 86]   Connolly, P., *Experimental JSD Rule System*, Project ToolUse, Insight.PC86h, Vector Software Ltd., Dublin, 1986

[Dijkstra 76]   Dijkstra, E.W., *A Discipline of Programming*, Prentice-Hall, 1976

[Greenspan 85]   Greenspan, S., Borgida, A., Mylopoulos, J., *Knowledge Representation as the basis for Requirements Specifications*, IEEE Computer, April 1985

[[Horgen 86]   Horgen, H. et al., *Workplan for ESPRIT Project 510 ToolUse*, Phase 2, Oct. 1986

[Jackson 83]   Jackson, M., *System Development*, Prentice-Hall, 1983

[Jackson 85]   Jackson, M.I., Denvir, B.T., and Shaw, R.C., *Experience of Introducing the Vienna Development Method into an Industrial Organisation*, in: Proceedings of the TAPSOFT Conference, Berlin, 1985, Springer-Verlag, Lecture Notes in Computer Science **186**, 1985

[Jones 80]   Jones, C.B., *Software Development: A Rigorous Approach*, Prentice-Hall, 1980

[Jones 85]   Jones, C.B., *The Role of Proof Obligations in Software Design*, in: Proceedings of the TAPSOFT Conference, Berlin, 1985, Springer-Verlag, Lecture Notes in Computer Science **186**, 1985

[Jones 86]   Jones, C.B., *Systematic Software Development Using VDM*, Prentice-Hall, 1986

[Kearney 86]   Kearney, S., *OOD/VDM Methodology*, Project ToolUse, Generics.sk86t, Generics (Software) Ltd., November 1986

[Koch 83]   Koch, G., Epple, W., *Sars, A System for Application Oriented Requirements Specification*, 1983

[Krieg-Brückner 83]   Krieg-Brückner, B., Luckham, D., Von Henke, F. and Owe, O., *Draft Reference Manual for Anna: A Language for Annotating Ada Programs*, DARPA/RADC, 1983

[Kugler 87]   Kugler, H.-J. et al., *GenericsAdaM - Handbook for the Generics Ada Development Method*, Generics (Software) Ltd., 1987 (to appear)

[Lemaitre 85]   Lemaitre, M., *A Synthesis of VDM*, Project ToolUse, Cert.ML85b, 1985

[Lemoine 86]   Lemoine, *M., Evaluation of B.*,Cert.ML86f, June 1986

[Mac an Airchinnigh 86] Mac an Airchinnigh, M., *VDM and ADA, Relational Meta IV and Prolog*, Generics (Software) Ltd., 1986

[O'Neill 87]   O'Neill, D., *Support Tools for the Abstract Data Typing Approach to Software Development*, M.Sc. Thesis, Trinity College Dublin, 1987 (to appear)

[Prehn 83]   Prehn, S. et al., *Formal Methods Appraisal: Final Report - DDC Subprogramme*, ESPRIT Preparatory Study Report, 1983

[Ryan 86]   Ryan, K.T. (ed.) et al., TCD.KR86B, *An Experimental Basis for ToolUse - Task 5.2 Report*, Project ToolUse, Trinity College Dublin, Dec. 1986

[SLC 80]   Freeman, P. , Wasserman, A., *Tutorial on Software Design Techniques,* Third Edition, IEEE Computer Society, April 1980.

The Stepwise Development of Software Development Graphs

--

Meta-Programming VDM Developments

An Extended Abstract

Dines Bjørner

Department of Computing Science
Technical University of Denmark

Dansk Datamatik Center
Lundtoftevej 1C

DK-2800 Lyngby
Denmark

Summary

In VDM development of software proceeds from specification, via stages of design, to coding. A classical way of illustrating this is by the "waterfall- diagram" of fig.3.

As a planning aid, drawing such simple sequences of boxes as shown in fig. 3. really is of no help. In this paper we shall carefully develop an example, so-called software development graph. Thus from a graph like fig. 3. we shall arrive at a graph like that of fig. 9, which is claimed far more useful.

The meaning of nodes (boxes or vertices) and edges (arrows or arcs) is given relative to VDM, and in four different versions: one each for theoretical computer science, programming methodology, software engineering and management.

Our basic point is the following (see fig. 4.): before actually developing the various components (formulas) of the specifications (nodes s), before actually developing the design ($d1$) from the specification (s), or more concrete design ($d2$) from more abstract design ($d1$), and before actually developing the various components (formulas) of the designs (see figs.7-8), etc., we meta-develop the development, that is we decide on a development strategy, we specify which design choices to make (ie. the basic object and operation transformation ideas), and we specify which components our specifications and designs will then consists of.

Our derived point is then the following: even the development of the final, so-called consistent & complete software development graph, will take place as a stepwise development, from that almost meaninglessly expressed by fig. 3, via those of the more and more detailed figs. 4-5-6-7-8, to fig. 9!

The paper is discursive. An appendix will show some of the actual formulas whose construction are being planned by the software meta-development method of this paper.

1. Introduction

We "self-referentially" apply the dogma of specification, design and coding to our paper itself: the specification of the present paper is by a **pre-/post-**condition, which we shall shortly give; the design is by a explaining the structure of the paper; and the coding is then the body of the paper itself!

1.1 Paper Specification

You are supposed (**pre-condition**) to have some acquaintance with the VDM rigorous approach to software development as for example illustrated in either of the books: [Jones 80, Bjørner & Jones 82, Jones 85].

The aim of the paper (**post-condition**) is then to make you aware of the concept of 'software development graphs' [Bjørner 86a, Bjørner 86b], and show you its application to a typical problem.

1.2 Paper Design

The way we hope to achieve fulfilment of the pre-/post-condition is by first stating, in sect. 2, the particular problem at hand, ie. the application on which we wish to illustrate the idea of stepwise development of software development graphs. Then in sect. 3 we indeed do the stepwise development of this graph. In sect. 4 we assign attributes, in a more systematic way than implied in sect. 3, to the nodes and edges of the final (consistent & complete) software development graph (fig. 9). These attributes examplify the four mutually related, but otherwise separable concerns of the 'resident project scientist', the project programmers, the project software engineers, and project management.

1.3 Paper Coding

The remainder of this paper forms the final implementation, the coding, which is hoped to fulfil the design, and hence the specification.

2. The Example Problem

The problem, seen from the point of view of the customer, in the abstract, is quite simple-minded:

We are given a simple, block-structured programming language with GOTOs, and we wish to instrument a number of software tools for the analysis (including debugger-like execution) of programs in this language.

In the more concrete the customer/supplier problem can be phrased as follows:

Given a linear, textual, external representation of programs (in a language), implement a suitable internal ("storage") [data- structure] representation such that reasonable, transparent procedures can be written implementing the desired analysis functions.

The problem, seen from the point of view of us, in this paper, with its particular aims, is to present this customer/supplier problem as an application for our idea of software development graphs.

But first we present the customer/supplier problem before we, from sect.3 on, turn to our problem, that of talking about the customer/supplier, and the suppliers (internal development) problems!

2.1 Informal Definition of the Programming Language

We shall primarily concentrate of defining the syntax -- assuming that the reader will readily be able to fill in the missing semantical details!

-- **An Example Program**

```
begin      var v1,v2;
    11:    a1;
    12:    if b2 goto 112;
    13:    begin      var v2,v3;
               14:    a4;
               15:    if b5 goto 113;
               16:    a6;
               17:    begin      var v3,v4;
                          18:    a8;
                          19:    if b9 goto 112;
                          110:   a10
                      end;
               111:   a11
           end;
    112:   a12;
    113:   if b13 goto 13
end
```

Figure 1
An Example Program

-- **Syntax**

Programs are Blocks. Blocks consists of two parts: a unordered set of type-less Variable declarations, and an ordered list of Commands. A Variable declaration consists of just the Variable name. A Command has two parts: a Label and a Statement. No two Commands of the same Command list of a Block have identical Labels. A Statement is either a Block (so Blocks can be nested), an Assignment, or a Conditional GOTO. An Assignment Statement consists of two parts: a (left hand side [lhs]) Variable, and an Expression. We leave Expressions further undefined. A Conditional GOTO consists of two parts: a boolean valued Expression and a Label.

-- **Semantics**

Instead of tackling the perhaps more interesting problems of specific program analysis functions [such as control and data flow analysis, assertion and induction invariant verification, etc.], we limit ourselves to the more conventional one of program semantics.

Executing Blocks proceed in three stages: (Block Prologue) first Storage Locations for all declared Variables are Allocated. (Block Body) Then we execute the Command list by executing its Statements in the order listed. Provided no GOTOs have occured leading out of the Block execution of the Command list terminates with the execution of the last Statement of the list, after which the third, normal stage of Block execution takes place, namely (Block Epilogue) the Freeing of all those Variable Locations Allocated in the Block Prologue. Assignments are executed as you would expect it! So is execution of nested Blocks. Conditional GOTOs are executed by first evaluating their Expression. If the resulting value is false then execution proceeds to the next Statement, if any, otherwise to Block Epilogue. If the value is instead true, then a 'jump' is made to the lexicographically nearest surrounding Statement whose Command Label is that of the Conditional GOTO just executed. [We asume that the reader understands the notions of 'lexicographic', 'nearest', 'surrounding', etc.] To make a 'jump' means to let execution of the next Statement be that of the so Labeled Statement. If a jump is 'within' a Block, ie. is local to a Block, then no further actions are required. If the jump is to a Statement in a surrounding, outer Block, then, for eack such Block "boundary" traversed, the actions corresponding to their Block Epilogue are taken, ie. Variable Locations of Blocks left are Freed.

2.2 Informal Exposition of Data-Structure Representation Idea

In this particular example we choose to focus, in our decisive step of development, on the data-structure representation of programs in storage.

[We could have chosen to tackle other problems, to pursue other approaches -- that really is immaterial for what we really want to illustrate: the stepwise development of software development graphs.]

The basic data-structure design idea is to storage represent Statements as Nodes in a possibly cyclic graph, to represent Labels as Pointers to such Nodes, to represent Assignment Nodes by one pointer leading out, to represent Conditional GOTO Nodes by two pointers leading out, and by representing Blocks almost by their syntactic counterparts: one Node (the Begin Node) for **begin** and one Node (the End Node) for **end**. A GOTO leading out of a Block will have its 'true' arc leading through as many distinct End Nodes as the GOTO is traversing Blocks. All these Nodes will be contained in a single design state component which maps Pointers to such Nodes.

The derived data-structure coding idea is to represent each Node as a separately and dynamically allocated based, or unnamed variable in the coding language (eg. Pascal, using **new**).

-- Example Data-Structure

Fig. 2. shows the cyclic graph corresponding to the example program of fig. 1:

83

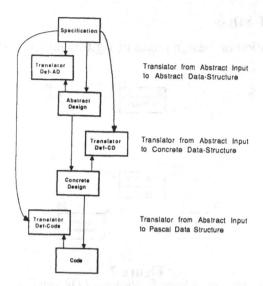

Figure 5
An Enriched Four Stage Development

And then there is one more problem: the syntax of external programs of fig.5s topmost box is abstract, to make definition of language semantics easy to read. In real life a syntax, eg. a BNF grammar, which specifies the concrete linear form of textual programs must be specified, and translation into internal representation must be wrt. such a concrete input language. This is intended illustrated by fig. 6:

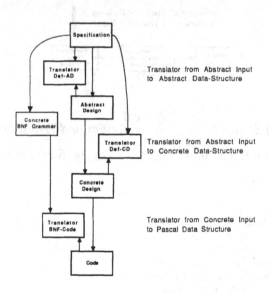

Figure 6
A Finally Enriched Four Stage Development

3.2   Refinement of SDGs

Each of the Specification or Design boxes of fig.6 really consists of three parts, as illustrated by fig.7:

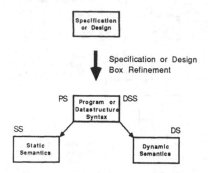

Figure 7
Refinement of Specification and Design Boxes

And the Static and the Dynamic Semantics definition boxes of fig.7, and the Translator boxes of fig. 6 [call then X bozes], all can be decomposed into three boxes: X domain definition, X domain invariants, and X functions, as illustrated by fig. 8:

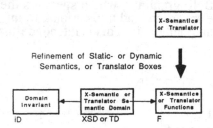

Figure 8
Refinement of Static- & Dynamic Semantics and Translator Boxes

Applying each of these refinement schemas to all of fig. 6 we get fig. 9.

Legend:

PS:	Program Syntax
SSi:	Static Semantics Functions
SSDi:	Static Semantics Domain
iSSDi	Invariance of SSDi
Ji:	Semantic Elaboration Functions
J3:	(eg. Pascal) Interpreter Procedures
DSDi:	Dynamic Semantics Domain
iDSDi:	Invariance of DSDi
DSSi:	Data Structure Syntax
Ti:	Translator (from i-1 to i)

T3:	(eg. Pascal) Translator Procedures
TDi:	Translator Domain
iTDi:	Invariance of TDi
BNF:	BNF Grammar and Syntax Analyser
iBNF:	Invariance/Static Semantics of BNF
DICT:	Dictionary/BNF Semantics Domain
iDICT:	Invariance of DICT Domain
DS type:	(eg. Pascal) type definition of program data structure
Aux.type:	(eg. Pascal) type definition of auxiliary data types

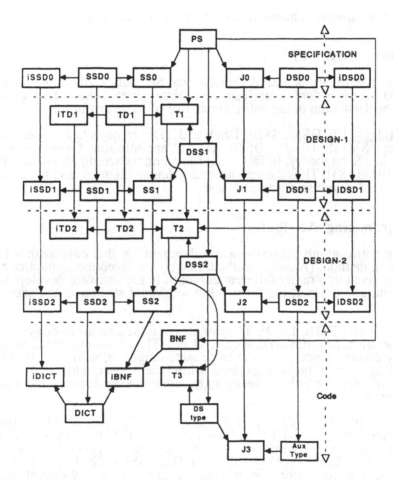

Figure 9
Consistent & Complete Software Development Graph

[We assume the reader sufficiently familiar with the denotational semantics (and hence the VDM) notions of domain (or abstract syntax) definitions, their well-formedness constraints (ie. invariants), and semantics elaboration or translation functions (from syntactic to semantic objects).]

Consistency & Completeness of the software development graph of fig.9 follows from our ability, as shown in the next section, to assign meaningful, in this case, VDM oriented attributes to each node and edges. In a subsequent report we shall make the consistency & completeness notion more precise.

4. Assignment of Attributes

To the resulting software development graph, fig.9, and its nodes and edges, we now assign theory, programming, engineering, and management attributes. Each of the below four subsections have two parts, both informal: assignment of attributes to the entire graph, and assignment of attributes to respectively nodes and edges.

In a bit unstructured manner, to save typing space, we list:

4.1 Theory Attributes

Graph: The base theory is that of Denotational Semantics. Since the nodes denote theories and the edges denote morhisms, we might, given some orderly development obtain, as the denotation of the entire graph, that of some institution.

Nodes & Edges: PS, DSSi, SSDi, DSDi and TDi are objects in a Scott theory of retracts; and SSi, iSSDi, Ji, iDSDi, Ti, etc. are minimal fixpoints of function definitions in a Scott theory. In fact, from some i on we would choose a naive Blikle semantics [Blikle 83]. Thus the various nodes denote theories, and the edges denote various kinds of morphisms between these.

4.2 Programming Attributes

Graph:The entire graph prescribe a development, in this case within the VDM programming method. [Another method, like eg. an algebraic semantics approach, would have given us a rather different approach to the software development graph development, and its resulting form -- but we would still have had such an SDG. Etc., etc.

Nodes: PS, DSSi, SSDi, DSDi, TDi are all expressed as abstract syntaxes in the MEta-IV notation. SSi, $\jmath$i, iSSDi, iDSDi, Ti and iTDi are all expressed as potentially recursively defined functions in the same meta-language, with SS0, iSSD0, J0 and iDSD0 being applicatively expressed while the subsequent developments are imperatively expressed. We use an **exit** semantics to express the meaning of GOTOs.Etc., etc.

Edges: Edges (PS,SS0), (PS,Jo), DSSi,SSi), (DSSi,Ji), etc., denote simple "inclu-sion" relations. Edges (Ji-1,Ji), (iDSDi-1,iDSDi), (iSSDi-1,iSSDi) and (Ti-1,Ti) denote operation transformations (ie. refinement of functions), while edges (PS,DSS1), (DSS2,DS Type), (DSDi-1,DSDi), (SSDi-1,SSDi) and (TDi-1,TDi) denote object transformations (ie. refinement, or reification of data structures).We will develop the software systematically in some cases, in other cases rigorously -- in no cases will we actually, in this development (that we are still planning) prove any transformations correct. Edges also denote injection functions, almost like those of Ti, and abstraction (or retrieve) functions -- from DSS1 to PS, from DSS2 to DSS1, and from DS type to DSS2. Edges finally denote proof of correctness obligations and their discharge.

[We assume familiarity with the spectrum of notions: systematic, rigorous and formal, with the meaning of procing correctness, injection and retrieve functions, etc.]

4.3 Engineering Attributes

Graph: We are only going to develop one product based on this graph; no versions, no special configurations. The DDC Meta-IV Toolset [Prehn 87] will be used for this purpose. Etc., etc.

Nodes: We may wish to symbolically execute certain functions, for example: T2 and J2 before proceeding to code T3, respectively the Code. We adopt certain document presentation standards, ie. require certain pretty printer routines. All documents, ie. documents of all nodes are to be syntactically (type) checked. Etc., etc.

Edges: Certain transformations, notably the quadrant ((PS,Jo),(DSS1,J1)) is to be validated under the translator function T0. Validation will be in the form of some symbolic test runs. Etc., etc.

4.4 Management Attributes

An SDG is almost like a PERT Diagram. Our attributes have to do with allocation of overall resources to the entire project (ie. graph), and decomposing these in assignments to nodes and edges. Resources consists of three facets: people, time, and machine-facilities.

-- Manpower Resources

Graph: Typically we could determine to set aside 3 people for 3 months on this little exercise. Etc., etc.

Nodes: PS, DSSi, etc. each take 2 man days to construct; Ji each 1 man day; iSSDi and iDSSi 1/2 each a man day; Ti each 4 man days. Etc., etc.

Edges: Most edges, in this sometimes systematic, sometimes rigorous, but never formal development, are expected to take 2 man days each to settle.

-- Other Resources

Similar assignments can be made for other resources.

5. Conclusion

We have cursorily shown what goes into the planning of a software development project to be actually carried out within the VDM framework. We have not shown what follows this planning, namely the actual development, the actual production of documents (nodes), and their motivation and justification (edges).

In other reports we have outlined more general aspects of software development graphs [Bjørner 86a, Bjørner 86b].

In a project, **DiProGS**, we are now designing, formalising [Nørgaard et al. 86] and implementing the architecture of a **D**istributed, advanced work station based **S**ystem for supporting the development and use (execution) of software development **Pro**ject **G**raphs.

References

[Jones 80]   C.B.Jones: **Software Development - a Rigorous Approach,** Prentice-Hall International, 1982.

[Bjørner 82]   D.Bjørner & C.B.Jones: **Formal Specification and Program Development,** Prentice-Hall International, 1982.

[Jones 86]   C.B.Jones: **Systematic Software Development using VDM,** Prentice-Hall International, 1986.

[Bjørner 86a]   D.Bjørner: **Project Graphs and Meta-Programs, Towards a Theory of Software Engineering,** Capri Conference on *Innovative Software Engineering Environments and Ada,* May 1986, Springer Lecture Notes in Computer Science, 1987, ed. U.Montanari.

[Nørgaard 86]   M. Frendorf, N.Nørgaard, & I.Lysgaard Andersen: **A Formal Specification of A Project Graph System,** M.Sc.Stud.Proj. Rept., June 1986, 61 pages.

[Bjørner 86b]   D.Bjørner: **Software Development Graphs - a Unifying Concept for Software Development?,** 6th Conf. on *Foundations of Software Technology and Theoretical Computer Science ,* **FST&TCS,** New Delhi, India, Springer Lecture Notes in Computer Science, vol. 241, pp. 1-9, ed. Kesav V. Nori, 1986.

[Prehn 87]   S.Prehn: **The DDC Meta-IV Toolset,** these proceedings.

APPENDIX

Below follows a number of sections. Each section relates directly to a distinct node or edge of fig.9, and thus illustrates the formulas to be constructed (ie 'programmed') after the 'meta-programming' outlined in this paper.

PS: Program Syntax

$$P \quad = \quad B$$
$$B \quad :: \quad V\text{-}set \times C\!+$$
$$C \quad = \quad E \times S$$
$$S \quad = \quad A \mid H \mid B$$
$$A \quad :: \quad V \times U$$
$$H \quad :: \quad U \times E$$
$$V \cap E \quad = \quad \{\}$$
$$V, E \quad = \quad TOKEN$$

SS$_0$: Static Semantics 0

$$is\text{-}wf\text{-}P(p) \quad \underline{\Delta} \quad is\text{-}wf\text{-}B(b)\{\}$$

$$is\text{-}wf\text{-}B(\underline{mk}\text{-}B(vs,cl))\delta \quad \underline{\Delta}$$
$$\quad (\forall i,j \varepsilon \underline{ind} \; cl)(i \neq j \supset s\text{-}E(cl[i]) \neq s\text{-}E(cl[j]))$$
$$\wedge \; (\forall(,s)\varepsilon \underline{elems} \; cl)(is\text{-}wf\text{-}S(s)(\delta \cup vs \cup \{l \mid (,l)\varepsilon \underline{elems} \; cl\})$$

$$is\text{-}wf\text{-}H(\underline{mk}\text{-}H(u,e))\delta \quad \underline{\Delta} \quad e \varepsilon \delta \wedge \ldots$$

$$is\text{-}wf\text{-}A(\underline{mk}\text{-}A(v,x))\delta \quad \underline{\Delta} \quad v \varepsilon \delta \wedge \ldots$$

$$\underline{type}: \quad S \to (DICT \to BOOL)$$

SSD$_0$: Static Semantics Domain

$$\delta: \; DICT = (V \mid E)\text{-}set$$

iSSD$_0$: Invariance of SSD$_0$

$$inv\text{-}DICT(\delta) \quad \underline{\Delta} \quad true$$

$\underline{DSD_0}$: $\underline{Dynamic\ Semantics\ Domain}$

$$ENV \quad = \quad V \xrightarrow{m} L$$
$$STG \quad = \quad L \xrightarrow{m} VAL$$
$$\Sigma \quad = \quad Stg \xrightarrow{m} STG$$
$$\underline{dcl}\ Stg := []\ \underline{type}\ STG$$

$\underline{iDSD_0}$: $\underline{Invariance\ of\ DSD_0}$

$$inv\text{-}ENV(\rho) \triangleq true$$
$$inv\text{-}STG(\sigma) \triangleq true$$

$\underline{J_0}$: $\underline{Dynamic\ Semantics\ Functions}$

$$I_p(p) \triangleq I_B(p)[]$$

$$I_B(\underline{mk\text{-}B}(vs,cl))\rho \triangleq$$
$$\quad (\underline{def}\ \rho':\ \rho + [v \mapsto A()\,|v \varepsilon vs];$$
$$\quad \underline{always}\ Stg := (\underline{c}Stg) \backslash \{\rho'(v)\,|v \varepsilon vs\}\ \underline{in}$$
$$\quad I_{CL}(cl)\rho')$$

$$I_{CL}(cl)\rho \triangleq$$
$$\quad (\underline{tixe}\ [e \mapsto E_{CL}(cl,j)\rho\,|j \varepsilon \underline{ind}\ cl:\underline{s\text{-}E}(cl[i])=e]\ \underline{in}$$
$$\quad E_{CL}(cl,1)\rho)$$

$$E_{CL}(cl,i)\rho \triangleq$$
$$\quad \underline{if}\ i>\underline{len}\ cl$$
$$\quad\quad \underline{then}\ I$$
$$\quad\quad \underline{else}\ (I_S(cl[i])\rho;$$
$$\quad\quad\quad\quad E_{CL}(cl,i+1)\rho)$$

$$I_S(\underline{mk\text{-}C}(\ ,s))\rho \triangleq$$
$$\quad \underline{cases}\ s:\ (\underline{mk\text{-}A}(v,x) \to Stg := \underline{c}Stg + [\rho(v) \mapsto V(x)\rho],$$
$$\quad\quad\quad\quad\quad \underline{mk\text{-}H}(u,e) \to \underline{if}\ V(u)\rho\ \underline{then}\ exit(e)\ \underline{else}\ I,$$
$$\quad\quad\quad\quad\quad T \quad\quad\quad \to I_B(s)\rho)$$

$$A() \triangleq (\underline{def}\ l \varepsilon STG \backslash \underline{c}Stg;$$
$$\quad\quad Stg := \underline{c}Stg \cup [l \mapsto \ldots];$$
$$\quad\quad \underline{return}\ l)$$

DSS₁: Data Structure Syntax 1

$$D \quad = \quad L \times M$$
$$M \quad = \quad L \underset{m}{\rightarrow} N$$
$$N \quad = \quad A1 \mid B1 \mid H1$$
$$A1 \quad :: \quad A \times L$$
$$B1 \quad = \quad Beg \mid End$$
$$Beg \quad :: \quad \underline{V\text{-}set} \times L$$
$$End \quad :: \quad [L]$$
$$H1 \quad :: \quad U \times L \times L$$
$$L \quad = \quad TOKEN, \; L \cap (V \cup E) = \{\}$$

iDSS₁: Invariance of DSS₁

$inv\text{-}D(l,m) \;\underline{\Delta}$

   $(l \; \varepsilon \; \underline{dom} \; m \; \wedge \; is\text{-}Beg(m(l)))$

$\wedge \; (\forall l', l'' \; \varepsilon \; \underline{dom} \; m)$

     $(l' \neq l'' \; \wedge \; is\text{-}Beg(m(l')) \; \wedge \; is\text{-}Beg(m(l'')))$

    $\supset \; ((\underline{let} \; (i'',e') = L(l',m),$

           $(i'',e'') = L(l',m) \; \underline{in}$

       $(i' \cup e') \cap (i'' \cup e'') = \{\})$

$\wedge \; (\underline{dom} \; m = All(m))$

$\wedge \; (\exists! l' \varepsilon \underline{dom} \; m)$

     $((m(l') = \underline{mk\text{-}End}(\underline{nil}))$

      $\wedge \; (\neg \exists l' \varepsilon \underline{dom} \; m \backslash L(l,m))(m(l') = \underline{mk\text{-}End}(\underline{nil})))$

   $\underline{type}: \quad L: (L_0 \times M) \rightarrow (L_0\text{-}\underline{set} \times L'\text{-}\underline{set})$

$L(l,m) \;\underline{\Delta}$

   $(\underline{let} \; \underline{mk\text{-}Beg}(vs,l') = m(l) \; \underline{in}$

    $C(l',m)(\{l'\},\{\}))$

$type:$ $C: (L \times M) \to (L_1\text{-}set \times L_1\text{-}set)$
$$\to (L_0\text{-}set \times L'\text{-}set)$$

$C(l,m)(i,e)$ $\triangle$
  $cases$ $m(l):$
    $(mk\text{-}A_1(,l')$ $\to C(l',m)(i\cup\{l'\},e),$

    $mk\text{-}Beg(vs,l') \to$ $(let$ $(i',e') = L(l',m)$ in
                $Mrg\{C(el,m)(i\cup(let$ $mk\text{-}End(l'') = m(el)$ in
                      $\{l''\},e) \mid el\varepsilon e'\}),$

    $mk\text{-}End(l')$ $\to (i\backslash\{l'\},e\cup\{l'\}),$

    $mk\text{-}G_1(,l',l'') \to (let$ $(i',e') = C(l',m)(i\cup\{l'\},e),$
                $(i'',e'') = C(l'',m)(i\cup\{l''\},e)$ in
              $(i'\cup i'',e'\cup e'')))$

$type:$ $Mrg: (L_0\text{-}set \times L'\text{-}set)\text{-}set \to (L_0\text{-}set \times L'\text{-}set)$

$Mrg(s) = (union\{i\mid(i,)\varepsilon s\},union\{e\mid(,e)\varepsilon s\})$

$type:$ $All: M \to L_1\text{-}set$

$All(m)$ $\triangle$
    $\{l \mid mk\text{-}A_1(,l) \varepsilon$ rng $m\}$
  $\cup \{l \mid mk\text{-}Beg(l) \varepsilon$ rng $m\}$
  $\cup \{l \mid mk\text{-}End(l) \varepsilon$ rng $m \wedge l\neq nil\}$
  $\cup \{l',l'' \mid mk\text{-}G_1(,l',l') \varepsilon$ rng $m\}$

$\underline{DSS_1},\underline{PS}:$ Abstraction: $\underline{DSS_1}$ to $\underline{PS}$

$retr\text{-}P(l,m)$ $\triangle$ $s\text{-}B(retr\text{-}B(l,m))$

$retr\text{-}B(l,m)$ $\triangle$ $(let$ $mk\text{-}Beg(vs,l') = m(l)$ in
              let $(cl,l'') = retr\text{-}CL(l',m)<>$ in
              $(mk\text{-}B(vs,cl),l''))$

$$retr\text{-}CL(l,m)cl \;\underline{\Delta}$$

$\underline{cases}\;m(l):$

$\underline{mk}\text{-}A1(a,l')$	$\rightarrow\; \underline{retr}\text{-}CL(l',m)(cl^\wedge<\underline{mk}\text{-}C(l,a)>),$
$\underline{mk}\text{-}Beg(\;)$	$\rightarrow\; (\underline{let}\;(b,l'') = \underline{retr}\text{-}B(l,m)\;\underline{in}$
	$\quad\underline{retr}\text{-}CL(l'',m)(cl^\wedge<\underline{mk}\text{-}C(l,b)>)),$
$\underline{mk}\text{-}End(l')$	$\rightarrow\; (cl,l'),$
$\underline{mk}\text{-}H1(u,l1,l2)$	$\rightarrow\; (\underline{let}\;l' = goto\;(l1,m)\;\underline{in}$
	$\quad\underline{retr}\text{-}CL(l_a,m)(cl^\wedge<\underline{mk}\text{-}C(l,\underline{mk}\text{-}H(u,l')>))$

$$goto(l,m)\;\underline{\Delta}\;\underline{cases}\;m(l):\;\underline{mk}\text{-}End(l') \rightarrow goto(l',m),T \rightarrow l$$

$\underline{TD_1}$: Translator Domain 1

$bn:$	BN	$= L_0 \underset{m}{\rightarrow} N_1$
$n:$	BL	$= N_1$
$lp:$	LP	$= L_0 \underset{m}{\rightarrow} Ptr$
$li:$	LI	$= L_0 \underset{m}{} N_1$
$il:$	IL	$= N_1 \underset{m}{} Ptr$
$p:$	Ptr	$= L_0$

$\quad\underline{dcl}\;L := A(p_0)\;\underline{type}\;L_0\text{-}\underline{set}$

$\quad\underline{get}\;Ptr()\;\underline{\Delta}\;(\underline{def}\;p\epsilon Ptr\backslash \underline{\subseteq} L;$

$\quad\quad\quad\quad\quad\;L := \underline{\subseteq}L\cup\{p\};$

$\quad\quad\quad\quad\quad\;\underline{return}\;p)$

$\quad Ptr \subseteq L_0$

$\underline{T_1}$: Translator 1

$\underline{Type}:\quad GP:\;(L_0 \times B_0) \rightarrow (Ptr \times M)$

$GP(l,\underline{mk}\text{-}B_0(vs,cl))\;\underline{\Delta}$

$\quad(\underline{def}\;(p_b,p_e):\;(\underline{get}\;Ptr(),\underline{get}\;Ptr());$

$\quad(p_b,GB(vs,cl)(([],0),(p_b,p_e),([l\mapsto p_b],[])$

$\quad\quad\cup\;[p_e\mapsto\underline{mk}\text{-}End(nil)]))$

type: GB: C+ → ((BN × BL) → ((Ptr × Ptr) → ((LP × LI) → M)))

GB(vs,cl)((bn,n),(p_b,p_e),(lp,li)) ≜
    (*def* il: [i↦*get* Ptr()|i∈*ind* cl] ∪ [*len* cl+1↦p_e];
    let bn' = bn + [l↦n+1|(l,)∈*elems* cl],
        lp' = lp + [s-L_0(cl[i])↦il(i)|i∈*ind* cl],
        li' = li + [s-L_0(cl[i])↦i|i∈*ind* cl] *in*
    [p_b↦*mk-Beg*(vs,il(1))] ∪
    merge{G(cl,i)((bn',n+1),(lp',li),il)|i∈*ind* cl})

type: G: (C+ × N_1) → ((BN × BL) × (LP × LI) × IL) → M)

G(cl,i)((bn,n),(lp,li),il) ≜
    cases cl[i]:
        mk-A_0(...)   → [il(i)↦*mk-A_1*(cl[i],il(i+1))],
        mk-B_0(vs,cl') → (*def* (p_b,p_e): (*get* Ptr(),*get* Ptr());
                GB(vs,cl')((bn,n),(p_b,p_e),(lp,li))
                ∪[p_e↦*mk-End*(il(i+1))]),
        mk-G_0(e,l)   → (*let* d = n-bn(l) *in*
                if d = 0
                  then [il(i)↦*mk-G_1*(e,il(li(l)),il(i+1)]
                  else (*def* p: *get* Ptr();
                      Chain(d,p,lp(l))
                    ∪[il(i)↦*mk-G_1*(e,p,il(i+1))]))

Chain(d,p_e,p_f) ≜
    if d = 1 *then* [p_e↦*mk-End*(p_f)]
    else (*def* p: *get* Ptr();
        [p_e↦*mk-End*(p')] ∪ Chain(d-1,p',p_f))

type: Chain: N_1 × Ptr × Ptr → M

Correctness: Diagram Commutation (PS, T_1, DSS_1)

$type: \quad Q: P_0 \times P_0 \to BOOL$

$Q(p,p') \triangleq (\exists f \; \varepsilon \; (L_0 \xrightarrow{m} L_0))(X(p')(f) = p)$

$type: \quad X: P_0 \to (L_0 \xrightarrow{m} L_0) \to P_0$

$X((l,b))(f) \triangleq (f(l), X_B(b)(f))$

$X_B(\underline{mk\text{-}B}_0(cl))(f) \triangleq$
$\quad \underline{mk\text{-}B}_0 < (f(\underline{s\text{-}L}_0(cl[i])), X_S(\underline{s\text{-}S}_0(cl[i]))(f)) \mid 1 \underline{\leq} i \underline{\leq} \; \underline{len} \; cl >$

$X_S(s)(f) \triangleq$
$\quad \underline{cases} \; s: \; \underline{mk\text{-}A}_0(\ldots) \to s,$
$\qquad\qquad\quad \underline{mk\text{-}B}_0(\ldots) \to X_B(s)(f),$
$\qquad\qquad\quad \underline{mk\text{-}G}_0(e,l) \to \underline{mk\text{-}G}_0(e,f(l))$

Theorem:

$(\forall p \; \varepsilon \; P_0)$
$\quad \underline{is\text{-}wf\text{-}P}_0(p) \supset$
$\qquad (\underline{let} \; p_1 = GP(p) \; \underline{in}$
$\qquad\quad \underline{inv\text{-}p}_1(p_1)$
$\qquad \wedge \; Q(p, \underline{retr\text{-}P}_0(p_1)))$

$\underline{DSD}_1$: Dynamic Semantics Domain 1

$STK = ACT*$
$ACT = (V \xrightarrow{m} VAL)$

$\underline{dcl}: \; Stk := <> \; \underline{type} \; STK$

$\Sigma \;\; = Stk \xrightarrow{m} STK$

$\underline{call}: \; F(d)$

<u>iDSD$_1$</u>: <u>Invariance of DSD$_1$</u>

$\quad$ *inv-A(act)* $\underline{\Delta}$ *true*

<u>J$_1$</u>: <u>Semantic Elaboration Functions 1</u>

$\quad$ *F(l,m)* $\underline{\Delta}$
$\quad\quad$ *(<u>if</u> l=<u>nil</u> <u>then</u> I*
$\quad\quad$ *<u>else</u> (<u>cases</u> m(l):*
$\quad\quad\quad\quad$ *<u>mk-Beg</u>(vs,l')* $\quad\quad\quad\quad$ →
$\quad\quad\quad\quad\quad$ *(Stk := <[v↦...|v∈vs]>^<u>c</u>Stk;*
$\quad\quad\quad\quad\quad$ *F(l',m)),*
$\quad\quad\quad\quad$ *<u>mk-End</u>(l')* $\quad\quad\quad\quad$ →
$\quad\quad\quad\quad\quad$ *(Stk := <u>tl</u> <u>c</u>Stk;*
$\quad\quad\quad\quad\quad$ *F(l',m)),*
$\quad\quad\quad\quad$ *<u>mk-Al</u>(<u>mk-A</u>(v,u),l')* →
$\quad\quad\quad\quad\quad$ *(<u>def</u> val: V(u);*
$\quad\quad\quad\quad\quad$ *<u>def</u> i: Search(v);*
$\quad\quad\quad\quad\quad$ *Insert(v,val,i);*
$\quad\quad\quad\quad\quad$ *F(l',m)),*
$\quad\quad\quad\quad$ *<u>mk-Hl</u>(u,l$_c$,l$_a$)* $\quad\quad\quad$ →
$\quad\quad\quad\quad\quad$ *(<u>def</u> b: V(u);*
$\quad\quad\quad\quad\quad$ *<u>if</u> b <u>then</u> F(l$_c$,m) <u>else</u> F(l$_a$,m)))*

$\quad$ *Search(v)* $\underline{\Delta}$ *Lookup(v)(<u>c</u>Stk)(1)*

$\quad$ *Lookup(v)(stk)(i)* $\underline{\Delta}$
$\quad\quad$ *<u>if</u> v ε <u>dom</u> stk[i]*
$\quad\quad\quad$ *<u>then</u> i*
$\quad\quad\quad$ *<u>else</u> Lookup(v)(stk)(i+1)*

$\quad$ *Insert(v,val,i)* $\underline{\Delta}$
$\quad\quad$ *Stk := <u>c</u>Stk + [i↦[v↦val}]] + (<u>c</u>Stk)[i]]*

HEAP STORAGE SPECIFICATION AND DEVELOPMENT

Chris George
Software Technology Division, STC Technology Ltd,
London Road, Harlow, Essex CM17 9NA, UK

1.   Introduction

The specification is intended to describe the NEW and DISPOSE operations of the heap in Pascal. It contains several levels of specification, each intended to implement the previous one. It is intended to
show how an efficient implementation may be gradually created from an
abstract specification by successive commitments to data structures and
algorithms.

2.   Level 0

Level 0 is an attempt to be as abstract as possible. The free space is
simply a set of locations; disposal is then simply a matter of set
union. Allocating free space with NEW0 involves finding a sufficiently
long sequence.

```
State0—State is

FREE0 : Loc-set
Loc = Nat0

NEW0 (REQ:Nat)  RES:Loc-set
ext   FREE0 : wr Loc-set
pre   (∃ s ∈ Loc-list)(has_seq(s,req,free0))
post  (∃ s ∈ Loc-list)
      (has_seq(s,req,free0) ∧
       res = elems s ∧
       free0' = free0 - res)

DISPOSE0 (RET:Loc-set)
ext   FREE0 : wr Loc-set
pre   ret ∩ free0 = {}
post  free0' = free0 ∪ ret

has_seq: Loc-list X Nat X Loc-set → Bool
has_seq(s,n,free) ≙
  is_sequential(s) ∧
  elems s ⊆ free ∧
  len s = n

is_sequential: Nat0-list → Bool
is_sequential(s) ≙
  (∃ i,j ∈ Nat0)(s = interval(i,j))

end
```

3. Level 1

Level 1 tries to tackle the inefficiency of NEW, which in level 0 consisted of a search for a suitable set. The free space is now held as a set of non-overlapping, non-abutting pieces. NEW is now a matter of finding a suitable piece. It was originally intended that it would be undecided at this stage whether the pieces were non-abutting, but it was pointed out that if they were allowed to abut then either the precondition of NEW1 would need changing to show that there existed a set of pieces that could be assembled to form the requirement, or there would be cases where NEW2 at the next level would satisfy its precondition and NEW1 would not. Hence the level 1 invariant now insists on non-abutting pieces.

The retrieve function is

  retr1_0 ≙ locs

Note that the normal refinement rules, as for example in [1], will not work for NEW1 and DISPOSE1 since their signatures have changed.

    State1—*State is*

    FREE1 : Piece-set
    Piece :: LOC:Loc
            SIZE:Nat
    Loc = Nat0

    inv ≙ is_ok1(free1)

    NEW1 (REQ:Nat) RES:Piece
    ext   FREE1 : *wr* Piece-set
    pre   (∃ p ∈ free1)(SIZE(p)⩾req)
    post locs(free1') = locs(free1) - locs_of(res) ∧
            locs_of(res) ⊆ locs(free1) ∧
            SIZE(res) = req

    DISPOSE1 (RET:Piece)
    ext   FREE1 : *wr* Piece-set
    pre   locs_of(ret) ∩ locs(free1) = {}
    post locs(free1') = locs(free1) ∪ locs_of(ret)

    locs: Piece-set → Loc-set
    locs(ps) ≙ *union*{locs_of(p) | p ∈ ps}

    locs_of: Piece → Loc-set
    locs_of(p) ≙ {LOC(p) : LOC(p)+SIZE(p)-1}

    is_ok1: Piece-set → Bool
    is_ok1(ps) ≙
      (∀ p1,p2 ∈ ps)
      (p1 = p2 ∨ locs_of(p1) ∩ locs_of(p2) = {} ∧
       LOC(p1)+SIZE(p1) ≠ LOC(p2))

      /* pieces must be disjoint and non abutting */

end

4.   Level 2

Having tried to deal with the problem of NEW in level 1, it still seems
that DISPOSE has a problem of checking for abutment of the pieces it
tries to add to the free space with those already there - apparently
checking each of the free set of pieces. The level 2 state now holds
the pieces in a recursive and ordered structure allowing for a simple
search.

The retrieve function to level 1 is

>   retr2_1: [Fp] → Piece-set
>   retr2_1(free) ≙
>   {*mk*-Piece(FPLOC(fp),FPSIZE(fp)) | fp ∈ Fp ∧ is_reachable(fp,free)}

but it is perhaps easier to give that back to level 0 as

>   retr2_0 ≙ locs2

since the post-conditions of NEW2 and DISPOSE2 use locs2.

Note that it would be more convenient to represent the level 2 state by

>   State2-*State is*
>
>   FREE2 : Piece-list
>   ...

when the type 'Fp' and the function 'is_reachable' are no longer necessary - the quantification in the pre-condition of NEW2 can be done over
the *elems* of the state. This example was written without using the
list data type of VDM, but effectively modelling it, to show how recursive structures may be defined, and to show the use of predicates like
'is_reachable' with such structures.

>   State2-*State is*
>
>   FREE2 : [Fp]
>   Fp :: FPLOC:Loc
>   FPSIZE:Nat
>   FPNEXT:[Fp]
>   Piece :: LOC:Loc
>   SIZE:Nat
>   Loc = Nat0
>
>   *inv*-Fp ≙ is_ok2
>   is_ok2: [Fp] → Bool
>   is_ok2(fp) ≙
>   *if* fp = NIL *then* TRUE
>   *else if* FPNEXT(fp) = NIL *then* TRUE
>   *else* FPLOC(fp)+FPSIZE(fp) < FPLOC(FPNEXT(fp)) ∧
>   is_ok2(FPNEXT(fp))

```
/* Note that the pieces are in ascending order.
   Note also that the use of '<' rather than '≤' forces the pieces
   not to abut. */

NEW2 (REQ:Nat) RES:Piece
ext   FREE2 : wr [Fp]
pre   (∃ fp ∈ Fp)
      (FPSIZE(fp) ≥ req ∧
       is_reachable(fp,free2))
post  locs2(free2') = locs2(free2) - locs_of(res) ∧
      locs_of(res) ⊆ locs2(free2) ∧
      SIZE(res) = req

DISPOSE2 (RET:Piece)
ext   FREE2 : wr [Fp]
pre   locs_of(ret) ∩ locs2(free2) = {}
post  locs2(free2') = locs2(free2) ∪ locs_of(ret)

locs2: [Fp] → Loc-set
locs2(fp) ≙
  if fp = NIL then {}
  else {FPLOC(fp) : FPLOC(fp)+FPSIZE(fp)-1} ∪
       locs2(FPNEXT(fp))

is_reachable: Fp X [Fp] → Bool
is_reachable(fp,start) ≙
  if start = NIL then FALSE
  else if fp = start then TRUE
  else is_reachable(fp,FPNEXT(start))

end
```

5. Level 3

Having achieved a state structure that will allow reasonably efficient
procedures for NEW and DISPOSE (or at least procedures that are an
improvement on searching sets), there is still the problem that in
implementing this structure much storage will be used. We wish instead
to use the free storage as the space in which the information about its
structure is held. Hence in level 3 we model storage as a map from
location to value, where a value may also represent a location. Since
each piece of free space must now store its length and a pointer to the
next, a new requirement is added that NEW and DISPOSE will not work on
pieces of length 1.

The retrieve function is

```
retr3_2: [Loc] X Store → [Fp]
pre-retr3_2(start,store) ≙ is_ok3(start,store)
retr3_2(start,store) ≙
  if start = NIL then NIL
  else mk-Fp(start,store(start),retr3_2(store(start+1),store))
```

but as with level 2 it might be easier to use

retr3_0 ≙ locs3

Neither of these retrieve functions will be adequate, of course, because of the ban on pieces of length 1.

State3−*State is*

START : [Loc]
STORE : Store
Store = Loc → [Nat0]
Piece :: LOC:Loc
         SIZE:Nat
Loc = Nat0

inv ≙ is_ok3(start,store)
is_ok3: [Loc] X Store → Bool
is_ok3(a,store) ≙
  if a = NIL *then* TRUE
  else {a,a+1} ⊆ *dom* store ∧
         store(a) ≠ NIL ∧
         store(a) > 1 ∧
         store(a+1) ≠ NIL ⇸
             (a+store(a) < store(a+1) ∧ is_ok3(store(a+1),store))

/* Note the new restriction, carried into NEW3 and DISPOSE3, that
   the size of a piece must be at least 2 */

NEW3 (REQ:Nat) RES:Piece
ext   START : *wr* [Loc]
         STORE : *wr* Store
pre   req > 1 ∧
         (∃ a ∈ *dom* store)
         (store(a) ≠ NIL ∧
          (store(a) = req ∨ store(a)−req > 1) ∧
          is_reachable3(a,start,store))
post   locs3(start',store') = locs3(start,store) − locs_of(res) ∧
         locs_of(res) ⊆ locs3(start,store) ∧
         SIZE(res) = req ∧
         (∀ loc ∈ *dom* store − locs3(start,store))
         (loc ∈ *dom* store' ∧ store'(loc) = store(loc))

DISPOSE3 (RET:Piece)
ext   START : *wr* [Loc]
         STORE : *wr* Store
pre   SIZE(ret) > 1 ∧
         locs_of(ret) ∩ locs3(start,store) = {}
post   locs3(start',store') = locs3(start,store) ∪ locs_of(ret) ∧
         (∀ loc ∈ *dom* store − locs3(start',store'))
         (loc ∈ *dom* store' ∧ store'(loc) = store(loc))

is_reachable3: Loc X [Loc] X Store → Bool
pre−is_reachable(a,start,store) ≙ is_ok3(start,store)
is_reachable3(a,start,store) ≙
  if start = NIL *then* FALSE
  else if a = start *then* TRUE

```
        else is_reachable3(a,store(start+1),store)

  locs3: [Loc] X Store → Loc-set
  pre-locs3(start,store) ≙ is_ok3(start,store)
  locs3(start,store) ≙
    if start = NIL then {}
    else  {start : start+store(start)-1} ∪
          locs3(store(start+1),store)
```

6. NEW4 and DISPOSE4

NEW4 and DISPOSE4 are new versions of NEW and DISPOSE working on the
level 3 state, but supplying explicit instead of implicit specifications. For each of the previous definitions of NEW and DISPOSE there
is no algorithm — the specifications are in terms of the sets of locations represented and the state invariants. It is an interesting question whether it would have been better to try to introduce these algorithms at level 2. In the opinion of the author the algorithms are
difficult to introduce, but would have been no easier at level 2.

```
  NEW4 (REQ:Nat) RES:Piece
  ext    START : wr [Loc]
         STORE : wr Store
  pre    req > 1 ∧
         (∃ a ∈ dom store)
         (store(a) ≠ NIL ∧
          (store(a) = req ∨ store(a)-req > 1) ∧
          is_reachable3(a,start,store))
  post   start' = if store(start) = req then store(start+1)
                    else start ∧
         (store',res) = remove4(NIL,start,store,req)

  remove4: [Loc] X [Loc] X Store X Nat → (Store X Piece)
  pre-remove4(prev,current,store,n) ≙
    n > 1 ∧
    (∃ a ∈ dom store)
    (store(a) ≠ NIL ∧
     (store(a) = req ∨ store(a)-req > 1) ∧
     is_reachable3(a,current,store)) ∧
    (prev = NIL ∨ current = NIL ∨ prev < current) ∧
    is_ok3(prev,store) ∧
    is_ok3(current,store)
  remove4(prev,current,store,n) ≙
    if (store(current) < n) ∨ (store(current) = n+1)
    then remove4(current,store(current+1),store,n)
    else let storel ≙
      if store(current) = n
      then if prev = NIL then store
            else store † [prev ↦ store(current+1)]
      else store † [current ↦ store(current)-n]
    in (storel,mk-Piece(current+store(current)-n,n))

  DISPOSE4 (RET:Piece)
  ext    START : wr [Loc]
```

```
        STORE : wr Store
 pre    SIZE(ret) > 1 ∧
        locs_of(ret) ∩ locs3(start,store) = {}
 post   let ret ≙ mk-Piece(a,s) in
        start' = if start = NIL then a
                    else min(start,a)
        ∧ store' = insert(NIL,start,store,a,s)

insert: [Loc] X [Loc] X Store X Loc X Nat → Store
pre-insert(prev,current,store,a,s) ≙
    s > 1 ∧
    (prev = NIL ∨ current = NIL ∨ prev < current) ∧
    is_ok3(prev,store) ∧
    is_ok3(current,store)
insert(prev,current,store,a,s) ≙
    if current ≠ NIL ∧ a > current
    then insert(current,store(current+1),store,a,s)
    else
    let store1 ≙ store † [a ↦ s, a+1 ↦ current] in
    let store2 ≙ if prev = NIL then store1
                    else store1 † [prev+1 ↦ a] in
    let store3 ≙ if current = NIL ∨ a+s < current
                    then store2
                    else (store2\{current,current+1}) †
                         [a ↦ s+store2(current),
                          a+1 ↦ store2(current+1)] in
    let store4 ≙ if prev = NIL ∨ prev+store(prev) < a
                    then store3
                    else (store3\{a,a+1}) †
                         [prev ↦ store3(prev)+store3(a),
                          prev+1 ↦ store3(a+1)] in
    store4
    /* store1 has new piece hooked up to next
       store2 has new piece hooked up to previous one
       store3 has new piece merged with next if possible
       store4 has new piece merged with previous if possible */

    /* DISPOSE4 is an implementation of DISPOSE3 */

    end
```

7. Further refinements

The removal of domain elements from the store map in DISPOSE4 is difficult to model, and should be deleted on the basis that the presence of
unreachable elements in the domain of the the map is irrelevant.

The pre-conditions for DISPOSE4 and NEW4 should be replaced by exception conditions, and the exceptions raised at appropriate points in the
algorithms. Note that this is more than encapsulation in some operation whose body (for NEW, say) is effectively

    if pre-NEW(req) then NEW(req) else raise exception

since an implementation of this implies in general two searches for a suitable piece!

The type Loc should then be replaced by some range of values representing possible heap locations. (This introduction of bounds is, of course, an inadequate refinement.) An extra exception for exhaustion of heap space should also be added.

The operations could then be implemented in some suitable programming language, though of course we would only be modelling heap space by some (presumably large) array.

A development along these lines into Pascal has in fact been completed and is documented in [3].

8. Logic

This specification has been written assuming LPF ([2]) for the logic, which allowed the use of terms like

    (∃ a ∈ *dom* store)
    (store(a) ≠ *NIL* ∧ store(a) = n)

where n ∈ Nat. The problems of rewriting it for a two valued logic are probably worth examining.

9. Proofs

No proofs of adequacy or correctness of refined operations have been attempted. The proofs look tedious but may be worth study.

10. More interesting data structures

It could be argued that the data structures used are still fairly trivial. A more interesting level 2 structure would use a B-tree instead of the linear recursive structure, and a further refinement to the operations would be to keep the tree balanced. This involves a further restriction on the minimum size of pieces to 3.

An even more interesting structure can be obtained by noting that the balanced B-tree gives an O(log(n)) algorithm for DISPOSE but still leaves NEW as O(n), where 'n' is the number of pieces. If most NEW and DISPOSE operations are of the same size, or from a small range of sizes, this should not be too much of a problem. If NEW is also required to be O(log(n)) some other structure might be used.

11. Acknowledgements

This study was originally intended to provide an example of development for use in courses on VDM, and has benefited from the comments of course participants. Several colleagues have also provided suggestions and pointed out errors, particularly A.J. Evans, P. Goldsack and C.B. Jones.

This work was partially funded by the Commission of the European

Communities (CEC) under the ESPRIT programme in the field of software technology, project number 315 "Rigorous Approach to Industrial Software Engineering (RAISE)"

12. References

[1] C.B. Jones, 'Systematic software development using VDM', Prentice-Hall International, 1986.

[2] H. Barringer, J.H. Cheng and C.B. Jones, 'A logic covering unde-finedness in program proofs', Acta Informatica, vol. 21 pp 251-259, 1984.

[3] A.J. Evans, 'Heap storage specification and refinement to a target language', RAISE/STC/AJE/1, 1986.

VDM as a Specification Method for Telecommunications Software
(Summary)

Thomas Letschert

Philips Kommunikations Industrie AG

Nürnberg, West Germany

1. Demands

Recent advances in technology have made it possible to construct large systems of
interconnected processing units. Such a system consists of nodes that are connected
via a communication network. We find longhaul and shorthaul networks. A telephone
network is longhaul, but increased demands for functionality and faulttolerance
have lead to the use of special multiprocessor systems as switching nodes (exchanges).
Here we consider specification, design and implementation of telecommunication software for the shorthaul network formed by such a node.

Special attention has to be paid to:
- Real time

  The systems have to meet severe time constraints.
- Continuous service

  The systems have to provide continuous service in the face of errors and crashes
  of varying severity.

In addition to these, the last years have brought several new demands. The most
important of them are:
- Distribution and configuration

  The software has to run on hardware consisting of several more or less
  independent nodes with a change in configuration fequently.
- Reusability of software

  In order to provide a rather wide range of products at low cost, reusability of
  software in differing systems is of prime concern.
- Version and configuration control

  Improved interface descriptions and appropriate tools should reduce the cost of
  software integration.
- Transition to a new uniform implementation language.

  Software engineering methods and tools have to be adapted to new language (CHILL).

The use of improved design and specification methods has been considered to be one of
the most important means to achieve these goals.

2. Background

In an industrial environment you cannot replace the way software is produced by whole departments by a new one over night, even if the new one is considerably better than the old way. So we tried to improve only local aspects of the software life cycle in isolation and according to an existing environment.

The local experience in producing switching nodes is reflected in a sophisticated documentation system with strong connections to software integration and configuration tools. Software is organized as systems, subsystems, and packages. Packages are the most fine grained units with a formally organized life cycle. Package specifications and designs are written in a CHILL-like pseudo code according to some standards. A first and very effective step towards the introduction of rigorous software development was the introduction of improved package specification and design standards.

3. A Library of Specified Programs

The number and variety of objects - specifications, documentations, source code, compiled code,etc. - is a principle source of complexity in large systems. A library (database) concept that integrates all these objects into a uniform conceptual framework and provides appropriate tools would be the philosophers stone of software engineering. Unfortunately such stones tend to be found not very early before doomesday. So we sought a relatively simple concept for one kind of objects that may serve as a robust backbone for bearing the others.

Modern languages like Modula-2, ADA, CHILL, provide linguistic features to specify units and their interfaces. A specification language may offer much more for these purposes. If we maintain units of specification, we have to take additional care of those of the implementation language and the relation between these two kinds of units. If we use the implementation language as conceptual framework, much of the expressional power of the specification language has to be sacrificed.

A compromise between these alternatives can only be found by taking the specification language, the implementation language, and the intended area of application into account. Some remarks concerning the latter will follow in the next section.

Take for example a generic data type. Let us say a priority queue with two parameters: the type of queued objects and a function to compare them. Obviously the specification language should be able to express such a thing. The generic queue may be used to

create special ones by passing appropriate parameters to it. If the priority queue
is implemented and made a reusable component of our library, we have to provide
this implementation with guidelines, that restrict its use to one that corresponds to
this parameter passing. But - the other way round - as our implementation language
(CHILL) only provides static instantiations of types, we have to state that the
priority queue may not be compiled, but only used as code macro, thus - if we unify
units of specification and implementation - the use of the queue specification is
restricted to situations where its implementation may be used in this way. To
summarize: The demand to structure specifications and implementations uniformly
leads to some restrictions in the use of specifications, but we claim that these are
paid back by a considerably more simple development environment.

4. Layered Systems

To a large extend telecommunication software resembles that of other (real time)
systems. Its main purpose however is the transmission of messages. Message transmission usually is defined in terms of layered systems. Two instances at layer n
communicate according to some protocol using services of layer n-1. There is a long
tradition to define such systems as consisting of communicating (finite) state
machines (e.g. using SDL).

Rigorous software development in this area means (among other things) using a well
defined and founded programming related notation to express the same. Some form of
communicating sequential processes are appropriate here. This however does not always
reflect the actual software structure. The desire to use the same conceptual units in
specification as in implementation language would either fix too much implementation
details or devate too much from common practice. This has led us to the decision to
introduce a new abstraction mechanism, the semantics of which may be based on
processes, but does not correspond directly to CHILL processes. As this abstraction
is based in its notation on local package specifications they are called "packages".

A package is organized like a data abstraction (abstract variable). It has an internal
state and exports services which may be seen as message passing to and from the
package. Additional features of package specifications are concerned with error
handling, recovery and configuration.

Package specifications and implementations are currently under investigation
mainly by rewriting existing specifications according to modified demands and by deriving new implementations for them.

5. Conclusion

Improved software development techniques can be introduced only if their advantage can be demonstrated even without major investments. We suggested to start by change-ing low level specifications while still keeping them close to the implementation language and to a smoothly extended environment.

So use and adaption to a given context of "the Method" have been of interest here. Our message was: create libraries of specified programs close to the area of appli-cation and the implementation language.

Things reported on here are still in their infancy and the author would like to thank all those who have and will answer his bothering questions about telephones.

Support Environments for VDM

Kevin D. Jones
Department of Computer Science
The University
Manchester M13 9PL
kevin@uk.ac.man.cs.ux, mcvax!ukc!man.cs.ux!kevin

Abstract

This paper discusses the experiences and issues of building two different levels of system to support the use of VDM.

The MULE system is an example of an environment giving support in the syntactic generation of formal objects, such as specifications.

The IPSE 2.5 system is an attempt to produce an industrial scale system to support the use of formal methods over the whole of a software development life cycle.

1 Introduction

The aim of this paper is to discuss some of the issues that have to be addressed if one wishes to build support environments for formal methods. Of course, most of these issues are more generically applicable than just to VDM [Jon86].In view of the context of presentation, however, VDM is a better focus of attention than most.

1.1 Why do we need support environments?

The need for some mechanised support of formal/rigorous development becomes obvious as the size of the examples tackled grows beyond the trivial. There are many extra classes of detail (such as proof obligation) that have to be kept track of. It would also be beneficial if the system could help to discharge some of these obligations. Furthermore, since formal languages have well-defined syntax, it is possible for the system to help in constructing objects, removing some of the inconveniences from the user. In fact, it could be argued that it is only after the extra "house-keeping" details are removed from the user's concern that it will be possible to convince the "general (programming) public" that the benefits of Formal Methods outweigh the overheads.

1.2 Are Support Environments for Formal/Rigorous development special?

An obvious claim is that all support environments have to tackle the same problem and that there is nothing special involved in supporting formal methods. However, a little further thought should show that there are certain features of such methods that differ from "general" software support.

1. Formal methods involve formal languages (obviously!). This means that more is known about the structure of correct texts than in the case of natural languages, for example. This leads naturally to the use of structure editors [Wil86c] as an interaction medium.

2. In general there will be a stronger type system than for informal languages and dependencies between objects will be easily categorizable. For example, the relationship between *specification, refinement* and *proof obligation* is well defined and can be tracked by the system.

3. The granularity of information and the degree of interconnectivity is likely to differ from most support environments. In traditional cases (e.g. [Bou82]), the normal level of granularity is the *file*. This would normally be a fairly large "chunk" of data. Dependencies and relationships can only be tracked by the system at this level of granularity — references within these boundaries are usually the domain of special tools. When the environment is intended to support formal methods, this is not an adequate model. It is more often the case that references will be to small objects (e.g. a line within a proof, a variable within an expression) and that there will be a great deal of interconnection between these objects. The file system view imposes an unnatural boundary between tools making full integration almost impossible to achieve.

This would seem to imply that a file system is not sufficient to support an environment intended for formal methods and that it would be necessary to build such a system on a "fine-grain" database. Past (and present) experience at Manchester would seem to strongly support this claim.

To illustrate the issues involved in building such environments, the next section examines two differing systems with which Manchester University has had some involvement.

2 Principal Examples of Support Environments

The examples presented below can be taken as illustrative of

a. an experimental academic environment;

b. an experimental industrial environment;

Obviously, the latter supports a much wider range of facilities and relationships than the former. Roughly speaking they represent the past (the laboratory) and the future (the "real world") respectively.

2.1 The Past — MULE

The MULE project [Wil86a] was a SERC supported project intended to investigate the issues involved in providing mechanised support for VDM development. A prototype environment was produced and runs on an ICL Perq under PNX.

2.1.1 Description of the system

MULE represents a fairly early attempt at building a support environment for VDM. Most of the assistance offered is at the syntactic level.

The system ensures that objects which are constructed conform to an appropriate grammer. This removes many of the common errors due to incorrectly formed definitions.

The mule system can be roughly divided into three parts

1. The Database (MDB) [Nip82]

2. The User Interface [Wil86a]

3. The GRAPL language [Nip83].

2.1.2 MDB

The database, MDB [Nip82], is a "fine-grain" system designed and built specifically for the task of supporting MULE.

Basically, MDB is a graph based persistent[1] database providing a procedural interface (in Pascal). There is a great deal of similarity between MDB and conventional binary relational databases — in that there are entities and relations between them. Entities can have values (either *NILVALUE*, a string or a user defined type). Relations are "represented" by labelled arcs, where the labels are in turn entities. In addition, there are three special kinds of relations

1. MAP — linking entities to entities

2. SET — linking entities to sets of entities

3. LIST — linking entities to lists of entities.

The interface to MDB is a set of procedures that support navigation within the database. These primitives are generally invisible to a user of the MULE system.

On top of this basic level, there are more sophisticated interface levels providing additional support, such as type information [Wil86b].

---

[1]following the notions of [Per85]

2.1.3 The User Interface

The UI makes use of the Perq's bit-mapped display and pointing device. At the lowest level, it provides an independent tiled windowing environment working within one of the Perq windows.

The UI provides the mechanism for activating the other components of the system and displaying the results of the invocation. The philosophy of this interface is that of *syntax-directed editing*. The interface provides a projection of a database construct containing *holes*. These *holes* represent components of the structure. When the appropriate action is invoked at a *hole*, a menu of possible constructs is displayed.

By this use of projections from the database, the UI presents *views* of the current database state. Modifications are done directly on this representation, with database actions being invoked implicitly by the interface.

A noteworthy difference between MULE and other similar systems (such as [Mel84]) is the influence of graphs structures. Other such systems are based on a tree representation, allowing less generality in structure without redundant copying. The MULE system is based on graphs and this is reflected in the views that can be presented to a user.

2.1.4 GRAPL

GRAPL [Nip83] is a database manipulation language, derived from PROLOG. It is specifically intended to work over MDB graphs. It is possible to attach GRAPL programs to MULE structures. On activating the "hole", the GRAPL program is invoked with the attached parameters. Conceptually, there is a spectrum of rôles for GRAPL within the overall system. These range from a simple database query language, up to all of the interaction with the system being via GRAPL programs[2]. Originally, the system was query only, since the output was always sent to the standard output. More recently the system has been extended to allow manipulation of the database to be done via attached GRAPL code.

2.1.5 MULE for VDM

MULE is in fact a generic support environment in that it is grammer driven. However, the system has been instantiated to provide the originally intended VDM support environment. This involved providing a grammer for MULE-VDM [CJNW83] (an extended version of the usual VDM Metalanguage [Jon86]) which provides CLEAR-like modularisation features.

2.1.6 Lessons learned from MULE

The development and subsequent experimentation with the MULE system brought to light some important factors relating to support environments for formal methods.

---

[2]implicitly invoked of course!

Firstly, it became obvious that while the "fine-grain" approach is necessary, it is a difficult goal to realise efficiently. MDB is basically fully memory resident during a session and uses the "core dump" model of persistence [KDJ86]. This places heavy reliance on the virtual memory system. In the case of MULE's chosen workstation (Perq 2), this was found to be unsatisfactory as page thrashing severely limited the systems performance. Obviously, usable systems must adopt a better approach to this problem.

2.2   The Future — IPSE 2.5

IPSE 2.5 [SU85] is an Alvey-supported project. It is a large collaboration involving five industrial companies in addition to Manchester University and RAL. The aim of the project is to build an industrial scale integrated project support environment supporting formal methods[3].

2.2.1   IPSE 2.5 — The system

The major difference between a system like MULE (above) and IPSE 2.5 is that of complexity of task tackled. IPSE 2.5 intends to support the entire software development process. In view of this, tools are to be provided to support management processes, design processes (both formal and semi-formal), etc. In addition, the system is to be a support environment generator (i.e. a generic support environment that can be instatiated for any particular system).

The basic structure of the IPSE 2.5 system (in general terms, since the detailed design is still an on-going process) consists of

1. An Object Management System
   This will provide persistent storage of all objects within the system. The OMS provides the basic mechanism for integration, since all communication between tools will be done via this, using a common type system.

2. A User Interface
   This will take full advantage of the workstation type facilities and will provide a uniform interface to all tools. Specific tool interfaces can be constructed on top of the "primitive" UI.

3. Configuration Management System
   This system will provide the basic mechanism for controlling the use of, and dependencies between, objects within the OMS. This has to be more sophisticated than is currently available, since Formal Reasoning (in particular) requires CM over unusually small objects having a large number of interdependencies.

---

[3]The term IPSE 2.5 comes from the fact that it is believed that this project fits in somewhere between an IPSE 2 and an IPSE 3 on the Alvey scale [Alv83]

4. Interaction Language

   This language will be the main medium of communication with the system. In many cases, this will be hidden by use of the pointing capability of the UI. This language will have to be sufficiently expressive to handle objects such as process descriptions, plans and theorem proving tactics.

5. Process Control Engine

   One of the most interesting features of IPSE 2.5 is the inclusion of an active process model. This defines the activities which a user can perform via the concept of a *rôle* such as manager, designer, etc. The PCE supports the execution of such *rôle descriptions* to drive the system.

6. Various Tools Specific To Individual Interest Areas

   This includes the tools specific to Formal Reasoning, Management support, design support, etc.

2.2.2   Specific support for Formal Reasoning

Within this overall framework, it is necessary to provide (generic) support for formal development methods[JLW86].

The intended goal is to provide a logic independent theorem proving environment that can be instantiated for any given system. This may,of course, prove an unattainable goal and the level of genericity that is feasible is still under investigation.

The pragmatic aim of the formal reasoning aspects of IPSE 2.5 is to make theorem proving a more useful tool for the purpose of software engineering. It is believed that there are two key factors involved in achieving this aim:

1. The User Interface of the Theorem Proving System

   If the system provides a "modern"[4] interface tailored to TP tasks, in place of the "glass teletype" standard found on most existing systems, it is believed that this will be a major step forward. In particular, a large screen with good selection mechanisms should encourage the "proof at the terminal" style of working that has not been realistically possible with contemporary systems.

2. A Theory Database

   The second important feature is that of a database of stored objects. This should include theories, theorems, proofs, tactics, etc. Most currently existing theorem proving systems do not provide this facility at anything beyond the "text to file" level. As well as providing for greater power in use by allowing sophisticated searching/retrieval mechanisms, this facility also encourages the reuse of formal objects. It is also believed that the correct approach to the Theory database will enable the system to be extended to a multiple user environment in a convenient way, making use of the CM system (above).

---

[4]i.e. large bit-mapped screen, windows, pointing device, etc.

In addition, the system will provide other tools useful in a formal reasoning context such as a symbolic execution system.

One of the examples of an instantiated IPSE 2.5 system will be an environment tailored to VDM. This instantiation will involve

- providing appropriate drivers for the structure editor interfaces

- providing the appropriate logic for the TP system (e.g. LPF[BCJ84])

- building a library of appropriate theories (e.g. sets, lists, etc.)

The work at Manchester is primarily concerned with building the Theorem Proving Environment and the investigation of the theoretical issues associated with a generic system. Current investigations include :

1. User Interfaces for Proof Editors (Muffin [Moo86])

2. The uses and structure of a Theory Database

3. Description of Generic Logics

4. Object-oriented approaches to Theorem Proving

5. The infrastructure of a TP environment

6. symbolic execution of specifications.

3 Summary

It is obvious to anyone who has attempted serious use of a formal method that the advantages of such an approach would show more clearly if the mechanical detail could be handled automatically. Existing systems generally provide assistance with the syntax of the languages involved. Current research work is aimed at providing support for the process of proof.

Future systems will provide support for both the construction of specifications and the discharge of proof obligations, in the context of the complete life cycle of software development.

4 Acknowledgements

Thanks should be given to the staff of the IPSE 2.5 project for providing much of the information included in here and to SERC for providing the necessary financial support.

References

[Alv83]   The Alvey Directorate. The Alvey software engineering stratagy. 1983.

[BCJ84]   H. Barringer, J.H. Cheng, and C.B. Jones. A logic covering undefinedness in program proofs. *Acta Informatica*, 21:251 – 269, 1984.

[Bou82]   S.R. Bourne. *The Unix System*. Addison Wesley, 1982.

[CJNW83] I.D. Cottam, C.B. Jones, T. Nipkow, and A.C. Wills. The 2nd annual report on the MULE project. 1983.

[JLW86]   C.B. Jones, P. Lindsey, and C.P. Wadsworth. IPSE 2.5 : the theorem proving concept paper. 1986.

[Jon86]   Cliff B. Jones. *Systematic Software Development using VDM*. Prentice Hall International, 1986.

[KDJ86]   K.D.Jones. A review of persistence in programming languages. 1986.

[Mel84]   B. Melese. Practical applications of a syntax directed program manipulation environment. In 7th *Int. Conf. on Software Engineering*, 1984.

[Moo86]   R.C. Moore. The specification of Muffin. 1986.

[Nip82]   T. Nipkow. A user guide to the MULE database. 1982.

[Nip83]   T. Nipkow. A graph manipulation language — GRAPL. 1983.

[Per85]   The Persistent Programming Research Group. *The PS-Algol Reference Manual*. Universities of St. Andrews and Glasgow, 2nd edition, 1985.

[SU85]   STC and The University of Manchester. The IPSE 2.5 project proposal. 1985.

[Wil86a]   A.C. Wills. The book of MULE. 1986.

[Wil86b]   A.C. Wills. Description of MDB-T. 1986.

[Wil86c]   A.C. Wills. Structure of interactive systems. 1986.

DEVELOPMENT AND APPLICATION OF A META IV COMPILER

Manfred Haß

Institut für Informatik und Praktische Mathematik der
Christian-Albrechts-Universität zu Kiel
Olshausenstr. 40 - 60, D-2300 Kiel 1

Abstract:

A method using **VDM** and its meta language **META IV** for systematic semi-automated compiler development is outlined. Then the construction of a **META IV** compiler sophisticated enough to extend that method to a fully automated one is described. After the introduction of a compilable subset of **META IV** the implementation of fixpoints and implicitly defined sets, maps and tuples will be discussed. Another issue is the question how to manage I/O for a compiled **META IV** specification. The automatic generation of a compiler for the example language PLO [Wir 77] will show that the new **META IV** compiler enables automatic transformation of VDM compiler specifications into executable programs.

1 Introduction

This paper describes development and implementation of a compiler for **META IV**, the meta language used in the Vienna Development Method (VDM, [BjJ78]). The **META IV** compiler serves two purposes. Firstly, it may be employed for rapid prototyping. By translating specifications of software products into executable programms it will be possible to test their consistency as well as their dynamic semantics. Secondly, the development of a **META IV** compiler is a step towards a compiler-compiler system that automatically transforms **VDM** compiler specifications into programs.

The **META IV** compiler project has its origin in the **CAT** project. The latter was started in 1982 by NORSK DATA and the University of Kiel, Germany, with the aim of searching for practical tools to reduce the costs of compiler development and maintainance. In the **CAT** project **VDM** was used to design a multi language and multi target compiler system. Abstract syntax, static and dynamic semantics of source and target language were formally specified in **META IV** and served as a basis for the development of compile algorithms also specified in **META IV**. These compile algorithms together with the abstract syntaxes and the is-wf- functions for testing the static semantics of the source language form a **VDM** compiler specification.

In the **CAT** project compiler front ends, translating source languages into **CAT**, a machine independent intermediate language, suitable for compiling ALGOL-like source languages into different machine languages, were implemented by systematic transformation of such specifications into Pascal code [Sch83, Völ83].

In 1985 NORSK DATA completed a parser generator system, which for a given specification of concrete and abstract syntax of a programming language automatically generates a parser module. The systematic manual conversion of **META IV** specifications into compiler modules and their combination with parser modules produced automatically by the parser generator represent a semi-automated compiler compiler [CaC85]. Our approach to proceed to a fully automated system is the automatic translation of compiler specifications written in **META IV** into executable programs. Therefore a compiler from **META IV** into Pascal was developed at the University of Kiel within the framework of two master theses.

We start with an outline of the semi-automated method of compiler development used in the **CAT** project. Then we will describe how the design of the **META IV** compiler was influenced by its intended use in a compiler generating system. In the second part the compiler itself is treated. The compilable subset of **META IV** is introduced and some interesting aspects of the semantics of **META IV** are pointed out. Remarks to the implementation of fixpoints follow and the benefit of lazy evaluation for the implementation of implicit sets, maps and tuples will be described. Another interesting aspect is I/O for translated **META IV** specifications because **META IV** functions work on abstract mathematical objects, the concrete representation of which can heavily depend on the subject of specification.

The use of a fully automated **VDM** based compiler generating system with the **META IV** compiler as a central element will be described in the third part of the paper by example of generating a compiler for the simple test language PL0 [Wir 77]. Some data about the system performance will show that it is indeed practically useful. Finally,

there will be a short outlook on future use and development of the
META IV compiler.

2 Systematic Semi-automated Compiler Development

As mentioned already this method relies on systematic manual transformation of **META IV** specifications into Pascal code and on the
parser generator system of NORSK DATA (see fig. 1).

The complete specification of a compiler consists of five parts,
which are shown on the left in figure 1. The lexical scanner and the
parser used in the front ends are automatically generated from a
lexical specification and a LR(1) grammar respectively. Static
semantics and compile algorithms are specified in **META IV**, so the
corresponding compiler modules need an abstract syntax tree as input.
Therefore the concrete syntax obtained from the parser module has to
be explicitly transformed into the abstract one. The transformer
generator can produce the required transformer module automatically
from the transform rules in the compiler specification.

In contrast to the automatic parser generation the remaining
compiler modules for static semantics check and code generation up to
now had to be manually developed from their **META IV** specifications.
Our main intention during the development of the **META IV** compiler was
to eliminate these manual steps.

Therefore the definition of the compilable subset is mainly
oriented towards those **META IV** language elements occuring in the
compiler and static semantics specifications used in the **CAT** project.
This subset was implemented in a pragmatic way, i.e. in spite of some
weaknesses the existing semantic definitions [BjJ78, BjJ82 and BlT83]
were employed without deeper research. Further investigations about
formal semantics of **META IV** are part of the RAISE project and have
not yet been finished [Rai86].

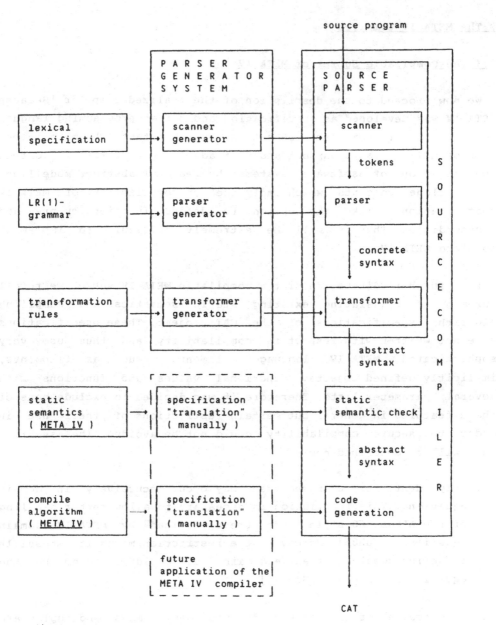

fig 1 :   Systematic semi-automated compiler development

3 The META IV Compiler

3.1 The Compilable Subset of META IV

We now proceed to the description of the realized compiler. Because META IV was developed as specification and not as programming langua- ge a look at its compilable subset is very important. The main inten- tion of META IV is to support short, readable and formally correct specification of software systems by means of abstract modelling. This includes concepts, which imply the non-compilability of META IV specifications, like the option to define functions by pre- and postcondition. Thus it will be extremely difficult to implement complete META IV.

For further discussion of the compilable META IV subset we recall our aim of translating existing static semantics and compiling algorithm specifications of the CAT project. These specifications were not written with respect to compilability and thus use very sophisticated META IV language elements, such as fixpoints, implicitly defined objects, functional values and functions with several parameter lists. Therefore it was decided to exclude none of these features in general but certain restrictions of their use in order to secure compilability could not be avoided. The essential ones will be described now:

1. Only identifiers of named trees may occur recursively in domain equations. This restriction is necessary to allow better handling of the ALGOL 68-style mode trees defined by META IV domain equations [Juh86]. Moreover, the restriction makes it impossible to define complex reflexive domains as could be done by the equation $D = D --> D$ [Sco 76].

2. Predicates of implicitly defined sets, maps and tuples are translated from left to right and after the first applied identifier occurrence no more defining ones may follow [Juh86]. Otherwise it would be impossible to distinguish between defining and applied occurences of identifiers as the following example shows:

   { mk_Mem(i,loc) : (i ε N1) & (i<10) & (loc ε { STACK, HEAP })}

If no context has to be considered this specification describes a set of 20 memory locations, 10 on the stack and 10 on the heap. But if "loc" has already been defined in some context the occurence of "loc" in the predicate might be applied. Thereby dependent on the value denoted by the global "loc" a set of 10 memory locations or an empty set would be defined.

3. **META IV** functions must be algorithmically specified. The option of simply giving a type clause or a pre- and postcondition could not be implemented.

4. Variable Access of local functions is restricted to their formal parameters, their own local variables and to variables of static level 0, i.e. to variables which are global to all defined functions. As functional values are available in **META IV**, access to variables of all static predecessors would require complex analysis concerning life-time of stack items referenced by functional results.

5. The use of domain identifiers in the **META IV** <u>let-be</u> constructs which causes a (partial) enumeration of the domain at runtime is restricted. Only the standard domains BOOL, INTG, N0, N1 and TOKEN as well as domains consisting of a quotation list may be enumerated. Implementing this feature for arbitrary domains, especially structured domains like trees or sets, was not considered because the enormous runtime of the translated specification would not permit useful applications.

6. Test for domain membership must be done using the is-operator, not the ε-operator.

7. Binding and scope rules for identifiers must be strictly obeyed. Some informal although conveniently short notations in this area, such as

```
    if (E x ....) ( P(x)) then c(x) else I
instead of
    if (E x ....) ( P(x)) then let x be s.t. P(x) in c(x) else I,
```

which were explicitly introduced in [BjJ78] are not supported [Juh86].

8. The fixpoint operator has been implemented to deliver the least fixpoint with respect to an appropriate ordering (see fig. 3). In fact this is no restriction of **META IV** but it will prohibit the custom to use parallel and recursive let expressions in an informal way to define fixpoints different from the least one (see 3.3).

The remaining part of **META IV** has been implemented. However, to get around certain weaknesses in the actual semantics of **META IV** (e.g. [BlT83]) pragmatic assumptions concerning careful use of complex language constructs could not be avoided.

3.2 The Structure of the META IV Compiler

After the introduction of the compilable subset of **META IV** the structure of the compiler will be outlined.

The compiler (fig. 2) consists of three subprograms, each of them written in Pascal. First, a given **META IV** specification is parsed according to a LR(1)-grammar for **META IV**, which has been developed in Kiel [Juh86]. For a syntactically correct specification the parser generates an abstract syntax tree serving as input for the static semantic analyser.

The latter analyses the static semantics of **META IV** specifications. Especially the binding relation between identifier occurences is tested for correctness and a type check is done. Tests for correct application of **META IV** operators are included and, on condition that a type clause is present, function calls will result in checks for correct parameter passing and correct result types. Since the static semantics of **META IV** are not algorithmically determinable [Juh86], certain errors occuring in connection with union domains can not be recognized at compile time. Therefore suitable checks had to be programmed into the runtime system (see below) to guarantee the validity of all computed results.

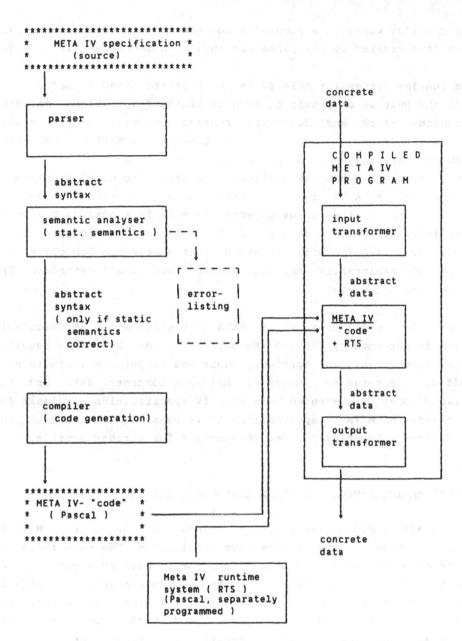

fig. 2: Structure of META IV compiler and generated program

The compiler works in a recursive descent manner, uses the abstract syntax tree created by the parser as input and generates Pascal code.

The runtime system for **META IV** is a seperate Pascal module. It serves the purpose of providing **META IV** standard operations, managing the runtime stack and detecting runtime errors. As the static semantic analyser does not reveal all type errors **META IV** operations and runtime actions handling procedure calls are not invoked until a dynamic type check has taken place. In contrast to usual programming languages the **META IV** runtime system does not contain any I/O routines because the input objects for **META IV** functions belong to the individually defined domains of the compiled specification. Later in chapter 3.4, it will be shown, that a standard I/O coding for objects of arbitrarily defined domains and hence standard I/O routines are not useful.

After the compilation of a **META IV** specification an executable program is obtained by linking the generated code and the required runtime system routines. Moreover, input and output transformers must be added. They serve as interface between concrete data and the abstract model represented by a **META IV** specification. At least for some classes of **META IV** applications it is possible to generate the transformers automatically. See chapter 3.4 for further details.

3.3 Challenging Aspects of the Semantic of META IV

Now we are ready to discuss some points in the actual **META IV** semantics which create problems for compilation. The main issue is, that no complete formal semantic definition of **META IV** itself is at hand to serve as a basis for the implementation of a **META IV** compiler. So in spite of their somewhat informal character, the papers by Bjørner and Jones [BjJ78 and BjJ82] were used under consideration of some critical remarks by Blickle and Tarlecki [BlT83]. If necessary, code generation for a **META IV** language element additionally takes into account the semantics in its original area. Examples are mathematical operators and quantifiers.

The problem which restrictions for the combined use of **META IV** constructs must be employed in order to make sure that the semantics of a whole specification is well defined, has not yet been solved. Due to the complexity of this issue it was only treated to a small extent in this project. Further research on this subject has been started at the University of Kiel and within the ESPRIT Project RAISE.

3.3.1 The Compilation of Domain Equations

The compilation of domain equations is based on the "universal set approach" by Blikle and Tarlecki which is possible due to the fact that the use of reflexive domains has been prevented by an appropriate restriction (see 3.1). Thus a domain equation defines a subset of an universal set which depends on certain basic domains like INTG, BOOL etc. [BlT83]. One of the reasons why the static semantics of **META IV** is not algorithmically computable is the option to define union domains. Therefore information about all defined domains has to be passed to the runtime system in order to enable runtime type checks. This is done by compiling the abstract syntax of a **META IV** specification into specific domain denotations, which are put into an interface file. They can be regarded as constants for the generated program.

When a "META IV program" is started a runtime system routine reads the interface file and by means of Pascal pointer structures creates the real domain denotations, which are structured like ALGOL 68 mode trees. Using these trees all runtime type checks can be done and so, at the expense of increased computer time, every error concerning illegal use of operators and illegal parameter transfer to functions can be recognized. Moreover, code generation for **META IV** is-functions relies on the presence of runtime domain denotations because there is only one is-function in the runtime system, taking a domain denotation and a **META IV** object as arguments.

3.3.2 **The Implementation of the Fixpoint Operator**

Now we turn to the realization of the fixpoint operator. The fixpoint operator is used to define the semantics of applicatively recursive and parallel let expressions and delivers the least fixpoint solution of the set of simultaneous equations represented by the let construct. It was necessary to choose the least fixpoint with respect to a special ordering because this is the only way to secure its existence and uniqueness for arbitrary sets of equations. Among others Tennent [Ten76] provides further information about the mathematical foundation of the fixpoint operator and its use in the framework of denotational semantics. The crucial point is that for a proper implementation of the fixpoint operator a special undefined or bottom ($\perp$) element has to be introduced. Unfortunately the least fixpoint with respect to a useful ordering (see fig. 3) in many cases will turn out to be $\perp$, especially if the **META IV** let construct is not carefully used. Up to now many users of **META IV** have not payed enough attention to this point and used parallel let constructs not to specify the least but a "convenient" fixpoint solution. The following example is taken from Jones [BjJ78]

```
begin    p1: proc ... p2 ...;
         p2: proc ... p1 ... p2 ...;
         ...
end
```

For a block of some source language allowing mutually recursive procedures (see above) the following lines are meant to specify the building of the usual environment.

```
let nenv = env + [ p1 --> e-proc-den( (..p2..), nenv),
                   p2 --> e-proc-den( (..p1..p2..), nenv)]
   in ...
```

"nenv" describes the final environment containing proper denotations of all defined identifiers and "e-proc-den" computes a procedure denotation. In that process it will use its actual "nenv" parameter to determine the denotation of identifiers occuring in the procedure body. In fact $\perp$ is specified. To justify this claim we employ the well known fixpoint iteration method [e.g. Ten76].

According to this method the least fixpoint solution with respect to an appropriate ordering can be obtained by simultaneous iteration of all fixpoint defined objects presuming each of them has been initialized with $\perp$ and the iteration is order preserving. In the example "nenv" will be initialized with $\perp$. So during iteration "e-proc-den" will always receive $\perp$ when trying to get a denotation from its "nenv" parameter. Of course, that will cause a $\perp$ as result of "e-proc-den" and the iteration stops with unchanged "nenv", i.e. nenv = $\perp$.

Although an inconsistency in the specification above has been discovered it still may be considered to be a useful, short and readable one. Therefore investigations were started to implement a sophisticated fixpoint operator delivering a "more user convenient" fixpoint than ´ the least one. But it turned out, that from the point of implementation uniqueness and existence are absolutely necessary. So the compilation of a parallel or recursive let will result in fixpoint iteration code designed for computing the least fixpoint with respect to the ordering <<= shown in fig. 3. One iteration consists of the sequential evaluation of all expressions on the right hand side of the let with all left hand side identifiers bound to their previous values. The **META IV** user has to take care that this iteration is order preserving. Non order preserving iterations will cause a runtime error. Refer to the next chapter for more details about the implementation.

$$
a \ll= b \quad :\Leftrightarrow \quad
\begin{array}{ll}
(a = \perp &) \\
\lor (a \subseteq b & ,\text{if } a,b \text{ are sets} \quad) \\
\lor (a \subseteq b & ,\text{if } a,b \text{ are maps} \quad) \\
\lor (\exists c : a ^\wedge c = b & ,\text{if } a,b,c \text{ tuples} \quad)
\end{array}
$$

fig. 3 : Ordering for evaluation of fixpoints

It is important to stress, that a parallel or recursive let in a compilable **META IV** specification may only be used if it is supposed to denote the least fixpoint solution of the set of equations belonging to it with respect to the order <<=. Otherwise the desired fixpoint has to be specified algorithmically.

3.3.3 The Compilation of Implicit Sets, Maps and Tuples

The power of **META IV** heavily relies on the option to define sets, maps and tuples implicitly, that is by giving a predicate to test whether certain candidates belong to the defined object or not. Let us, for example, have a look at the (infinite) set of all prime numbers:

```
let primset = { x  : (x ε N1) & isprim(x) } in ...
where
  isprim(x)= (∀ y ε { 2 .. (x div 2) } ) (( x mod y) <> 0)
```

To be able to implement the main features of implicitly defined objects, even the option to describe infinite sets, the lazy evaluation strategy is used. For efficiency reasons it is also applied to fixpoint defined objects. That is, the fixpoint iteration will not automatically be done, but only if one of the fixpoint values is explicitly needed. Thus unnecessary iterations are avoided.

The implementation is based on Hendersons [Hen80] force/delay mechanism which originally has been designed for a LISP interpreter system. According to that approach the evaluation of an expression is delayed by generating a "recipe". A recipe in principle consists of the expression to be evaluated and the actual environment at delay time. Access to recipes is possible by means of a force procedure which takes the recipe expression and evaluates it according to the recipe environment. Corresponding to the lazy evaluation strategy calling this procedure will be avoided as long as possible. For adaptation to the **META IV** runtime system the outlined approach had to be extended in order to be used in a non applicative context by a compiler system.

First of all it is essential to distinguish carefully between compile time and runtime actions. At runtime the relevant data for the evaluation of a delayed expression is stored in an own data segment, which is kept apart from the runtime stack in a special memory area. The data segment is used to implement the environment part of the recipe. It contains the delay time values of all memory locations which will be accessed during the evaluation of the delayed expression. In particular the data segment of a delayed expression

itself may contain a delayed expression. In this case the evaluation
of the outermost expression will recursively force the evaluation of
all needed subexpressions.

During compilation of an implicitly defined object, as for example
the set of all prime numbers, two tasks have to be managed.   On the
one hand the implicit object itself must be compiled in order to get
the evaluation code, which will be delivered as a Pascal procedure.
The procedure name forms the expression part of the recipe. As the
expression evaluation may be forced anywhere in the target program,
variable access in this procedure has to be done carefully. Of
course, the compiler will care about this by managing the environment
part of the recipe. Before the compilation of an implicit object
starts, a special initially empty object environment is created.
Whenever a variable global to the object is first accessed an address
in the data segment is allocated and added to the object environment.
Further, during the compilation of the implicit object, access to
these variables is managed via the address in the data segment and
not via the static chain. The second task is to produce code for
dynamic allocation of the data segment and for copying all relevant
data into it, i.e. the delay time values denoted by the identifiers
reallocated in the object environment.

The runtime system also supports the partial evaluation   of
implicitly defined **META IV** objects. One call of the evaluation
procedure for delayed objects will only deliver the next element of
the implicit set, map or tuple. In this way an expression like
$$7 \in primset$$
will not result in the computation of all prime numbers.

In a similar manner the fixpoint iteration for parallel _let_
constructs has been implemented. A "fixpoint recipe" is created,
consisting of the name of the fixpoint iteration procedure and a
data segment. In the segment the relevant values are kept which are
global to the equation set defined by the _let_. It is important to
store these values at execution time of the _let_ as they are because
fixpoint iteration will only be done if the value of a fixpoint
defined object is explicitly needed and may therefore be activated
anywhere in the target program. Additionally the actual values of the
fixpoint objects, according to the present state of iteration, are
kept in the segment. Because an appropriate ordering on fixpoint

values has been defined (fig. 3) they may be used as "approximations" for the real values. The iteration procedure contains the code for one (simultaneous) iteration of all objects defined by the <u>let</u>. In the code global values and the old approximations of the fixpoint values are accessed via the data segment.

At runtime implicitly defined and fixpoint defined objects are essentially represented by the start address of their data segment, their evaluation or iteration procedure, and the current approximation of their value. This data structure is implemented by means of Pascal records.

3.4 I/O for META IV Target Programs

An important point concerning practical use of the **META IV** compiler is the question how to manage I/O for the generated program. **META IV** functions take elements from individually defined **META IV** domains as inputs, i.e. abstract mathematical objects like trees or sets. Accordingly the code generated during compilation of a **META IV** function needs such objects as input. The user of the **META IV** compiler on the other hand has written his specification as an abstract model for some software system. Therefore he does not want the generated program to process abstract objects but concrete data.

In all applications of the **META IV** compiler a suitable interface between abstract model and concrete data has to be provided because all software products specified in **META IV** must support some user convenient external data format. A "**META IV** program", i.e. a program automatically generated from a **META IV** specification, on the other hand uses the internal data representation for **META IV** objects as defined by the **META IV** compiler. Therefore the concrete input data format has to be transformed into the internal data structure according to the definition of the domain they belong to. An analogous process is the transformation of a character string representing an integer number to its binary form by the runtime systems of common programming languages.

Of course, the I/O transformation for **META IV** is more complex. As a **META IV** specification relies on abstract domain equations, it contains no information concerning common or desired external representations for the specified abstract mathematical objects. Because **META IV** can be used for modelling a wide variety of software systems in many different ways it would make no sense to define a standard external representation for the **META IV** abstract objects. In any case a compiled "**META IV** program" would be unable to meet user I/O requirements and probably violate existing conventions for specified software products. Therefore the **META IV** runtime system does not contain conventional I/O routines. Instead, a set of procedures generating the internal **META IV** representations of standard objects (INTG, BOOL etc.) and structured objects (sets, tuples, trees and maps) is provided to support the programming of a suitable transformer module. This task must be carried out in conjunction with the specification of the specific software product.

For restricted areas of application however it is possible to generate a transformer module automatically. In the area of compiler construction for example the parser generator system used in the **CAT** project produces a source language parser, i.e. an input transformer, from specifications without any human programming effort.

4 The Automatic Generation of a PLO Compiler

Using the language PLO [Wir 77] as an example we will describe in this chapter the automatic compiler generating system, obtained by integration of the semi-automated method (chapter 2) and the **META IV** compiler. We start from a compiler specification as it is needed for the semi-automated method. To show what a compilable specification of static semantics and compile algoritm looks like, a small extract of it is shown in fig. 4. The complete PLO compiler specification including the parts concerning concrete syntax is given in [CaC85].

The generation of the PLO compiler proceeds exactly as shown in figure 1. The only difference to the semi-automated method is that the transformation of the **META IV** specified static semantics and compile algorithm ("is_wf_prog" resp. "c-prog" in fig. 4) into executable code is no longer done manually but by the **META IV** compiler. Now the generated compiler and its relationship to the specification will be outlined.

First the parser module checks, whether the input string is a syntactically correct PLO program. In this case the input string is a concrete representation of a abstract PLO syntax tree, i.e. of an element of the Domain "Prog" of the PLO specification (see fig. 4). Then the (automatically generated) PLO parser transforms the input string into the internal **META IV** representation of the abstract syntax tree and thus in this specific application realizes the generally required input transformer.

The compiler module needs a PLO abstract program tree as input. is-wf-prog yields a Boolean value as result of the static semantics check for the PLO program. On condition that it is _true_, c-prog is activated to generate a **CAT** abstract syntax tree. Again, its internal representation has to be transformed to a concrete external data format (not shown in fig. 1). As the PLO compiler was designed for use as front end in the CAT system, the required output format is the one accepted by the **CAT** back ends of that system. An existing output module transforming abstract **CAT** trees, i.e. elements of the domain Cat-program in the abstract syntax of **CAT**, into the concrete **CAT** representation was incorporated into the PLO compiler. It represents the specific implementation of the output transformer mentioned in chapter 3.4 .

Finally some statistics about the size of the specifications and the computer time needed for the automatic generation of the PLO compiler are given. They show that the **META IV** compiler is not merely of academic interest but that there are encouraging aspects for future practical use.

specifications used in compiler generation:

```
A. lexical specification of  PLO         :  ≈   60  lines
   ( token definition )
B. LR(1) grammar for PLO (concrete syntax) :  ≈   40    "
C. PLO transformer specification         :  ≈  120    "
D. specification PLO compiler ( META IV ) :  ≈  575    "
```

```
{ PLO abstract syntax }

   Prog            =  Body
   Body            ::  s-const   : Cconst*
                       s-var     : Vvar*
                       s-proc    : Proc*
                       s-stat    : Stmt*
   Cconst          ::  s-cname   : Identifier
                       s-cval    : Number
   Vvar            ::  s-var     : Identifier
   Proc            ::  s-pname   : Identifier
                       s-body    : Body
   Stmt            = Ass-stmt | Call-stmt | If-stmt | While-stmt
   ....

{  PLO semantic domains }

   Lenv            = Identifier -m-> Den
   Den             = Constden | Varden | Procden
   Constden        :: Number
   Varden          :: [ Varname | Comname ]
   Procden         :: [ Procname | Globpname]
   Env             = Lenv*

{  static semantics of PLO }

 is-wf-prog(p)=

   let env=<[],
            [ mk-Identifier(PRINT) --> mk-Procden(nil),
              mk-Identifier(VALUE) --> mk-Varden (nil)]> in
       is-wf-body(p,env)

 type : Prog --> BOOL


 is-wf-body(mk-Body(bconst,bvar,bproc,bstat),env)=

   let (wf1,env1) = is-wf-cconsts(bconst,env ) in
   let (wf2,env2) = is-wf-vvars  (bvar  ,env1) in
   let (wf3,env3) = is-wf-procs  (bproc ,env2) in
       wf1 & wf2 & wf3 & is-wf-stmts(bstat,env3)

 type : Body  Env  --> BOOL
  ...
```

fig. 4a: PLO abstract syntax and static semantics specification
(extract)

```
{ CAT abstract  syntax }

  Cat-program    :: s-name        : Procname
                    s-glob-obj  : Obj-dec*
                    s-init      : Init*
                    s-body      : Statement
                    s-opt       : Stringconst
  Obj-dec        = Var-dec | Typ-dec | Proc-dec
  Var-dec        :: s-vn         : [Varname | Comname]
                    s-typ        : Type
  Comname        :: String   [ Nodeptr ]
  Proname        :: String   [ Nodeptr ]

  ...

  { compile algorithm for PL0 }

c-prog(p)=

let env =
    <[],
     [mk-Identifier('PRINT') --> mk-Procden(mk-Globpname('PRINT',
                                            gen-node())),
      mk-Identifier('VALUE') --> mk-Varden (mk-Comname('VALUE',
                                            gen-node()))]>
  let (decls,stmts)= c-body(p,<[]> ^ env) in
     mk-Cat-program (mk-Procname('MAIN',gen-node()),
                     decls,
                     <>,
                     mk-Sequence(stmts),
                     mk-Stringconst(' '))

type : Prog  --> Cat-program

c-body(mk-Body(cdcl,vdcl,prdcl,stl),env) =

  let env0              = c-consts(cdcl,env)      in
  let (decls1,env1)     = c-vvars (vdcl,env0 )    in
  let (decls2,env2)     = c-procs (prdcl,env1)    in
        ( decls1 ^ decls2 ,c-stmts(stl,env2))

type :   Body  Env   --> ( Obj-dec* Statement*   )

  ...
```

fig. 4b: CAT abstract syntax and compile algorithm for PL0
                    (extract)

   These specifications were processed on a ND 570/CX by the parser
generator system and the **META IV** compiler respectively. The automatic
generation of a Pascal source for the PL0 parser module (from specifications A-C) took about 320 sec cpu time. This seems to be
acceptable when we consider that test and validation of the parser
can be done on the basis of those specifications instead of debugging

a much longer and less readable Pascal program.

The performance of the **META IV** compiler is discussed in more detail:

generation of a PL0 compiler module from specification D

```
    1. parse of specification      :    ≈     17 sec
    2. static semantics check      :    ≈     12 sec
    3. code generation             :    ≈     37 sec
    4. compiling generated         :    ≈    150 sec
       Pascal code
    5. linking Parser module,
       compiler module and
       META IV runtime system      :    ≈    100 sec

    total                          :    ≈    320 sec
```

The real **META IV** compilation consists of steps one to three and proceeds at a speed of approximately 10 lines per second. About 1800 lines Pascal code are generated. Thus the **META IV** compiler is not much slower than the Pascal compiler. This result is very encouraging although it is surely more complicated to generate machine code than Pascal code. As the whole specification of an existing language has been treated we hope that this result holds for common programming languages too.

```
 compile(p) =

     ( let p₁ be e Targetprog s.t. sem_A (p) = sem_B (p₁ )
       in
           p₁                                              )

 type :  Sourceprog  --> Targetprog


 where  sem_A     source language semantics
        sem_B     target language semantics
```

fig. 5: Non algorithmical compiler specification

At the end of this chapter the efficiency of the generated compiler will be discussed. When used on a ND 570/CX to translate a 22 line PL0 program the compiler took 17 sec for static semantics analysis and 24 sec for generation of **CAT** code. Of course that cannot stand comparison with a manually developed PL0 compiler but it enables rapid prototyping of complex software systems including their test with non trivial examples.

For further discussions it has to be taken into account that the style of a specification has a crucial influence on the performance of the specified system. Specifying in a non algorithmic way, as shown in fig. 5, does not make much sense at this time. Instead, efficient algorithmic specifications are required. But according to the present stage of development even from such specifications no competetive software product can be generated. Certainly not an unexspected result, especially since code optimization was not among the primary project goals. So restrictions of the compilable subset of **META IV** for efficiency reasons have been turned down in order to get a tool for a wide range of applications. Particularly, specifications extensively using the complex options of **META IV**, which normally occur in the initial phases of software development projects, are compilable and therefore may be animated to test the project concept in an early stage. Since code optimization has not been treated until now, considerable progress should be possible in this area.

5 Conclusion and Future Work

The main issue for further research will be the performance improvement of the generated code. Apart from restrictions of the compilable subset the following two ideas may be of value. First of all, it would be useful to store sets and maps no longer as unordered lists but in the form of binary search trees. That requires the runtime system to be able to set up a total ordering of all possible runtime objects for any set of domain equations. Secondly, the use of union domains should be restricted to secure that complete type checking could be done at compile time.

We now turn to special applications of the **META IV** compiler in connection with the **CAT** system. Obviously, an improvement will be achieved, if **CAT** code is generated by the **META IV** compiler directly. This is supposed to result in a 25% decrease of compile time for an average **META IV** specification.

The developed **META IV** compiler represents a tool, that, even in early phases of a software development project, can be used for rapid prototyping. This provides an opportunity to test the consistency of drafts, recognize errors and check, whether customer demands can be met. Furthermore, the compiler is an important step forward on the way to a (**VDM** based) compiler compiler that is of pratical use.

ACKNOWLEDGEMENTS

The author wants to thank Prof. Dr. Hans Langmaack, Computer Science Department, University of Kiel, as well as Dr. Reinhard Völler and Dr. Uwe Schmidt from NORSK DATA, Kiel for valuable discussions about earlier drafts of this paper.

REFERENCES

[BjJ78]   Bjørner, D., Jones, C.B. :
            The Vienna Development Method: The Meta-Language
            LNCS 61, Springer, Berlin 1978

[BjJ82]   Bjørner, D., Jones, C.B. :
            Formal Specification and Software Development
            Prentice-Hall 1982

[BlT83]   Blikle, A., Tarlecki, A. :
            Naive Denotational Semantics
            Information Processing 1983, North Holland 1983

[CaC85]   CAT Cookbook
            NORSK DATA GmbH, Mülheim 1985

[Hen80]   Henderson, P. :
            Functional Programming, Application and Implementation
            Prentice-Hall, London 1980

[Juh86]   Juhl, B. :
            Überprüfung der Syntax und statischen Semantik von META IV
            master thesis, Christian-Albrechts-Universität Kiel, 1986

[Rai86]   Meiling, E. (ed.) :
            Outline of the RAISE Specification Language
            Dansk Datamatic Center, Lyngby 1986

[Sch83]   Schmidt, U. :
            Ein neuartiger auf VDM basierender Codegenerator - Generator
            dissertation, Christian-Albrechts- Universität Kiel, 1983

[Sco76]   Scott, D. :
            Data Types as Lattices
            SIAM Journal on Computing, volume 5, 1976

[Ten76]   Tennent, R. D. :
            The Denotational Semantics of Programming Languages
            Communications of the ACM, volume 19, 1976

[Völ83]   Völler, R. :
            Entwicklung einer maschinenunabhängigen Zwischensprache
            und zugehöriger Übersetzeroberteile für ein Mehrsprachen-
            übersetzersystem mit Hilfe von VDM
            dissertation, Christian-Albrechts- Universität Kiel, 1983

[Wir77]   Wirth, N. :
            Compilerbau
            Teubner Studienbuch, Berlin 1977

From VDM to RAISE

Søren Prehn

Dansk Datamatik Center

Lundtoftevej 1 C

DK-2800 Lyngby

Denmark

Abstract

Although VDM — the Vienna Development Method — has probably been the most widespread and popular so-called formal method for software development in use so far, it is clear that VDM suffers from a number of deficiencies. In this paper, the transition from VDM to a new, "second generation" formal method — RAISE — is discussed. Problems with VDM are discussed, and their solutions within RAISE are outlined. The reader is assumed to be familiar with VDM.

1 Introduction

Since VDM emerged from the IBM Vienna Labs in the early seventies, VDM has has been put to increasingly widespread use in both academe and industry. Unlike most other proposed methods for formal specification and development of software, VDM has been succesfully applied to a number of different projects concerned with the development of major (large) systems. However successful, VDM is subject to criticism. There is a number of problems with VDM that has surfaced in various context, many of which are due to lack of features in the notation employed in VDM (e.g.: structuring, concurrency), or to the lack of a proper definition of those present.

Experiences from various applications of VDM to larger projects seem to suggest that a major problem in ensuring a widespread, industrial acceptance of a software development method like VDM is the lack of powerful, computerised tools. Alone the sheer size of specification and design documents arising in real-life projects prohibits a reasonable working style supported by paper-and-pencil only. An important criteria for evaluating a method's capability for industrial usage is its ability to "scale up".

Another important criteria is the ability to cope with a wide variety of application areas, such as the development of telecommunications software, systems software, software tools, etc., and possibly also hardware. In particular is it important that the notion of concurrency is adequately catered for, in specification, development, and implementation alike.

Over the last decade, numerous proposals has been made for specification and development methodologies, each offering various improvements over existing ones. For example, the massive amount of research on so-called *algrebraic specification* techniques has contributed rather much to the understanding of how to structure specifications and developments. But none of the thus proposed methodologies have otherwise enjoyed any significant interest from the user community.

In this paper we describe the transition from VDM to RAISE. RAISE is a formal, mathematically based method for software development that retains many of the charcateristics of VDM that we believe have accounted for its success in practise, while incorporating missing features developed elsewhere over the last decade, or being developed within the RAISE project itself. RAISE includes not only a wide-spectrum language for expressing specifications and designs, but also a formalization of development steps (i.e.: method), and massive computerised tool support.

The RAISE project is expected to finish at the end of 1989; this paper is thus a report on work in progress.

The remaining part of the paper is organised as follows. Section 2 contains an overview of what is believed to be the intrinsic features of VDM, while section 3 summarises the major problems with VDM. Section 4 describes the RAISE project in general, while sections 5 and 6 presents the RAISE languages and tool environment, respectively, to some level of detail.

2   What is VDM?

There is no easy way to precisely answer the posed question. Ever since VDM emerged in the seventies, several individuals and groups have extended, modified, redefined, and reinterpreted what was to go into "VDM". However, there is a number of notions that appear to remain stable across this diversity.

At the heart of VDM is the principle of *model oriented* specifications, that is, specifications (or designs, or whatever) where object or value classes are explicitly constructed (by means of domain equations), in separation from functions over them. And, even more specifically, the set of value class constructors needed appears to be rather generally agreed upon: sets, cartesian products, finite mappings, lists, and functions.

By constructing first a number of domains (or types), and then a number of functions over them, a *model* results. In VDM, a model may serve several purposes: it may express a specification, high- or low-level design or even implementation of a system, an abstract data type for use in a wider context, or merely a recording of ideas believed to be interesting for the work at hand.

The class of models that one may express in VDM have been found to be appropriate for expressing various kinds of abstractions, for example: representational abstraction (using the notion of "abstract syntax") and computational abstraction (using post conditions), as well as being appropriate for expressing less abstract, more implementation oriented system descriptions. The judicious use of the linguistic features offered by VDM to catch particular views of a system is probably a fundamental characteristic of "VDM-style".

An important aspect of model oriented specifications is the ability to capture central aspects of a specification alone by recording domain equations; that is: designing the "grand state".

A common feature of the various dialects of VDM notation is the availability of both *constructive* expressions and *implicit* expressions, such as set-comprehension, for denoting values. Likewise for functions, that may be either denoted by a "body expression" or characterised by a post condition.

There is less agreement and consistency when one consider development steps, apart from the overall classification of developement steps into data transformations and operation transformations [Bjørner 82a]. Certain types of data transformations, *data reification*, is a rather well investigated area in the context of VDM [Jones 86], whereas in particular operation transformations appear to be invented and applied in a rather ad-hoc manner.

3 Problems with VDM

In this section we will concentrate on concrete, technical problems, and not discuss the appropriateness of the various styles of abstraction, development steps, and so on, advocated by VDM workers. Then, we may view VDM as consisting of: a language, and a number of development principles, together with criteria for their correctness.

For such a language to be truly useful in a purportedly formal method, it must have a mathematical semantics and be equipped with a set of (useful) proof rules consistent with such a semantics. It is a fundamental problem to the VDM community that such provisions have not really been catered for. When reviewing the various features of VDM notation, and attempting to ascribe them a mathematical semantics, a number of troublesome issues crop up [Prehn et al 83], for example:

- the distinction between types, sets, and algebras is not clear

- are infinite objects (e.g.: infinite sets) allowed?

- does predicative (implicit) notions imply non-determinacy?

A number of attempts to solve these problems have been made. In [Monahan 85] a semantic system for a version of VDM allowing for finitary types, viewed as sets, is given, and is shown to closely match the mathematics of Scott domain theory as used in "classical" denotational semantics. In [Jones 86] proof rules are given for a similar version of VDM notation. [Blikle 84] again views domains as sets, and extends the semantics to cover (some) infinitary types as well. In [Reggio et al 86], a semantics is established by specifying the VDM domain constructions algebraically.

With the possible exception of [Reggio et al 86] it is common to the mentioned approaches that they fail to ascribe a mathematical semantics for an exhaustive version of VDM notation including also a structuring mechanism and concurrency.

The lack of a well-designed structuring mechanism is major problem with VDM. Structuring mechanisms are needed in order to be able to produce and reason about individual documents such as specifications and designs, and in order to be able to decompose development steps into sub-steps presenting proof obligations of managable complexity.

Various attempts have been made to extend VDM notation with some means for expressing concurrency. The most well-exercised attempts are the combination of VDM and CSP as used in for example [Haff et al 80] and the combination of VDM and SMoLCS as described in [Reggio et al 86]. The former features an attractive style of presentation of "operational intuition", but fails to have been given a satisfactory semantics, whereas the latter indeed has a full, mathematical semantics, but is probably much too intricate. What is needed is a combination that allows for a mathematical semantics, that integrates well with structuring mechanisms, and that offers the user a range of abstraction levels for expressing concurrency.

VDM seriously lacks a formal way of describing development steps. Even though the concept of for example data reification is formally well-understood, there is still the lack of a notation that allows a user to express a data reification as an "object" and a notation in which one can express its application to a particular (part of a) document.

Given the above considerations it is perhaps not too surprising that the VDM tools that have been constructed so far, have been rather limited in scope.

4 The RAISE Project

The RAISE project is a 115 staff-years effort undertaken by the following four companies:

- Dansk Datamatik Center (DDC), Denmark
- Standard Telephone and Cables, plc (STC), United Kingdom

- Nordisk Brown Boveri (NBB), Denmark

- International Computers Limited (ICL), United Kingdom

The project is carried out in the period from 1985 to 1989, and is partially funded by the Commission of the European Communities under the ESPRIT programme.

The project aims at providing the following products:

- A wide-spectrum language for expressing specifications and designs,

- A method for rigorous development, including a language for expressing development steps,

- A computerised tool set for supporting the use of RAISE,

- Educational and training material for use in industry.

RAISE stands for *Rigorous Approach to Industrial Software Engineering.* The term *rigorous* has deliberately been chosen rather than *formal*: it is believed that, in order to be of practical value, a development method cannot insist on formality in every detail — e.g. that each and every development step is formally proved correct — nor can it fail to provide the potential for carrying out (local) formal proofs. That is, RAISE is intended to support the rigorous style of work so often advocated in the context of VDM (see e.g. [Jones 80], [Jones 86], [Bjørner 82], [Bjørner 82a]).

As implied by the title of the project, RAISE is specifically aimed at producing results that will be acceptable to industry. This is sought achieved by maintaining the features and characteristics of VDM discussed above; by providing tools and educational and training material; and finally by having project results tried out in actual industrial applications, as they emerge during the project conduct.

During the two out of five project years elapsed so far, about one year has been spent on studying and analyzing published results on formal specification and development, providing both sources of inspirations and particular results directly adopted by RAISE, while the second of the years elapsed has been spent on producing outline designs of the RAISE products.

The philosophy of the RAISE project is discussed in more detail in [Bjørner 85] and [Meiling et al 86].

5   The RAISE Languages

The RAISE Specification Language, RSL[1], is a wide-spectrum language in which the user may express specifications, high-level designs, algorithmic designs, etc. "Wide-spectrum" is used in

---

[1]Not a very good name, as a matter of fact!

the sense advocated by the CIP group [CIP 85]. RSL preserves many of the well-known features of VDM notation(s): domain equations, the usual predefined operations on the various sorts of domains (although these are now termed *types*), imperative features, explicit function definitions, function definitions by pre-post conditions, etc.

RSL differs radically from the VDM notation in providing a powerful structuring mechanism, in treating types in a rather more general way than the well-known VDM domains, and in gracefully incorporating concurrency.

The most fundamental concept in RSL is that of a *strucure*. A structure is, to the user, a collection of named entities (i.e. a piece of "environment"), where the named entities can be types, values, functions, and so on. Semantically, a structure denotes a class of many-sorted algebras. "Class" here stems from possible *underspecification* of structures, and signals an adoption of the principle of *loose semantics* as advocated by the CIP group [CIP 85]. Structures may be parameterised, combined, and enriched in the sense developed for algebraic specification techniques (e.g. [Sanella et al 83]). The user is offered a range of ways to present, i.e. define, a structure, the general principle being that the denotation of a structure definition is the class of algebras satisfying all axioms presented in the structure definition. As axioms, one can provide (exhaustive) explicit function definitions, function post-conditions, or just equations over terms, etc. Types, ultimately denoting the carrier sets of the algebras being denoted by a structure definition, may be defined explicitly using domain equations, or *abstractly* as in algebraic specifications, i.e. being determined by axioms for functions. When defined explicitly, a type may be deemed *opaque*, i.e. the operations coming along with the domain constructors defining it are not included in the algebras denoted by the structure definition in which the type is defined.

For concurrency, RSL offers features closely following CSP as described in [Hoare 85]. That is, both abstract notions of concurrency, expressed as trace assertions, and operational notions, expressed as CSP programs, are provided. Semantically, CSP is integrated in RSL by considering CSP processes to be algebras having sequences of communication events as carrier sets, and CSP operators denoting functions over such sets [2].

VDM has, alongside with any other method or approach we can think of, been limited to express specifications that denotes, ultimately, "computable systems". This is fair enough, since specifications are usually intended to be implemented! But furthermore, the components out of which specifications may be built, has been restricted to this same universe. The relevance of this restriction is not evident [3]. For example, the *real* real numbers are not "computable", but may still serve as a rather welcomed abstraction in certain applications, such as numerical analysis. In RSL, we break with the principle that every clause must have a computational justification.

---

[2] Other, alternative ways are currently being investigated.

[3] The Larch project [Guttag et al 85] specifically distinguishes between specifying entities to be implemented and providing abstractions out of which such specifications may be built, by providing two different languages: an interface language, and the so-called shared language.

This adds expressive power and potential for abstraction (while incurring more proof obligations on the user in the form of proofs of existence of reasonable solutions to certain equations) , and — hopefully — aids in settling the ever-so-long discussions on the provision for infinitary objects, types as sets or not, etc.

The RAISE Development Language, RDL, is used to manipulate development steps, i.e. relations between pairs (or more complex groupings) of RSL specification and design documents. RDL is intimately connected with the RAISE Data Model that describes ongoing or complete developments (or projects). The RAISE Data Model may be depicted as graphs whose nodes are RSL documents, such as entire specifications, designs, abstract data types, etc., and whose arcs represent relations between such objects. The arcs, thus, is (or contains) RDL documents describing development steps, such as a particular data reification. An entire graph represents a (snapshot of a) project.

6   The RAISE Environment

The RAISE environment is a computerised tool set, with tools from three different classes:

- Syntactic Tools

- Semantic Tools

- Pragmatic Tools

The tools are invoked from an environment implementing a number of basic facilities and paradigms.

From a technical viewpoint, the entire tool set will be based on PCTE [PCTE 86] hosted on Unix System V, and two different user interfaces will be provided: one for use on personal workstations with a bit-mapped display, window environment, etc., and one for for use on standard terminals, such as the DEC VT220.

Wherever possible, meta-tools (such as attribute-grammar evaluator generators) will be used in implementing the RAISE tool set. This means that the entire tool set will be straightforwardly adaptable in various ways; for example, an organisation may elect to adapt the tool set to specific syntactic standards or conventions.

On top of PCTE the RAISE tool set support environment will be implemented. The support environment provides storage and retreival facilities for objects being manipulated by the tools and offers a rather general structure editing paradigm to be utilized by individual tools. Furthermore, the support environment implements certain aspects of the RAISE method, in the sense that the environment controls that the individual tools are used to create, manipulate, and destroy objects (e.g.: specifications, development steps) in a manner consistent with the RAISE method.

The *syntactic tools* are a collection of tools for manipulating individual objects, e.g:

- RSL and RDL structure editors

- RSL and RDL type checkers

- RSL cross reference generator

- Proof editor

The *semantic tools* are a collection of tools for creating new objects from existing ones, that is, the tools that serve as the active vehicles during development, e.g.:

- "unfold the appointed application of the function f"

- "apply the data refinement described in ... to this document"

- "translate this RSL document into Modula-2 code"

The *pragmatic tools* are a collection of tools supporting the following activities:

- Version control

- Configuration control

- Journaling, undo, and replay of development steps

- Status reporting

Certain tools where originally envisaged as being part of the RAISE tool set: theorem provers, transformation tools (transformation taken in the sense of [CIP 85]), and interpretation/rapid-prototyping tools.

Numerous experiments done in the RAISE project with various theorem proving tools and tools for interpretation (e.g.: ML and Prolog implementations) convinced us, however, that little is to be gained from such tools, at the current state of the art, when aiming at providing tools for use in large development projects.

Experiences from other experiments and from studies of larger projects having applied formal methods, have convinced us that development by (only) application of correctness-preserving transformations, one after the other, is just not practical. Even very simple, yet realistic, development steps whose correctness can be reasoned about either rigorously or even formally, defies being easily formulated as transformations or sequences of such.

7 Conclusions

VDM has been characterised, and some problems with VDM have been identified. An outline has been given of the RAISE project and the manner in which RAISE is hoped to overcome these problems and combine well-known, useful aspects of VDM with well-researched areas of algebraic specification techniques and CSP, thereby providing a full-fledged, mathematically based method for software systems specification and development, suitable for use in industrial contexts.

References

[Bjørner 82]	D. Bjørner & C.B. Jones: "Formal Specification and Software Development", Prentice/Hall, 1982.
[Bjørner 82a]	D. Bjørner, S. Prehn: "Software Engineering Aspects of VDM", in: D. Ferrari et al: "Theory and Practice of Software Technology", North-Holland, 1983.
[Bjørner 85]	D. Bjørner et al: "The RAISE Project — Fundamental Issues and Requirements", RAISE/DDC/EM/1, Dansk Datamatik Center, 1985.
[Blikle 84]	A. Blikle: "A Metalanguage for Naive Denotational Semantics", Progretto Finalizzato Informatica, C.N.R. Progretto P1, CNET 104, Pisa, 1984.
[CIP 85]	F.L. Bauer et al: "The Munich Project CIP", Volume I: The Wide Spectrum Language CIP-L, Springer Verlag LNCS 183, 1985.
[Guttag et al 85]	J. Guttag et al: "Larch in Five Easy Pieces", Report #5, DEC Systems Research Center, Palo Alto, 1985.
[Haff et al 80]	P. Haff, D. Bjørner (eds.): "A Formal Definition of CHILL. A Supplement to the CCITT Recommendation Z.200", Dansk Datamatik Center, 1980.
[Hoare 85]	C.A.R. Hoare: "Communicating Sequential Processes", Prentice/Hall, 1985.
[Jones 80]	C.B. Jones: "Software Development: A Rigorous Approach", Prentice/Hall, 1980.
[Jones 86]	C.B. Jones: "Systematic Software Development Using VDM", Prentice/Hall, 1986.
[Meiling et al 86]	E. Meiling, C.W. George: "The RAISE Language and Method", RAISE/DDC/EM/21, Dansk Datamatik Center, 1986.
[Monahan 85]	B. Monahan: "A Semantic Definition of the STC Reference Language", STC Technology Ltd., 1985.
[PCTE 86]	"A Basis for a Portable Common Tool Environment", Fourth Edition, Volumes I+II, Bull S.A., 1986.
[Prehn et al 83]	S. Prehn et al: "A Critical Examination of VDM", ESPRIT Formal Methods Appraisal Study Final Report, Dansk Datamatik Center, 1983.
[Reggio et al 86]	G. Reggio, P. Inverardi, E. Astesiano, A. Giovini, F. Mazzanti, E. Zucca: "The Draft Formal Definition of Ada, The User Manual of the Meta-Language", CRAI/IEI/University of Genoa, September 1986.

[Sanella et al 83]   D. Sanella, M. Wirsing: "A Kernel Language for Algebraic Specification and Implementation", University of Edinburgh, CSR-131-83, 1983.

DENOTATIONAL ENGINEERING
OR
FROM DENOTATIONS TO SYNTAX

Andrzej Blikle
Project MetaSoft
Institute of Computer Science
Polish Academy of Sciences
PKiN, P.O.Box 22, 00-901 Warsaw

December 1986

CONTENTS

ABSTRACT

This paper is devoted to the methodology of using denotational
techniques in software design. Since denotations describe the
mechanisms of a system and syntax is only a user-visible
representation of these mechanisms, we suggest that denotations be
developed in the first place and that syntax be derived from them
later. That viewpoint is opposite to the traditional (descriptive)
style where denotational techniques are used in assigning a meaning
to some earlier defined syntax. Our methodology is discussed on an
algebraic ground where both denotations and syntax constitute
many-sorted algebras and where denotational semantics is a
homomorphism between them. On that ground the construction of a
denotational model of a software system may be regarded as a
derivation of a sequence of algebras. We discuss some mathematical
techniques which may support that process especially this part where
syntax is derived from denotations. The suggested methodology is
illustrated on an example where we develop a toy programming language
with rendezvous mechanisms.

~~~~~~~~~~~~~~~~   ~~~~~~~~~~~~~~~~

Research reported in this paper contributes to project **MetaSoft**.

> "The authors have the peculiar
> idea that domains of our concepts
> can be quite rigorously laid out
> before we make the final choice of
> the language in which we are going
> to describe these concepts. (...)
> What we suggest is that in order to
> sort out your ideas, you put your
> domains on the table first."
> [Scott,Strachey 71]

1. INTRODUCTION

Denotational semantics is most frequently understood as a method of assigning meaning to syntax. It is implicit in such an understanding that syntax comes first into the play and semantics is assigned to it later. In typical textbooks on denotational semantics such as e.g. [Stoy 77] or [Gordon 79] or in the monographs devoted to applications, e.g. [Bjoerner, Oest 80] or [Bjoerner, Jones 82] the construction of a denotational model of a software system is regarded as a four-step process:

- first we describe a concrete syntax of the system,
- then we derive a corresponding abstract syntax,
- next we define the domains of denotations,
- finally we assign denotations to syntax.

The way in which that process is organized is typical to the case where denotational techniques are used in formally defining some existing programming languages. In that case concrete syntax is always given ahead and what remains to be done is to define its meaning in formalizing some previously given informal description.

Giving formal definitions to existing programming languages was the first practical problem tackled on the ground of denotational semantics. Since the early experiment with ALGOL—60 [Mosses 74], many programming languages have been formalized on that ground, frequently in supporting a later compiler writing (e.g. [Bjoerner, Oest 80]). On the other hand, the formalization of an existing software is not a goal in itself. From the very beginning denotational semantics has been aimed primarily as a tool for the development of new software.

This paper is devoted to studying the methodology of using denotational techniques in software design. Since denotations describe the mechanisms of the system and syntax is only a user-visible representation of these mechanisms, we suggest that denotations be developed in the first place and that syntax be derived from them later. More precisely, we suggest that the development of a denotational model of a software system be organized in four following steps:

1) We develop a mathematical model of the mechanisms of the future system. We define the types of objects which the system is going to manipulate and operations on these objects. We also define the mechanisms which are offered by a computer environment such as storing and retrieving data in computer memory, combining single operations into programs, etc.

2) Among the mechanisms defined in the first step we select these which are to be seen (accessible) by the user.

3) We define a prototype syntax for the system defined in the second step.

4) We modify the prototype syntax in making it more convenient for the user.

Of course, each of these steps usually splits into several substeps.

As a framework for our discussion we have chosen an algebraic model advocated in early ADJ's papers (c.f. [Goguen, Thatcher, Wagner, Wright 74]. In that model a software system is described by two many-sorted algebras: **Syn** of syntax and **Den** of denotations. A homomorphism between them:

$$S : \textbf{Syn} \rightarrow \textbf{Den}. \tag{1.1}$$

represents the denotational semantics of **Syn** in **Den**. The fact that S is a homomorphism reflects the compositionality property of denotational semantics, i.e. the fact that the meaning of a whole is the composition of the meanings of its parts.

According to the chosen algebraic framework in each of the four steps described above, as well as in the intermediate steps, we define a certain algebra. In our examples all algebras are constructed on the ground of *naive denotational semantics* [Blikle,Tarlecki 83] where semantic domains are usual sets rather than reflexive domains. The used notation is very closed to META-IV, the definitional metalanguage of VDM.

For the benefit of readers less familiar with many—sorted algebras we recall basic algebraic concepts in Sec.2 and Sec.3. In Sec.4 we discuss the definability of the algebras of syntax by context—free grammars. This leads to a few observations of a technical character which are useful when syntax is derived from denotations. In Sec.5 we very briefly discuss the process of the construction of an algebra of denotations. Sec.6 is devoted to the derivation of syntax from an algebra of denotations. In Sec.7 we illustrate our method in showing how to develop a simple programming language with rendezvous—based concurrency. We construct a denotational model of such a language where we combine the ideas of trace semantics with state—transition semantics.

An earlier version of the discussed method was described in [Blikle 84]. In that paper prototype syntax corresponds to an *abstract syntax* in the sense of VDM, whereas now it is closer to an abstract syntax in the algebraic sense [Goguen,Thatcher,Wagner, Write 74].

2. INTRODUCTORY CONCEPTS

In this section we introduce a notation and we recall basic algebraic concepts. We start from a notation which we shall use in the denotational definitions of software systems. That notation is a dialect of META—IV (the metalanguage of VDM, see [Bjoerner, Jones 82]) and has been thoroughly described in [Blikle 86].

For any sets A and B:

> A|B   denotes the union of A and B,
>
> A\B   denotes the difference of sets,
>
> A+B   denotes the set of all total functions from A into B,
>
> $A \tilde{\rightarrow} B$ denotes the set of all partial functions from A into B,
>
> $A \underset{m}{\rightarrow} B$ denotes the set of all finite—domain functions, called **mappings** from A into B,
>
> A^{c^*} denotes the set of all finite tuples $\langle a_1,...,a_n \rangle$ over A including the empty tuple $\langle \rangle$,

A^{c+} denotes A^{c*} without the empty tuple $\langle\rangle$,

A-**set** denotes the set of all subsets of A,

A-**finset** denotes the set of all finite subsets of A.

By "^" we denote the operation of concatenation both for single tuples and for languages. If L is a language, i.e. if $L \subseteq A^{c*}$ for some A, then L^* denotes the usual Kleene-iteration of L. Observe that "c*" is applicable to any set whereas "*" is applicable only to languages. Moreover:

$$(A^{c*})^* = A^{c*} \neq (A^{c*})^{c*}.$$

From [Tennent 76] we borrow a convention of writing domain equations in the form:

d : D = (domain expression)

by which we mean that d possibly with indices denotes an element of domain D.

For indexed families $\{A_i\}_{i \in I}$ we use alternatively the notation $\{A.i \mid i \in I\}$.

By $f:A \rightarrow B$, $f:A \overset{3}{\rightarrow} B$ or $f:A \underset{m}{\rightarrow} B$ we denote the fact that f is respectively a total function, a partial function, or a mapping from A to B. For **curried functions** like $f:A \rightarrow (B \rightarrow (C \rightarrow D))$ we write $f:A \rightarrow B \rightarrow C \rightarrow D$. We also write f.a for f(a) and f.a.b.c for ((f.a).b).c . For uniformity reasons each many-argument non-curried function is regarded as a one-argument function on tuples. Consequently we write $f.\langle a_1, \ldots, a_n \rangle$ for $f(a_1, \ldots, a_n)$. If $f:A \overset{3}{\rightarrow} B$ and $g:B \overset{3}{\rightarrow} C$, then $f \cdot g:A \overset{3}{\rightarrow} C$ where $(f \cdot g).a = g.(f.a)$. In the definitions of functions we frequently use conditional expressions of the form $b \rightarrow c, d$ which stand for **if** b **then** c **else** d. This may be iterated in which case the expression $b_1 \rightarrow (a_1, (b_2 \rightarrow \ldots (b_n \rightarrow a_n, a_{n+1}) \ldots))$ is written in a column:

$b_1 \quad \rightarrow a_1$,

$\ldots$

$b_n \quad \rightarrow a_n$,

TRUE $\rightarrow a_{n+1}$

Sometimes in conditional expressions we shall nest "local constants' declarations" of the form **let** x=exp **in** borrowed from VDM. The scope of such a declaration is the expression which follows this declaration.

For any partial function $f:A \overset{?}{\to} B$, by f[b/a] where $a \varepsilon A$, $b \varepsilon B$ and $f[b/a]:A \overset{?}{\to} B$ we denote the following modification of f:

$$f[b/a].x = x=a \to b, f.x$$

Now we shall briefly recall some basic concepts associated to many—sorted algebras. Our notation is close to that of [Cohn 81]. By a **signature** we mean a four—tuple

$$Sig = (Sn, Fn, sort, arity)$$

where Sn is a nonempty possibly infinite set of **sort names**, Fn is a nonempty possibly infinite set of **function names** and where

$$sort : Fn \to Sn$$
$$arity : Fn \to Sn^{c*}$$

are functions which associate sorts and arities to function names. By an **algebra** over the signature **Sig**, or shortly by a **Sig—algebra**, we mean a triple **Alg** = (Sig,car,fun) where car and fun are functions interpreting sort names as nonempty sets and function names as total functions on these sets. More precisely, for any $sn \varepsilon Sn$, car.sn is a set called the **carrier** of sort sn, and for any $fn \varepsilon Fn$ with sort.fn=sn and arity.fn=$\langle sn_1, \ldots, sn_n \rangle$, fun.fn is a total function between corresponding carriers, i.e.

$$fun.fn : car.sn_1 \times \ldots \times car.sn_n \to car.sn$$

If arity.fn=ε, then fun.fn is a zero—ary function, i.e. accepts only the empty tuple "$\langle \rangle$" as an argument. The fact that f is a zero—ary function with value in A is denoted by $f: \to A$. Zero—ary functions are also called **algebraic constants**. For simplicity we frequently identify them with their unique values.

In applications we in general do not show the signature of an algebra explicitly. A signature is only an abstraction of the structure of an algebra and serves the purpose of talking about a class of algebras with the same structure. As we shall see later, a signature may also constitute a starting point for the construction of a formal language of expression over a given algebra. When we talk about a concrete (one) algebra we usually describe it as a collection of carriers (sets) and operations (total functions) on these carriers. For instance, we may consider a two-sorted algebra of integers and booleans with the carriers $Int = \{\ldots,-1,0,1,\ldots\}$ and $Bool = \{tt,ff\}$ and with the following operations:

```
1  :  → Int              an integer constant "one"
+  :  Int x Int → Int    an integer operation of addition
tt :  → Bool             a boolean constant "true"
<  :  Int x Int → Bool   a boolean function "less than"
~  :  Bool → Bool        a boolean function "not"
```

The signature of this algebra is implicit (up to the choice of the names of sorts and functions) in the above description. For instance we may choose:

```
Sn = {int,bool}   and
Fn = {one,plus,true,less,not}
```

in which case the functions of sort and arity are defined as follows:

```
arity.one  = <>,           sort.one  = int
arity.plus = <int,int>,    sort.plus = int
etc.
```

Now, our algebra may be more formally defined as $Arith = (Sig, car_a, fun_a)$, where Sig has been defined above and where:

```
car_a.int  = Int          fun_a.one  = 1
car_a.bool = Bool         fun_a.plus = +
                          etc.
```

Two algebras with the same signature are called **similar**. If $Alg_i = (Sig, car_i, fun_i)$ for $i=1,2$ are two similar algebras, then we say that Alg_1 is a **subalgebra** of Alg_2 if for any $sn \varepsilon Sn$,

$car_1.sn \quad car_2.sn$

and for any $fn\varepsilon Fn$, $fun_1.fn$ coincides with $fun_2.fn$ on the appropriate carriers of $\textbf{Alg}_1$. By a **homomorphism** from $\textbf{Alg}_1$ (a **source algebra**) into $\textbf{Alg}_2$ (a **target algebra**) we mean a family of functions $H = \{H.sn \mid sn\varepsilon Sn\}$ such that for any $sn\varepsilon Sn$ and for any $fn\varepsilon Fn$ with $sort.fn=sn$:

    1) $H.sn : car_1.sn \rightarrow car_2.sn$ $\hspace{4cm}$ (2.1)

    2) if $arity.fn = \langle\rangle$, then
       $H.sn.(fun_1.fn.\langle\rangle) = fun_2.fn.\langle\rangle$

    3) if $arity.fn = \langle sn_1,\ldots,sn_n\rangle$ with $n>0$, then for any tuple
       of arguments $\langle a_1,\ldots,a_n\rangle$ ε $car.sn_1 \times \ldots \times car.sn_n$ we have
       $H.sn.(fun_1.fn.\langle a_1,\ldots,a_n\rangle) =$
          $fun_2.fn.\langle H.sn_1.a_1,\ldots,H.sn_n.a_n\rangle$

If all the component functions $H.sn$ are onto-functions, then H is called an **onto-homomorphism**. Otherwise it is called a **strictly into-homomorphism**. If each component of a onto-homomorphism H is reversible, then H is called an **isomorphism**. The componentwise reverse of H is then denoted by H^{-1}. All the elements of $\textbf{Alg}_2$ which are the images of some elements from $\textbf{Alg}_1$ trough H constitute a subalgebra of $\textbf{Alg}_2$ called the **image** of $\textbf{Alg}_1$.

By $H : \textbf{Alg}_1 \rightarrow \textbf{Alg}_2$ we denote the fact that H is a homomorphism from $\textbf{Alg}_1$ into $\textbf{Alg}_2$. If

    $H_{12} : \textbf{Alg}_1 \rightarrow \textbf{Alg}_2$ and
    $H_{23} : \textbf{Alg}_2 \rightarrow \textbf{Alg}_3$,

then $\quad H_{12}\cdot H_{23} = \{H_{12}.sn\cdot H_{23}.sn \mid sn\varepsilon Sn\}$ is a homomorphism from $\textbf{Alg}_1$ into $\textbf{Alg}_3$.

As we already mentioned before the signature of an algebra may constitute a basis for the construction of a language (syntax) of expressions over that algebra. Starting from a signature $\textbf{Sig} = (Sn,Fn,sort,arity)$ we construct the least family $\{car_t.sn \mid sn\varepsilon Sn\}$ of formal languages of **terms** over the alphabet $Fn|\{(,),",\"\}$ such that for any $sn \varepsilon Sn$ and any fn with sort.fn = sn:

1) if arity.fn = <>, then $fn \varepsilon car_t.sn$
2) if arity.fn = $<sn_1,...,sn_n>$, then for any terms
   $ter_i \varepsilon car_t.sn_i$,
   $fn^\wedge(^\wedge ter_1^\wedge,^\wedge...^\wedge,^\wedge ter_n^\wedge) \varepsilon car_t.sn$

If all the sets $car_t.sn$ are not empty, then we may define a so called **Sig—algebra of terms**

$$Term = (Sig, car_t, fun_t)$$

where the operations are defined as follows: for any fn with sort.fn=sn

1) if arity.fn = <>, then $fun_t.fn.<> = fn$,   (2.2)
2) if arity.fn = $<sn_1,...,sn_n>$ and $ter_i \varepsilon car_t.sn_i$, then
   $fun_t.fn.<ter_1,...,ter_n> = fn^\wedge(^\wedge ter_1^\wedge,^\wedge...^\wedge,^\wedge ter_n^\wedge)$

For instance, in the case of the algebra **Arith** we have:

$car_t.int$ = {one, plus(one,one), plus(one,plus(one,one)),...}
$car_t.bool$ = {true, not(true), less(one,one),...}
$fun_t.plus.<plus(one,one),one>$ = plus(plus(one,one),one)
etc.

The algebra **Term** over **Sig**, if it exists, constitutes a universal language of expressions for the class of all **Sig**-algebras. Formally, for any **Sig**-algebra **Alg** = (Sig,car,fun) there exists exactly one homomorphism

$$T : Term \rightarrow Alg$$

This homomorphism represents the "semantics" of **Term** in **Alg** and is called the **canonical term—homomorphism** or the **evaluating homomorphism** for **Alg**. It maps terms into their corresponding values in **Alg** and is defined in the following way:

1) for any primitive term fn with sort.fn = sn and
   arity.fn = <>,   (2.3)
   T.sn.fn = fun.fn.<>

2) for any compound term $fn(ter_1,\ldots,ter_n)$, where $sort.fn=sn$
   and $arity.fn = \langle sn_1,\ldots,sn_n\rangle$,
   $$T.sn.fn(ter_1,\ldots,ter_n) =$$
   $$fun.fn.\langle T.sn_1.ter_1,\ldots,T.sn_n.ter_n\rangle$$

E.g. in **Arith** we have

   $T.int.one = 1,$
   $T.int.plus(one,one) = 2,$
   $T.bool.less(one,one) = ff,$
   etc.

Observe that the definition of T is an instance of the general definition (2.1) of a homomorphism. This implies that **T** is indeed a homomorphism. On the other hand, since any homomorphism from **Term** into **Alg** must satisfy (2.3) and since these equations define **T** unambiguously, **T** is the unique homomorphism between our algebras.

Let $Sig_i = (Sn_i,Fn_i,sort_i,arity_i)$ for $i=1,2$ be two arbitrary signatures and let $Alg_i = (Sig_i,car_i,fun_i)$ be two algebras over these signatures.

We say that Sig_2 is an **extension** of Sig_1, or that Sig_1 is a **restriction** of Sig_2, if $Sn_1 \subseteq Sn_2$, $Fn_1 \subseteq Fn_2$ and the functions $sort_2$ and $arity_2$ coincide with $sort_1$ and $arity_1$ on Fn_1.

We say that Alg_2 is an **extension** of Alg_1, or that Alg_1 is a **restriction** of Alg_2 if:

   1) Sig_2 is an extension of Sig_1,
   2) for any $sn \varepsilon Sn_1$, $car_1.sn \ car_2.sn,$
   3) for any $fn \varepsilon Fn_1$, $fun_1.fn$ coincides with $fun_2.fn$ on
      appropriate carriers of Alg_1.

In other words, we extend an algebra if we add new carriers, new functions and new elements.

3. REACHABILITY, AMBIGUITY AND INITIALITY

In general, not every element of an algebra is a value of a term. E.g. in **Arith** terms of sort int assume only positive values, whereas car_a.int contains all integers. The elements of an algebra which are the values of some terms are called **reachable elements**. Elements which are not reachable are referred to as the **junk** of an algebra. For each sort the set of all reachable elements of that sort is called the **reachable carrier** of that sort.

As is easy to see, an element is reachable in an algebra **Alg** if and only if it can be constructed from the constants of **Alg** in using the operations of **Alg**. This immediately implies that reachable carriers are always closed under all the operations of **Alg** and therefore, if they are all not empty, then they constitute the least subalgebra of **Alg**. We call this subalgebra the **reachable subalgebra** of **Alg** and denote it by Alg^R. If **Alg** and Alg^R are equal, then **Alg** is called a **reachable algebra**.

Reachable algebras play a very important role in our applications. In particular the algebras of syntax **Syn** (cf. (1.1)) are always reachable since syntax is always defined in a constructive way. Below we recall some important properties of reachable algebras.

PROPOSITION 3.1 The following properties are equivalent:
  1) **Alg** is reachable,
  2) the (unique) evaluating homomorphism $T: \textbf{Term} \rightarrow \textbf{Alg}$ is onto,
  3) any homomorphism which has **Alg** as a target is onto.   [ ]

PROOF. The equivalence between 1) and 2) is an immediate consequence of the reachability definition. Now consider an arbitrary $\textbf{Alg}_1$ with a homomorphism $H: \textbf{Alg}_1 \rightarrow \textbf{Alg}$ and let $T_1: \textbf{Term} \rightarrow \textbf{Alg}_1$. Since $T_1 \cdot H$ is a homomorphism from **Term** into $\textbf{Alg}_1$ and T is a unique such a homomorphism we must have $T_1 \cdot H = T$. Therefore H is onto iff T is onto.

                                                                    [ ]

PROPOSITION 3.2   If   **Alg**$_1$ and   **Alg**$_2$ are   similar   and   if   **Alg**$_1$
is reachable, then there exists at most one homomorphism:

    H : **Alg**$_1$ → **Alg**$_2$

If that homomorphism exists, then the   image   of   **Alg**$_1$ in   **Alg**$_2$
is reachable.   []

PROOF. Let **Term** be the common algebra of terms   of   both   algebras and
let T_1 and T_2 be   the   unique   corresponding   homomorphisms
(Fig.3.1).

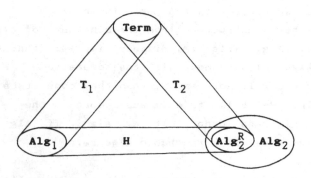

Fig.3.1

If **H** exists, then $T_1 \cdot H$ is   a   homomorphism   from **Term** into
Alg$_2$ and   since T_2 is   a   unique   such   a   homomorphism   the
following equation must hold:

    $T_1 \cdot H = T_2.$ (3.1)

Therefore,   since T_1 and T_2 are   unique   and   **Alg**$_1$ is
reachable, **H** must be unique as well. The   reachability of the image
of **Alg**$_1$ in **Alg**$_2$ also follows from (3.1).   []

In   our   applications   the   diagram   of Fig.3.1 usually   represents   a
denotational   model   of a software system   where **Alg**$_2$ is   an   algebra
of denotations, **Alg**$_1$ is   a   corresponding   algebra of (final) syntax
and **Term** is the algebra of prototype (abstract) syntax (cf.   Sec.1).
The   homomorphism   **H** represents   the   denotational   semantics   of
Alg$_1$ in **Alg**$_2$.

So far we have proved that between syntax and denotations there may be at most one denotational semantics. As turns out, there may be also none. Below we shall formulate a condition under which such a semantics exists.

We say that Alg_1 is not more ambiguous then Alg_2, in symbols

$$\text{Alg}_1 \sqsubseteq \text{Alg}_2$$

if T_1 glues not more than T_2, i.e. if for any $sn \varepsilon Sn$ and any $t_1, t_2 \varepsilon car_t.sn$:

$$T_1.sn.t_1 = T_1.sn.t_2 \quad \text{implies} \quad T_2.sn.t_1 = T_2.sn.t_2$$

Of course, for the sake of this definition we do not need to assume that Alg_1 is reachable. The relation $\sqsubseteq$ is defined in the class of all Sig-algebras, although not any two algebras are comparable in it. The ambiguity relation constitutes a **preordering**, i.e. is reflexive and transitive.

The defined preordering has a natural intuitive interpretation. Observe that for each of the algebras Alg_i each term $t \varepsilon car_t.sn$ describes a way of construction of a (reachable) element $T_i.sn.t$. If two different terms have the same value in the target algebra, then they describe two different ways of the construction of the same element. E.g. in **Arith** the terms plus(one,plus(one,one)) and plus(plus(one,one),one) describe two different ways of the construction of the integer 3. The more ways we have to construct one element in an algebra, the more that algebra may be called ambiguous. Moreover, each term may be regarded as a parsing tree of a reachable element. In fact, if **Alg** is an algebra of syntax generated by a CF-grammar (Sec.4), then terms correspond exactly to parsing trees.

PROPOSITION 3.3 If Alg_1 and Alg_2 are similar and if Alg_1 is reachable, then the (unique) homomorphism

$$H : \text{Alg}_1 \to \text{Alg}_2$$

exists if and only if $\text{Alg}_1 \sqsubseteq \text{Alg}_2$. []

PROOF. If **H** exists, then by (3.1) T_2 must glue at least as much as T_1. (It glues exactly as much as T_1 iff **H** is an isomorphism). If $\textbf{Alg}_1 \sqsubseteq \textbf{Alg}_2$, then the homomorphism **H** may be constructed in the following way: For any $sn\epsilon Sn$ and any $a\epsilon car_1.sn$ take an arbitrary $t\epsilon car_t.sn$ such that $T_1.sn.t = a$ and set

$$H.sn.a = T_2.sn.t$$

Since $\textbf{Alg}_1$ is reachable t always exists and since T_2 glues at least as much as T_1, the choice of t does not matter. It is not difficult to prove that **H** is indeed a homomorphism.   []

As is easy to see, the algebra **Term** is less ambiguous than any other algebra **Alg** with the same signature, i.e. **Term** $\sqsubseteq$ **Alg**. An algebra for which the opposite relationship, i.e. **Alg** $\sqsubseteq$ **Term**, is satisfied is called **unambiguous**. In an unambiguous algebra each reachable element is the value of exactly one term, i.e. may be constructed in exactly one way. If that property is not satisfied, then the algebra is called **ambiguous**.

An algebra **Alg** is called **initial** in the class of all **Sig**-algebras, or is simply called **Sig-initial**, if for any other **Sig**-algebra $\textbf{Alg}_2$ there is exactly one homomorphism from **Alg** into $\textbf{Alg}_1$.

PROPOSITION 3.4 The following properties are equivalent:
1) **Alg** is initial,
2) **Alg** is reachable and unambiguous,
3) **Alg** is isomorphic to **Term**

Proofs are immediate from previous propositions.

4. ALGEBRAS VERSUS GRAMMARS

In the denotational model of a software system syntax is represented by an algebra. This allows us to express the compositionality principle of denotational semantics and to formulate the rules governing the systematic derivation of syntax (Sec.6). It turns out, however, that in applications it is rather inconvenient to describe the algebras of syntax in the style used for the algebras of denotations, i.e. by defining each function by an equation. In case of syntax this leads to unnecessarily long definitions with a lot of superfluous technical notation.

Below we discuss the techniques of defining the algebras of syntax by context-free grammars. Such definitions are shorter, better fit to the style of syntax derivation through successive refinements and last but not least provide an adequate starting point for the construction of parsers.

The idea of defining algebras by grammars in not new. It has been already proposed in [Goguen et al 74] where grammars are used to define the algebras of parsing trees. In this paper we slightly redefine the classical concept of a context-free grammar by associating with it a signature. Let $Sig = (Sn,Fn,sort,arity)$ be an arbitrary signature with finite sets Sn and Fn, and let T be an finite (terminal) alphabet disjoint with Sn. By a **Sig-grammar** we mean a triple

$$Gra = (Sig,lan,pro)$$

where lan and pro are functions assigning languages over T to the elements of Sn and productions to the elements of Fn:

$$lan : Sn \rightarrow T^{c^*}\text{-set}$$
$$pro : Fn \rightarrow (Sn \times (T|Sn)^{c^*})$$

We assume that the elements of Sn play the role of nonterminals and that the functions lan and pro are defined in the following way: For any $fn \varepsilon Fn$ with $sort.fn = sn$ and $arity.fn = \langle sn_1, \ldots, sn_n \rangle$,

$$pro.fn = \langle sn, x_0 sn_{i_1} \cdots x_{n-1} sn_{i_n} x_n \rangle$$

where $\langle i_1, \ldots, i_n \rangle$ is a permutation of $\langle 1, \ldots, n \rangle$ and where each x_i is a word over the alphabet T. For the sake of uniqueness we shall assume that T is the smallest alphabet such that all x_i's from all productions are words over T. Let $P = \{pro.fn \mid fn \varepsilon Fn\}$ be the set of all productions of our grammar. With every $sn \varepsilon Sn$ we can associate a traditional context-free grammar $G_{sn} = (T,Sn,P,sn)$ where sn plays the role of an initial nonterminal. The language lan.sn is now the language defined by G_{sn} in the usual sense (see e.g. [Harrison 78]).

The notion of a grammar contains a redundancy since the family of languages $\{lan.sn \mid sn\varepsilon Sn\}$ is implicit in the remaining components of the grammar. We deliberately accept this redundancy in order to make grammars closer to algebras.

With every **Sig**-grammar **Gra** = (Sig,lan,pro) we unambiguously associate a **Sig**-algebra of words **AL.Gra** = (Sig,car,fun), where:

  1) for any $sn\varepsilon Sn$, car.sn = lan.sn   (4.1)
  2) for any $fn\varepsilon Fn$ with sort.fn = sn, arity.fn = $\langle sn_1,...,sn_n\rangle$
     and pro.fn = $\langle sn, x_0 sn_{i_1}...x_{n-1}sn_{i_n}x_n\rangle$ we have,
     fun.fn.$\langle y_1,...,y_n\rangle = x_0 y_{i_1}...x_{n-1}y_{i_n}x_n\rangle$

We say that **Gra** defines **AL.Gra**. We say that a **Sig**-algebra **Alg** is a **context-free algebra** (abbr. **CF-algebra**) if there exists a **Sig**-grammar **Gra** which defines that algebra, i.e. such that AL.**Gra** = **Alg**.

By a **syntactic algebra** we mean any reachable algebra of words with finite sets of sorts and operations. Of course, every context-free algebra is a syntactic algebra. The converse implication is not true. First of all in every context-free algebra every carrier must be a context-free language. It is also easy to show, that this property is only necessary but not sufficient for the context-freeness of an algebra. As an example we may consider a one-sorted algebra with a carrier $\{a\}$ and two operations:

  h.$\langle\rangle$ = a
  f.y = a   (4.2)

This algebra is not context-free since f is not expressible by a production.

Now we shall formulate a property of syntactic algebras which is necessary and sufficient for context-freeness. This requires the introduction of some auxiliary concepts. Let **Alg** = (Sig,car,fun)

with **Sig** = (Sn,Fn,sort, arity) be an arbitrary syntactic algebra
over some (minimal) alphabet T. If for an operation fun.fn with
arity.fn = $(sn_1,\ldots,sn_n)$ where $n \geqslant 0$ there exists a word
$x_0 sn_{i_1} \ldots x_{n-1} sn_{i_n} x_n$ over T|Sn such that for any
argument $\langle y_1,\ldots,y_n \rangle$ of that function:

$$fun.fn.\langle y_1,\ldots,y_n \rangle = x_0 y_{i_1} \ldots x_{n-1} y_{i_n} x_n$$

then $x_0 sn_{i_1} \ldots x_{n-1} sn_{i_n} x_n$ is called a **skeleton** of
fun.fn and we say that fun.fn is a **skeleton function**.

A function in a syntactic algebra may have from none to many
skeletons. Consider the following one-sorted algebra with a carrier
$\{a\}^{c+}$:

$$h_1.\langle\rangle = a$$
$$f_1.y = ya \qquad\qquad\qquad\qquad (4.3)$$

and let the unique sort name be A. Function h_1 has exactly one
skeleton, namely a, and function f_1 has two skeletons: Aa and aA.
Function f from (4.2) has no skeleton at all. A function which has
exactly one skeleton is called a **monoskeleton function**.

If every operation of **Alg** is a skeleton function, then **Alg** is
called a **skeleton algebra** and by a **skeleton** of **Alg** we mean any
function:

$$sk : Fn \rightarrow (T|Sn)^{c^*}$$

such that sk.fn is a skeleton of fun.fn. Of course, similarly to
functions, also algebras may have from none to many skeletons. An
algebra which has exactly one skeleton is called a **monoskeleton
algebra**.

With every skeleton algebra **Alg** = (Sig,car,fun) and a chosen
skeleton sk of that algebra we may unambiguously associate a grammar
GR.$\langle$**Alg**,sk$\rangle$ = (Sig,lan,pro) defined as follows:

1) for any $sn \varepsilon Sn$, lan.sn = car.sn
2) for any $fn \varepsilon Fn$ with sort.fn = sn, pro.fn = $\langle sn,sk.fn \rangle$

As is easy to check, that grammar defines **Alg**, i.e.

    AL.(GR.<**Alg**,sk>) = **Alg**.

Consequently, **Alg** is context—free. Since every context—free algebra is, of course, a skeleton algebra — cf. (4.1) — we can formulate the following proposition:

PROPOSITION 4.1 A syntactic algebra is context—free if and only if it is a skeleton algebra.
[]

In Sec.6 we shall discuss a systematic method of the derivation of an algebra of syntax **Syn** for a given algebra of denotations **Den**. This consists in constructing a sequence of syntactic algebras

    $Syn_0, \ldots, Syn_n$

such that Syn_0 = **Term**, Syn_n = **Syn** and each Syn_i is a homomorphic image of Syn_{i-1}. Of course, **Term** is a skeleton algebra (cf. (2.2)), hence is context—free. It turns out, however, that a homomorphism may destroy this property. Indeed, take as a source algebra the algebra (4.3) which is obviously context—free, and as a target algebra the algebra (4.2) which is not context—free. The (unique) homomorphism between them is $H_1.x = a$ for any $x \varepsilon \{a\}^{c+}$.

In our example the context—freeness of an algebra is destroyed by a homomorphism which is "glueing" too much. We can show that also an isomorphism may destroy this property. Consider again (4.3) as a source, and as a target a one—sorted algebra with the carrier $\{a^n b^n c^n \mid n=1,2,\ldots\}$ and with the following operations:

    $h_2.<>$ = abc
    $f_2.a^n b^n c^n = a^{n+1} b^{n+1} c^{n+1}$ for $n=1,2,\ldots$

Of course, our new algebra is not context—free and the corresponding (unique) isomorphism between them is defined by:

    $I.a^n = a^n b^n c^n$ for $n=1,2,\ldots$

Let $Alg_i = (Sig, car_i, fun_i)$, $i=1,2$ be two syntactic algebras over a common signature $Sig = (Sn,Fn,sort,arity)$ and let $H:Alg_1 \rightarrow Alg_2$ be a homomorphism. We say that H is a **skeleton homomorphism** if there exists a function

$$sk : Fn \rightarrow (T|Sn)^{C^*}$$

called **a skeleton of** H such that for every $fn \varepsilon Fn$ with $sort.fn=sn$, $arity.fn=\langle sn_1,...,sn_n \rangle$, $n \geqslant 0$ and $sk.fn = x_0 sn_{i_1} \cdots$
$\cdots x_{n-1} sn_{i_n} x_n$

$$H.sn.(fun_1.fn.\langle y_1,...,y_n \rangle) = \qquad\qquad (4.4)$$
$$x_0(H.sn_{i_1}.y_{i_1}) \cdots x_{n-1}(H.sn_{i_n}.y_{i_n})x_n$$

for any argument $\langle y_1,...,y_n \rangle$ of $fun_1.fn$. Similarly to functions, also homomorphisms may have from none to many skeletons. E.g. both our formerly defined homomorphism which have (4.3) as a source have no skeletons.

PROPOSITION 4.2 For any syntactic algebra **Alg** the following properties are equivalent:

1) **Alg** is context free,

2) ever homomorphism which has **Alg** as a target is a skeleton
homomorphism,

3) there exists a skeleton homomorphism which has **Alg** as a
target.   []

PROOF. Let Alg_2 be context free and let sk be one of its skeletons. Consider an arbitrary Alg_1 with a homomorphism $H:Alg_1 \rightarrow Alg_2$. For every $fn \varepsilon Fn$ with $sort.fn=sn$ and $arity.fn=\langle sn_1,...,sn_n \rangle$ we have

$$H.sn.(fun_1.fn.\langle y_1,...,y_n \rangle) = \qquad\qquad (4.5)$$
$$fun_2.fn.\langle H.sn_1.y_1,...,H.sn_n.y_n \rangle =$$
$$x_0(H.sn_{i_1}.y_{i_1}) \cdots x_{n-1}(H.sn_{i_n}.y_{i_n})x_n$$

where $x_0 sn_{i_1} \cdots x_{n-1} sn_{i_n} x_n = sk.fn$. This proves that **H** is a skeleton homomorphism, i.e. that 1) implies 2). The implication from 2) to 3) is obvious because the set of homomorphisms which point to Alg_2 is not empty since it contains the canonical term-—homomorphism. Now assume that there exists Alg_1 with $H:Alg_1 \rightarrow Alg_2$ which is a skeleton homomorphism. Let sk be the skeleton of this homomorphism and take an arbitrary $fn \varepsilon Fn$ with sort.$fn=sn$ and arity.$fn=\langle sn_1,\ldots,sn_n\rangle$ and an arbitrary argument tuple $\langle w_1,\ldots,w_n\rangle$ for $fun_2.fn$. Since $\mathbf{Alg_2}$ is reachable H must be onto (Prop.3.1) and therefore there exists a tuple $\langle y_1,\ldots,y_n\rangle$ of elements of $\mathbf{Alg_1}$ such that $H.sn_i.y_i = = w_i$. Consequently

$$fun_2.fn.\langle w_1,\ldots,w_n\rangle =$$
$$fun_2.fn.\langle H.sn_1.y_1,\ldots,H.sn_n.y_n\rangle =$$
$$H.sn.(fun_1.fn.\langle y_1,\ldots,y_n\rangle) =$$
$$x_0(H.sn_{i_1}.y_{i_1})\ldots x_{n-1}(H.sn_{i_n}.y_{i_n})x_n$$

where $x_0 sn_{i_1}\ldots x_{n-1} sn_{i_n} x_n = sk.fn$. This proves that sk is a skeleton of $\mathbf{Alg_2}$. Hence $\mathbf{Alg_2}$ is context free.   [ ]

Observe that the grammar of a target algebra is always implicit in the definition of a corresponding skeleton homomorphism. Indeed, for any equation of the form (4.4) the corresponding production is (cf. the proof of Prop.4.1):

$$sn \rightarrow x_0 sn_{i_1}\ldots x_{n-1} sn_{i_n} x_n$$

Examples will be shown in Sec.6. In the same section we shall also see that our approach to the derivation of syntax will allow us, and encourage, to use ambiguous grammars. Below we define that property formally in our framework.

A **Sig**-grammar **Gra** is said to be **ambiguous** if for any $sn \varepsilon Sn$ the corresponding traditional grammar $\mathbf{Gra_{sn}}$, is ambiguous in the usual sense (cf. [Harrison 78]). In the opposite case **Gra** is said to be **unambiguous**.

PROPOSITION 4.3 A grammar **Gra** is unambiguous if and only if the algebra AL.**Gra** is unambiguous.   [ ]

The proof of this proposition (which we leave to the reader) bases on the fact that terms over the signature of **Gra** unambiguously represent parsing trees over **Gra**. More formally, if $T:\mathbf{Term} \rightarrow AL.\mathbf{Gra}$ is the canonical term-homomorphism for AL.**Gra**, then for any $sn \varepsilon Sn$ and any $x \varepsilon car.sn$ the elements of the set

$$T^{-1}.sn.x = \{t \mid T.sn.t = x\}$$

represent — and in fact may be regarded as — all parsing trees of x
in the grammar Gra_{sn}.

5. DESIGNING DENOTATIONS

The method which we discuss in this paper consists in developing the
denotational model (1.1) of a software system in two stages: first we
develop the algebra of denotations **Den**, then we derive from it a
corresponding algebra of syntax **Syn**. Of course, each of these
stages consists of many steps. In this section we briefly discuss the
development of **Den**. The derivation of **Syn** is discussed in Sec.6.

The development of the algebra **Den**, or more generally of an
algebraic model of a software system, may be compared to programming
in a high-level functional language. As in the usual programming,
also here, there may be many different styles depending on the case
under consideration and/or on the personal preference of a
programmer. In this section we discuss a method which roughly
corresponds to the bottom-up style. In Sec.7 we illustrate a top-down
method.

A software system may be regarded as a computer environment which
supports the manipulation of objects of certain types by means of
some operations. First step towards the development of **Den** may
consist, therefore, of defining an algebra over these objects and
operations. This is called the **algebra of data types**. We shall
denote it by **Dat**. For instance, if we design a data-base system,
then the carriers of **Dat** will typically contain such objects as
numbers, logical values, character strings, records, files, reports,
etc. whereas operations will be arithmetic-, Boolean- and string
operations, the operations of the creation and the updation of
records and files, the operations which generate reports from files,
etc.

When **Dat** has been defined we may proceed to the next step where we
describe a system which "implements" **Dat** in a computer environment.

Formally, we define another algebra — we call it **Sys** — which models this system. Since at that level data are usually not available in isolation (as in **Dat**) but only as objects stored in a memory, the operations on data are represented in **Sys** by operations on memory states. Besides, we usually also have a number of pure store—oriented operations such as e.g. declarations and assignments. Finally, a software system usually provides means for combining single operations on stores into compound such operations. This corresponds to programming. In order to describe that mechanism all operations on stores must be regarded as the elements of **Sys**. The operations of that algebra must be, therefore, second—order functions. In our example functions from states to data (expression denotations) and from states to states (command denotations) will constitute typical elements of **Sys**, whereas typical operations of that algebra will correspond to program constructors such as e.g. ";", IF_THEN_ELSE_FI, WHILE_DO_OD, etc.

By definition, the algebra **Sys** covers all the mechanisms of the system, including also these which we do not want to show to the user. For instance, in the definition of an operation of file modification we may wish to use a function which temporarily destroys the structure of a file. Such a function corresponds to a procedure in a future implementation and therefore should be included in **Sys**. On the other hand, we certainly do not want to make it accessible to the user. In order to make our contract with the user explicit we identify in **Sys** all these operations and carriers which we wish to make user—visible. In this way we define a restriction of **Sys** which constitutes our algebra of denotations **Den**. This will be showed in a small example at the end of this section and in a larger example in Sec.7.


```
Dat -----------> Sys -----------> Den
basic            full             user's
tools            workshop         interface
                 Fig.5.1
```

The process of developing **Den** is summarized on the diagram of Fig.5.1. The algebra **Dat** defines a collection of basic tools which must be provided by the future system. The algebra **Sys** defines a workshop where the former tools may be used in a computer environment. This includes the mechanisms of storing data and combining simple universal tools into complex problem—oriented tools. The algebra **Den** contains a selection of the mechanisms of **Sys** which are available to the user.

Now, let us briefly discuss the techniques which may be chosen in defining our three algebras. Essentially they may be split into two classes: axiomatic techniques and constructive (model—oriented) techniques.

Axiomatic techniques have been intensively studied on the ground of algebraic semantics approach and several of them were implemented (see [Ehrig,Mahr 85] and references there). Their major advantage is abstractness. An axiomatic definition lists the intended properties of the future system. The only obligation of the implementation designer is to satisfy these properties, no matter how. The disadvantage of axiomatic specifications is that the consistency of such specifications is usually far from evident and may be difficult to prove. This problem is, of course, the more critical the larger and more complicated is the system. Axiomatic definitions require also more mathematical maturity from the designer. At the same time they provide less hints about how to implement the system, besides, of course, a standard solution by rewriting rules (cf. [Dershowitz 85] or [Meseguer,Goguen, 85] and references there) which is restricted to a rather narrow class of applications.

Constructive techniques lead to definitions which are, of course, less abstract. Each such a definition describes a concrete mathematical model of a system and therefore it is much easier to be checked for consistency and gives more hints about a future implementation. On the other hand, the adequacy of such a definition, i.e. the satisfaction of some expected properties of the defined system, may be not easy to prove.

Of our algebras of Fig.5.1 only **Dat** seems to be a candidate for an axiomatic definition. Of course, this always depends on the system under design, but in general **Dat** is much simpler and of a lower functionality order than **Sys**. It should be emphasized at this point that an axiomatic definition of **Dat** does not imply any (mathematical) obligation to define **Sys** axiomatically as well. If we have a sufficiently rich definitional metalanguage, then we may define **Dat** axiomatically and later refer to this definition in a constructive definitions of **Sys**. Since **Den** is a restriction of **Sys** their definitions are always formulated in the same style. In applications, the definition of **Den** is just a list of selected operations and carriers of **Sys**.

A few more remarks about constructive techniques are in order. At the ground of denotational-semantics approach it is usually assumed that all operations of **Sys** should be defined within a certain meta-algebra of functions and (generic) functional constructors such as functional composition, conditional union, fixed-point operators etc. Indeed, in general, it is advisable to do so, but in some situations we may prefer to define some operations by different means. E.g. we may wish to define an operation on strings via a stack-machine. In that case our definition appears more operational which does not mean, however, that it becomes less denotational. Independently of the techniques which we use in defining **Den**, as long as **Den** is a homomorphic image of **Syn** our model is fully denotational. We shall see an example of such a situation in Sec.7.

EXAMPLE 5.1

Assume that we want to define a simple programming language with only two types: natural numbers and Boolean values. The carriers of **Dat** may be the following:

Carriers (of objects)

    n : Nat = {1,...,N,err}
    b : Bool = {tt,ff,ee}

In each of these carriers we have included a so called **abstract error** (cf.[Goguen 78]) which represents an error message. We assume to have in **Dat** the following operations:

    one   :   → Nat
    plus : Nat x Nat → Nat
    times : Nat x Nat → Nat
    less : Nat x Nat → Bool
    and   : Bool x Bool → Bool

In order to keep our example short we explicitly define only three of these operations. Other definitions are left to the reader. The reader may also wish to check that our algebra is reachable.

    one.<> = 1

    plus.$\langle n_1,n_2 \rangle$ =   less.$\langle n_1,n_2 \rangle$ =
        n_1=err → err, n_1=err → ee,
        n_2=err → err, n_2=err → ee,
        n_1+n_2>N → err, n_1<n_2 → tt,
        TRUE   → n_1+n_2 TRUE   → ff

Now we are ready to define the algebra **Sys**. We start from the definition of some (semantic) domains.

    sta : State   = Identifier → Value
    ide : Identifier = {x,y}
    val : Value   = Nat | Bool
    mes : Message   = Value x Value
          Reading   = Message → State
          Writing   = State → Message
    eva : Evaluator = State → Value   (denotations of expressions)
    exe : Executor   = State ⇸ State   (denotations of commands)

These domains have been defined under the assumption that our system will contain only two memory cells (visible to the user), will communicate with the external word by receiving and sending ordered pairs of values (called messages) and internally will be able to compute a value from a state and to transform a state. The denotations of expressions are assumed to be total functions since in our language the evaluation of an expression will always terminate. The denotations of commands are partial functions since we are going to have a loop construction. Below we define the mechanisms of our system represented by the following operations on domains:

    create_x : → Identifier   (5.1)
    create_y : → Identifier

    evaluate : Identifier → Evaluator

    e_one   :   → Evaluator
    e_plus   : Evaluator x Evaluator → Evaluator

```
e_times   : Evaluator  x Evaluator  → Evaluator
e_less    : Evaluator  x Evaluator  → Evaluator
e_and     : Evaluator  x Evaluator  → Evaluator

read      :                                      → Reading
write     :                                      → Writing
assign    : Identifier x Evaluator               → Executor
continue  : Executor   x Executor                → Executor
while     : Evaluator   x Executor               → Executor
if        : Evaluator   x Executor   x Executor  → Executor
```

For clarity these functions have been split into four groups. In the
first group we have two functions which generate identifiers.
Intuitively this corresponds to the fact that each identifier may be
typed (used) by the user. Formally, this makes the carrier Identifier
reachable. In the second group we have only one function. It makes
evaluators from identifiers. Intuitively this corresponds to the fact
that every identifier may be used as an expression. In the third
group we have five functions which correspond in a one-to-one way to
data-type operations. The association of data-type operations to
evaluator operations is implicit in the names of the latter. Prefix
"e_ " stands for "evaluator's". Functions of the fourth group describe
these mechanism of our system which are additional to the mechanisms
of data types. Again, for the sake of brevity we give only a few
typical examples of the definitions of our functions.

```
create_x.<> = x

evaluate.x.sta = sta.x

e_plus.<eva₁,eva₂>.sta =
   let val₁=eva₁.sta in
   let val₂=eva₂.sta in
   val₁∉Nat → err,
   val₂∉Nat → err,
   TRUE      → plus.<val₁,val₂>

read.<>.<val₁,val₂> = [val₁/x,val₂/y]

assign.ide.eva.sta = sta[eva.sta/ide]
```

```
continue.<exe₁,exe₂>.sta = exe₂.(exe₁.sta)
```

In this way we have defined the algebra **Sys**. Formally we may assume that it contains only these carriers which appear in the signature (5.1). Other domains play only an auxiliary role (there are no operations defined on them) and therefore they do not need to be included in the algebra.

In the last step of designing denotations we have to identify the algebra **Den**. This, of course, depends on the decision of a designer. In our example we shall assume that both input/output operations are to be implemented in hardware and therefore they are not included in our programming language. Formally this means that we restrict **Sys** to **Den** by removing the carriers "Reading" and "Writing" together with the corresponding operations. The carriers of **Den** are therefore:

    Identifier
    Evaluator
    Executor

and operations are the corresponding operations of (5.1).

                                                    End of example.

6. DESIGNING SYNTAX

In this section we discuss the process of designing a "custom-made" syntax for given denotations. More formally, given an algebra **Den** we construct an algebra **Syn** with four following properties:

    1) **Syn** is a syntactic algebra,
    2) there is a homomorphism from **Syn** into **Den**,
    3) **Syn** is context free,
    4) the notation offered by **Syn** is sufficiently convenient.

Property 2) is called the **correctness** of **Syn** with respect to **Den**. This property guarantees that **Syn** may be used as a syntax for **Den**. The (unique) homomorphism between these algebras is the corresponding denotational semantics.

Of course, in order to be correct **Syn** must have the same signature as **Den**. This implies that these algebras must fit into the diagram of Fig.6.1

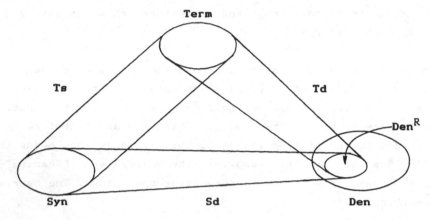

Fig.6.1

where **Term** is a common algebra of terms and **Ts** (term-to-syntax), **Td** (term-to-denotation) and **Sd** (syntax-to-denotation) are the corresponding unique homomorphisms (see Sec.3).

As our diagram shows, **Term** is correct and any other correct syntax is a homomorphic image of **Term**. Since **Term** is unambiguously defined by the signature of **Den**, and since it is contex-free, we suggést that **Syn** be derived from **Term** through a sequence of stepwise homomorphic refinements which preserve both the correctness and context-freeness. Formally this should lead to a sequence of algebras $Syn_0, \ldots, Syn_n$ such that:

1) Syn_0 = **Term**
2) each Syn_i is a homomorphic refinement of Syn_{i-1},
   i.e. there exists a homomorphism $Ss_i : Syn_{i-1} \rightarrow Syn_i$,
3) each Syn_i is correct,
   i.e. there exists a homomorphism $Sd_i : Syn_i \rightarrow$ **Den**
4) each Syn_i is context-free,
5) Syn_n = **Syn**

The initial step in this derivation, i.e. the derivation of **Term**, is quite routine since this algebra is unambiguously determined by the signature of **Den**. Although in applications this signature is usually not defined explicitly, it is always implicit in the notation chosen in the definition of **Den** (see Example 6.1 and Sec.7). Further steps are, of course, much less routine, since they describe design decisions, such as e.g. passing from a prefix to an infix notation, introducing key—words, omitting superfluous parentheses etc.

In the sequel, the algebra **Term** is called a **prototype syntax** and the algebra **Syn** is called a **final syntax**. From a traditional viewpoint this roughly corresponds to the classification into an **abstract syntax** and a **concrete syntax** (see [McCarthy 61], [Goguen,Thatcher,Wagner, Write 77], [Bjoerner, Jones 82]). We use different terms here in order to emphasize the methodological fact that our derivation of **Syn** from **Term** proceeds within one abstraction level where we transform a concrete prototype syntax into an equally concrete but more convenient final syntax.

In the derivation of **Syn** each Syn_i is an algebra of syntax since homomorphic transformations obviously preserve this property (cf. Prop.3.2). In each step we should check, however, whether Syn_i is correct. Here two cases are possible:

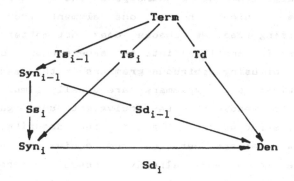

Fig.6.2

1) If Ss_i is an isomorphism, then the correctness of Syn_i follows from the correctness of Syn_{i-1} since in that case

$$Sd_i = Ss_i^{-1} \cdot Sd_{i-1}.$$

2) If Ss_i is not an isomorphism, which means that it glues

some elements of Syn_{i-1} together, then Syn_i may turn out to be incorrect. In order to prove that Syn_i is correct we have to prove that it is not more ambiguous than **Den**. This in turn amounts to proving that Ts_i does not glue more than **Td** (cf. Fig.6.2), or - which is equivalent, but may be easier to prove - that Ss_i does not glue more than Sd_{i-1}. Intuitively this requirement is quite obvious: one expression cannot mean two different things. Observe that due to the reachability of syntax all the diagrams of Fig.6.2 commute.

There is one more point which we should clarify about our treatment of syntax. We do not assume that **Syn** is unambiguous, i.e. that the corresponding grammar is unambiguous (Prop.4.3). Apparently this may lead to an ambiguous (or nondeterministic) parsing algorithms since for a given element x of **Syn** the corresponding set of parsing trees (cf.Sec.4)

$$Ts^{-1}.sn.x = \{t \mid Ts.sn.t=x\}$$

may contain more than one element. Observe, however, that the ambiguity of **Syn** is allowed only if all these trees are mapped into the same element of **Den**. This implies that we can transform our ambiguous parsing algorithm into a unambiguous one by adding to it an arbitrary procedure which chooses one element from each set $Ts^{-1}.sn.x$. Which parsing tree we choose does not matter since they are all interpreted (or compiled) into the same element of **Den**. A practical advantage of using ambiguous grammars in the description of syntax is twofold: First such grammars are usually simpler and more intuitive (easier to read) than the equivalent unambiguous ones. Second, parsers constructed from them in the described way are usually faster than parsers derived from equivalent unambiguous grammars. Both these facts were already discussed in [Aho, Johnson, Ullman 75] although without any semantic considerations. A practical implementation of that idea may also be found in an algebraic--specification language OBJ [Goguen,Messeguer,Plaisted 83] under the name of **coercions**.

EXAMPLE 6.1

Here we shall derive a syntax for the algebra of denotations **Den** defined in Example 5.1. This requires an explicit establishment of

the signature of that algebra together with the interpretation
functions car and fun. Let then **Den** = (**Sig**,car,fun) and
Sig = (Sn,Fn,sort,arity). We set:

    Sn = {<identifier>, <expression>, <command>}
    Fn = {t_generate_x, t_generate_y, t_evaluate,...,t_while}

    car.<identifier> = Identifier
    car.<expression> = Evaluator
    car.<command>   = Executor

    fun.t_create_x   = create_x   (6.1)
    ...
    fun.t_while   = while

Functions "sort" and "arity" are implicit in (5.1). After having
defined the signature of **Den** we have a unique corresponding algebra
of terms **Term**. We describe it by a grammar **Gra**$_1$ which can be
effectively derived (in an obvious way) from the signature of **Den**:

    <identifier> ::=
        t_create_x
      | t_create_y

    <expression> ::=
        t_evaluate(<identifier>)
      | t_e_one
      | t_e_plus(<expression>,<expression>)
      . . .

    <command> ::=
        t_assign(<identifier>,<expression>)
      | t_continue(<command>,<command>)
      | t_while(<expression>,<command>)
      | t_if(<expression>,<command>,<command>)

For simplicity we omit in these BNF equations curly brackets and
concatenation symbols, e.g. we write t_evaluate(<identifier>) rather
than {t_evaluate}^{(}^<identifier>^{)}.

The prototype syntax which is defined by **Gra**$_1$ is, of course, rather inconvenient. Therefore we modify this syntax by introducing an infix notation and simplifying key-words. This modification is described by a homomorphism $Ss_1 : Term \rightarrow Syn_1$. The algebra Syn_1 is implicit in the definition of that homomorphism and therefore we first define that homomorphism and only then the algebra. In what follows we use abbreviated sort names and we assume that ide, exp and com possibly with indices range over the corresponding carriers of **Term**.

$$Ss_1.<id>.t\_create\_x \qquad = x$$
$$Ss_1.<id>.t\_create\_y \qquad = y$$
$$Ss_1.<ex>.t\_evaluate(id) \quad = id$$
$$Ss_1.<ex>.t\_e\_one \qquad\quad = 1$$
$$Ss_1.<ex>.t\_plus(exp_1,exp_2) =$$
$$(Ss_1.<ex>.exp_1+Ss_1.<ex>.exp_2)$$

. . .

$$Ss_1.<co>.t\_assign(ide,exp) \qquad =$$
$$Ss_1.<id>.ide:=Ss_1.<ex>.exp$$
$$Ss_1.<co>.t\_continue(com_1,com_2) =$$
$$(Ss_1.<co>.com_1;Ss_1.<co>.com_2)$$
$$Ss_1.<co>.t\_if(exp,com_1,com_2) \quad =$$
$$IF\ Ss_1.<co>.exp$$
$$THEN\ Ss_1.<co>.com_1\ ELSE\ Ss_1.<co>.com_2\ FI$$
$$Ss_1.<co>.t\_while(exp,com) \qquad =$$
$$WHILE\ Ss_1.<ex>.exp\ DO\ Ss_1.<co>.com\ OD$$

This homomorphism is, in fact, an isomorphism and therefore our new syntax is correct. Moreover, this is a skeleton homomorphism, which means that Syn_1 is context free. A grammar of that algebra may be derived directly (and mechanically) from the definition of Ss_1 and is the following:

```
<id> ::= x | y
<ex> ::= x | y | 1 | (<ex>+<ex>) | ...
<co> ::= <id>:=<ex> | (<co>;<co>)
         | IF <ex> THEN <co> ELSE <co> FI | WHILE <ex> DO <co> OD
```

This syntax is nearly acceptable as a final syntax, with one exception: the use of ";" requires the introduction of semantically superfluous parenthesis such as e.g. in (((x:=1);(y:=1));(x:=x+1)).

We make therefore another modification of syntax which corresponds to the second homomorphism $Ss_2 : Syn_1 \rightarrow Syn_2$. This homomorphism should be defined in such a way that the grammar of the new algebra is a modification of the former grammar by replacing the production $\langle co \rangle \rightarrow (\langle co \rangle ; \langle co \rangle)$ by the production

$\langle co \rangle \rightarrow \langle co \rangle ; \langle co \rangle$

This homomorphism may be defined more explicitly, but the reader has probably noticed already that an explicit definition of a homomorphism is much less readable, then the corresponding transformation of grammars. It seems, therefore, advisable that in applications homomorphism between context-free algebras be described by the corresponding transformations on grammars. This requires, of course, some care since not every transformation of grammars corresponds to a homomorphism. We shall not tackle this problem here leaving it as a litte research problem.

Of course, our second homomorphism is not an isomorphism and therefore we have to prove that Syn_2 is not more ambiguous than **Den**. This proof may be carried out by structural induction.

End of example []

7. A CASE STUDY

In this section we discuss an example of the development of a toy programming language of concurrently cooperating processes. Our processes can run forever and are synchronized by a rendezvous mechanism. We have chosen this example since it provides an opportunity of showing a construction which is not quite routine. In our model we combine two different approaches to the semantics of programs: a trace approach in the sense of [Mazurkiewicz 72] and [Hoare 85] and a common state-transition approach. The former provides a convenient ground for the description of rendezvous, but does not cover the computational effect of processes. The latter describes that effect but is inconvenient for the treatment of concurrency. Their combination leads to a denotational model which provides an adequate description of both these aspects.

For the sake of our example we extend the notation introduced in Sec.2. For any sets A and B:

$A^{C\infty}$ denotes the set of all infinite sequences over A

$A^{C\omega}$ denotes the set of all finite and infinite sequences over A

For any set $A^{C\omega}$ its elements are called **generalized words** and its subsets **generalized languages**. If x and y are generalized words, then their **concatenation** $x{^\wedge}y$ is x if x is infinite and is the extension of x by y otherwise. The concatenation, finite power and iteration of generalized languages are defined in an obvious way. Let $X, Y \subseteq A^{C\omega}$:

$$X{^\wedge}Y = \{x{^\wedge}y \mid x\varepsilon X \textbf{ and } y\varepsilon Y\}.$$
$$X^0 = \{<>\},$$
$$X^n = X^{n-1}{^\wedge}X \quad \text{for} \quad n>1,$$
$$X^* = U_{n=0}^{\infty}X^n.$$

If $z=x{^\wedge}y$ then x is called a **prefix** of z in symbols x pre z. As is easy to check pre is a chain-complete partial ordering in $A^{C\omega}$. For any chain in $A^{C\omega}$, i.e. any sequence of words of the form $\{x_i\}_{i=1}^{\infty}$ with x_1 pre x_2 ... its least upper bound is denoted by $\lim.\{x_i\}_{i=1}^{\infty}$.

Let $X \subseteq A^{C\omega}$ and let $\{x_i\}_{i=1}^{\infty}$ be a chain in $A^{C\omega}$. We say that $\{x_i\}_{i=1}^{\infty}$ is an **iteration chain** over X, if $x_1 \varepsilon X$ and for each i$>$1 there exists a $y_i \varepsilon X$ such that $x_{i+1}=x_i{^\wedge}y_i$. By IC.X we denote the set of all iteration chains over X. By the **infinite power** of X we mean the generalized language:

$$X^\infty = \{\lim.\{x_i\}_{i=1}^{\infty} \mid \{x_i\}_{i=1}^{\infty} \varepsilon \text{ IC.X}\}.$$

Functions "head" and "tail" are extended in an obvious way to infinite words.

In domain equations we shall use a notation borrowed from VDM. In the place of equality sign "=" we also allow the use of "::" in which case we define a domain of objects marked "by the name of their domain". E.g. if we define:

```
ide : Identifier  = ...
eva : Evaluator   = ...
asg : Assignment :: Identifier x Evaluator
```

then the elements of Assignment are all of the form

```
<mk-assignment,<ide,eva>>
```

and according to VDM convention are denoted by

```
mk-assignment(<ide,eva>).
```

7.1 An informal description of the language

Our language is a toy version of a programming language which could be used in the development of distributed computer systems such as e.g. a reservation system of an airline where several concurrently cooperating workstations permanently receive orders, issue confirmations and update a central data base.

The main conceptual category of our language is a process. A process can transform some global memory states and can communicate with other processes and with an external environment via a finite number of input-output channels. Each process is either an elementary process consisting of a single command, or is composed of other processes. There are four constructors of compound processes in the language: while-loop, nondeterministic alternative, sequential composition and parallel composition. Each of these constructors may be nested to an arbitrary depth.

Processes which are subject to a parallel composition may communicate via shared channels. The set of such channels is in each case specified by a programmer and is called a **link**. Channels which belong to a link are invisible for other processes and for the external environment. Processes which share a channel in a link can use this channel exclusively in a common rendezvous action. Channels

which do not belong to a link are called **free** in a given process.
They can be used for the communication with the external environment
or with other processes. In the latter case they must belong to a
"higher-level" link. If two processes share a free channel, then they
can never use this channel simultaneously.

The type of concurrency which we want to deal with is a CSP-like
interleaving [Hoare 85]. This means that in the case of cooperating
processes only one action of one process is performed at a time. An
certain exception is a rendezvous which consists of a joint execution
of an input command from one process with an output command from
another process. A rendezvous, however, is a single action of a
compound process which is the parallel composition of the two.

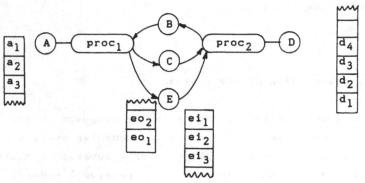

Fig.7.1.1

By a root process in a program we mean a process which is not a
component of another process. The external environment of a root
process is represented in our model by infinite sequences of
to-be-consumed inputs associated to free input channels and by finite
sequences of so-far-produced outputs associated to free output
channels. A channel may be at the same time an input channel and an
output channel in which case it has two associated sequences. If such
a channel is shared by two subprocesses, as on Fig.7.1, then both
processes are using the same channel in accessing the corresponding
input- or output sequence. However, they cannot communicate through
that channel and they cannot use it simultaneously.

For the simplicity of our example we assume that all variables are
global and that we only have three primitive commands: an assignment,
an input and an output. Depending on the context inputs and outputs
may either serve in a communication with the external environment, or

may be reserved for a rendezvous with other processes. We also assume
to have only two data types: Nat and Bool defined as in Example 5.1.
In Sec.7.5 we briefly discuss possible enrichments of our model by
some typical mechanisms of real-life programming languages.

7.2 Processes and their behaviors

In classical   denotational models of programming languages the
denotations of programs   (and   therefore   also   of commands,
declarations, expressions, etc.) are most frequently assumed to be
functions. These functions describe the so called **input-output
behaviors**, i.e. the ways in which inputs are transformed into
outputs. Each such a function is a set of input-output pairs, each
pair describes the effect of one execution of a program. An
input-output function of a program describes its full user-visible
effect. Its specification defines, therefore, programmer's obligation
about <u>what</u> a program in supposed to do.

In the case of our language an input-output model of behavior would
be rather inadequate. First, the execution of a process may never
terminate in which case there is no ultimate output. Second, whether
an execution terminates or not, its expected effect, i.e. the one for
which a programmer should be responsible, may only be described as a
step-by-step recording of program's activity. Such a recording, which
we shall call an **execution**, is represented in our model by a
sequence of   environments   and may be regarded as a natural
generalization of an input-output pair of the former model. Sets of
executions,   which we call **behaviors**, are generalizations   of
input-output functions. This leads us to the following domains:

```
    beh   : Behavior      = Execution-set
    exe   : Execution      = Environment^{Cω}
    env   : Environment    = Input-env x Output-env x Message x State
    i-env : Input-env      = Channel ⇸ₘ Input-stream
    o-env : Output-env     = Channel ⇸ₘ Output-stream
    mes   : Message        = Error | {OK}
    sta   : State          = Identifier ⇸ₘ Data
    chan  : Channel        = Identifier
    i-str : Input-stream   = Data^{C∞}
```

```
o-str  : Output-stream = Data^{c*}
ide    : Identifier    = ... (some set of identifiers)
dat    : Data          = Value \ {err,ee}
val    : Value         = Nat | Bool
nat    : Nat           = {1,...,N,err}
bool   : Bool          = {tt,ff,ee}
er     : Error         = {err,ee,ERROR}
```

An **environment** consists of an input environment, an output environment, a message and a (memory) state. An **input environment** is a mapping which assigns input streams to (free input) channels. A **channel** is just an identifier and an **input stream** represents a sequence of data which may be consumed by the process in the future. This sequence is infinite since a process may run forever. An **output environment** is a mapping which assigns output streams to (free output) channels. An **output stream** represents a sequence of data produced by the process since its birthday till present. This sequence is finite since we assume that each process is finitely old. A **data** is a value which is not an abstract error. **Values** have been defined as in Example 5.1, i.e. may be either natural numbers from a fixed interval, or Boolean values or appropriate abstract errors. A **message** is either an error or an "OK". A **state** is a mapping which assigns arbitrary data to identifiers. An **error** is either a data-type error or a system error "ERROR".

Above we have defined the concept of a behavior (of a process) plus a number of auxiliary concepts used in the definition of the former. The programming language which we design should provide means of specifying (programming) systems with given behaviors. On the ground of our model this leads to the necessity of defining appropriate constructors (functions) which create some elementary behaviors and which combine simple behaviors into compound ones. According to our earlier requirements about the language these constructors should express such mechanisms as assignments, input commands, output commands, while loops, sequential compositions of processes, alternative compositions of processes and parallel composition of processes with rendezvous-type synchronization.

As is known from elsewhere (cf.[Hoare 85]), the mechanism of rendezvous can hardly be described on the ground of behaviors. It is so because a rendezvous is defined as a joint execution of an input

action of one process with an output action of another process. In
order to talk about rendezvous we have to construct a less abstract
model of processes with an explicit concept of an action. Such a
model is well known from the literature as a **trace model**. We shall
apply it here with a certain modification which is explained later.

In a trace model every **process** is represented by a set of traces
where a **trace** is a finite or an infinite sequence of actions. Each
action corresponds to a primitive execution step which results an
environment transformation. With every trace we associate a behavior
— the set of all executions generated by that trace. With every
process we also associate a behavior which is the union of behaviors
of all its traces, and we call it the **behavior of that process**. In
this way processes can be used to specify behaviors. Formally, we
define a function which leads from processes to behaviors and which
is our unique constructor of behaviors. Of course, now we have to
define appropriate constructors of processes. It is a well-known fact
that all mentioned earlier programming constructions can easily be
expressed on that ground. This leads us to a two-level model where
processes constitute another major semantic concept. Below we define
the corresponding domains. The constructors of processes are defined
in Sec.7.4.

```
proc : Process        = Trace-set
tra  : Trace          = Action^{Cω}
act  : Action         = Executor | Rendezvous | Test

       Executor       = Assignment | Input | Output  (com. denot.)
       Assignment    :: Identifier x Evaluator
       Input         :: Identifier x Channel
       Output        :: Channel x Evaluator
eva  : Evaluator      = State → Value                (exp. denot.)

       Rendezvous    :: Lab-Input x Lab-Output
       Lab-Input      = Label x Input
       Lab-Output       Label x Output
       Label         = {1,2}

       Test           = Positive-test | Negative-test
       Positive-test :: Evaluator
       Negative-test :: Evaluator
```

        link : Link   = Channel-**finset**

A **process** is a set of traces and a **trace** is a finite or an
infinite sequence of actions. Intuitively a trace may be regarded as
a history of process activity recorded by an observer who is local to
that process and who can only see which actions were activated in
which order, but who does not see their effect on environments. The
locality of the observer means that if an input command or an output
command is activated and if this command does not take part in an
internal rendezvous, then our observer does not know whether this
command takes place in an external rendezvous or in a communication
with the environment.

In the traditional trace approach to concurrency (e.g. in [Hoare 85)
or [Mazuriewicz 84]) actions are merely symbols without any meaning.
Only later they may be interpreted as, for instance, functions on
environments. In our model actions are "semantic objects" , although
they do not need to be always functions.

At the classical denotational ground it is always tacitly assumed
that the executional effect of a component of a program does not
depend on the context where that component is executed. E.g. the
meaning of an assignment or an expression is always the same function
on environments. We say that these components are **context-
-independent**. The denotations of such a components describe their
ultimate executional effect. We shall call them **executional
denotations**.

In our case, where we describe rendezvous mechanism, the situation is
different. The commands of inputs and outputs, may "do" different
things depending whether they are activated in order to take part in
a rendezvous or in order to interact with the external environment.
These commands are **context-dependent** and their denotations should
only identify tools which are used later in the construction of
appropriate functions. E.g. the denotation of an output command is a
pair channel-evaluator and is used later either in the construction
of a function which corresponds to a rendezvous and modifies the
state or which corresponds to a communication with the external word
and modifies the output environment. The executional meanings of
program's components are defined in our model by a function which
assigns behaviors to processes (Sec.7.3).

Components whose ultimate effect depends on the context of execution will be called **context—dependent**. Their denotations will be called **instrumental denotations**, since they only define instruments which can be used later in achieving the ultimate effect.

Our denotational model of processes is instrumental in the above sense. Only evaluators represent executional denotations. All actions have been defined in the instrumental style. As we shall see later, assignments and tests are context—independent and therefore they could have been defined as functions on environments. We keep them, however, instrumental in order to to make our model more uniform.

Now let us proceed to an intuitive explanation of our domains. An **action** is either an executor, or a rendezvous, or a test. Executors are these actions of a process which can be explicitly specified by a programmer. As we shall see in Sec.7.6, they have a syntactic representation. Intuitively they correspond to single commands. Test and rendezvous are actions which are implicit in the semantics of processes. They do not have a direct syntactic representation.

All actions have been defined as marked tuples. This makes the corresponding domains disjoint and helps in the definition of a function run—a in Sec.7.3.

An **executor** is either an assignment or an input or an output.

An **assignment** is a labeled tuple consisting of an identifier and an evaluator. Its intuitive interpretation is usual.

An **input** consists of an identifier and a channel. When an input action mk—input(<ide,chan>) is executed by a process, two effects should be considered: an internal effect (local to the process) and an external effect. The internal effect is context—independent and consists of receiving a data which is transported through chan and stored under ide. The external effect depends on whether chan is free or not. In the former case the inputted data comes from an input environment and that environment is modified (7.3.1). In the latter case the inputted value comes from another process and an effect of synchronization takes place (7.3.1).

An **output** consists of a channel and an evaluator. The execution of mk-output(<chan,eva>) also has an internal and an external effect. The former consists of outputting a value generated by eva through channel chan. The external effect depends on the freeness of chan in a way analogous to the case of inputs.

A **rendezvous** is a marked pair which consists of a labeled input and a labeled output:

$$mk-rendevous(<<lab_1,mk-input(<ide,chan_1>)>,$$
$$<lab_2,mk-output(<chan_2,eva>)>>)$$

Labels are indicating from where the corresponding component of a rendezvous comes in a parallel composition of processes (7.4.2). A channel is just an identifier. This does not lead to any clashes with variable identifiers since channels are never used to "store" values, but only to identify these pairs of input- and output commands of two different processes which can take part in a common rendezvous (7.4.2).

A **test** is an action activated by a process at a control-branching point. In our case this may happen only at the entrance to a while-loop. Formally a test is a labeled evaluator. In a correct program this evaluator should return only boolean values.

A **link** is a finite set of channels and is used as an argument of a parallel composition of processes (7.4.2).

7.3 Assigning behaviors to processes

We assume that all actions are deterministic, i.e. that each of them may be associated with a function which transforms a current environment into a new one. Let

env-t : Env-transformation = Environment $\tilde{\to}$ Environment

The association of environment transformations to actions is described by the following function run-a (run-action):

```
run-a : Action → Env-transformation

run-a.act.<i-env,o-env,mes,sta> =                                    (7.3.1)
   mesεError → <i-env,o-env,mes,sta>,
   actεAssignment →
      let mk-assignment(<ide,eva>) = act in
      let val = eva.sta in
      valεError → <i-env,o-env,val,sta>,
      TRUE       → <i-env,o-env,val,sta[val/ide]>,
   actεInput →
      let mk-input(<ide,chan>) = act in
      let dat = head.(i-env.chan) in
      let i-str = tail.(i-env.chan) in
      <i-env[i-str/chan],o-str,mes,sta[dat/ide]>,
   actεOutput →
      let mk-output(<chan,eva>) = act in
      let val = eva.sta in
      valεError → <i-env,o-env,val,sta>,
      TRUE →
         let o-str = <val>^(o-env.chan) in
         <i-env,o-env[o-str/chan],mes,sta>,
   actεRendezvous →
      let mk-rendezvous((<lab₁,mk-input(<ide,chan₁>)>,
                   <lab₂,mk-output(<chan₂,eva>)>)) = act in
      let val = eva.sta in
      valεError → <i-env,o-env,val,sta>,
      TRUE       → <i-env,o-env,val,sta[val/ide]>,
   actεPositive-test →
      let mk-positive-test(eva) = act in
      let val = eva.sta in
      val∉{tt,ff} → <i-env,o-env,ERROR,sta>,
      val=tt       → <i-env,o-env,mes,sta>,
      TRUE         → UNDEFINED
   actεNegative-test →
      let mk-negative-test(eva) = act in
      let val = eva.sta in
      val∉{tt,ff} → <i-env,o-env,ERROR,sta>,
      val=ff       → <i-env,o-env,mes,sta>,
      TRUE         → UNDEFINED
```

The informal reading of this definition is the following. If the current environment bears an error message, then the new environment is a copy of the former. This describes the fact, that the occurrence of an error blocks any further activity of a process. If there is no error message, then the execution of an action depends on its type.

An **assignment** evaluates the corresponding evaluator and then, if the generated value is an abstract error, passes this value as an error message, otherwise assigns this value to the corresponding identifier in the state. An **input** command removes the top value from the corresponding input stream and assigns it to the corresponding identifier. An **output** command evaluates the corresponding evaluator and then, if this generates an error, passes this error as an error message, otherwise sends the corresponding value to the top of the corresponding output stream.

A **rendezvous** does exactly the same as an assignment, since it is nothing else but an assignment executed jointly by two processes. As we shall see later, a rendezvous can only take place if $chan_1=chan_2$ and if both these channels have been declared as internal. This restriction is formally expressed in (7.4.2) where we define the synchronization mechanisms of our language. Here we only define the executional effect of a rendezvous whenever it takes place.

Tests constitute a certain singular case. A **test**, whether positive or negative, may either issue an error message, if the value of the corresponding evaluator is not a proper boolean value, or may copy the environment, if the value of the evaluator is appropriate (i.e. tt for positive case and ff for negative case), or may issue no environment at all. In contrast to all former actions, environment transitions which correspond to tests are partial functions. This is expressed in our definition in an ad hoc (and a not quite formal notation) using the UNDEFINED. The undefinedness of the environment transition which corresponds to a test means that the current state has failed the test. Why are we modeling test—failure in that way will be partly seen below and partly in Sec.7.4 where we define the process constructor corresponding to while—loops.

Each trace may be regarded as a sequential program without loops and branchings where actions correspond to primitive commands. With every such program we associate the set of all corresponding executions. We introduce a function run-t (run trace):

    run-t : Trace → Behavior

which we define as follows (a more algebraic definition is left to the reader):

    run-t.<act_1,act_2,...> =   (7.3.2)
        {<env_1,env_2,...> | env_{i+1} = run-a.act_i.env_i for
        i=1,2,...}

The behavior of a trace consists of all finite or infinite executions which are generated in executing the actions of the trace one after another. Observe that in each such execution no test could have failed. Formally this is the consequence of the partiality of environment transformations which correspond to tests. Intuitively this corresponds to the fact that at every branching point a process chooses this branch where the branching condition (in our case a while-condition) is satisfied.

The behavior of a process is defined as the union of the behaviors of all its traces. This is expressed by the function:

    run : Process → Behavior
    run.proc = U{run-t.tra | tra∈proc}

7.4 The constructors of processes

In the former section we have defined the executional effect of each action in (7.3.1) and we have assumed in (7.3.2) that if two actions are executed one after another, then the second inherits the output environment of the first. We have not defined, however, any mechanism which would allow the programmer to set a desired order between actions. In other words, we have not defined any control mechanism of the language. In this section we shall fill this gap and describe the control mechanisms of the language expressed by the constructors of processes. First let us establish the names and types of these constructors:

```
asg    : Identifier x Evaluator              → Process
in     : Identifier x Channel                → Process
out    : Channel    x Evaluator              → Process
while  : Evaluator  x Process                → Process
alt    : Process    x Process                → Process
seq    : Process    x Process                → Process
par    : Link       x Process    x Process   → Process
```

These constructors should be defined in such a way that the corresponding processes' behaviors reflect our intuitive understanding of assignments, input commands, output commands, while-loops etc. Intuitively each process should contain all the traces, and only such traces, which are not excluded by the control structure of that process. Some of these traces may be "dynamically infeasible" but this is only seen at the level of behaviors. Let us start from the constructors of primitive processes, i.e. from constructors which do not take processes as arguments:

```
asg.<ide,eva>  = {<mk-assignment(<ide,eva>)>}
in.<ide,chan>  = {<mk-input(<ide,chan>)>}
out.<chan,eva> = {<mk-output(<chan,eva>)>}
```

Each of the constructed process corresponds to a single primitive command and therefore consists of a single one-action trace. In the next step we define sequential-programming operations on processes:

```
while.<eva,proc> =
   [{<mk-positive-test(eva)>}^proc]*^{<mk-negative-test(eva)>}
  |[{<mk-positive-test(eva)>}^proc]°
alt.<proc₁,proc₂> = proc₁|proc₂
seq.<proc₁,proc₂> = proc₁^proc₂
```

The "while" constructor gives a process which contains all possible traces corresponding to finite and infinite runs through the while-loop. In general, not all these traces will have non-empty behaviors but none of them can be excluded on the ground of the control structure of the loop. The operation "alt" corresponds to a nondeterministic branching, the operation "seq" to a sequential composition of processes.

Now we proceed to the definition of the parallel composition of processes. This definition is more complex than the others and requires the introduction of a few auxiliary domains and functions. The reader should remember in this place that trace model has been introduced exclusively in order to define this operation. All other operations could have been defined on the level of behaviors.

Intuitively, the parallel composition of processes $proc_1$ and $proc_2$ with a given link between them, denote it by

$$proc_{12} = par.<link,proc_1,proc_2>$$

should contain all and only such (global) traces which can be constructed from (local) traces of component processes by interleaving their independent actions and by combining each pair of cooperating (linked) input and output actions into a common rendezvous. In order to formalize this construction we first introduce some auxiliary domains:

```
g-tra : Glo-trace    = Glo-action^Cω
g-act : Glo-action   = Lab-Action | Rendezvous
l-act : Lab-action   = Label x Action
lab   : Label        = {1,2}
        Pseudotrace = [Action|{INCONSISTENCY}]^Cω
```

A **global trace** is a finite or an infinite sequence of global actions. A **global action** is either a labeled action or a rendezvous. A **labeled action** is an action labeled by 1 or 2 depending which process is supposed to host this action. In particular a labeled action may be a labeled rendezvous in which case this is a rendezvous of an "inner block", i.e. between some subprocesses of $proc_1$ or of $proc_2$. A non-labeled rendezvous describes an interaction between $proc_1$ and $proc_2$.

Intuitively each trace of $proc_{12}$ should be an interleaving of some traces from $proc_1$ and $proc_2$. An interleaving of two traces tra_1 and tra_2 may be defined as a trace tra which consists only of the actions of tra_1 and tra_2 and has the property that the removal from tra of all actions which belong to $proc_1$ gives tra_2 and similarly for $proc_2$. Trace tra with removed $proc_1$-actions ($proc_2$-actions) will be called a **projection** of tra on $proc_2$ ($proc_1$). More formally, we define a **projection function**:

$$\text{proj} : \{1,2\} \times \text{Link} \times \text{Glo-trace} \rightarrow \text{Pseudotrace}$$

which given a label i, a link and a global trace g-tra returns a pseudotrace which represents the contribution of proc_i to the global trace. This projection contains all actions which are labeled by i in g-tra plus input and output commands which come from rendezvous's with channels from the link. In addition a projection may contain **inconsistency marks** "INCONSISTENT", and therefore the projection of a trace is in general only a pseudotrace. An inconsistency mark appears in a projection either if g-tra contains a rendezvous with two different channels, with a common channel which does not belong to the link, or if it contains inputs and/or outputs with channels which do belong to the link. A pseudotrace with an occurrence of an inconsistency mark is called an **inconsistent pseudotrace**. The parallel composition of two processes with a given link is defined as follows:

$$\text{par.}\langle \text{link}, \text{proc}_1, \text{proc}_2 \rangle =$$
$$\{\text{dl.g-tra} \mid \text{proj.1.link.g-tra} \varepsilon \text{proc}_1 \text{ and}$$
$$\text{proj.2.link.g-tra} \varepsilon \text{proc}_2\}$$

where dl.g-tra denotes g-tra with removed labels (dl is a function and stands for "delabeling"). This new process contains all traces which can be labeled in such a way that their projections belong to corresponding component processes. Observe that an inconsistent pseudotrace never belongs to a process and therefore if a projection of a global trace g-tra is inconsistent, then dl.g-tra cannot belong to the parallel composition of processes.

It should be emphasized that inconsistency marks play a different role than abstract errors. Whereas the latter represent erroneous situations which may happen in program execution, the former correspond to situations which cannot happen. The mechanism of abstract errors is installed in the language in order to protect the programmer and the end-user of programs from their own errors. It is their responsibility to write/use programs in such a way that error messages do not appear, but it is always possible to write/use programs in such a way that errors will appear. Inconsistency marks describe the control mechanism of the system and are used by system designer in order to define the obligation of system's implementor. It is the responsibility of the latter to implement the language in such a way that global traces with inconsistent projections will never happen.

The formal definition of projection function is split into two steps. In the first step we express the fact that the projection of a sequence (finite or infinite) of global actions is the concatenation of the projections of these action:

$$\text{proj.lab.link.}\langle\rangle = \langle\rangle, \qquad\qquad (7.4.1)$$
$$\text{proj.lab.link.}\langle g\text{-act}_1,\ldots,g\text{-act}_n\rangle =$$
$$\quad \text{proj.lab.link.}\langle g\text{-act}_1\rangle^\wedge\text{proj.lab.link.}\langle g\text{-act}_2,\ldots,g\text{-act}_n\rangle;$$
$$\text{proj.lab.link.}\langle g\text{-act}_1,g\text{-act}_2,\ldots\rangle =$$
$$\quad \lim\{\text{proj.lab.link.}\langle g\text{-act}_1,\ldots,g\text{-act}_n\rangle\}_{n=1}^{\infty}$$

Of course, by the projection of a single action we formally mean a projection of a one-element trace which contains this action. In the second step we define the projections of single-action traces:

```
proj.lab.link.<g-act> =                          (7.4.2)
    g-actεrendezvous →
        let mk-rendevous(<<lab₁,mk-input(<ide,chan₁>)>,
                         <lab₂,mk-output(<chan₂,eva>)>>) = g-act in
        lab₁=lab₂    → <INCONSISTENT>,
        chan₁≠chan₂  → <INCONSISTENT>,
        chan₁∉link   → <INCONSISTENT>,
        lab=lab₁     → <mk-input(<ide,chan₁>)>,
        lab=lab₂     → <mk-output(<chan₂,eva>)>,
    g-actεLab-action →
        let <lab_a,act> = g-act in
        lab≠lab_a    → <>,
        actεAssignment|Test|Rendezvous → <act>,
        actεInput →
            let mk-input(<ide,chan>) = act in
            chanεlink → <INCONSISTENT>,
            TRUE      → <act>,
        actεOutput →
            let mk-output(<chan,eva>) = act in
            chanεlink → <INCONSISTENT>,
            TRUE      → <act>,
```

If a global action is a (unlabeled) rendezvous then we first check three consistency conditions which are the following:

- the corresponding input and output must belong to different
  processes, i.e. their labels must be different,
- the input and the output must share a common channel,
- this common channel must belong to a link.

If at least one of these conditions is not satisfied, then we set an
inconsistency mark into the trace. Otherwise the projection of our
rendezvous is the input or the output depending which of the
corresponding labels is the projection label.

If a global action is a a labeled action, then we check if its label
coincides with the projection label. If this is not the case, then
the projection is an empty trace. Otherwise it is the delabeled
action with the exception of an input or an output action with a
channel which belongs to the link. In both these cases we set the
inconsistency mark to express the fact that a channel which belongs
to a link cannot be used for a communication with the external
environment.

As we already mentioned before, a rendezvous may appear in a global
trace also as a labeled action. In that case it represents a
rendezvous which is local to one of our component processes. This is
possible only if that local process is itself a parallel composition
of processes.

7.5 The constructors of evaluators, channels, links and identifiers

In this section we define the constructors of all these objects which
were used in the construction of processes. Since this part of our
example is rather routine we shall not go here into details. First
the names and types of our constructors:

```
create_x  :                      → Identifier  for all x∈Identifier
set-chan  : Identifier     → Channel
set-link  : Channel        → Link
add-link  : Link      x Link → Link
create_one :                     → Evaluator
```

```
evaluate    : Identifier                    → Evaluator
e-plus      : Evaluator x Evaluator → Evaluator
e-less      : Evaluator x Evaluator → Evaluator
```

Notice that for each identifier x we have a different constructor create_x. The definitions of constructors are the following:

```
create_x.<> = x        for any xεIdentifier
set-chan.ide = ide
set-link.ide = {ide}
add-link.<link₁,link₂> = link₁ | link₂
```

The remaining constructors, i.e. the constructors of evaluators, are defined as in Example 5.1.

7.6 Syntax

So far we have constructed the algebra **Sys** which describes our future computer system of concurrent processes. In this section we shall derive a syntax for that system. In the first step we have to decide, therefore, which mechanisms of our system should be accessible to the user.

The ultimate goal of our system is to provide the user with some means of creating processes with given behaviors. In order to do that he must be able to construct behaviors hence also to construct processes since

    run : Process → Behavior

is the only constructor of behaviors in **Sys**. In order to construct processes he must be able to construct evaluators, links, channels and identifiers. Hence the algebra **Den** must contain all these carriers with the corresponding constructors. It seems also rather obvious that we shall not include in **Den** any other carriers. Of course, our user does not need to construct actions, traces, executions, states, etc. in isolation. We have implicitly taken this decision earlier by constructing **Sys** in such a way that the corresponding carriers have empty reachable subsets. Now, even if we would have included these carriers and operations on them to **Den**, their corresponding syntactic carriers of terms would have been empty.

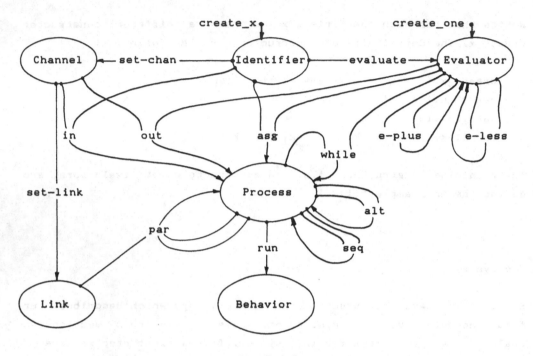

Fig.7.6.1

It should be emphasized that keeping in **Den** all the carriers of **Sys** which contain reachable elements is not at all a rule. It just happened so in our example, but in general we may wish to exclude some of these carriers as well (cf.Example 5.1).

The signature of **Den** is shown on Fig.7.6.1. Below we show the grammar of the corresponding prototype syntax of terms and a grammar of a slightly modified intermediate syntax. The reader may wish to check that our intermediate syntax is an isomorphic modification of the prototype syntax. This implies that it is correct. Of course, it is still rather inconvenient due to the superfluous parentheses in many constructs. Therefore we should not accept it as a final syntax. Further transformations are, however, left to the reader.

PROTOTYPE SYNTAX	INTERMEDIATE SYNTAX

<ide> ::=
    create_a|create_b...
	<ide> ::=
	    a|b|c|...

<chan> ::= set-chan(<ide>)	<chan> ::= <ide>

<eva> ::=
    e-one
  |evaluate(<ide>
  |e-plus(<eva>,<eva>)
  |e-less(<eva>,<eva>)
  |...
	<eva> ::=
	    1
	  |<ide>
	  |(<eva>+<eva>)
	  |(<eva><<eva>)
	  |...

<link> ::=
    set-link(<chan>)
  |add-link(<link>,<link>)
	<link> ::=
	    <chan>
	  |(<link>,<link>)

<proc> ::=
    asg(<ide>,<eva>)
  |in(<ide>,<chan>)
  |out(<chan>,<eva>)
  |while(<eva>,<proc>)
  |alt(<proc>,<proc>)
  |seq(<proc>,<proc>)
  |par(<link>,<proc>,<proc>)
	<proc> ::=
	    <ide>:=<eva>
	  |<ide>?<chan>
	  |<chan>!<ide>
	  |**while** <eva> **do** <proc> **od**
	  |**alt** <proc>,<proc> **endalt**
	  |(<proc>;<proc>)
	  |**par**
	       link <link>:<proc>;<proc>
	    endpar

<beh> ::=
    run(<proc>)
	<beh> ::=
	    run <proc> **endrun**

Observe that in both grammars processes and behaviors have nearly identical carriers. This somewhat unusual situation is the consequence of the fact that in **Den** the only way of constructing a behavior is the application of a function "run" to a process. The existence of such two carriers allows for the construction of a denotational semantics which looks like a two-level semantics: given a program (i.e. the syntax of a behavior we first assign to it a

process and then we assign a behavior to that process. Of course,
this is an ordinary denotational semantics and the two-level effect
is hidden in the existence of two corresponding carriers. From the
perspective of a traditional (descriptive) denotational semantics
this may appear as a trick, but in our approach this construction
came out in a natural way and was well motivated.

Let us make one more remark about isomorphic transformations of
syntax. As we know, such transformations are always safe in the sense
that they preserve the correctness of syntax (Sec.6). If in addition
they have a skeleton property, then they also preserve the
context-freeness of syntax (Sec.4). This is the case which we have in
our example. It should be emphasized however, that even a skeleton
isomorphism cannot be regarded as merely a sugaring transformation,
since it can seriously change the parsing-complexity of a grammar. As
is easy to see each prototype syntax of terms is of type LL(1).
However, if e.g. we change a prefix- to an infix notation, then we
usually go to a higher LL(k)-ness or we can even lose this property
at all. For instance in our example the intermediate syntax of input-
and output processes is LL(2), whereas the syntax of plus-evaluators
is not LL(k) for any k>0.

7.7 Concluding remarks

Let us start from analyzing our definition regarded as a
specification addressed to the implementor and user of the language.
From that viewpoint it provides the following information:

1) It states that the execution of a program (i.e. of an element
of <beh>) consists of a consecutive execution (one at a time) of
primitive actions. Each action transforms an environment inherited
from a preceding action. This is formally expressed by (7.3.2).

2) It specifies the executional effect of each action in (7.3.1)
and in the definitions of the constructors of evaluators.

3) It specifies the mechanism of control and synchronization in
the definition of the constructors of processes (Sec.7.4).

Such a description of a language, although slightly different from traditional denotational style, seems sufficiently adequate for language implementation and use. The user of the language may also wish to develop an appropriate logic where to formulate and prove program properties. In that case our definition provides a framework where one can formulate usual invariant-type properties of programs plus such properties as successful termination or deadlock. Due to the fact that behaviors include infinite executions and that we have introduced abstract errors, we can distinguish between divergence and abortion.

In a traditional denotational semantics the meaning of a program is defined as a combination of the meanings of its parts. In our case, although the compositionality principle is formally satisfied (our semantics is a many-sorted homomorphism) the meaning of a program, i.e. of the syntax of a behavior is defined as the behavior of a certain process and only this process has a "true" compositional definition. Strictly speaking, our denotational semantics is defined by the following tuple of functions:

        I : <ide> → Identifier   E : <eva> → Evaluator
        C : <chan> → Channel   P : <proc> → Process
        L : <link> → Link   B : <beh> → Behavior

where the relationship between B and P is the following:

        B[run s-proc endrun] = run.P[s-proc]   (7.7.1)

The element s-proc stands for "the syntax of a process" and belongs to <proc>.

Equation (7.7.1) describes formally what we have informally called in Sec.7.6 a "two-level semantics". This two-levelness reflects the fact that in our model the mechanisms of data manipulation and control are described separately. The separation of these mechanisms is typical to the treatment of concurrency and may be observed in many models, e.g. in Petri nets, trace languages [Mazurkiewicz 84], failures [Brookes,Hoare,Roscoe 84] or in the processes of [Maggiolo--Schettini,Winkowski 86]. Consequently, all these models could be used within our approach. The general philosophy of that approach is expressed by the signature of Den on Fig.7.6.1. Within that philosophy we have chosen — in our example — certain concepts of a process and a behavior. Other choices, however, are also possible.

Of course, a denotational model of a programming language with concurrency does not need to fit always into our signature. An interesting example of a model written in a more classical style has been shown in [Roscoe 84] where a denotational semantics of OCCAM^{TM} [Inmos 84] has been defined. In that model the semantics of programs assigns to them curried functions:

P : Program → Environment → Store → [Failure x Termination]

where failures and terminations involve the concept of a trace. Traces in that model are finite sequences of symbols. Terminations, which roughly correspond to our behaviors describe an input—output effect of programs. They glue, however, abortion and divergence into a common undefinedness ⊥.

It may be worth mentioning that our model could easily be transformed into a style similar to that of Roscoe's model. In order to do that we should replace the carrier Process by ProcessxBehavior and accordingly modify all corresponding constructors. Such a transformation, however, would probably lead to a longer and less readable definition.

As the last issue of this section let us convey a few remarks about the possible extensions of our model towards the mechanisms of OCCAAM and ADA.

It seems rather easy to extend our model to OCCAM except for the mechanisms which refer to time. Quite evidently we can define the omitted process constructors FOR and IF, we can expand our "seq", "alt" and "par" to more than just two arguments and we can introduce guards to "alt". It is also a rather routine task to define more data—type mechanisms and the declarations of variables and channels. The introduction of OCCAM's procedures, called "named processes" seems also not very difficult. Simplifying a little this requires four new domains:

Proc—declaration = Identifier x Form—par x Process
Form—par   = Identifier | Channel

```
Proc-call         = Identifier x Act-par
Act-par           = Identifier | Channel
```

the redefinition of two old domains:

```
Channel           :: Identifier
Action            = Executor | Rendezvous | Test | Proc-call
```

and the introduction of a new constructor:

```
prefix : Proc-declaration x Process + Process
```

The replacement of simple CSP-like input and output commands by ADA-like **accept statements** and **entry calls** is also possible although this requires a more substantial modification of the concept of an action. Roughly speaking, since accept statements may be nested and may also contain entry calls, actions which correspond to accept statements and to rendezvous's must contain global traces as components. In this case traces are no more "flat" sequences, but may be sequences, of sequences, of sequences, etc. to an arbitrary finite depth. This, of course, requires also the appropriate redefinition of projection function. On the other hand, it is not obvious whether the other mechanisms of ADA, such as e.g. exceptions or procedures, can be conveniently described in our model.

It is also worth noticing that the mechanism of rendezvous in our language can easily be modified both at the level of synchronization (7.4.2) and execution (7.3.1). In the most general case a rendezvous may be regarded as a simultaneous (joint) execution of two actions coming from two different processes. The types of these actions, the rules of their synchronization and their joint executional effect may be defined in many different ways.

REFERENCES

AHO A.V., JOHNSON S.C., ULLMAN J.D. **Deterministic parsing of ambiguous grammars**, Com. ACM no 8, vol. 18 (1975), 441-452

BJOERNER D., JONES C.B. **The Vienna Development Method: The Meta Language**, LNCS Vol.61,Springer Verlag 1978

BJOERNER D., JONES C.B. **Formal Specification and Software Development**, Prentice Hall Int. 1982

BJOERNER D., OEST O.N. (eds.) **Towards a Formal Description of ADA**, LNCS 98, Springer 1980

BLIKLE A. **Proving programs by sets of computations**, MFCS Proc. Symp. Warsaw-Jadwisin 1974, LNCS 28, Springer 1975, 313-358

BLIKLE A. **Noninitial algebraic semantics**, Proc. conf. Nyborg 1984, to be published by North Holland

BLIKLE A. **Denotational constructors**, a manuscript 1986

BLIKLE A., TARLECKI A. **Naive denotational semantics**, in: Information Processing 83 (Proc. IFIP Congress 1983, R.E.A.Manson ed.), North Holland 1983

BROOKES S.D., HOARE C.A.R., ROSCOE A.W. **A theory of communicating sequential processes**, J.ACM 31 (1984), 560-599

COHN P.M. **Universal Algebra**, D.Reidel Publishing Company 1981

DERSHOWITZ N. **Computing with rewrite systems**, Information and Control 65 (1985), 122-157

EHRIG H., MAHR B. **Fundamentals of Algebraic Specification 1**, Springer 1985

GOGUEN J.A. **Abstract errors for abstract data types**, in: Formal Description of Programming Concepts (Proc. IFIP TC-2 Working Conf. 1977, ed. E.Neuhold), North-Holland 1978

GOGUEN J., MESEGUER J., PLAISTED D. **Programming with perameterized abstract objects in OBJ**, in: Theory and Practice of Software Technology, North Holland 1983, 163-194

GOGUEN J.A., THATCHER J.W., WAGNER E.G., WRIGHT J.B. **Initial algebra semantics and continuous algebras**, J. ACM 24 (1974), 68-95

GORDON M.J.C. **The Denotational Description of Programming Languages**, Springer 1979

HARRISON M.A. **Introduction to Formal Language Theory**, Addison-Wesley Publishing Company 1978

HOARE C.A.R. **Communicating Sequential Processes**, Prentice Hall
    Int.1985

INMOS Ltd. **OCCAM^{TM} Programming Manual**, Prentice-Hall Int. 1984

MAGGIOLO-SCHETTINI A., WINKOWSKI J. **An algebra of processes**,
    Journal of Computer and System Science, to appear

MAZURKIEWICZ A. **Recursive algorithms and formal languages**, Bull.
    Acad. Polon. Sci., Sér. Sci. Math. Astronom. et Phys. 20
(1972), 799-803

MAZURKIEWICZ A. **Semantics of concurrent systems: a modular
    fixed-point trace approach**, Advances in Petri Nets 1984
    (G.Rozenberg ed.), LNCS 188, Springer 1984, 352-371

MESEGUER J., GOGUEN A.J. **Initiality, induction and computability**,
    in: Application of Algebra to Language Definition and
    Compilation, (M.Nivat, J.Reynolds eds.), Cambridge Univ. Press
    1985, 459-541

MOSSES P. **The mathematical semantics of Algol 60**, Technical
    Monograph PRG-12, Oxford University 1974

McCARTHY J. **A basis for a mathematical theory of computation**,
    Western Joint Computer Conf. 1961, since then published in
    Computer Programming and Formal Systems (P.Braffort, D.Hirschberg
    eds.), North-Holland, Amstardam 1967, 33-70

SCOTT D., STRACHEY Ch. **Toward a mathematical semantics for computer
    languages**, Technical Monograhp PRG-6, Oxford University 1971

STOY J.E. **Denotational Semantics: The Scott-Strachey Approach to
    Programming Language Theory**, The MIT Press, Cambridge Mass. 1977

TENNENT R.D. **The denotational semantics of programming languages**,
    Communication of ACM, Vol.19 (1976), 437-453

A type model for VDM

B.Q.Monahan

Imperial Software Technology Ltd.
60, Albert Court, Prince Consort Road, Kensington, LONDON, SW7

Abstract

A model of types for use in VDM specifications is presented. Standard VDM types consisting of finitary values are given set-theoretic denotations, restricting the use of Scott domain theory to the provision of types for the continuous functions and *Bekic* mappings. An objective of this work was to give a simple account of recursively defined data types not involving the full apparatus surrounding the use of Scott domain theory. To do this, various "type universes" are introduced axiomatically for use as semantic denotation spaces for type expressions. Basic constructions of these universes are given to show that these axiomatic requirements can be satisfied. As these type universes indirectly specify the "values" that each type consists of, it also gives a framework for building a full semantic model of VDM.

1 Introduction.

In VDM, types are simply taken to be sets of values; the idea being that each VDM expression will denote a value from its type. Hence, every type stands for an *a priori* well-defined set that contains the values of (ground) terms which hold that type.

Their usage in VDM is to place a semantic constraint upon the formation of terms. Each function symbol has a type that describes its source (i.e. a set containing its domain of definition) and its target (a set containing its image). Hence, functions are not assumed to be total with respect to their type. Quantified variables also possess types to indicate their range of variation.

This notion of type corresponds to that of "sort" in the algebraic school of specification. Our objective here is to discuss the concept of type to assist in giving semantics to recursive type definitions in as simple a way as possible and to provide motivation for a VDM type system (forthcoming). To do this, a (rather humble) universe of types is postulated axiomatically without reference to any specific value manipulating functions or morphisms.

The Appendix contains a number of set theoretical definitions, in an attempt to be reasonably self-contained. However, the reader may also wish to consult standard works such as [Enderton] and the first chapters of [Cohn] for further details.

2 A language for type definition.

In VDM specifications, types are introduced using type definitions whose syntactic form is described here (see [Bjorner,Jones],[Jones]).

Each type definition introduces a named set of a particular form, and may be either a type equation or a tagged definition. This may be more precisely stated using an obvious BNF-like formalism:-

$$\text{s-td} \quad ::= \quad \text{ty-nm} = \text{ty}$$
$$| \quad \text{ty-nm} :: \text{ty}$$

where s-td stands for (simple) type definitions and ty-nm stands for the name of the type being defined.

A syntactic form for type expressions, ty, is defined below:-

$$
\begin{aligned}
\text{ty} \quad ::= \quad & \text{Bool} \,|\, \text{Nat} \,|\, \text{Int} \,|\, \text{Real} \cdots \\
| \quad & \text{ty-nm} \\
| \quad & \textbf{record} \; \text{s-id}_1 : \text{ty}_1, \; \text{s-id}_2 : \text{ty}_2, \; \ldots, \; \text{s-id}_n : \text{ty}_n \; \textbf{end} \\
| \quad & \{\underline{OB}_1, \underline{OB}_2, \cdots, \underline{OB}_n\} \\
| \quad & \textbf{list of} \; \text{ty}_1 \\
| \quad & \textbf{set of} \; \text{ty}_1 \\
| \quad & \textbf{map} \; \text{ty}_1 \; \textbf{to} \; \text{ty}_2 \\
| \quad & \textbf{opt} \, \text{ty} \\
| \quad & (\text{ty}_1 \,|\, \text{ty}_2 \,|\, \cdots \,|\, \text{ty}_k)
\end{aligned}
$$

Each of the ty_i's is a type expression and each of the s-id_i's is the name of a corresponding selector function, for $1 \leq i \leq n$. The names $\underline{OB}_i$ stand for primitive, atomic objects whose only distinguishing characteristic is the name by which it is known. It is assumed that each ty-nm, other than the base types Nat etc. will be introduced via a type definition in the specification.

The language of types given above is very regular and structural. As such, it is rather over generous for specification purposes in that a tighter description of the permissable values is required. This, of course, means that the VDM notion of *invariant* has to be included into our language. This should strictly involve specifying the VDM metalanguage for predicates; however, for our purposes, we shall assume that these are simple first order predicate calculus formulae, ranged over by Ψ.

The syntax for full type definitions is now as follows:-

$$
\begin{aligned}
\text{td} \quad ::= \quad & \text{s-td} \\
| \quad & \text{s-td} \; \textbf{where inv} - \text{ty-nm}(args) \triangleq \Psi
\end{aligned}
$$

Note that Ψ should contain no free occurrences of variables other than those given within args.

In addition, the following notation for integer ranges is also included:-

$$\{n, \cdots, m\}$$

with the obvious changes to the type expression syntax, assuming that n and m are simple arithmetic expressions.

The remainder of the paper will present semantic structures which could be used to assign phrases from this language meaning. Our approach to this is to consider type definition's as a set of simultaneous equation's to be solved between sets. The role of the type universes considered later is to provide the solution spaces for these simultaneous equations. Hence, a type definition in this language is said to be *valid* if there exists at least one simultaneous "solution" of all of it's clauses[1].

3 Type Universes and their Axiomatic properties.

The standard VDM doctrine concerning values and types states that the "typing" relation between well formed values and their types consists precisely of set membership.

Our task is to specify what all VDM values look like, and to say which types they belong to. However, it is very complicated to give a universal space of denotations for all the required values, upon which a type structure with the correct properties can be imposed by *fiat*.

Instead, the approach taken here is to first specify and define what all the needed types look like and from that determine what all the VDM values are. This can be done conceptually, by examining the elements of each type belonging to the type universe.

A *type universe* is, first of all, a collection of sets which must satisfy certain properties if the elements of this universe (i.e the types) are to be rich enough to contain enough values. To ensure that this space of types is sufficently rich, it is required that the type universe is closed under certain type forming operations (e.g set union, sequence construction etc.). To show that our requirements are consistent, a construction is given for a particular type universe called $\overline{U}$. It will turn out that $\overline{U}$ is, in a well defined way, a *minimal* type universe.

Further requirements are made to ensure that the type universe contains enough sets of the right kind so that solutions to recursive type definitions exist. In essence, this means that all the basic type operators must be *monotonic* and *continuous*, with respect to set inclusion. Moreover, these operators should also possess *least fixed points* within type universe's.

The basic structure of the type universes given here is well known in Mathematical Logic, where they are known as the *hereditarily finite* sets. The idea of describing universes of admissable sets derives from foundational studies in Mathematics. For example, similar descriptions are given in [Blikle], [Cohn] and [Mac Lane]. Thorough expositions of general set theory may be found in [Enderton] or [Devlin]; a more introductory treatment can be found in [Halmos].

---

[1] Each solution consists of an assignment of *non-empty* sets belonging to the type universe, for each type being defined

3.1 Basic Types

It is assumed that there is some collection, Bty, of specific sets that are to be regarded as basic types. Such a collection of basic types should satisfy the following conditions:-

$$\{\underline{\text{TRUE VALUE}}, \underline{\text{FALSE VALUE}}\} = \mathbf{B} \in \text{Bty} \land |\mathbf{B}| = 2 \tag{1}$$

$$\forall S \in \text{Bty} \cdot (\mathbf{B} \cap S) \neq \{\} \Rightarrow \mathbf{B} = S \tag{2}$$

The elements $\underline{\text{TRUE VALUE}}$ and $\underline{\text{FALSE VALUE}}$ are chosen as a fixed pair of distinct values. The set of truth values, $\mathbf{B}$, consists precisely of these two elements and is also disjoint from any other base type in Bty.

$$|\text{Atom}| = \omega \tag{3}$$

$$\text{Text} \in \text{Bty} \land |\text{Text}| = \omega \tag{4}$$

$$\text{Atom} \cap \text{Text} = \{\} \tag{5}$$

There exist two *disjoint* countably infinite sets called Text and Atom. It is assumed that all of their elements can be literally expressed; values belonging to Text are given by quotation, for example, "this is a Text value"; Atom values are given as (possibly hyphenated) underlined upper case words, for example, $\underline{\text{THIS IS AN ATOM}}$.

$$(\forall S \in \text{Bty} \cdot \text{Text} \cap S = \{\} \lor \text{Text} = S) \tag{6}$$

$$\forall S \in \text{Bty} \cdot (S \neq \{\} \land |S| \in \omega) \Rightarrow S \in \text{Bty} \tag{7}$$

$$\forall S \in \text{Bty} \cdot (|S| \notin \omega \land \text{Atom} \cap S \neq \{\}) \Rightarrow \text{Atom} = S \tag{8}$$

The set Text is included as a basic type. Although Atom itself is *not* a base type, any finite non-empty subset of Atom may serve as a basic type (i.e enumerated types).

$$\text{Bty} \subseteq \text{U} \tag{9}$$

Every set belonging to Bty is a base type and, as such, belongs to type universe U.

3.2 Operators

At this stage, some notation is introduced for various operations for combining arbitrary sets to form new ones. So suppose that S, S_1 and S_2 are any sets.

- $\mathcal{S}(S)$ - the set of all *finite* sequences of elements from S.

- $\mathcal{F}(S)$ - the set of all *finite* subsets of the set S.

- $\mathcal{M}(S_1, S_2)$ - the set of all partial graphs of mappings from S_1 to S_2 with *finite* domain of definition.

- $\mathcal{R}(F)(rt)$ - the set of all *record values* that conform to the finite mapping, rt, from names to sets (i.e $rt \in \mathcal{M}(Atom, F)$, where F is a family of sets). Each record value, rv, is, in essence, a finite function from names to values. Informally, it is said to *conform* to the mapping rt if it has at least as many named fields as rt and that values of fields common to both rt and rv belong to the corresponding type in rt. Note that field selection corresponds to the application of the field name to the mapping representing the record.

These set operations, including record types, are further described in the Appendix.

We assume that there is a *tagging* operation that takes a token tk $\in$ Text and an arbitrary set S and produces an isomorphic "copy" of S, denoted by (tk :: S). This operation is assumed to have the following properties:-

$$\forall x \cdot \forall tk \in \text{Text} \cdot \mid tk :: \{x\} \mid = 1 \tag{10}$$

Tagging a singleton set produces another singleton.

$$\forall tk \in \text{Text} \cdot (tk :: S) = \bigcup \{(tk :: \{a\}) \mid a \in S\} \tag{11}$$

The tagged set, (tk :: S) is entirely determined by the tagging of the elements of S.

$$\forall tk_1, tk_2 \in \text{Text} \cdot (tk_1 :: S_1) \subseteq (tk_2 :: S_2) \Leftrightarrow (tk_1 = tk_2) \wedge (S_1 \subseteq S_2) \tag{12}$$

The tagging function is monotonic in it's second argument, assuming that the tags in the first argument agree. It can be shown, from the above axioms, that unions and intersections are preserved, where tk $\in$ Text:-

$$(tk :: S_1) \cap (tk :: S_2) = (tk :: (S_1 \cap S_2))$$

$$(tk :: S_1) \cup (tk :: S_2) = (tk :: (S_1 \cup S_2))$$

In general, we have for an arbitrary family of sets F and token tk:-

$$\bigcap_{S \in F} (tk :: S) = (tk :: (\bigcap_{S \in F} S))$$

$$\bigcup_{S \in F} (\text{tk} :: S) = (\text{tk} :: (\bigcup_{S \in F} S))$$

Note that if tk_1 and $\text{tk}_2 \in$ Text are distinct tokens and S_1 and S_2 are any sets, then by property (12),

$$(\text{tk}_1 :: S_1) \cap (\text{tk}_2 :: S_2) = \{\}$$

3.3 Closure conditions.

Any type universe should be closed with respect to certain specific operations upon sets. This means that when these operations are applied to any appropriate choice of sets from U, the resulting set should also belong to U.

So, suppose that $A, B \in U$, $F \subseteq U$, $rt \in \mathcal{M}(\text{Atom}, F)$ and that $\text{tk} \in$ Text,

$$\text{Seq}(A) \quad = \quad (\text{"seq"} :: \mathcal{S}(A)) \in U \tag{13}$$

$$\text{Set}(A) \quad = \quad (\text{"set"} :: \mathcal{F}(A)) \in U \tag{14}$$

$$\text{Optional}(A) \quad = \quad (A \cup \{\underline{\text{NIL VALUE}}\}) \in U \tag{15}$$

$$\text{Record}(F)(rt) \quad = \quad (\text{"record"} :: \mathcal{R}(F)(rt)) \in U \tag{16}$$

$$\text{Map}(A, B) \quad = \quad (\text{"map"} :: \mathcal{M}(A, B)) \in U \tag{17}$$

$$(A \cup B) \quad \in \quad U \tag{18}$$

$$(A \times B) \quad \in \quad U \tag{19}$$

$$(\text{tk} :: A) \quad \in \quad U \tag{20}$$

Finally, it is necessary to ensure that U contains unions of countable ascending chains within U. This requirement will ensure that well-formed recursive type definitions will always have a solution within the type universe U. More formally, this condition is:-

$$\forall S \in U^{\omega} \cdot (\forall i \in \omega \cdot S_i \subseteq S_{i+1}) \Rightarrow (\bigcup_{i \in \omega} S_i) \in U \tag{21}$$

This says that for every sequence $< S_i >_{i \in \omega}$ of sets from U, if the sequence is increasing monotonicaly (i.e it is a chain), then the union of the chain also belongs to U.

This completes the closure conditions for an arbitrary type universe, U. Each of the basic type constructors (e.g sequences, records) are appropriately tagged, to prevent any undesired identifications within our model. For example, if these tags were omitted, then the empty set would represent both the empty sequence and the empty mapping.

However, these tags will have to be manipulated by all data operations defined for each kind of data. Fortuneatly, all of these manipulations are encapsulated within the primitive data operations for types in the model and so insulates the specifier from having to deal with these tags explicitly.

4 Extended type universes.

The notion of type universe covered so far only provide (set theoretic) types for simple data structures used in the VDM metalanguage. For example, it does not possess type denotations for general (user defined) functions or operations.

4.1 The subset closure operator.

To permit an arbitrary subset of type's to also be type's the operator **Sub** may be used:-

$$\mathbf{Sub}(F) = \{s | \exists t \in F \cdot s \subseteq t\} = \bigcup \{P(t) | t \in F\} \tag{22}$$

Observe that $\mathbf{Sub}(F)$ is well defined for an arbitrary family of sets, F, and we have that $F \subseteq \mathbf{Sub}(F)$ and $\mathbf{Sub}(\mathbf{Sub}(F)) = \mathbf{Sub}(F)$. Hence, if U is a type universe (i.e satisfies the conditions given in Section 3) then $\mathbf{Sub}(\mathrm{U})$ is also a type universe but extended by all subsets of types.

4.2 Flat domain embedding operator.

Our approach to function types for the VDM metalanguage is to "inject" each type into a space of "flat" domains and to consider the Scott continuous functions between these structured sets. So, as a preliminary step to this, an embedding of an arbitrary family of sets into flat domain objects is given.

Let $\boxed{\perp}$ be an arbitrary value and let F be an arbitrary family of sets. Consider the following set function defined for any $s \in F$:-

$$\forall s \in F \cdot s_\perp = s \cup \{\boxed{\perp}\} \tag{23}$$

and consider the ordering relation $\sqsubseteq_s \subseteq (s_\perp \times s_\perp)$ defined by:-

$$\forall x, y \in s_\perp \cdot (x \sqsubseteq_s y) \Leftrightarrow (x = \boxed{\perp}) \vee (x = y) \tag{24}$$

It can be easily shown that $\sqsubseteq_s$ is a *complete partial order* for $s_\perp$ with a least element $\boxed{\perp}$. We can now define the flat domain operator, **FD**, that takes any set from F to a corresponding flat domain:-

$$\mathbf{FD}(F) = \{< s_\perp, \sqsubseteq_s, \boxed{\perp} > | s \in F\} \tag{25}$$

As is the usual practice, the dependance upon $\sqsubseteq_s$ can be suppressed whenever this can be determined from the context.

4.2.1 Extending set operators for flat domains.

Each set combining operation can be uniquely extended to operate upon flat domains in a standard way. Let $m, n \in \omega$ and consider any (set) operator $f : F^m \to F^n$. This extends uniquely to a (flat domain) operator $f_\perp : \mathbf{FD}(F)^m \to \mathbf{FD}(F)^n$ in the following way:-

$$f_\perp(a_{1_\perp}, a_{2_\perp}, \cdots, a_{m_\perp}) = (b_{1_\perp}, b_{2_\perp}, \cdots, b_{n_\perp}) \tag{26}$$

where $f(a_1, a_2, \cdots, a_m) = (b_1, b_2, \cdots, b_n)$.

This extension property can also be specified in terms of the following commuting diagram:-

$$
\begin{array}{ccc}
F^m & \xrightarrow{\;f\;} & F^n \\
\downarrow{-_{\perp_m}} & & \downarrow{-_{\perp_n}} \\
\mathbf{FD}(F)^m & \xrightarrow{\;f_\perp\;} & \mathbf{FD}(F)^n
\end{array}
$$

where $-_{\perp_k}$ (for $k \geq 1$) is defined to be:-

$$(a_1, a_2, \cdots, a_k)_{\perp_k} = (a_{1_\perp}, a_{2_\perp}, \cdots, a_{k_\perp}) \tag{27}$$

If F is a type universe then it is closed under union and cartesian product. From the above, both of these operations extend directly to operations upon $\mathbf{FD}(F)$, the corresponding universe of flat domains. For example, the union operation becomes, for any $a, b \in F$:-

$$a_\perp \cup_\perp b_\perp = (a \cup b)_\perp$$

and the cartesian product operation corresponds to:-

$$a_\perp \times_\perp b_\perp = (a \times b)_\perp$$

Within Scott's theory of domains, these domain operators are known as the *coalesced sum* and the *smash* product respectively.

4.3 Scott universes.

Having now defined how to embed a given family of sets into a family of flat domains, we show how this family can be endowed with enough (continuous) functions and domain products to give a type model rich enough to interpret the VDM metalanguage.

A *Scott universe* is a family of domains *closed* under the formation of product domains, Scott continuous function domains and the (so called) Bekič mapping domains. Suppose that f is an arbitrary flat domain and that d, d_1, d_2 are arbitrary domains.

Scott Continuous Function Space $[d_1 \to d_2]$ denotes the domain of all Scott continuous functions from d_1 to d_2 that is ordered "point-wise" with respect to d_2. The least value in this domain is the function that returns the least value of d_2 for all inputs.

Full Cartesian Product $(d_1 \times d_2)$ denotes the domain of all ordered pairs of values drawn from d_1 and d_2. This is ordered "component-wise" with respect to the orderings upon the domains d_1 and d_2. The least value is given by the pair of least values from each of the component domains.

Note that this operation is *not* the same as the *smash* product for flat domains.

Bekic Mappings $f\underset{B}{\longrightarrow}d$ denotes the domain of all (strict) finite mappings from flat domain f to the domain d. These mappings are comparable if they have the same finite domain of definition and, if so, are ordered "point-wise" with respect to d. The least value in this domain is the function whose result is the least value from d everywhere. Carefully note that this is not the same as the *empty* Bekic mapping, which is a perfectly well-defined "data" value.

Note also that the Bekic maps are, in effect, finite mappings whose range elements belong to Scott domains This, of course, implies that the application of arguments to these maps could produce "partially defined" values, in the sense of Scott.

Let both D, S be arbitrary families of domains. Then, S is a *Scott universe* for D iff

$$D \subseteq S \tag{28}$$

$$\forall d_1, d_2 \in S \cdot [d_1 \to d_2] \in S \tag{29}$$

$$\forall d_1, d_2 \in S \cdot (d_1 \times d_2) \in S \tag{30}$$

$$\forall f, d \in S \cdot (f \text{ is a flat domain}) \Rightarrow (f\underset{B}{\longrightarrow}d) \in S \tag{31}$$

Scott universes are (almost) examples of Cartesian Closed Categories; such structures play a central role within the theory of Topoi (See [Goldblatt]). This completes the discussion of the main properties of Scott universes; in the next section, a construction is given for a "minimal" Scott universe containing a given family of domains.

5 Constructions

A particular construction of the type universes previously discussed is presented here, by giving a specific collection of base types and tagging operator.

5.1 Base types

The specific collection of base types, named **BT**, includes the set Bool defined in Section 3.1. However, the VDM metalanguage uses a number of other types, such as $\mathbf{N}_0$ and $\mathbf{Z}$, which should be taken as fundamental and not composite. Hence, the appropriate set of base types for interpreting VDM specifications is defined as follows:-

$$\mathbf{BT} = \{\mathbf{B}, \text{Text}, \mathbf{N_0}, \mathbf{N_1}, \mathbf{Z}, \mathbf{A}\} \cup (\mathcal{F}(\text{Atom}) \setminus \{\emptyset\}) \qquad (32)$$

where

$$
\begin{aligned}
\mathbf{N_1} &= \text{the set of natural numbers} = \{1, 2, 3, \cdots\} \\
\mathbf{N_0} &= \{0\} \cup \mathbf{N_1} = \{0, 1, 2, 3, \cdots\} \\
\mathbf{Z} &= \text{the set of integers} = \mathbf{N_0} \cup \{-n | n \in \mathbf{N_1}\} \\
\mathbf{A} &= \text{a countable subfield of the set of the real numbers} \supseteq \mathbf{Q}
\end{aligned}
$$

Note that $\mathbf{N_1} \subset \mathbf{N_0} \subset \mathbf{Z} \subset \mathbf{A}$. The usual operators over values associated with each of base type is given within the semantic mapping for the metalanguage.

5.2 The Tag Operator

In Section 3.2, the properties expected of a tag operator for the "trademarking" of types was given. Naively, the use of the "tag" operator is to explicitly seperate sets of values with different tags and so guarantee their disjointness. The tag operator is also used to ensure the semantic integrity of the use of abstract data types. A specific set operator is now defined to provide a set-theoretical implementation of such a tag operator.

Essentially, the values of a "tagged" type are pairs consisting of a "tag" together with the untagged value; the important additional property required for type integrity is that it is logically impossible to inadvertently "fake" tag values. This is done by ensuring that the set of tag values used is chosen *not* to belong to the particular type universe $\overline{U}$.

So, choose a countable Tag that is *isomorphic* to the countable set Text such that Tag does not intersect any set belonging to $\overline{U}$ (i.e no tag value belongs to any type). This is consistent since the class of all countable sets cannot itself be countable — therefore there exists a countable set disjoint from any countable set of countable sets(!)

By definition, there exists at least one bijection between Tag and Text; choose any bijection pair GenTag : Text $\rightarrow$ Tag and GetTag : Tag $\rightarrow$ Text which therefore satisfies:-

$$\forall \text{tk} \in \text{Text} \cdot \text{GetTag}(\text{GenTag}(\text{tk})) = \text{tk} \qquad (33)$$

$$\forall \text{tg} \in \text{Tag} \cdot \text{GenTag}(\text{GetTag}(\text{tg})) = \text{tg} \qquad (34)$$

Note that, by definition, Tag will not be a standard VDM type (i.e it does not belong to $\overline{U}$) the two functions above cannot be used within VDM specifications as they will not possess VDM types. Using these functions, the standard tag operator can be defined as follows:-

$$\forall S \cdot \forall tk \in \text{Text} \quad \cdot \tag{35}$$

$$(tk :: S) = \{\text{GenTag}(tk)\} \times S$$
$$= \{< \text{GenTag}(tk), s > | s \in S\}$$

This defines a tag operator because GenTag is a bijection and that the cartesian product operation on sets is continuous with respect to set inclusion.

5.2.1 Tags and the *mk*-notation

Apart from the use of tags to seperate basic data type constructors, the VDM specifier may also introduce tagged types directly using the ":" form of type declaration. This aspect of the VDM metalanguage can now be given semantics using the machinery developed above.

Let $tk \in \text{Text}$ and S be any set; now consider the following *dependently typed* family of bijections:-
$MK_{tk,S} : S \rightarrow (tk :: S)$ defined as follows:-

$$\forall s \in S \cdot MK_{tk,S}(s) = < \text{GenTag}(tk), s > \tag{36}$$

with the inverse bijection defined as:-

$$\forall x \in (tk :: S) \cdot MK_{tk,S}^{-1}(x) = \text{snd}(x) \tag{37}$$

The parametric function $\text{snd}[A, B] : (A \times B) \rightarrow B$ is easily defined by:-

$$\forall x \in A \cdot \forall y \in B \cdot \text{snd}(< x, y >) = y$$

Clearly, we have, for arbitrary $tk \in \text{Text}$ and set S, the following isomorphism properties:-

$$\forall s \in S \cdot MK_{tk,S}^{-1}(MK_{tk,S}(s)) = s \tag{38}$$

and

$$\forall x \in (tk :: S) \cdot MK_{tk,S}(MK_{tk,S}^{-1}(x)) = x \tag{39}$$

The VDM metalanguage "mk-" constructor function corresponds to a direct use of the MK family of bijections, with appropriate parameters put in place. For example, suppose that some set called Foo is introduced in a VDM specification by the type declaration:-

$$\text{Foo} :: \textbf{record} \ \ N:\text{Nat0}, B:\text{Bool} \ \textbf{end}$$

then there is a corresponding "mk" function for constructing values in this set, named as "mk-Foo", such that:-

$$\forall n \in \mathbf{N}_0 \cdot \forall b \in \mathbf{B} \cdot \tag{40}$$

$$\text{mk-Foo}(\{B \mapsto b, N \mapsto n\}) = \text{MK}_{\text{``Foo''}, \text{Foo}}(< n, b >)$$
$$= < \text{GenTag}(\text{``Foo''}), < n, b >>$$

Note that the VDM constructor function **mk-Foo** has type **record** N:Nat0, B:Bool **end** $\to$ Foo.

5.3 Building $\overline{U}$.

A construction of a particular family of sets, called $\overline{U}$, is given satisfying the basic requirements for a type universe. The technique used for this construction is standard and well-known within Universal Algebra (see Ch.3,Sec.2 of [Cohn]).

The basic idea is to form a "tower" of (families of) sets by the iteration of a function mapping families to families, starting from a given family, the base types. The type universe $\overline{U}$ is then obtained by taking the union over this tower of families to give a single family of sets, and then closing up under union's of countable chains of sets.

The following operators on families of *arbitrary* sets are now defined; let F stand for an arbitrary family of sets.

$$\text{SEQ}(F) = \{\text{Seq}(s)|s \in F\} \tag{41}$$

$$\text{SET}(F) = \{\text{Set}(s)|s \in F\} \tag{42}$$

$$\text{RECORD}(F) = \{\text{Record}(F)(\text{rt})|\text{rt} \in \mathcal{M}(\text{Atom}, F)\} \tag{43}$$

$$\text{MAP}(F) = \{\text{Map}(a,b)|a,b \in F\} \tag{44}$$

$$\text{OPTIONAL}(F) = \{\text{Optional}(s)|s \in F\} \tag{45}$$

$$\text{UNION}(F) = \{(a \cup b)|a,b \in F\} \tag{46}$$

$$\text{PRODUCT}(F) = \{(a \times b)|a,b \in F\} \tag{47}$$

$$\text{TAG}(F) = \{(\text{tk} :: a)|\text{tk} \in \text{Text} \wedge a \in F\} \tag{48}$$

Define the following sequence of sets $< T_i >_{i \in \omega}$ by primitive recursion on the index i as follows:-

$$T_0 = \mathbf{BT}$$
$$\forall i \in \omega \cdot T_{i+1} = \text{SEQ}(T_i) \cup \text{SET}(T_i) \cup \text{MAP}(T_i) \cup$$
$$\text{RECORD}(T_i) \cup \text{OPTIONAL}(T_i) \cup \text{UNION}(T_i) \cup$$
$$\text{PRODUCT}(T_i) \cup \text{TAG}(T_i)$$

Each T_i is clearly a family of sets for each $i \in \omega$ such that $T_i \subseteq T_{i+1}$, for each $i \in \omega$. Finally, $\overline{U}$ can now be defined by the following equation:-

$$\overline{U} = \text{OMEGA}(\bigcup_{i \in \omega} T_i) \tag{49}$$

where OMEGA is the closure operator defined as follows:-

$$\text{OMEGA}(F) = \{\bigcup_{j \in \omega} S_j | S \in F^\omega \wedge (\forall i \in \omega \cdot S_i \subseteq S_{i+1})\} \tag{50}$$

5.4 Building the Scott Universe.

In Section 4.3, the notion of Scott Universe was introduced; in this Section a construction of a particular Scott Universe will be given, named $\underline{SU}$, following along similar lines to the construction of $\overline{U}$ above. So, let D stand for the family of *flat* domains given by $\mathbf{FD}(\mathbf{Sub}(\overline{U}))$.

The following domain operators are now defined, where G is an arbitrary family of domains-

$$\begin{aligned}
\text{FUNCTION}(\mathcal{G}) &= \{[d_1 \to d_2] | d_1, d_2 \in \mathcal{G}\} \\
\text{CARTESIAN}(\mathcal{G}) &= \{(d_1 \times d_2) | d_1, d_2 \in \mathcal{G}\} \\
\text{BEKICMAP}(\mathcal{G}) &= \{(f \underset{B}{\to} d) | f \in D) \wedge d \in \mathcal{G}\}
\end{aligned}$$

As before, a "tower" of families (of domains), $< D_i >_{i \in \omega}$, is constructed by primitive recursion upon the index i.

$$\begin{aligned}
D_0 &= D = \mathbf{FD}(\mathbf{Sub}(\overline{U})) \\
\forall i \in \omega \cdot D_{i+1} &= D_i \cup \text{FUNCTION}(D_i) \cup \\
&\quad \text{CARTESIAN}(D_i) \cup \text{BEKICMAP}(D_i)
\end{aligned}$$

Finally, define $\underline{SU}$ by the equation:-

$$\underline{SU} = \bigcup_{i \in \omega} D_i \tag{51}$$

5.5 Polymorphism.

The VDM metalanguage contains several forms of "polymorphism" — the capacity for a multitude values of similar structure to be encapsulated by some single value. Polymorphism arises in this language in various ways; one way is as a result of set-theoretical subtyping, so that a single type may include values from several different types of interest. This is already delt with by using the type universes given above.

Our interest lies with *type parametric* polymorphism for functions values and with type operators. In this kind of polymorphism, polymorphic objects are families of ground monomorphic values indexed by *type parameter's*; it is briefly illustrated below:-

```
reverse [A] : seq A ⟶ seq A
reverse(1) ≜
    case 1 of
        [] → [],
        [a] ⌢ l₁ → reverse(l₁) ⌢ [a]
    end
```

This describes the reverse function upon sequences of elements of type A; the identifier A is a type parameter and is intended to range over elements belonging to $\text{Sub}(\overline{U})$. This function can also be specified in the pre/post condition style by:-

```
reverse [A] (s:seq A) r:seq A
post
    let ls ≜ len s in
        ls = len r ∧ ∀i ∈ { 1,...,ls} . r(i) = s(1+ls-i)
```

Various examples of type instance's of this function are stated below:-

```
reverse[A\Int] : seq Int ⟶ seq Int
reverse[A\seq Bool] : seq (seq Bool) ⟶ seq(seq Bool)
reverse[A\set of B] : seq(set of B) ⟶ seq(set of B)
```

Note that reverse is not type instantiated within it's own definition; this is because polymorphic functions are defined *assuming that all of it's type instances are constant throughout it's definition*. More generally, type instances for functions can be omitted to simplify notation if they can be deduced from the context of use; Milner's type inference algorithm[2] may be used for this calculation (see [Milner]).

In general, the rule is that all occurrences of a polymorphic function within it's defining right hand side *must* have the same type instance as it's defining left hand side. For clusters of polymorphic functions defined by *mutual* recursion, this rule applies transitively to all *relevent* defining right hand side's.

Naively, a polymorphic function is a second order functional, mapping types into functions whose monomorphic type is *dependent* upon the given type instance. Type instantiation of a polymorphic

---

[2]Unfortuneatly, to take account of subtypes, this algorithm probably has to use associative-commutative unification of type expressions. Consequently, the user may in practice need to specify more type instance information than might have been thought necessary.

function therefore produces a function belonging to the function space corresponding to the type instance. More precisely, consider the following:-

$$foo \; [A,B,C] \; : \; ty_1[A,B,C] \longrightarrow ty_2[A,B,C]$$
$$foo(u) \; \triangleq \; e[foo,A,B,C,u]$$

The semantics of this definition is a function:-

$$\lambda(A_1,B_1,C_1):\mathrm{Sub}(\overline{U})^3.$$
$$fix(\lambda(F:[\![ty_1[A_1,B_1,C_1]]\!] \longrightarrow [\![ty_2[A_1,B_1,C_1]]\!]) \; .$$
$$\lambda(x:[\![ty_1[A_1,B_1,C_1]]\!]) \; . \; [\![e[F,A_1,B_1,C_1,x]]\!])$$

An important point to note is that the fixed point is taken *within* the type abstraction; hence, recursive definitions of polymorphic functions may not use different type instances of themselves within their own definition.

A relatively straightforward semantics of type operators is made possible by the explicit use of type universes. Informally, a type operator is an inclusion continuous function from types to types; such operators could be given by an equation of the form:-

$$Graph(Node) \; = \; map \; Node \; to \; set \; of \; Node$$
$$where \; inv\text{-}Graph[Node](m) \; \triangleq \; \bigcup rng \; m \subseteq dom \; m$$

Inclusion continuity is assured by the use of continuous type constructors; the application of invariants is also continuous. The continuity requirement ensures that type operators can be used with impunity when forming recursive types.

6 Type universes and VDM types

In the following sections, some of the consequences that this type model has for the usage of types in VDM specifications are presented, followed by a discussion of type checking and equivalence issues.

6.1 Implications for VDM types

As already mentioned in Section 3, the type universe $\overline{U}$ is intended to be the space of denotations for the regular type denotations, disregarding any invariants and other means of taking subsets. Well formed type definitions (which may be recursive) are taken to specify the *least assignment of sets* that satisfies the definition; well formedness criteria essentially rule out type definitions that do not possess such a solution.

To ensure that enough solutions exist, $\overline{U}$ is closed under countable unions; a given collection of type definition clauses (i.e equations and record definitions) specifies an inclusion-continuous function from $(\overline{U} \cup \{\emptyset\})^n$ to itself, where n is the number of such clauses. The desired solution of the type definition is given by by taking the least fixed point of this function. The non-emptiness constraint can be formulated and efficiently checked syntactically (as it is equivalent to the non-emptiness problem for context-free languages).

An important property of the types in $\overline{U}$ is that, generally speaking, each one is an infinite (but countable) set whose elements, or instances, are finitely generated. Each instance can be given using a literal, constant expression of finite size.

The subset-enriched universe $\mathbf{Sub}(\overline{U})$ is used to give the denotations for the full type language where invariants are taken into account. This has the consequence that an invariant applied to a recursively defined type also holds for any of it's nested uses.

For instance, consider the example below in Figure 1. This invariant requires that each tree be

```
Node :: record
    left  : Tree,
    data  : Bool,
    right : Tree
end

Tree = Nat | Node
where  inv-Tree(t) ≜
        if t ∈ Nat then is_even(t)
        else  let mk-Node({|data=b,left=t₁,right=t₂|}) ≜ t
              in
                  b ∧ (t₁ = t₂)
```

Figure 1: Recursive invariant example

either an even number or a record containing a data field of value **true** and where the left and right sub-trees are equal. The invariant also applies recursively to the Tree components belonging to Node also. For instance, **mk-Node(true, 6, 6)** satisfies the invariant inv-Tree and so is a bona fide element of type Tree (and of course, Node). However the element **mk-Node(true, 5, 5)** does not satisfy the invariant since 5 is not an even number. Note also that the element **mk-Node(false, 26, 26)** is an element of Node, but not of Tree itself.

In other words, taking the least solution in $\mathbf{Sub}(\overline{U})$ of the equations specified by a type definition, ensures that invariants also hold recursively when forming terms of any type, including sequences etc.

The next universe, $\mathrm{FD}(\mathrm{Sub}(\overline{U}))$, maps every set (i.e type) in $\mathrm{Sub}(\overline{U})$ into a flat Scott domain. This is a preparatory stage to constructing the hierarchy of Scott continuous functions of arbitrary finite type. Flat domains are obtained by adding an extra element, conventionally denoted $\perp$, to a given data type and which stands for the "result" of executing a program not returning sensible output. In short, the improper element "$\perp$" denotes "improper termination" or "nonsense".

The last universe considered above was the so-called "Scott universe" $\underline{SU}$ containing the continuous function spaces between domains. The choice of Scott continuous functions is for correctly dealing with function's defined by recursion, at arbitrary functional type.

The basic idea is to treat all function specifications, which can be mutually recursive, as a set of equations to be solved for the functions involved. There are several possible solutions, but the one justified by computational intuition is the so-called least fixed point solution. Further details may be found in [Stoy] or in [Schmidt], for example.

One of the main motivations for the structure of this type model was to draw a firm distinction between "finitary" values which mimic standard computer data structures, and "infinitary" values, like the denotations of functions. Mathematically this distinction is made by using simple set theoretical types to contain the "finitary" values and domain theoretic types to contain "infinitary" values.

However, if this were applied too strictly, it might cause difficulties when using such a type model as a semantic basis for language processing systems, such as programming languages compilers. This is answered in the model presented above by including a family of mapping values called *Bekic mappings* whose range elements may contain "infinitary" values.

However, there is a price to be paid for using Bekic mappings; not all of the basic operations available over finitary mappings are available for Bekic mappings. In particular, these omitted operators are the equality, inequality and range operators. The motivation for these restrictions are that they are not computationally justifiable and is consistent with the omission of the same operators for values belonging to function domains.

Even so, Bekic mappings cannot be included within the state components of VDM state spaces (since these components are standard set-theoretic types), but they can serve as input and output data from semantic functions. It is important to note that if these objects were used in VDM states then their semantics could require the use of *reflexive domains*, which are not yet provided within this type model.

Recent work on Scott's reformulation of Domain Theory (see [Winskel, Larsen]) in terms of Information Systems (see [Scott]) seem to clear the way to extending this type model to include reflexive domains (together with dependent types).

While full recursive domain equations are not presently available, there are recursively defined set theoretical types that somewhat resemble reflexive domains; for instance consider the following:-

$$A = \text{seq of } A$$
$$B = \text{list of } B$$
$$C = \text{map } C \text{ to } C$$

These are each perfectly good type definitions with well defined least solutions in $\overline{U}$, because each of the corresponding empty values in each case. Moreover, because each type above belongs to $\overline{U}$ all values in each type can be given by a *finite* expression, such as:-

$$\texttt{<<>,<>,<<>,<<>>>>} \qquad (\in A)$$
$$\texttt{\{\{\{\}\},\{\}\},\{\{\}\}\}} \qquad (\in B)$$
$$\texttt{\{\{\} $\mapsto$ \{\{\} $\mapsto$ \{\}\},\{\{\} $\mapsto$ \{\}\} $\mapsto$ \{\}\}} \qquad (\in C)$$

Scott's reflexive domains consist of infinitary values, unlike the solutions of the set equations above.

6.2 Implications for type checking and equivalence.

The main objective of this paper was to give a denotational model of types for use in semantic definitions of languages containing type expressions. Although it does not directly address the type checking of value expressions or of type equivalence specifically, both can now be defined semantically. That is, an a priori correctness criteria for type-checking and type-equivalence can be specified with respect to a type model; different type models give rise to different notions of type checking and type equivalence.

Let TyExpr be a language of type language, and let Expr be a language of value expressions. Also suppose that $[\![\_]\!]$ produces the semantic meaning of either type or value expressions[3].

In our case, the natural type equivalence is the same as the standard equality of sets. The consequences for the notion of type checking that this imposes can be stated as follows:-

$$\forall v \in \text{Expr}, t \in \text{TyExpr} \cdot (v : t) \Leftrightarrow [\![v]\!] \in [\![t]\!]$$

$$\forall t_1, t_2 \in \text{TyExpr} \cdot (t_1 \equiv_T t_2) \Leftrightarrow ([\![t_1]\!] = [\![t_2]\!])$$

$$\forall v \in \text{Expr}, t_1, t_2 \in \text{TyExpr} \cdot (v : t_1) \wedge (t_1 \equiv_T t_2) \Rightarrow (v : t_2)$$

Because of the set-theoretical nature of types in this model, there is also a natural notion of subtype, denoted as $\_\preceq\_$, corresponding to that of set-theoretical subset. This may be defined by the following:-

$$\forall t_1, t_2 \in \text{TyExpr} \cdot t_1 \preceq t_2 \Leftrightarrow [\![t_1]\!] \subseteq [\![t_2]\!] \tag{52}$$

---

[3]The lack of precision in and the ambiguity of the $[\![]\!]$ notation is not significant here, since types and values are not mixed.

This has the following consequence for type checking:-

$$\forall v \in \text{Expr} \cdot \forall t_1, t_2 \in \text{TyExpr} \cdot (v : t_1) \wedge (t_1 \preceq t_2) \Rightarrow (v : t_2) \tag{53}$$

by the monotonicity of subset inclusion.

The semantics of VDM's type union should therefore correspond to set-theoretical union in the semantic space, and which has the following consequences:-

$$(A \mid B) \mid C = A \mid (B \mid C)$$
$$A \mid B = B \mid A$$
$$A \mid A = A$$
$$(A \subseteq B) \Leftrightarrow A \mid B = B$$

All of these semantic relations have an impact upon the complexity of practical type-checking; the computed type checking relation should simulate the semantic type checking relation specified above.

6.3 Type semantics in $\overline{U}$ and in $\text{Sub}(\overline{U})$

A type semantics with respect to $\overline{U}$ does not take type invariants into account; these are considered only when the type semantics is taken with respect to $\text{Sub}(\overline{U})$. Note that the family $\overline{U}$ is contained within $\text{Sub}(\overline{U})$. However, we also have that, by the definition of $\text{Sub}(\overline{U})$, every type in $\text{Sub}(\overline{U})$ is contained in some type in $\overline{U}$. Hence, $\overline{U}$ is an "approximation" to $\text{Sub}(\overline{U})$ in that type expressions interpreted in $\overline{U}$ will contain more values than if it had been interpreted in the latter.

More formally, by subscripting the semantic function $[\![\,]\!]$ with the space that interpretation is taken with respect to, we have that:-

$$\forall t \in \text{TyExpr} \cdot [\![t]\!]_{\text{Sub}(\overline{U})} \subseteq [\![t]\!]_{\overline{U}} \tag{54}$$

Note that this relationship is *anti-monotonic*; this is due to the fact that type equivalence relative to $\text{Sub}(\overline{U})$ is finer than the corresponding equivalence relative to $\overline{U}$.

For example, consider the following VDM type definitions:-

$$\text{Even} = \text{Nat0}$$
$$\text{where inv-}Even(n) \triangleq (n \bmod 2) = 0$$
$$\text{Odd} = \text{Nat0}$$
$$\text{where inv-}Odd(n) \triangleq (n \bmod 2) = 1$$

When interpreted with respect to $\overline{U}$, both type definitions equate the VDM types Even and Odd. But when interpreted with respect to $\text{Sub}(\overline{U})$, their meanings are the sets of even and odd numbers as appropriate and so are disjoint.

Because of this relationship between $\overline{U}$ and $\mathbf{Sub}(\overline{U})$, if an expression is badly typed with respect to $\overline{U}$ it is certainly badly typed with respect to $\mathbf{Sub}(\overline{U})$. Conversely, if an expression is well typed with respect to $\mathbf{Sub}(\overline{U})$, then it is also well typed with respect to $\overline{U}$. More formally, we have that, for any $v \in \text{Expr}, t \in \text{TyExpr}$:-

$$[\![v]\!] \notin [\![t]\!]_{\overline{U}} \Rightarrow [\![v]\!] \notin [\![t]\!]_{\mathbf{Sub}(\overline{U})}$$
$$[\![v]\!] \in [\![t]\!]_{\mathbf{Sub}(\overline{U})} \Rightarrow [\![v]\!] \in [\![t]\!]_{\overline{U}}$$

Type checking with respect to $\overline{U}$ broadly corresponds to structural data type checking in modern programming languages. Type checking with respect to $\mathbf{Sub}(\overline{U})$ involves checking that certain logical predicates are satisfied by given values. This kind of checking appears to broadly correspond to the verification of statements in Hoare like program logics, and is formally undecideable in the general case. Hence, any checking program for such conditions will probably have to make use of general purpose theorem proving techniques.

However the task of type checking with respect to $\mathbf{Sub}(\overline{U})$ can be broken down into a couple of stages, as follows:-

1. Type check with respect to $\overline{U}$. This will filter out a number of simple errors, such as applying a function to the wrong number of arguments, or assuming that a record has fields it does not possess.

2. Generate "proof obligations" corresponding to the invariant's that expressions have to satisfy, including pre and post conditions of functions and operations. The proofs of these formulae clearly depends upon the definitions of identifiers in scope; these definitions act as assumptions from which the formulae can be derived.

This second phase is not a purely automatic process, since correctness will depend upon strong, inductive properties of data types in general. Even so, strategies are known that can solve many of the proof obligations that arise in practice. User programmable proof assistants (such as LCF, Boyer-Moore and AFFIRM) that possess facilities for sophisticated user guidance could be of practical use in performing this kind of checking.

7 Conclusions and summary.

A rich, set-theoretical notion of type suitable for computing applications is given. Specific families of sets and Scott domains, called type universes, are introduced to precisely characterise those collections of values that may serve as types.

It has been informally argued that the two set-theoretical type universes, $\overline{U}$ and $\mathbf{Sub}(\overline{U})$ together with the domain-theoretical type universe $\underline{SU}$ are adequate for giving semantics to the VDM metalanguage for software specification.

The general impact of this type model for VDM specifications can be summarised as follows:-

- Data types are taken to be (usually infinite) collections of values belonging to $\overline{U}$(or Sub($\overline{U}$)). Since type universes are closed under the formation of the appropriate fixed points, set theoretical data types can be recursively constructed.

- All values belonging to sets in $\overline{U}$(and hence also Sub($\overline{U}$)) are *finitely generated*. This means that each value can be *named* by some ground expression of finite size.

- Arbitrary partial functions and other values whose denotation is either "infinite" are not values belonging to standard set-theoretical types. Scott universes consisting of Scott domains (based upon $\overline{U}$) are constructed to "house" these entities.

- The type equivalence implied by the use of the set theoretical type universes $\overline{U}$and Sub($\overline{U}$) is extensional and corresponds to the usual equality between sets. For example, if $A = B$ and $B = C$ then $A = C$ and also seq $A =$ seq $B =$ seq C.

  The effect of "name" equivalence can be easily obtained by explicit use of the tagging operator "::".

- Record types are included in this model; record values are mappings from field names to values belonging to the corresponding field type. Record values belonging to a particular record type must have fielde that conform to the specified field types. However, fields not mentioned in the field type are not constrained.

- There is a natural notion of *subtype* corresponding to the usual set-theoretical subset relationship. Hence, this relation is a partial ordering, possessing consequences for the equality on types such as if $A \subseteq B$ and $B \subseteq A$ then $A = B$.

- Optional types are defined to be opt$A = A \cup \{\underline{\text{NIL VALUE}}\}$. This has the immeadiate consequence that opt(opt$A$) = opt$A$.

- The semantics of type parametric polymorphism is made easier by having a closed collection of data types over which type parameters may range. Polymorphic functions are dependently typed functions from types to function's belonging to the appropriate instance of the function type.

8   Acknowledgements.

I would like to thank P.Aczel, H.Barringer, A.Blickle, W.T.Harwood, B.T.Denvir, C.B.Jones, T.Nipkow and J.E.Stoy for helpful remarks and useful criticism.

Many thanks to Julie Hibbs for typing the original version of this paper using the VUWRITER word processing package. This version was prepared using the LaTeX document preparation system.

This paper is based upon an internal technical report written while seconded to the University of Manchester by Standard Telecommunication Laboratories Ltd between September 1983 and January 1985 (see [Monahan]).

Appendix

A   Basic Set Theory.

All of the constructions in the paper are given within a "naive" set theory; that is, a rigorous, but informal, theory of arbitrary sets. It is widely accepted (amongst logicians) that this naive theory of sets can be formalised in several ways. One of the best known axiomatisations of sets is known as Zermelo-Fraenkel set theory (or ZF). It has been shown, in practice, that this theory is powerful enough for giving a set-theoretical account of much of classical mathematics, and hence adequate for our needs.

The remainder of this section will give a brief, whirlwind tour of set theory according to Zermelo-Fraenkel. Let $\Psi[x]$ be any first order formula that may contain free occurrences of the variable x. Assume that A, B and C stand for any sets; the binary predicate $\in$ stands for set membership.

Extensionality Principle.	$\forall A, B \cdot (A = B) \Leftrightarrow \forall x \cdot (x \in A) \Leftrightarrow (x \in B)$
Empty Set Postulate.	$\forall x \cdot (x \notin \emptyset)$
Pairing Postulate.	$\forall z \cdot (z \in \{x, y\}) \Leftrightarrow (z = x) \vee (z = y)$
Union Postulate.	$\forall z \cdot (z \in \bigcup A) \Leftrightarrow \exists y \in A \cdot (z \in y)$
Set Comprehension Schema.	$\forall z \cdot (z \in \{x \in A \vert \Psi[x]\}) \Leftrightarrow (z \in A) \wedge \Psi[z/x]$
Power Set Postulate.	$\forall z \cdot (z \in P(A)) \Leftrightarrow (z \subseteq A)$
Infinity Postulate.	$\exists N \cdot (\emptyset \in N) \wedge (\forall a \cdot a \in N \Rightarrow S(a) \in N)$
Foundation Principle.	$\forall x \cdot (x \neq \emptyset) \Rightarrow (\exists z \cdot (z \in x) \wedge ((z \cap x) = \emptyset))$
Axiom of Choice.	$\forall A, B \cdot (A \trianglelefteq B) \vee (B \trianglelefteq A)$

Figure 2: Axioms for Zermelo-Fraenkel set theory

The notation "$\{x\}$" is used to abbreaviate "$\{x,x\}$". The usual notation for binary union, $- \cup -$, is defined by:-

$$(A \cup B) = \bigcup\{A, B\}$$

The subset relation, $- \subseteq -$, is defined by the axiom:-

$$(A \subseteq B) \Leftrightarrow (\forall x \cdot x \in A \Rightarrow x \in B)$$

A successor function, S, can be explicitly defined by the simple axiom:-

$$\forall x \cdot S(x) = x \cup \{x\}$$

The cartesian product of two sets A, B is defined by:-

$$A \times B \triangleq \{(a, b) | (a \in A) \wedge (b \in B)\}$$

where the pairing operator $-, -$ satisfies the property:-

$$\forall a, b, c, d \cdot (a, b) = (c, d) \Leftrightarrow (a = c) \wedge (b = d)$$

The set of all binary relation graphs between sets A, B is defined as:-

$\forall$ A, B. $\forall$ r .
$\quad r \in (A \leftrightarrow B) \Leftrightarrow r \subseteq P(A \times B)$

The domain and range operators for a binary relation is defined as follows:-

$\forall$ A,B . $\forall$ r$\in$(A$\leftrightarrow$B) .
$\quad \partial_0(r) \triangleq \{ x \in A \mid \exists y. \ y \in B \wedge (x,y) \in r \}$
$\quad \partial_1(r) \triangleq \{ y \in B \mid \exists x. \ x \in A \wedge (x,y) \in r \}$

The set of all functions between sets A,B can be defined as follows:-

$\forall$ A, B. $\forall$ f .
$\quad f \in (A \rightarrow B) \Leftrightarrow$
$\quad (f \in (A \leftrightarrow B) \wedge$
$\quad (\forall a_1 \in A. \exists b_1, b_2 \in B. \ ((a, b_1) \in f \wedge (a, b_2) \in f) \Rightarrow b_1 = b_2)$

The size ordering $- \trianglelefteq -$ can then be defined by:-

$$(A \trianglelefteq B) \Leftrightarrow (\exists f \cdot (f \in (A \rightarrow B)) \wedge \forall x, y \in A \cdot f(x) = f(y) \Rightarrow x = y$$

B   Set operators.

Let A, B be any sets.

Finite Sequence Operator.

$$S(A) \triangleq \bigcup_{n \in \omega} (\{1, \cdots, n\} \to A)$$

Finite Set Operator.

$$\mathcal{F}(A) \triangleq \{S \in P(A)| \, |S| \in \omega\}$$

Finite Map Operator.

$$M(A, B) \triangleq \bigcup_{S \in \mathcal{F}(A)} (S \to B)$$

Finite Record Operator.

Let F stand for any family of sets.

$$\forall \, rt \in M(\text{Atom}, F).$$
$$\mathcal{R}(F)(rt) \triangleq$$
$$\{ \, m \in M(\text{Atom}, \bigcup F) \mid \partial_0(rt) \subseteq \partial_0(m) \wedge (\forall at \in \partial_0(rt) \, . \, m(at) \in rt(at)) \, \}$$

C   Basic Domain Theory

A *domain* $< D, \sqsubseteq_D, \bot_D >$ is a structure consisting of a carrier, D, together with a (ω-)chain complete partial ordering $\sqsubseteq_D$ and a least element, denoted by $\bot_D$. In more advanced work on domains, stronger requirements are place upon the structure of domains such as ω-*algebraicity* and *consistent completeness* (see [Winskel, Larsen]). The chain completeness property is stated as follows:-

$$\forall \, s \in D^\omega.$$
$$(\forall i \in \omega. \, s_i \sqsubseteq_D s_{i+1}) \Rightarrow \exists x \in D \, .(\forall i \in \omega \, . \, s_i \sqsubseteq_D x) \wedge (\forall y \in D.(\forall i \in \omega \, . \, s_i \sqsubseteq_D y) \Rightarrow x \sqsubseteq_D y)$$

The value x asserted above to exist is called the *least upper bound* of the sequence $< s_i >_{i \in \omega}$, and is conventionally denoted by $\bigsqcup_{i \in \omega} s_i$ (or even by $\bigsqcup s_i$). Sequences $< s_i >_{i \in \omega}$ such that $\forall i \in \omega. s_i \sqsubseteq_D s_{i+1}$ are called ω-*chains*. In the following, assume that each of D, D_1, D_2 stand for domains.

Scott Continuous Function Space.

Let $f: D_1 \rightarrow D_2$ (i.e a function upon the appropriate carrier sets), and define:-

$\quad$ f is-monotonic $\Leftrightarrow \forall\; x,y \in D_1\; .\; x \sqsubseteq_{D1} y \Rightarrow f(x) \sqsubseteq_{D2} f(y)$

and then

$\quad$ f is-continuous $\Leftrightarrow \forall s \in D_1^{\omega}.\; (\forall i \in \omega.\; s_i \sqsubseteq_{D1} s_{i+1}) \Rightarrow f(\bigsqcup_{i \in \omega} s_i) = \bigsqcup_{i \in \omega} f(s_i)$

The Scott continuous function space is defined to be the partial order with carrier:-

$\quad [D_1 \rightarrow D_2] \triangleq \{\; f \in (D_1 \rightarrow D_2) \mid f \text{ is-continuous} \}$

with the "pointwise" ordering given by:-

$\quad f \sqsubseteq g \Leftrightarrow (\forall x \in D_1\; .\; f(x) \sqsubseteq g(x))$

and where the least element is the function specified by:-

$\quad \lambda x \in D_1\; .\; \bot_{D_2}$

It can be shown that the function space $[D_1 \rightarrow D_2]$ forms a domain whenever D_2 is a domain.

Full Cartesian Product.

The *full cartesian product* of domains D_1 and D_2 has, as carrier, the cartesian product of the corresponding carriers; it is ordered "componentwise" in the following way:-

$\quad \forall\; a_1, a_2 \in D_1,\; b_1,b_2 \in D_2\; .\; (a_1,b_1) \sqsubseteq (a_2,b_2) \Leftrightarrow (a_1 \sqsubseteq a_2) \wedge (b_1 \sqsubseteq b_2)$

The least element in this partial order is the pair $< \bot_{D_1}, \bot_{D_2} >$. Assuming that D_1 and D_2 are both domains, the cartesian product with this ordering can also be shown to be a domain.

Bekic Maps.

Let D be a domain and let $F = A_{\bot}$ be an arbitrary *flat* domain. Let S be any *finite* subset of the set A (i.e not including $\bot$), and give $(S \rightarrow D)$ the "pointwise" ordering as in the case of the Scott continuous function space. Note that if S_1 and S_2 are different finite subsets of A then $(S_1 \to D) \cap (S_2 \to D) = \emptyset$. Moreover, note that $(\{\} \to D) = \{\emptyset\}$, containing the *empty* function, and is well-defined. The Bekic Maps can now be defined as:-

$$(F \xrightarrow{B} D) \triangleq \{\lambda x \in F \cdot \bot_D\} \cup \bigcup \{(S \to D) | S \in \mathcal{F}(F \setminus \{\bot_F\}\}$$

This is ordered as follows:-

$\forall\ m_1, m_2 \in (F \xrightarrow{B} D)$.

$\quad m_1 \sqsubseteq m_2 \Leftrightarrow (m_1 = \lambda x \in F.\bot_F)\ \vee$

$\qquad (\exists S \in \mathcal{F}(F \setminus \{\bot_F\} \cdot \{m_1, m_2\} \subseteq (S \to D) \wedge (\forall x \in S.m_1(x) \sqsubseteq m_2(x)))$

Bekic maps m_1 is less than m_2 whenever m_1 is the completly undefined function, or both have exactly the same domain of definition, and are ordered pointwise. Clearly, the least element is the undefined function $\lambda x \in F \cdot \bot_D$.

References

[Bjorner,Jones]

D.Bjorner, C.B.Jones, *Formal Specification and Software Development*, Prentice Hall, 1982

[Blikle]

A.Blikle, *A metalanguage for Naive Denotational Semantics*,
Progetto Finalizzato Informatica, C.N.R. Progetto Pl CNET 104, Pisa, 1984.

[Cohn]

P.M.Cohn, *Universal Algebra*, D.Reidel Pub. Co., 1980.

[Devlin]

K.J.Devlin, *Fundamentals of Contemporary Set Theory*,
Universitext, Springer-Verlag, 1979.

[Enderton]

H.Enderton, *Elements of Set Theory* Academic Press, 1975

[Goldblatt]

R.Goldblatt, *Topoi:The Categorical Analysis of Logic*,
Studies in Logic, Vol 98, North Holland Pub. Co., Amsterdam, 1979

[Halmos]

P.Halmos, *Naive Set Theory*, Springer-Verlag, 1979

[Jones]

C.B.Jones, *Systematic Software Development using VDM*, Prentice Hall, 1986

[Monahan]

B.Q.Monahan, *A type model for VDM*,
Internal technical report, STL Ltd/University of Manchester, July 1984

[Milner]

R.Milner, *A theory of type polymorphism in programming*,
J.Computer and System Sciences, Vol 17, p348-375, 1978.

[Schmidt]

D.A.Schmidt, *Denotational Semantics: A methodology for language development*, Allyn and Bacon, 198

[Scott]

D.S.Scott, *Domains for Denotational Semantics*, ICALP' 82, Aarhus, Denmark, July, 1982

[Stoy]

J.E.Stoy, *Denotational Semantics*, The MIT Press, 1977

[Winskel,Larsen]

G.Winskel, K.G.Larsen, *Using Information Systems to solve Recursive Domain Equations effectively*
Technical report 51, University of Cambridge Computer Laboratory, 1985.

A FORMAL DESCRIPTION OF OBJECT-ORIENTED PROGRAMMING USING VDM

Cydney Minkowitz* and Peter Henderson

Computing Science,University of Stirling,Stirling,FK9 4LA, Scotland

* also STC Technology Ltd., STL North West, Newcastle under Lyme, Staffordshire

1. Introduction

In this paper we present a formal definition of an object-oriented environment using the specification language VDM [1]. Object-oriented architectures have been of considerable importance in the Artificial Intelligence community [2,3,4] and are of increasing importance in a wider software engineering context [5]. The principal concepts to be defined are those of inheritance and message passing. Smalltalk [5] has a particular architecture which has gained immense popularity. Here we present an environment derived from the Smalltalk architecture, which is simpler but sufficiently powerful to support real applications and has the merit of having been given a concise formal specification.

We begin by giving an example of using an object-oriented class hierarchy to describe a simple network of nodes containing data. Then we present a VDM specification of a class hierarchy with a particular model of inheritance. We discuss the facility of passing messages between objects in the class hierarchy as a means of maintaining constraints on the data in our example network. Equipped with the full power of inheritance and message passing, we give examples of propagating constraints through the network in the styles of demand and data driven programming. When presenting the specifications we will assume that the reader has prior knowledge of VDM.

Finally, we discuss how the use of formal specification has allowed us to iterate upon the design of this particular object-oriented facility and how we have validated the design by turning the specification into a prototype using the *me too* method [6,7]. The software specified in this paper has eventually been implemented in LISP and is being used for the development of some business applications. We comment briefly on these matters.

2. Object Hierarchies and Inheritance

Consider the design of a simple database consisting of a hierarchy of *nodes* where each node will contain an integer value. A node is either a *leaf*, or a *root*, in which case it has two children which are other nodes in the hierarchy. A description of the types of these nodes is given in the following VDM specification.

$$Node = Leaf \cup Root$$

$$Leaf \; :: \; value: \mathbf{Z}$$

$$Root \; :: \; value: \mathbf{Z}$$

$$left: Node$$

$$right: Node$$

We have modelled *Leaf* and *Root* as composite types, which both have an integer value part, but *Root* has, in addition, *left* and *right* parts of type *Node*.

The above specification is structured in order to distinguish between nodes that are leaves and nodes that are roots by specifying that information which is specific to each type. In a sense, however, we have overspecified the types in that the information about integer values belongs to the more general type *Node* - not its two subtypes. A better structure for the information is suggested by the type hierarchy illustrated in Figure 1.

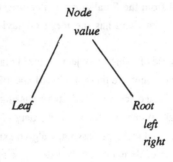

Figure 1 - A type hierarchy

Object-oriented architectures allow us to design such a type hierarchy. The items in this hierarchy are called *objects*. The objects appearing at lower levels in the hierarchy are more specialized than, and are said to *inherit* information from, those objects at higher levels.

Imagine that we have such an architecture in which we can embed our database design. Figure 2 is a pictorial description of the basic objects of the database. Each object has a name denoted by a string prefixed with the symbol '^', e.g. ^*Node*. Each object is a specialization of an object, which we refer to as its *class*, and may have its own local information. We depict the object as having a tag which contains the name of its class and a list of *associations* pertaining to its individual *attributes*. For example, ^*Root* has class ^*Node* and associations that relate values to the attributes *"left"* and *"right"*, which refer to its left and right subnodes respectively.

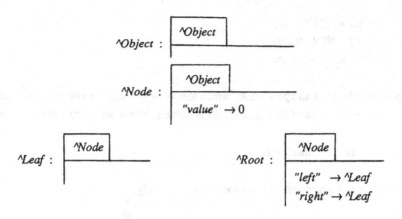

Figure 2. Database of Basic Objects

The class of the object *^Node* is *^Object* which is the name of the object that is the root of all others - that is, it is the most general of all objects. The class of *^Object* is itself. *^Node* includes an association that relates the attribute *"value"* to 0. This information assigns a *default* value to all nodes. Similarly, we have assigned the default value *^Leaf* to the attributes *"left"* and *"right"* in *^Root*. That is to say that the default root degenerates to having a single leaf at its left and right subnodes. This facility for declaring defaults is another feature of object-oriented programming. We will see later how objects can acquire their own specific data (see Figure 3).

Now imagine that we are provided with the operations *INITIAL-DB*, *NEW* and *AT-PUT* for setting up the database. The operation *INITIAL-DB* has no arguments and will establish an empty database containing the root object *^Object*. The operation *NEW* is used to introduce a new object into the database. It is given an argument which is the name of the class of the new object. The operation *AT-PUT* is used to assign local information to an object. Its arguments are the name of the object concerned, the name of the attribute to hold the information and the value given to that attribute. The following sequence shows how these operations are used to set up the database in Figure 2. We have used what we hope is a fairly obvious, single assignment language.

```
INITIAL-DB() ;
^Node = NEW(^Object) ;
AT-PUT(^Node,"value",0) ;
^Leaf = NEW(^Node) ;
^Root = NEW (^Node) ;
AT-PUT(^Root,"left",^Leaf) ;
AT-PUT (^Root,"right",^Leaf)
```

We can use *NEW* to introduce some data for leaves and roots as follows.

$$^\wedge L1 = NEW(^\wedge Leaf) ;$$
$$^\wedge L2 = NEW(^\wedge Leaf) ;$$
$$^\wedge R \ \ = NEW(^\wedge Root)$$

Suppose we also have an operation AT which allows us to retrieve an object's local information. Its arguments are the names of the object and the attribute in which we are interested. Then we have

$$AT(^\wedge L1,"value") = 0,$$

where $^\wedge L1$ inherits the zero default value for nodes. Similarly,

$$AT(^\wedge L2,"value") = 0 \ , \ AT(^\wedge R,"value") = 0 \ ,$$
$$AT(^\wedge R,"left") = \ ^\wedge Leaf \ , \ AT(^\wedge R,"right") = \ ^\wedge Leaf.$$

Of course we can override these default values using $AT\text{-}PUT$ in the following sequence of operations.

$$AT\text{-}PUT(^\wedge L1,"value",3) ;$$
$$AT\text{-}PUT(^\wedge L2,"value",4) ;$$
$$AT\text{-}PUT(^\wedge R,"value",7) \ ;$$
$$AT\text{-}PUT(^\wedge R,"left",^\wedge L1) \ ;$$
$$AT\text{-}PUT(^\wedge R,"right",^\wedge L2)$$

Figure 3 shows the rest of the data set up in the object hierarchy by this sequence of operations.

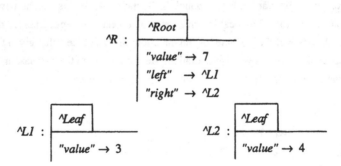

Figure 3. Example Data for Nodes

Now if we inspect these objects we have

$$AT(^\wedge L1,"value") = 3 \ , \ AT(^\wedge L2,"value") = 4 \ , \ AT(^\wedge R,"value") = 7 \ ,$$
$$AT(^\wedge R,"left") = \ ^\wedge L1 \ , \ AT(^\wedge R,"right") = \ ^\wedge L2 \ .$$

3. Specification of an Object Hierarchy

We now give a VDM specification of the types and the operations of the object hierarchy described in the previous section. The types we want to model are object hierarchies (*Db*), objects and their names (*Object* and *ObjectName*), and the associations containing an object's local information. The following mathematical types are used to model these.

$Object$ :: $class$: $ObjectName$

               $associations$: map $Attribute$ to $Value$

Db = map $ObjectName$ to $Object$

where

$inv\text{-}Db(db)$ $\triangle$

    $^\wedge Object \in$ dom db $\wedge$

      $\forall$ $on \in$ dom $db \cdot (class\,(db(on)) \in$ dom db $\wedge$ $inherits\text{-}from\text{-}^\wedge Object(db,on))$

and

    $inherits\text{-}from\text{-}^\wedge Object$: $Db \times Objectname \rightarrow \mathbf{B}$

    $inherits\text{-}from\text{-}^\wedge Object(db,on)$ $\triangle$

      $class(db(on)) = {^\wedge Object}$ $\vee$ $inherits\text{-}from\text{-}^\wedge Object(db,class(db(on)))$

Object is a composite type consisting of a *class* part, which refers to the class of the object, and an *associations* part, which refers to its local state. This information is represented as a map from attributes (*Attribute*) to values (*Value*). The type *Value*, as seen from the examples of the previous section, may contain object names as well as values of other types (including operations, as we will see in the examples of the next section).

Db is represented simply as a map from object names to objects. There is an invariant on hierarchies that specifies that the class of each object is contained in the domain of the hierarchy and that each object inherits from the root object $^\wedge Object$, which is defined to be the global constant

    $^\wedge Object$: $ObjectName$.

The operation *INITIAL-DB* is used to establish an initial database containing the root object $^\wedge Object$. We will also make it contain another object whose class is $^\wedge Object$ and whose name is given by the following global constant.

    $^\wedge undefined$: $ObjectName$

It is provided for use in the error cases which will arise in the definitions of other operations.

The definition of *INITIAL-DB* is given below

INITIAL-DB()

ext wr *db:Db*

post *db* = { ^*Object* ↦ *mk-Object(*^*Object*,{}) , ^*undefined* ↦ *mk-Object(*^*Object*,{}) }

This operation creates two objects of class ^*Object* with empty associations.

The operation *AT-PUT* updates the associations of object *on* with the attribute-value pair (a , v). It states a precondition that *on* is contained in the domain of the hierarchy. This precondition will reappear in the other operations.

AT-PUT(on:ObjectName,a:Attribute,v:Value)

ext wr *db:Db*

pre *on* ∈ dom *db*

post *db* = $\overline{db}$ † { *on* ↦ *mk-Object(class(*$\overline{db}$*(on))) , associations(*$\overline{db}$*(on))* † { *a* ↦ *v* }) }

The operation *AT* returns the value *(ans)* for an attribute *(a)* of an object *(on)*. It invokes an *inheritance* mechanism to search for it if necessary. It looks in *on*'s local associations to see if they contain *a*. If not, it searches for a value for *a* by recursively looking up *on*'s class hierarchy. It knows it has failed in the search if it has not found the attribute when it has reached the root object ^*Object*. In that case, it returns ^*undefined*.

AT(on:ObjectName,a:Attribute) ans:Value

ext rd *db:Db*

pre *on* ∈ dom *db*

post (*a* ∈ dom *associations(db(on))* ∧

      ans = *associations(db(on))(a)*) ∨

(*a* ∉ dom *associations (db(on))* ∧

    ((*on* = ^*Object* ∧ *ans* = ^*undefined*) ∨

      (*on* ≠ ^*Object* ∧ *post-AT(class(db(on)),a,db,ans)*)))

The final operation is *NEW*. *NEW* introduces a new object of a given class *(on)* into the hierarchy. It returns an unused object name and maps that name onto an object with empty associations.

NEW(on:ObjectName) ptr:ObjectName

ext wr *db:Db*

pre *on* ∈ dom *db*

post *ptr* ∉ dom $\overline{db}$ ∧ *db* = $\overline{db}$ ∪ { *ptr* ↦ *mk-Object(on,{})* }

4. Local Operations and Message Passing

The operations *NEW, AT-PUT* and *AT* allow us to create, update and query objects respectively. However, we want to do more with our database than these operations provide. For example, we want to specify constraints on the database, such as 'one may only assign a value to a leaf', and 'the value of a root is equal to the sum of its left and right subnodes'.

Consider our original VDM specification of the node hierarchy again and how we might extend the design to specify these constraints. We might maintain them by defining the following operations.

PUT-VALUE(i:$\mathbb{Z}$)

ext wr *n: Node*

post ($\overleftarrow{n}$ ∈ *Leaf* ∧ *n* = μ($\overleftarrow{n}$,*value* ↦ *i*)) ∨

($\overleftarrow{n}$ ∈ *Root* ∧ *n* = $\overleftarrow{n}$)   ;

GET-VALUE() ans: $\mathbb{Z}$

ext rd *n: Node*

post (*n* ∈ *Leaf* ∧ *ans* = *value(n)*) ∨

(*n* ∈ *Root* ∧ ∃*i,j* ∈ $\mathbb{Z}$ ·

(*post-GET-VALUE(left(n),i)* ∧

post-GET-VALUE(right(n),j) ∧

ans = *i* + *j*))

PUT-VALUE assigns a value (*i*) to a node (*n*) only if *n* is a leaf. *GET-VALUE* returns the value stored in a node (*n*) if *n* is a leaf, or the sum of *n*'s left and right subnodes if *n* is a root.

In order to know what action to perform on *n* these two operations have to carry out a case analysis on the type of the node to which it refers. An object-oriented view of the world would have each object possess its own knowledge about how it reacts to an operation. Thus, as well as having its own local data values, an object also contains its own local operations. An operation local to a leaf object that carries out its part of the operation *PUT-VALUE* is the operation *VALUE!* defined as follows:

VALUE!(self:ObjectName,i:**Z**)

ext wr *db:Db*

post *post-AT-PUT(self,"value",i,$\overline{db}$,db)*

When a leaf is told to assign an integer (*i*) to its attribute *"value"* it applies *VALUE!* on itself. The requirement is accomplished by the operation *AT-PUT* which is applied to an argument (*self*) which refers to the leaf.

We store an operation in an object by using *AT-PUT*. So we can store the operation *VALUE!* in the generic leaf object *^Leaf* alongside the attribute *"value!"* as follows.

AT-PUT(^Leaf,"value!",VALUE!)

where

VALUE!(self:ObjectName,i:**Z**)

ext wr *db:Db*

post *post-AT-PUT(self,"value",i,$\overline{db}$,db)*

However, we have not yet specified how that operation is invoked. The usual mechanism for doing this is to pass a *message* to the object. For example, if *^L1* is a leaf, we could tell *^L1* to apply the operation *VALUE!* on itself and the argument 3, say. We will adopt this idiom by defining operations *TELL*, *ASK* and *SEND* which have that effect. First we will give an example of their use. In the next section we will give a precise specification of them.

The arguments to *TELL* are the name of the receiver of the message, the attribute used to select the operation to be performed and a sequence of arguments that will be given to that operation. *TELL* will always perform some side-effect on the database. To give an example of how it is applied we tell *^L1* to assign 3 to its attribute *"value"* as follows.

TELL(^L1,"value!",[3])

A receiver will only respond to a message if it pertains to an operation that it contains or can inherit. If this is not the case, a call of *TELL* has no effect on the database. Thus, by leaving root objects without an operation for changing their values, the first constraint on the database can be satisfied.

Of course we will want to send messages to objects that will not alter their state but will merely retrieve data. For these we define an operation *ASK*. *ASK* has the same form as *TELL* but, instead of altering the database, it simply returns a value of interest. As an example of its use, suppose we add two operations to *^Leaf* and *^Root* (which divide up the task of the operation *GET-VALUE* defined above), respectively,

$AT\text{-}PUT(^\wedge Leaf,"value?",VALUE?)$

where

$VALUE?(self:ObjectName)\ ans:\mathbb{Z}$

ext rd $db:Db$

post $post\text{-}AT(self,"value",db,ans)$;

$AT\text{-}PUT(^\wedge Root,"value?",VALUE?)$

where

$VALUE?(self:ObjectName)\ ans:\mathbb{Z}$

ext rd $db:Db$

post $\exists l,r \in ObjectName \cdot \exists i,j \in \mathbb{Z} \cdot$

$\qquad (post\text{-}AT(self,"left",db,l) \wedge$

$\qquad\quad post\text{-}AT(self,"right",db,r) \wedge$

$\qquad\quad post\text{-}ASK(l,"value?",[],db,i) \wedge$

$\qquad\quad post\text{-}ASK(r,"value?",[],db,j) \wedge$

$\qquad\quad ans = i + j)$

And suppose we apply the following sequence of operations

$^\wedge L1 = NEW(^\wedge Leaf) ;$
$^\wedge L2 = NEW(^\wedge Leaf) ;$
$^\wedge R\ = NEW(^\wedge Root) ;$
$ATPUT(^\wedge R,"left",^\wedge L1) ;$
$ATPUT(^\wedge R,"right",^\wedge L2) ;$
$TELL(^\wedge L1,"value!",[3]) ;$
$TELL(^\wedge L2,"value!",[4])$

The leaves and root will respond differently to ASK by applying separate operations in order to compute their answers, and so

$ASK(^\wedge L1,"value?",[]) = AT(^\wedge L1,"value") = 3$

and

$ASK(^\wedge R,"value?",[]) = AT(^\wedge L1,"value") + AT(^\wedge L2,"value") = 7$

And we see that the second constraint on the database is satisfied.

Eventually, we shall want to send messages that both update a database and return a value. For these we will define an operation *SEND*. We shall see examples of the use of *SEND* later. But first we define these new, message passing operations.

5. Specification of Message Passing

The definition of the message passing operation *TELL* is given below. Its arguments are the name of the receiver (*rec*), the selector of an operation (*sel*) and arguments to that operation (*args*). We expect the effect of applying *TELL* is that an operation will be applied to *rec* and therefore change the state of the database. We use *AT* to find the operation stored in *rec* at *sel*. *AT* will either find the operation in *rec* itself or in one of the objects in its class hierarchy. We hope that the result of *AT* is an operation (*OP*). We use the predicate *is-operation* to determine whether *OP* is an operation. If it is not it will either be a data value or *^undefined*. If it is not an operation, then the message is not understood by *rec* and the database is unaffected. If it is, the operation will be applied to *rec* and the values in *args*. This amounts to saying in our definition that the predicate *post-OP* will have the form *post-OP(rec,arg1,...,argn,$\overline{db}$,db)*. (Note that we assume in our definition that *OP*'s precondition is true.)

*TELL(rec:ObjectName,sel:Attribute,args:*seq of *Value)*

ext wr *db:Db*

pre *rec* ∈ dom *db*

post ∃*OP* ∈ *Value* ·

$$(post\text{-}AT(rec,sel,\overline{db},OP) \wedge$$

$$((is\text{-}operation(OP) \wedge apply\text{-}postcondition(OP,rec,args,\overline{db},db))) \vee$$

$$(\neg is\text{-}operation(OP) \wedge db = \overline{db})))$$

We need to be specific about the meaning of apply-postcondition. In the case of an operation invoked by *TELL*, we assume that it has been defined and stored in an object *^X* by the statement

AT-PUT(^X,"op",OP)

where

OP(self:ObjectName,arg1:Value,...,argn:Value)

ext wr *db:Db*

post . . .

In this case, by

   apply-postcondition(OP,rec,[arg1,...,argn],$\overline{db}$,db),

we mean *post-OP(rec,arg1,...,argn,$\overline{db}$,db).*

To understand the definition better, we see its effect for the application

$$TELL\ (^{\wedge}L1,"value!",[3])$$

by breaking it down into the following predicates, where we suppose *dbs* is the value of the database before the operation is applied, and *dbf* is its value after it is applied . Thus, we have

$$post\text{-}TELL(^{\wedge}L1,"value!",[3],dbs,dbf) \Rightarrow$$

$$post\text{-}AT(^{\wedge}L1,"value!",dbs,VALUE!) \wedge is\text{-}operation(VALUE!) \wedge post\text{-}VALUE!(^{\wedge}L1,3,dbs,dbf) \Rightarrow$$

$$post\text{-}AT\text{-}PUT(^{\wedge}L1,"value",3,dbs,dbf)$$

The operation *ASK* is used to invoke an operation, such as the one defined and stored in the object ^*Y* shown below, that does not affect the database but returns a value.

   AT-PUT(^Y,"op",OP)

   where

   OP(self:ObjectName,arg1:Value,...,argn:Value) ans:Value

   ext rd *db:Db*

   post . . .

The meaning of *ASK* is, then, given by

   *ASK(rec:ObjectName,sel:Attribute,args:*seq of *Value) ans:Value*

   ext rd *db:Db*

   pre *rec* ∈ dom *db*

   post ∃*OP* ∈ *Value*

           (*post-AT(rec,sel,db,OP)* ∧

               ((*is-operation(OP)* ∧ *apply-postcondition(OP,rec,args,db,ans)*) ∨

                   (¬ *is-operation(OP)* ∧ *ans = ^undefined*)))

In this case, by

   apply-postcondition(OP,rec,[arg1,...,argn],db,ans),

we mean *post-OP(rec,arg1,...,argn,db,ans).*

The operation *SEND* is used to invoke an operation, such as the one defined and stored in the object ^Z shown below, that both affects the database and returns a value.

AT-PUT(^Z,"op",OP)

where

OP(self:ObjectName,arg1:Value,...,argn:Value) ans: Value

ext wr *db:Db*

post . . .

Then the meaning of *SEND* is given by

*SEND(rec:ObjectName,sel:Attribute,args:*seq of *Value) ans:Value*

ext wr *db:Db*

pre *rec* ∈ dom *db*

post ∃*OP* ∈ *Value* ·

$\qquad$ (*post-AT(rec,sel,$\overleftarrow{db}$,OP)* ∧

$\qquad\qquad$ ((*is-operation(OP)* ∧ *apply-postcondition(OP,rec,args,$\overleftarrow{db}$,ans,db)*)) ∨

$\qquad\qquad$ (¬ *is-operation(OP)* ∧ *db* = $\overleftarrow{db}$ ∧ *ans* = *^undefined)*))

And, in this case, by

$\quad$ *apply-postcondition(OP,rec,[arg1,...,argn],$\overleftarrow{db}$,ans,db)*,

we mean *post-OP(rec,arg1,...,argn,$\overleftarrow{db}$,ans,db)*.

6. A Demand Driven Design

We have now equipped ourselves with an environment in which we can easily embed some fairly complicated database applications. The first design we present is of a *demand driven* system. To understand what we mean by this, consider the following example of its use. Suppose we have a database of the basic objects ^*Node,* ^*Leaf* and ^*Root* as before, except that we will now relax our first constraint and allow values to be assigned to roots as well as leaves. Therefore we elevate the status of the operation *VALUE!* to belong to the more general object ^*Node.* We also assign the operation *VALUE?* to ^*Node* so that it behaves in the same way for leaves and roots in returning their stored integer values.

AT-PUT(^Node,"value!",VALUE!)

where

VALUE!(self:ObjectName,i:$\mathbf{Z}$)

ext wr *db:Db*

post *post-AT-PUT(self,"value",i,$\overline{db}$,db)* ;

AT-PUT(^Node,"value?",VALUE?)

where

VALUE?(self:ObjectName) ans:Value

ext rd *db:Db*

post *post-AT(self,"value",db,ans)*

Suppose that *^Leaf* responds to the message *SEND(^Leaf,"new-value!",[i])* by creating a new leaf and assigning to its value an integer (*i*) ,and that *^Root* responds to the message *SEND(^Root,"left!right!",[l,r])* by creating a new root and assigning *l* and *r* to its left and right subnodes respectively, and that we , then, pass the following messages to them to set up the database shown in Figure 4.

^L1 = SEND(^Leaf,"new-value!",[3]) ;
^L2 = SEND(^Leaf,"new-value!",[4]) ;
^L3 = SEND(^Leaf,"new-value!",[5]) ;
^R1 = SEND(^Root,"left!right!",[^L1,^L2]) ;
^R2 = SEND(^Root,"left!right!",[^L2,^L3]) ;
^R3 = SEND(^Root,"left!right!",[^L1,^L3]) ;
^R4 = SEND(^Root,"left!right!",[^R1,^R2])

At this stage the values at the leaves in the database will have been assigned but not those at the roots. To see this, suppose when passed the message *ASK(r,"value-set?",[])*, the root *r* will answer true or false according to whether its value has or has not been set. Then

$$ASK(^R1,"value\text{-}set?",[]) = ASK(^R2,"value\text{-}set?",[]) =$$
$$ASK(^R3,"value\text{-}set?",[]) = ASK(^R4,"value\text{-}set?",[]) = \text{false} .$$

We still want the second constraint on the database to hold, so that the value of a root is the sum of the values of its left and right subnodes, and we want the system to maintain this property for us. It could do this by calculating the values for each of the roots when the database is established. But if in

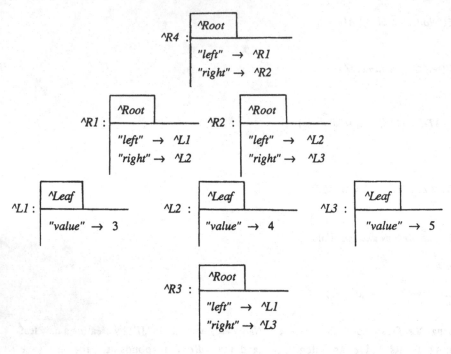

Figure 4. Example Data for Demand Driven Design

the end we are only interested in the values of a few of the roots, then this would be wasted effort. If this was to be the norm then we would be wiser to design a *demand driven* system which only calculates a root's value when it is required.

The *demand* side of our system is simulated by sending the message $TELL(n, "set\text{-}value", [])$, which tells a node to set its value. So, for example, if we apply

$$TELL(^\wedge R4, "set\text{-}value", []),$$

then

$$ASK(^\wedge R4, "value\text{-}set?", []) = \text{true}$$

and

$$ASK(^\wedge R4, "value?", []) = 16.$$

Since in calculating $^\wedge R4$'s value the system must also calculate those of $^\wedge R1$ and $^\wedge R2$, we expect the system to be clever enough to remember them, so that

$$ASK(^\wedge R1, "value\text{-}set?", []) = ASK(^\wedge R2, "value\text{-}set?", []) = \text{true}.$$

However, we still expect the following to hold.

$$ASK(^\wedge R3,"value\text{-}set?",[]) = \text{false}$$

To design the system we add some local operations to *^Leaf* and *^Root*. The operations *NEW-VALUE!* and *LEFT!RIGHT!* are used to set up the database, as we saw above.

AT-PUT(*^Leaf*,"*new-value!*",*NEW-VALUE!*)

where

NEW-VALUE!(self:ObjectName,i:$\mathbf{Z}$) ptr:ObjectName

ext wr *db:Db*

post $\exists db' \in Db \cdot$

      (*post-NEW(self,$\overline{db}$,ptr,db')* ∧

        post-TELL(ptr,"value!",[i],db',db))   ;

AT-PUT(*^Root*,"*left!right!*",*LEFT!RIGHT!*)

where

LEFT!RIGHT!(self:ObjectName,l:ObjectName,r:ObjectName) ptr:ObjectName

ext wr *db:Db*

post $\exists db',db'' \in Db \cdot$

      (*post-NEW(self,$\overline{db}$,ptr,db')* ∧

      post-AT-PUT(ptr,"left",l,db',db'') ∧

      post-AT-PUT(ptr,"right",r,db'',db))

The operation *VALUE-SET?* is added to *^Root* as a way of determining whether a root's value has been set. To help us with its definition, we add a special attribute *"set-flag"* to *^Root* whose default is false. The job of *VALUE-SET?* is simply to enquire of its object's flag.

AT-PUT(*^Root*,"*set-flag*",false) ;

AT-PUT (*^Root*,"*value-set?*",*VALUE-SET?*)

where

VALUE-SET?(self:ObjectName) ans:$\mathbf{B}$

ext rd *db:Db*

post *post-AT(self,"set-flag",db,ans)*

Next, the operation *SET-VALUE* is added to *^Root*. It has the hard task of calculating the value for a root. Its task will be lessened if the root's value has already been set. If not it must calculate it and all of the values of the root's subnodes. It does this by first telling the subnodes to set their values and then storing its own value as calculated from the affected database.

AT-PUT(^Root,"set-value",SET-VALUE)

where

SET-VALUE(self:ObjectName)

ext wr *db:Db*

post (*post-ASK(self,"value-set?",[],$\overline{db}$,true)* $\wedge$ *db = $\overline{db}$*) $\vee$

(*post-ASK(self,"value-set?",[],$\overline{db}$,false)* $\wedge$

$\exists l,r \in ObjectName \cdot \exists db0,db1,db2 \in Db \cdot \exists i,j \in \mathbf{Z} \cdot$

(*post-AT(self,"left",$\overline{db}$,l)* $\wedge$

post-AT(self,"right",$\overline{db}$,r) $\wedge$

post-TELL(l,"set-value",[],$\overline{db}$,db0) $\wedge$

post-ASK(l,"value?",[],db0,i) $\wedge$

post-TELL(r,"set-value",[],db0,db1) $\wedge$

post-ASK(r,"value?",[],db1,j) $\wedge$

post-TELL(self,"value!",[i+j],db1,db2) $\wedge$

post-AT-PUT(self,"set-flag",true,db2,db)))

The demand driven design we have just completed has the property that it does not compute unnecessary values but when values are required they are not recomputed unecessarily. In practice, we would probably subsume the functionality of *SET-VALUE* in the operation *VALUE?*.

7. A Data Driven Design

An alternative to our demand driven system is a data driven one. In a data driven system, properties of a database are established as soon as data is available to satisfy them. Such a system is attractive in that it is very receptive to change. Unlike in the demand driven system, if a leaf is allowed a change of data, then the data of its dependents automatically changes.

The system accommodates change by recording the dependence links which relate subnodes to their roots. When a change of data occurs that information is propagated up the dependence hierarchy.

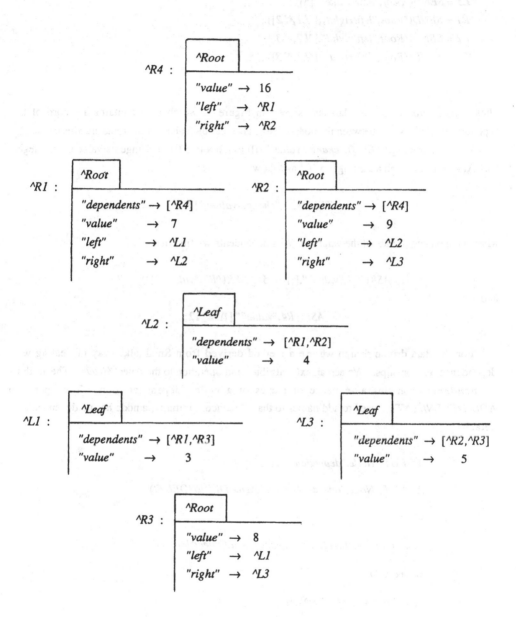

Figure 5. Example data for data driven design

The effect of a data driven system is shown by providing it with the data of the previous section using the same sequence of operations

$^\wedge L1 = SEND(^\wedge Leaf,"new-value!",[3])$;

$^\wedge L2 = SEND(^\wedge Leaf,"new-value!",[4])$;

$^\wedge L3 = SEND(^\wedge Leaf,"new-value!",[5])$;

$^\wedge R1 = SEND(^\wedge Root,"left!right!",[^\wedge L1,^\wedge L2])$;

$^\wedge R2 = SEND(^\wedge Root,"left!right!",[^\wedge L2,^\wedge L3])$;

$^\wedge R3 = SEND(^\wedge Root,"left!right!",[^\wedge L1,^\wedge L3])$;

$^\wedge R4 = SEND(^\wedge Root,"left!right!",[^\wedge R1,^\wedge R2])$

These operations set up the database shown in Figure 5, which now contains a record of the dependence relationships between the nodes. Note also that the values of the roots are already set.

We use the message $TELL(l,"change-value!",[i])$ to tell a leaf (l) to change its value to an integer (i). After sending such a message to $^\wedge L2$ as follows

$$TELL(^\wedge L2,"change-value!",[2]),$$

when we next enquire about the values of $^\wedge L2$'s dependents we find that

$$ASK(^\wedge R1,"value?",[]) = 5 \ , \ ASK(^\wedge R2,"value?",[]) = 7$$

and

$$ASK(^\wedge R4,"value?",[]) = 12 \ .$$

For the data driven design we use a method derived from Smalltalk's way of dealing with dependence relationships. We add an extra attribute and operation to the object $^\wedge Node$. The attribute *"dependents"* contains a sequence of names of a node's dependent roots. The operation *ADD-DEPENDENT!* is used to add names to that sequence. Initially, a node has no dependents by default.

AT-$PUT(^\wedge Node,"dependents",[])$;

AT-$PUT(^\wedge Node,"add-dependent!",ADD$-$DEPENDENT!)$

where

ADD-$DEPENDENT!(self:ObjectName,n:ObjectName)$

ext wr $db:Db$

post $\exists ds \in$ seq of $ObjectName$ ·

$(post$-$AT(self,"dependents",\overline{db},ds) \wedge$

$post$-AT-$PUT(self,"dependents",ds \frown [n],\overline{db},db))$;

A change of data is propagated with a message of the form $TELL(n,"value-changed",[])$, where n is the name of a node that has experienced a change. That message is dealt with by the operation

VALUE-CHANGED in *^Node*. It broadcasts the change to *n*'s dependents using the function broadcast, which (recursively) tells each dependent root to update the value in its state.

> *AT-PUT(^Node,"value-changed",VALUE-CHANGED)*
>
> where
>
> *VALUE-CHANGED(self:ObjectName)*
>
> ext wr *db:Db*
>
> post $\exists ds \in$ seq of *ObjectName* ·
>
> > (*post-AT(self,"dependents",$\overline{db}$,ds)* $\wedge$ *post-broadcast($\overline{db}$,ds,db)*)
>
> *broadcast(db:Db,ds:*seq of *ObjectName) newdb:Db*
>
> post (*ds* = [] $\wedge$ *newdb* = *db*) $\vee$
>
> > (*ds* ≠ [] $\wedge$ $\exists db' \in Db$ ·
> >
> > > (*post-TELL(*hd *ds,"update-value",[],db,db')* $\wedge$
> > >
> > > *post-broadcast(db',*tl *ds,newdb)*))

A root responds to a message to update its value by applying the operation *UPDATE-VALUE* in *^Root* to itself. This operation stores, in the root, a value recomputed from the new values stored at its subnodes, and then informs the root of the change to itself, thus propagating the information further up the dependency chain.

> *AT-PUT(^Root,"update-value",UPDATE-VALUE)*
>
> where
>
> *UPDATE-VALUE(self:ObjectName)*
>
> ext wr *db:Db*
>
> post $\exists l,r \in$ *ObjectName* · $\exists db' \in Db$ · $\exists i,j \in Z$ ·
>
> > (*post-AT(self,"left",$\overline{db}$,l)* $\wedge$
> >
> > *post-AT(self,"right",$\overline{db}$,r)* $\wedge$
> >
> > *post-ASK(l,"value?",$\overline{db}$,i)* $\wedge$
> >
> > *post-ASK(r,"value?",$\overline{db}$,j)* $\wedge$
> >
> > *post-TELL(self,"value!",[i+j],$\overline{db}$,db')* $\wedge$
> >
> > *post-TELL(self,"value-changed",[],db',db)*)

A change message is triggered off as a result of changing a value at a leaf. This will happen by sending a message of the form $TELL(l,"change\text{-}value",[i])$, where i is an integer that is different from the one already stored in the leaf (l). This message is dealt with by the operation $CHANGE\text{-}VALUE!$ in $^\wedge Leaf$.

$AT\text{-}PUT(^\wedge Leaf,"change\text{-}value!",CHANGE\text{-}VALUE!)$

where

$CHANGE\text{-}VALUE!(self:ObjectName,i:\mathbb{Z})$

ext wr $db:Db$

post $\exists j \in \mathbb{Z} \cdot \ post\text{-}ASK(self,"value?",[],\overleftarrow{db},j) \wedge$

$\qquad (i = j \wedge db = \overleftarrow{db}) \vee$

$\qquad (i \neq j \wedge \exists db' \in Db \cdot$

$\qquad\qquad\qquad (post\text{-}TELL(self,"value!",[i],\overleftarrow{db},db') \wedge$

$\qquad\qquad\qquad post\text{-}TELL(self,"value\text{-}changed",[],db',db))$

The only thing left unspecified is the formation of the dependency links when a database is established initially. This is done in a revised version of the operation $"LEFT!RIGHT!"$ in $^\wedge Root$, where the links are set up at the time of a root's construction. Also at this time the root is told to update its value.

$AT\text{-}PUT(^\wedge Root,"left!right!",LEFT!RIGHT!)$

where

$LEFT!RIGHT!(self:ObjectName,l:ObjectName,r:ObjectName) \ ptr:Value$

ext wr $db:Db$

post $\exists db0,db1,db2,db3,db4 \in Db \cdot$

$\qquad (post\text{-}NEW(self,\overleftarrow{db},ptr,db0) \wedge$

$\qquad post\text{-}TELL(l,"add\text{-}dependent!",[ptr],db0,db1) \wedge$

$\qquad post\text{-}TELL(r,"add\text{-}dependent!",[ptr],db1,db2) \wedge$

$\qquad post\text{-}AT\text{-}PUT(ptr,"left",l,db2,db3) \wedge$

$\qquad post\text{-}AT\text{-}PUT(ptr,"right",r,db3,db4) \wedge$

$\qquad post\text{-}TELL(ptr,"update\text{-}value",[],db4,db))$

The architecture we have designed for data driven programming is such that the consequences of changing data values are propagated through the network as far as possible. This type of organisation of computation has proved popular in object-oriented programming because it fits well with the associated notion of providing an up-to-date display of objects in the database.

8. Validation using *me too*

We began this design with an informal statement of requirements, which we eventually elaborated into two refinements, respectively a demand driven and a data driven architecture, built upon a common object space specification. The use of mathematical notation has allowed us to be precise about our intended meaning for each operation and our intended architecture for implementing that meaning. But even this modest amount of mathematics is difficult to construct without error. Apart from the inevitable typing slips (which probably persist even now), we will make errors of ommission and commission which will result in inconsistent definitions. Elimination of such bugs can be achieved by various means, including careful reading by others and by setting up and performing proofs of various properties of the specified operations. An alternative, which we have chosen, is to transform the specification into an executable program which can be *tested* in order to detect many, if not all, of the residual faults.

The method we have used to do this uses a functional language embedded in LISP. A satisfactory alternative of course would have been to use Prolog. The language we used is *me too* which has the singular advantage that it already implements all of the VDM mathematical types (sets, tuples, maps and sequences) with a wide range of library functions and forms. Consequently, converting the VDM specification into *me too* is relatively straightforward.

The basis for this conversion is as follows. For a VDM operation with the protocol [1, p 88]

$OP(p:Tp)\ r:Tr$
ext rd $v1:T1$, wr $v2:T2$
pre ... p ... $v1$ ... $v2$ ...
post ... p ... $v1$ ... $\overleftarrow{v2}$ ... r ... $v2$ ...

we know that the other operations can refer to the precondition and the postcondition by using predicates with the functionality

$pre\text{-}OP : Tp \times T1 \times T2 \rightarrow \mathbf{B}$

$post\text{-}OP : Tp \times T1 \times T2 \times Tr \times T2 \rightarrow \mathbf{B}$

In a similar fashion we define constructive operations

$pre\text{-}f\text{-}OP : T1 \times T2 \times Tp \rightarrow \mathbf{B}$

$f\text{-}OP : T1 \times T2 \times Tp \rightarrow T2 \times Tr$

with the intended meaning

$pre\text{-}OP(p,v1,v2) \equiv pre\text{-}f\text{-}OP(v1,v2,p)$

$post\text{-}OP(p,\overleftarrow{v1,v2},r,v2) \equiv (\ f\text{-}OP(v1,\overleftarrow{v2},p) = (r,v2)\ )$

Of course this conversion is only straightforward if the original post-condition is in some sense *constructive* . Knowing that one is aiming to use a *me too* prototype to validate the specification encourages one to write the original specification in this (not unnatural) way.

As an example of the correspondence between specification and prototype, the definition used to validate *AT* is

$f\text{-}AT(db,on,a)\ \Delta$

      if $a \in dom(associations(db[on]))$ then $associations(db[on])[on]$

      else if $on = {}^\wedge Object$ then ${}^\wedge undefined$ else $f\text{-}AT(db,class(db[on]),a)$

(The variation in the *me too* abstract syntax from the VDM syntax should be self-evident to the reader.)

All of the claims made for the specification presented here were borne out by tests on the prototype. After iterating on various architectures for an object-oriented system, using VDM as the specification language for communication among the designers and *me too* as a means of rapid prototyping to determine that our architecture would support our requirements, we eventually went on to implement, in LISP, the system specified here. We called it EMILY. EMILY is now being used to implement a range of business applications including discrete event simulation (based on Petri nets), which we hope to report elsewhere.

9. Conclusions

In order to design complicated systems, such as the database applications we have seen, we have to discover the right architecture. To help us do this we need the support of good tools and an infrastructure that is right for our designs. The tools we used for our designs was the VDM specification language. With that we were able to design an applications environment based on the AI object-oriented architectures. Using a specification language we were able to explore a space of alternative environments, endeavouring to understand difficult concepts such as inheritance, message passing and state change, and on the basis of our understanding, to choose the one that best suited our needs. Having found the right architecture, we could then exploit it to design seemingly complex applications very naturally. This paper has presented the results of that search.

As a further aid to our understanding of the design of our applications environment we were able to execute a version of it using a method described in [7]. That method allows us to translate VDM specifications into equivalent functional programs which we can then validate by testing. We also executed the designs of the two applications presented here as functional programs embedded in the applications environment. That same environment allowed us to explore other programming problems to which it is well suited, such as simulation, data-directed backtracking and user interfacing. After gaining confidence in our design, we then implemented the environment in LISP, and since then have used it to develop some realistic applications. The rigorous development route we took provided us, we believe, with software that, while powerful enough for our applications, is simpler than that which we might have invented had we done otherwise.

Acknowledgements

We would like to thank Cliff Jones, Mario Wolczko, Simon Finn, Val Jones and Simon Jones for their comments on an earlier draft of this paper.

References

[1] Jones, C.B. "Systematic Software Development Using VDM"
     Prentice-Hall International Series in Computer Science, 1986

[2] Charniak, E., Riesbeck, K. and McDermott, D.V. "Artificial Intelligence Programming"
     Lawrence Erlbaum Associates, Publishers, 1980

[3] Abelson, H. and Sussman, G.J. with Sussman, J. "Structure and Interpretation of Computer
     Programs" The MIT Electrical Engineering and Computer Science Series,
     The MIT Press, McGraw-Hill Book Company, 1985

[4] Winston, P.H. "Artificial Intelligence" - Second Edition
     Addison-Wesley Publishing Company, 1984

[5] Goldberg, A. and Robson, D "Smalltalk-80 the Language and its Implementation"
     Addison-Wesley Publishing Company, 1983

[6] Henderson, P. "Functional Programming, Formal Specification and Rapid Prototyping"
     IEEE Transactions on Software Engineering, Vol. SE-12, No.1, 1986

[7] Henderson, P and Minkowitz,C.J. "The *me too* method of software design"
     ICL Journal, Volume 5, Issue 1, May 1986

VDM Proof Obligations and their Justification*

C.B. Jones
Department of Computer Science
The University
Manchester M13 9PL
United Kingdom

abstract>
Abstract

"The Vienna Development Method" (VDM) uses specifications built in terms of models and operations specified by pre-/post-conditions. Steps of design by data reification or operation decomposition give rise to proof obligations. This paper provides examples of both sorts of design step but its main intention is to show that the proof obligations for operation decomposition are consistent with a semantics of the language combinators. A discussion of a recently discovered data reification rule and some observations about the underlying logic are also included.

1 Introduction

Of the many problems presented by the development of major computer systems, some can be ameliorated by the use of formal methods. The term "Formal Methods" applies to the use of mathematical notation in the specification, and the use of such specifications as a basis for the verified design, of computer systems. VDM ("Vienna Development Method") is such a formal method. Here, the concern is with the application of VDM to program development; it has also been used extensively on programming languages—see [5].

There are three more or less distinct approaches to the formal development of programs. Each approach starts with a formal statement of the required function of the program and uses formally provable steps to link the final program to the specification. The approaches and their emphases are:

- specification/design/verification: the specification is written in a distinct specification language but the design (and eventual code) are written in a normal implementation language; correctness of each step of the design is established by discharging defined *proof obligations*. VDM uses this approach.

- transformation: the "specification" is given as an executable function whose clarity is considered to be paramount (the execution of the function is likely to be extremely inefficient); an acceptable implementation is created by a series of syntactic transformations (with some of which are associated the obligation to prove applicability). The best known example of this approach is the CIP project (see [8]).

- constructive mathematics: here the specification is taken as the statement of a theorem from whose constructive proof, can be extracted a program (cf. [11]).

---

*The material in the talk given at the EEC VDM-Europe Symposium is covered by [20]; this paper explores one aspect of that material in more detail.

There are two things which make VDM specifications far shorter than programs: they use data objects (e.g. maps) which are not present in most programming languages and they use post-conditions which do not show how to compute a result. Both of these specification "tricks" have to be removed in the design of a program. The realization of data objects is handled in steps of *data reification*; the development of control constructs to satisfy post-conditions is handled by steps of *operation decomposition*. In the development of any significant system, development will take place in many steps. Experience with VDM suggests that the early, or high-level, design stages concern data reification and the later, low-level, steps concern operation decomposition.

It is important to appreciate the rôle of *compositionality* in a development method. In outline, the idea is that a decision at one step of development cannot be affected by subsequent decisions. This is, perhaps, easiest to see in terms of steps of operation decomposition. Starting with a specification, say *OP*, this might be decomposed into two sub-operations *OPA* and *OPB* with the design decision that they are to be executed one after the other. The sub-operations can be specified and the design decision verified by discharging the relevant proof obligations. Subsequent development might result in a loop construct being used to realize *OPA*. In a compositional development method, this step of design can be verified without any reference to the context in which *OPA* is to be used: only its specification need be considered. Compositional development methods are not too difficult to find for sequential programs. For programs which permit interference of parallel processes, the challenge is much greater. Some work in the VDM framework is reported in [22]; more recent work on Temporal Logic is described in [3].

This paper is structured as follows. Section 2 outlines the problems caused by the need to reason about partial functions in program specification and justification: a non-standard logic which copes with the problems is described. Sections 3 and 4 address the two main forms of development steps. In both cases, the proof obligations are presented together with examples. Section 4 provides a detailed justification—with respect to a denotational semantics—of the proof rules for operation decomposition.

2 Underlying Logic

Many of the operators on the basic VDM data types (e.g. hd , map application) are partial and arise in expressions like:

$$t = [\,] \lor t = append(\text{hd } t, \text{tl } t)$$

or, if ρ is a member of map *Id* to *Den*:

$$id \in \text{dom } \rho \land \rho(id) \in \textit{Proctype}$$

The fact that the operators are partial gives rise to terms which may fail to denote a value. Another obvious source of partial terms is recursion—for example:

$$subp : \mathbf{N} \times \mathbf{N} \to \mathbf{N}$$

$$subp(i,j) \quad \triangleq \quad \text{if } i = j \text{ then } 0 \text{ else } subp(i, j+1) + 1$$

Providing that $i \geq j$, this function yields a defined result. This prompts the writing of expressions like:

$$\forall i, j \in \mathbf{N} \cdot i \geq j \ \Rightarrow \ subp(i,j) = i - j$$

It can be seen how the problem of undefined terms affects the meaning of the logical operators: what does this last expression mean when the antecedent of the implication is false?

Such partial expressions arise frequently in the specification and design of programs but earlier treatments of logical operators have not been fully successful. This section offers some requirements for an appropriate logic and compares the proposal in [2] and [7] with those requirements.

Figure 1: Ordering for Truth Values

Approaches can be judged against the following criteria:

- Both a model and a proof theory should be given and the latter should be proved consistent and complete with respect to the former.

- There should be clear links to classical logic—for example:

  - The proof rules should be consistent with classical logic;
  - conjunction and disjunction should be commutative;
  - most standard laws of logic should hold;
  - and there should be a clear way of building a link to those which do not hold;
  - familiar operators should be monotone with respect to the ordering in Figure 1;
  - implication should fit the standard abbreviation($p \Rightarrow q$ as $\neg p \vee q$).

- If there is a need for non-classical, non-monotonic operators, their use should be localized and not inflicted on the developer of standard programs.

- It should be possible to prove results about functions (e.g. *subp*) without a separate proof of definedness of terms.

The logic presented in [2] is known as the *Logic of Partial Functions* (*LPF*). The model theory of its propositional calculus can be summarized in truth tables (in which * is used to denote a missing value). For example, the extended truth table for disjunction is:

$\vee$	true	*	false
true	true	true	true
*	true	*	*
false	true	*	false

Notice that the truth table is symmetrical—this indicates the general way in which the other tables can be constructed. (The truth tables for implication and equivalence are derived by viewing them as the normal abbreviations.)

The proof rules for this logic (derived from [26]) are presented in a way which is intended to be used in (linear-style) natural deduction proofs. The proof rules support the deduction of sequents of the form:

$\Gamma \vdash E$

where Γ is a list of expressions. The intended (model-theoretic) interpretation of such sequents is that E should be true in all worlds where all of the expressions in Γ are true. Notice that the sequent:

$$E_1 \vdash E_2$$

is satisfied if E_1 is false or undefined, whatever the value of E_2.

For the basic propositional operators ($\neg$, $\vee$) there are the obvious introduction and elimination rules:

$$\vee\text{-I} \qquad \frac{E_i}{E_1 \vee E_2 \vee \ldots \vee E_n}$$

$$\vee\text{-E} \qquad \frac{E_1 \vee \ldots \vee E_n; \quad E_1 \vdash E; \ldots; E_n \vdash E}{E}$$

$$\neg\neg \qquad \frac{E}{\neg\neg E}$$

(All of the rules are given in [20].) In addition, it is necessary to have rules for negated disjunctions:

$$\neg\vee\text{-I} \qquad \frac{\neg E_1; \neg E_2; \ldots \neg E_n;}{\neg(E_1 \vee E_2 \vee \ldots \vee E_n)}$$

$$\neg\vee\text{-E} \qquad \frac{\neg(E_1 \vee E_2 \vee \ldots \vee E_n)}{\neg E_i}$$

The need for these rules arises from the fact that the "law of the excluded middle" does not hold in this logic. Conjunction, implication and equivalence are introduced by definitions and their introduction and elimination rules are proved as derived results. An example of a natural deduction proof using these rules to show:

$$(E_1 \vee E_2) \wedge (E_1 \vee E_3) \vdash E_1 \vee E_2 \wedge E_3$$

is given in Figure 2—this proof would be valid in classical logic whereas the normal proof written in classical logic (cf. [13]) is not valid here because it uses the "law of the excluded middle".

The axiomatization of the predicate calculus follows a similar pattern with the existential quantifier being treated as basic and the universal quantifier being introduced as an abbreviation for which inference rules have to be derived[1]. The main point with this treatment is to constrain the bound variable of a quantified expression to range only over "proper elements".

The requirement to minimize the use of non-monotonic operators has proved the most elusive and several attempts have been made in order to minimize the use of non-monotonic operators in normal proofs. A first step is to choose appropriate rules for induction proofs. The basic characterization of sets like the natural numbers is given by constructor functions:

$$0: \mathbf{N}$$
$$succ: \mathbf{N} \to \mathbf{N}$$

and an induction axiom:

$$N\text{-}ind \qquad \frac{p(0); \quad n \in \mathbf{N}, p(n) \vdash p(n+1)}{n \in \mathbf{N} \vdash p(n)}$$

---

[1] Proofs of many of the derived rules for this logic are contained in [24].

```
    from (E₁ ∨ E₂) ∧ (E₁ ∨ E₃)
1         E₁ ∨ E₂                                    ∧-E(h)
2         E₁ ∨ E₃                                    ∧-E(h)
3         from E1
          infer E₁ ∨ E₂ ∧ E₃                         ∨-I(h3)
4         from E₂
4.1           from E₃
4.1.1             E₂ ∧ E₃                             ∧-I(h4, h4.1)
              infer E₁ ∨ E₂ ∧ E₃                     ∨-I(4.1.1)
          infer E₁ ∨ E₂ ∧ E₃                         ∨-E(2, 3, 4.1)
      infer E₁ ∨ E₂ ∧ E₃                             ∨-E(1, 3, 4)
```

Figure 2: LPF Proof of Distribution

Notice that the induction rule is presented via a turnstile rather than using implication. This simplifies subsequent proofs because it avoids the need to use the ⇒-I rule. The induction rule is presented without quantifiers since they can be inserted using:

$$\forall\text{-I} \qquad \frac{x \in X \vdash E(x)}{\forall x \in X \cdot E(x)}$$

For recursively defined types, an induction rule is generated for each type.

A more important step—to minimize the use of non-monotonic operators—is to decide on the treatment of (recursive) partial functions. The approach in [2] was to handle definitions like that for *subp* by generating inference rules. The justification of such rules (with respect to the definition of *subp*) does require the use of—and reasoning about—strong equality; but the proof of the appropriate property in the referenced paper only uses the rules themselves.

In [23] a slightly different approach is used which obviates the need to create the inference rules. The idea is to use definition rules in direct substitutions. This permits proofs to avoid mentioning undefined values.

The principal differences between *LPF* and classical logic are:

- The law of the excluded middle does not hold.

- The deduction theorem does not hold without an additional hypothesis.

- For weak equality, it is not necessarily true that $t = t$ for an arbitrary term t.

On the other hand:

- The operators ∧ and ∨ are commutative and monotone.

- Properties like $x \in \mathbf{R} \vdash x = 0 \vee x/x = 1$ are easily proved.

- The implication operator fits its normal abbreviation and also has an interpretation which fits the needs of the result on *subp*.

- Many of the results from classical logic do hold although simple tautologies have to be re-expressed as sequents.

- Where properties would otherwise fail to hold, they can be made valid by adding hypotheses about the definedness of expressions.

A fuller account of the development of LPF is contained in [20]. In [7] (which should also be consulted for a full list of references) a number of completeness results are given.

3 Data Reification

3.1 Data Types

There are two major schools in the area of data type specification. They are referred to here as the *property-oriented* and *model-oriented* approaches. Both approaches have their uses and can be used to complement each other. The principal differences are:

- In a property-oriented description, the meaning of the operators is fixed by equations[2]. Model-oriented specifications define operators in terms of an underlying model.

- In a property-oriented specification, it is important to notice that certain operators are capable of *generating* all possible elements of the type.

- The most cited advantage of a property-oriented description is that it is presented without reference to any underlying, or pre-defined, data type. In fact, the rôle of a model is provided by the valid terms (*word algebra*) built from the generators.

- A more subtle advantage derives from the fact that the property-oriented approach is built on a branch of mathematics (i.e. Algebra) where notions relevant to data types have been studied. In particular *signatures*, *sorts*, *equations* and *models* are all of interest. The generalisation, from a specific data type, to a type which is parameterized (by types) is most easily studied in the property-oriented approach.

- The basic property-oriented approach copes well with *total* operators but treatments of partial operators are more complex[3].

- *Interpretations* of equations must be fixed. The choice between *initial, loose* or *final* interpretations are too technical to pursue in detail here. The reader is referred to a textbook such as [4] or [10].

- A far deeper problem comes from the fundamental limit on the expressive power of a specification by properties. It has long been known that certain data types cannot be characterized by finite sets of equations. This gives rise to the need for, so-called, *hidden functions*. The presence of such hidden functions weakens the main advantage of a property-oriented specification: the ideal that a data type can be understood solely in terms of *its* operators (or functions) and their relationship is clearly lost if new functions are introduced to describe the inter-relationship.

- Both partiality and non-determinism present problems in property-oriented specification techniques[4].

---

[2] The use of such algebraic equations gives rise to the more commonly used names for this approach: *equational specifications* or *algebraic presentations* or even *algebraic specifications*.

[3] The first major approach to the handling of *error algebras* (cf. [12]) was less than satisfactory; more recent work (e.g. [6]) fits more closely the way in which partial operators are used.

[4] See, however, [27].

- A distinction can be made between data types like Set_N which possess no obvious state and those like a database where the concept of a state affecting, and being changed by, the execution of operations[5] is pervasive. In fact, even with the example of a *Stack*, there is a natural place for a state. It is possible to disguise this fact by separating *top* and *remove* functions. But this separates two parts of what is naturally a single *POP* operation which changes the state by side effect and delivers the required value as a result. There is no basic reason why property-based descriptions could not be extended to handle signatures with more than one result. It does, however, remove some of the elegance with which the defining equations can be presented.

3.2 Model-Oriented Specification

The remainder of this section is concerned solely with model-oriented specifications which tend to predominate in VDM specifications. They handle the operations separately. Each operation is characterized by pre- and post-conditions in which there is no difficulty in handling state-like objects. The obvious danger presented by basing a specification on a model is that of "over-specification". This problem has been characterized in [19] and [23] as *implementation bias*: a test is given there which establishes that the underlying state exhibits no bias.

A series of operations are specified with respect to a state; the state is constructed from combinations of known types. Picking up the example of a stack, the underlying state might be defined in terms of sequences. The *POP* operation could then be specified:

POP () $r: X$

ext wr st : seq of X

pre $st \neq [\,]$

post $[r] \frown st = \overleftarrow{st}$

The ext clause identifies the non-local objects to which the operation has access. In this case, there is only one variable to be considered since the state is so simple. In larger examples, listing only those variables required goes some way to solving the so-called "frame problem". Furthermore, distinguishing between read-only access (rd) and read-write access (wr) can also clarify the potential effect of an operation. The pre-condition is a predicate of a state and can be used to limit the cases in which the operation has to be applicable (here, the implementor of *POP* is invited to ignore states in which the initial st is an empty sequence). The post-condition is a predicate of two states: it specifies the relationship required between the states before and after execution of the operation. Here, then, it is necessary to distinguish two values of the same (external) variables. There are many possible conventions for doing this; in [23] the values from the old state are decorated with a hook (e.g. $\overleftarrow{st}$).

Such an operation specification could be translated into a more functional notation:

POP: seq of $X \rightarrow$ seq of $X \times X$

$\forall \overleftarrow{st} \in$ seq of $X \cdot$
    $pre\text{-}POP(\overleftarrow{st}) \Rightarrow$
        $\exists st \in$ seq of $X, r \in X \cdot POP(\overleftarrow{st}) = (st, r) \wedge$
        $\forall st \in$ seq of $X, r \in X \cdot POP(\overleftarrow{st}) = (st, r) \Rightarrow [r] \frown st = \overleftarrow{st}$

---

[5] The term *operations* is used in preference to "operators" in order to emphasize the rôle of side-effects.

Notice, from this translation, that operation specifications require termination over the specified domain (i.e. *total correctness* is being handled). The decision to separate the pre-condition in an operation specification is made on pragmatic grounds. Partial operations are very common in computing and the pre-condition focuses attention on the assumptions. The full power of the post-conditions becomes apparent on more complex examples. Here, the advantages are simply listed:

- the ability to specify non-deterministic (and thus under-determined) operations;

- results can often be conveniently specified by conjunctions of properties—this makes it far easier to specify, than it is to create, the result;

- the use of negation has a similar effect;

- it is often easy to specify an operation in terms of some inverse.

One disadvantage of model-oriented specifications by pre- and post-conditions is that it is possible to specify an operation which is unimplementable (e.g. producing an even prime number greater than 10). This gives rise to the first of the *proof obligations* which are an inherent part of VDM. An operation (e.g. *POP*) is *implementable* only if:

$$\forall \overleftarrow{st} \in \text{seq of } X \cdot \text{pre-}POP(\overleftarrow{st}) \;\Rightarrow\; \exists st \in \text{seq of } X, r \in X \cdot \text{post-}POP(\overleftarrow{st}, st, r)$$

These particular proof obligations are not normally subject to formal proof but do provide a convenient reminder that type information, pre-condition and post-condition all combine to govern whether an operation is implementable.

3.3 A Basic Proof Rule

In order to achieve full advantage from the application of formal methods, it is necessary to apply them to the early stages of development. Clearly, this implies the construction of formal specifications. After that, one must ask what activities are most common in the early (high-level) design stages? Typically the choice of data representations is made before detailed algorithm design. Thus VDM tends to put more emphasis on proof of data reification than on operation decomposition. The remainder of this section reviews the most straightforward rules for the justification of design steps of data reification, the shortcomings of these rules, and a new set of rules which are—in some sense—complete.

A specification in VDM normally defines a set of states and a collection of operations which rely on, and transform, these states. A specification of a single operation contains a pre- and a post-condition: this makes it possible to define partial and non-deterministic operations. Intuitively, it should be acceptable for an implementation to terminate on more inputs than are required in its specification (i.e. have a bigger domain—or be defined on more input values) or to produce some subset of the permitted answers for any required input (i.e. be more determined). An implementation is written in some implementation language and it is therefore necessary to have some common way of discussing the meaning of both specifications and of programs. One convenient model is to define both in terms of the set of states over which termination is required and the meaning relation which defines the possible results:

$$(S, R)$$

where S is a subset of the set of states, say Σ, and R is a relation on Σ.

It is clear that a given *pre*, *post* pair can be translated into this form by:

$$(\{\sigma \in \Sigma \mid pre(\sigma)\}, \qquad \{(\overleftarrow{\sigma}, \sigma) \in \Sigma \times \Sigma \mid post(\overleftarrow{\sigma}, \sigma)\})$$

The ideas of denotational semantics can be used to express programming language constructs in terms of the same model (see below).

In terms of the set/relation pairs, it is possible to define precisely the notion of *satisfaction* (sat), which is described intuitively above[6]:

$$(S_1, R_1) \text{ sat } (S_2, R_2) \Leftrightarrow S_2 \subseteq S_1 \land S_2 \lhd R_1 \subseteq R_2$$

This sat relation provides the basis against which steps of development must be shown to be correct. Notice that sat is a partial order. Its transitivity is the key to compositionality.

A basic set of data reification rules are now introduced with the aid of a simple example. Operation specifications are discussed below; initially, attention is focussed on the objects which comprise the states. A computing system which needs to access a large set of values can be specified in terms of a state:

$Set =$ set of X

with an initial object corresponding to the empty set:

$s_0 = \{\}$

Such an abstraction is very convenient in the specification precisely because it hides all of the implementation problem. Clearly, the design process must choose—and justify—a representation. One possible way of storing large volumes of data is in a binary tree. Such a set of trees can be described by[7]:

$Setrep = [Node]$

$Node ::$ $lt : Setrep$
          $mv : X$
          $rt : Setrep$

where

$inv\text{-}Node(mk\text{-}Node(lt, mv, rv)) \quad \triangle$
    $(\forall lv \in retrns(lt) \cdot lv < mv) \land (\forall rv \in retrns(rt) \cdot mv < rv)$

$retrns : Setrep \rightarrow$ set of X

$retrns(sr) \quad \triangle$ cases sr of
        nil $\rightarrow \{\}$
        $mk\text{-}Node(lt, mv, rt) \rightarrow retrns(lt) \cup \{mv\} \cup retrns(rt)$
        end

The set of objects (*Node*) is considered to be restricted by the invariant[8]. The initial object (which corresponds to the empty set) is:

$t_0 =$ nil

The representation, *Setrep*, must be related to the abstraction *Set*. In many cases of reification a one-to-many relation exists between elements of the abstraction and those of the representation. This is no accident. It is desirable to make states of specifications as abstract as possible; the structure of the implementation language (or machine) forces the introduction of extra information and redundancy; it is, therefore, very common that a one-to-many relationship arises. Precisely this situation holds here. There are many possible tree representations

---

[6] $S \lhd R \triangle \{(\sigma, \sigma') \in R \mid \sigma \in S\}$

[7] For efficiency, such trees should also be *balanced*; for brevity, this requirement is not treated formally here.

[8] This, more central, rôle for invariants is a change from [21].

of any (non-trivial) set object. Both [16] and [25] relate the set of abstractions to their representations by a function from the latter to the former. Here they are called *retrieve functions* because they get back the abstract values from the representation details. For the example in hand, *retrns* is the required function.

In the set of rules used most commonly in VDM, such retrieve functions must be total. That this property is satisfied by *retrns*, follows from the operators used in its definition. Another property required of the representation (strictly—with respect to the retrieve function) is *adequacy*: there must be at least one representation for each abstract element. For the case in hand this proof obligation becomes:

$$\forall s \in Set \cdot \exists sr \in Setrep \cdot retrns(sr) = s$$

It is straightforward to prove this by induction on s. It is, in fact, worth providing a function which inserts elements into a tree and use this. In practice, it would be worth defining a number of functions and developing the *theory* of the data type (cf. [17]).

One of the advantages of this set of proof rules is that they do isolate useful proof obligations about the state alone and, in practice, these proofs are a very useful check on a representation before proceeding to look at the individual operations. It is, however, also necessary to consider the operations. The initial states are trivially related:

$$retrm(t_0) = s_0$$

On *Set*, the insert operation is specified trivially:

$ADD\ (e{:}X)$

ext wr s : set of X

pre $e \notin s$

post $s = \overleftarrow{s} \cup \{e\}$

The corresponding operation on *Setrep* could be defined:

$ADD_1\ (e{:}X)$

ext wr sr : *Setrep*

pre $e \notin retrns(sr)$

post $retrns(sr) = retrns(\overleftarrow{sr}) \cup \{e\}$

this is intended to mirror the behaviour of ADD. Notice that this post-condition is non-deterministic in that there are—except in trivial cases—many possible results which would be acceptable. This illustrates the way in which non-determinism can be used to structure a design. Even if the final program would be deterministic, this post-condition makes it possible to record and justify the design decision to use binary trees whilst postponing the decision about the tree balancing algorithm.

For the sake of simplicity, a more definite post-condition is used here:

$ADD_1\ (e{:}X)$

ext wr sr : *Setrep*

pre $e \notin retrns(sr)$

post $\overleftarrow{sr} = $ nil $\wedge sr = mk\text{-}Node(\text{nil}, e, \text{nil})\ \vee$

$\quad \overleftarrow{sr} \in Node\ \wedge$

$\quad$ let $mk\text{-}Node(\overleftarrow{lt}, mv, \overleftarrow{rt}) = \overleftarrow{sr}$ in

$\quad\quad e < mv \wedge \exists lt \in Setrep \cdot post\text{-}ADD_1(e, \overleftarrow{lt}, lt) \wedge sr = mk\text{-}Node(lt, mv, \overleftarrow{rt})\ \vee$

$\quad\quad e > mv \wedge \exists rt \in Setrep \cdot post\text{-}ADD_1(e, \overleftarrow{rt}, rt) \wedge sr = mk\text{-}Node(\overleftarrow{lt}, mv, rt)$

This records (the idea of *operation quotation* is employed for illustration) the essential recursion which could be used in ADD_1 but preserves the requirement that post-conditions are simply predicates (it is not possible to invoke an operation from within a predicate).

At this level of design, the obligation to prove implementability is non-trivial. That this algorithm yields an object which satisfies the data type invariant (*inv-Node*), should be proved. Thus:

$$\forall \overleftarrow{sr} \in Setrep, e \in X \cdot pre\text{-}ADD_1(e, \overleftarrow{sr}) \;\Rightarrow\; \exists sr \in Setrep \cdot post\text{-}ADD_1(e, \overleftarrow{sr}, sr)$$

The relevant data reification proof obligations for this operation are:

$$\forall sr \in Setrep \cdot pre\text{-}OP(retrns(sr)) \;\Rightarrow\; pre\text{-}OP_1(sr)$$

for the domain part of the rule; and:

$$\forall \overleftarrow{sr}, sr \in Setrep \cdot$$
$$pre\text{-}OP(retrns(\overleftarrow{sr})) \wedge post\text{-}OP_1(\overleftarrow{sr}, sr) \;\Rightarrow\; post\text{-}OP(retrns(\overleftarrow{sr}), retrns(sr))$$

for the result part. (These rules require obvious extensions to cope with arguments and results.) The first of these requires that the domain of the operation on the representation is large enough; the second requires that the transition on the representation—when viewed under the retrieve function—nowhere contradicts the specification on the abstract states. Proofs of these results are straightforward.

These proof rules are more general than required for this situation but it should be remembered that the post-condition of ADD_1 could have been non-deterministic. Furthermore, at the next stage of development, the operations on *Setrep* would play the part of the specification so the rules need to cater with partial, non-deterministic operations in both the specification and the representation.

The interest here, however, focuses on the *incompleteness* of the above rules. It was known at the time the rules were published in [21] that there were valid steps of development which they would not support. In particular, it was obvious that any step of development which reversed the normal one-to-many relationship between abstraction and representation (e.g. to have *Setrep* in the specification and *Set* in the design) could not be justified since a retrieve function could not be found. This restriction was viewed as a virtue in so far as it tended to minimize the danger of biased specifications. Lockwood Morris also pointed out a technical problem in the need to tighten invariants so as to fulfil the requirements on retrieve functions.

What has become apparent more recently is that there are perfectly good specifications for which valid implementations cannot be justified by the above set of rules. A simple example of this situation results from the specification:

$$s_0 = \{\,\}$$

ARB () r: **N**

ext wr s : set of **N**

pre true

post $r \notin \overleftarrow{s} \wedge s = \overleftarrow{s} \cup \{r\}$

This requires that each invocation of the operation ARB returns a result which it has never returned before. The state is initialized to the empty set and ARB adds each element which it returns. This specification is (unboundedly!) non-deterministic. An implementation which simply returns the "next" natural number on each invocation violates none of the specified requirements—thus:

$$n_0 = 0$$

ARB_n () $r:\mathbf{N}$

ext wr n : $\mathbf{N}$

pre true

post $r = \overleftarrow{n} \wedge n = \overleftarrow{n} + 1$

Intuitively ARB_n is correct with respect to the specification ARB: it has the same domain and yields answers which do not contradict the specification. Thus, with appropriate use of the retrieve function, it can be seen that ARB_n satisfies ARB but it cannot be proved by the rules used above for the development of *Setrep*. Were this the only sort of counter-example, it would be possible to introduce special steps of development for the situation where a reduction in non-determinacy reduces the complexity of states. There is, unfortunately, another class of counter-examples. The root of the further weakness discovered in the proof obligations used above is that they were formulated around the aim of showing that each individual operation on the representation satisfied the corresponding abstract operation. This property is not necessary since it is the external behaviour of the collection of operations which needs to be preserved. Once this point is recognised it is a simple matter to generate further counter-examples. (It is, of course, the case that the above rules can be—straightforwardly—proved consistent with sat .)

3.4 An Alternative Rule

The problems discussed above have been overcome by a rule which is based on a relation between the abstract and representation state spaces:

$$\_ \sqsubseteq \_: Rep \times Abs \to \mathbf{B}$$

There are no proof obligations such as adequacy on $\sqsubseteq$; those for the operations are:

$$\forall a \in Abs, r \in Rep \cdot r \sqsubseteq a \wedge pre_A(a) \Rightarrow pre_R(r)$$

$$\forall \overleftarrow{a} \in Abs, \overleftarrow{r}, r \in Rep \cdot$$
$$\overleftarrow{r} \sqsubseteq \overleftarrow{a} \wedge pre_A(a) \wedge post_R(\overleftarrow{r}, r) \Rightarrow \exists a \in Abs \cdot post_A(\overleftarrow{a}, a) \wedge r \sqsubseteq a$$

(It is possible to avoid the need for special rules on the initial states if an initialization operation is included which behaves like a (possibly non-deterministic) constant.) A form of this rule is given in [27] where it is shown to be consistent and—in a sense made precise there—complete. The rule of the preceding sub-section can also be seen to be a specialization of this one.

4   Operation Decomposition

The need to have post-conditions which relate final to initial states is illustrated above. It is such a natural way of thinking about the specification of a system that it comes as a surprise that much of the work on program proofs uses post-conditions of the final state alone. VDM uses post-conditions of two states [9]. What form are the proof rules for operation decomposition to have when post-conditions do relate final to initial states? Unfortunately, the proof obligations given in [21] are rather heavy. They do succeed in splitting the task of checking a decomposition step into small, separate, proof steps. But the rules are certainly not memorable. The suggestions made by Peter Aczel (cf. [1]), however, have led to rules which bear comparison with those in [15].

---

[9] Another issue which divides some specification methods from VDM is its separation of the pre-condition. It should be clear that (a form of) the pre-condition could be conjoined to the post-condition so as to yield a single predicate which comprises the whole specification of an operation. In Z, for example, there is one predicate to define an operation (cf. [14]).

4.1 The Proof Rules

The most basic way of combining two operations is to execute them in sequence. It would be reasonable to expect that the first operation must leave the state so that the pre-condition of the second operation is satisfied. In order to write this, a distinction must be made between the relational and single-state properties guaranteed by the first statement. The names of the truth-valued functions have been chosen as a reminder of the distinction between:

$$P: \Sigma \to \mathbf{B}$$
$$R: \Sigma \times \Sigma \to \mathbf{B}$$

Writing:

$$R_1 \mid R_2$$

for:

$$\exists \sigma_i \cdot R_1(\overleftarrow{\sigma}, \sigma_i) \wedge R_2(\sigma_i, \sigma)$$

the sequence rule is:

$$\frac{\{P_1\}S_1\{P_2 \wedge R_1\}, \ \{P_2\}S_2\{R_2\}}{\{P_1\}S_1; S_2\{R_1 \mid R_2\}}$$

The predicate P_2 can be seen as the designer's choice of interface between S_1 and S_2 whereas R_1 and R_2 fix the functionality of the two components.

Proof obligations for conditional statements are given by:

$$\frac{\{P \wedge B\}TH\{R\}, \ \{P \wedge \neg B\}EL\{R\}}{\{P\} \text{ if } B \text{ then } TH \text{ else } EL\{R\}}$$

Some proofs also use a rule which permits the use of stronger pre-conditions or weaker post-conditions:

$$\frac{PP \ \Rightarrow \ P, \ \{P\}S\{RR\}, \ RR \ \Rightarrow \ R}{\{PP\}S\{R\}}$$

The proof obligation for iteration is the most interesting—the general form is:

$$\frac{\{P \wedge B\}S\{P \wedge R\}}{\{P\} \text{ while } B \text{ do } S\{P \wedge \neg B \wedge R^*\}}$$

R is required to be well-founded[10] and transitive. In order to be well-founded, the logical expression R must be irreflexive (e.g. $x < \overleftarrow{x}$). Since the body of the loop might not be executed at all, the state might not be changed by the while loop. Thus the overall post-condition can (only) assume R^* which is the reflexive closure of R (e.g. $x \leq \overleftarrow{x}$). The rest of this rule is easy to understand. The expression P is an invariant which is true after any number of iterations (including zero) of the loop body. This is, in fact, just a special use of a data type invariant. The falseness of B after the loop follows immediately from the meaning of the loop construct. Examples of using these rules to annotate programs are given in Figures 3 and 4. The use of these rules in development is illustrated in [20].

The remainder of this section provides a semantic model against which the proof rules for operation decomposition can be judged and proves that the rules are consistent with that model. Some other important properties of the model are also discussed.

---

[10] There is a significant advantage in requiring that R be well-founded since the proof obligation then establishes termination.

POSMULT
ext wr $i, m: \mathbf{Z}$, rd $j: \mathbf{Z}$
pre $0 \leq i$

    $m := 0$

    ;

    pre $0 \leq i$

        while $i \neq 0$ do
        inv $0 \leq i$

            $i := i - 1;$
            $m := m + j;$
        rel $m = \overleftarrow{m} + (\overleftarrow{i} - i) * \overleftarrow{j} \wedge i < \overleftarrow{i}$
        post $m = \overleftarrow{m} + \overleftarrow{i} * \overleftarrow{j}$
post $m = \overleftarrow{i} * \overleftarrow{j}$

Figure 3: Development for Multiplication Example

POSMULT
ext wr $i, j, m: \mathbf{Z}$
pre $0 \leq i$

    $m := 0$

    ;

    pre $0 \leq i$

        while $i \neq 0$ do
        inv $0 \leq i$

            ext wr $i, j: \mathbf{Z}$
            pre $i \neq 0$

                while *is-even*(i) do
                inv $1 \leq i$

                    $i := i/2$
                    $j := j * 2$
                rel $i * j = \overleftarrow{i} * \overleftarrow{j} \wedge i < \overleftarrow{i}$
              post $i * j = \overleftarrow{i} * \overleftarrow{j} \wedge i \leq \overleftarrow{i}$

            ;

            $m := m + j;$
            $i := i - 1$
        rel $m + i * j = \overline{m} + \overleftarrow{i} * \overleftarrow{j} \wedge i < \overleftarrow{i}$
        post $m = \overline{m} + \overleftarrow{i} * \overleftarrow{j}$
post $m = \overleftarrow{i} * \overleftarrow{j}$

Figure 4: Alternative Development for Multiplication Example

4.2 A Denotational Semantics

The constructs used for operation decomposition above are sequential composition, conditional statements and a repetitive construct. The following abstract syntax fixes the language:

$Stmt = Atomic \mid Composition \mid If \mid While$
$Composition :: Stmt\ Stmt$
$If :: Expr\ Stmt\ Stmt$
$While :: Expr\ Stmt$

The semantic definition of this language has to cope with both non-termination and non-determinacy. It is clear that the *While* construct could result in non-termination; it is also assumed that the elements of *Atomic* might be undefined for some states. Non-determinacy[11] can arise from the *Atomic* statements and it is shown below that specifications in the pre-/post-condition form can be used in place of such statements. The semantic model used here to cope with these problems consists of a pair with a first element which is a termination set (of elements of Σ) and a second element which is a meaning relation (from $\Sigma \times \Sigma$)[12]. Thus, two semantic functions:

$$\mathcal{M}: Stmt \rightarrow \mathcal{P}(\Sigma \times \Sigma)$$

$$\mathcal{T}: Stmt \rightarrow \mathcal{P}(\Sigma)$$

are given. The set given by $\mathcal{T}$ is the set over which termination is guaranteed; the domain of the relation $\mathcal{M}$ can be thought of as showing a set over which termination is possible. Thus, it is possible to distinguish between:

$$(\{a\}, \{a \mapsto z, b \mapsto z\})$$

and:

$$(\{a, b\}, \{a \mapsto z, b \mapsto z\})$$

This becomes important when the relational composition of R_1 and R_2 is considered:

$R_1 = \{a \mapsto m, b \mapsto m, b \mapsto n\}$
$R_2 = \{m \mapsto z\}$
$R_1; R_2 = \{a \mapsto z, b \mapsto z\}$

If this were defined as the semantics of sequential composition, an implementation would be obliged to realize *angelic non-determinism*.

Intuitively, it should be clear that:

$$\forall s \in Stmt \cdot \mathcal{T}[\![s]\!] \subseteq \text{dom}\, \mathcal{M}[\![s]\!]$$

That this property holds for non-atomic statements is proved below: it is an assumption on the meaning of the *Atomic* statements:
Assumption (A1)

$$\forall s \in Atomic \cdot \mathcal{T}[\![s]\!] \subseteq \text{dom}\, \mathcal{M}[\![s]\!]$$

The meaning relation for the sequential composition of two statements is defined as the relational composition[13] of the meaning relations of these two statements:

$$\mathcal{M}[\![mk\text{-}Composition(S_1, S_2)]\!] \triangleq \mathcal{M}[\![S_1]\!]; \mathcal{M}[\![S_2]\!]$$

---

[11] An additional source of non-determinacy can be brought in by using guarded conditional or loop constructs as discussed in [9]; the semantics is given for the former (and the relevant properties proved) in [18].
[12] This follows the approach used in [18] which was, in turn, prompted by [28].
[13] $R_1; R_2 \triangleq \{(\sigma, \sigma'') \mid \exists \sigma' \cdot (\sigma, \sigma') \in R_1 \wedge (\sigma', \sigma'') \in R_2\}$

This would, taken alone, require angelic nondeterminism; this is avoided by showing the required termination set to be (only)[14]:

$$T[\![mk\text{-}Composition(S_1, S_2)]\!] \triangleq T[\![S_1]\!] - \text{dom}\,(\mathcal{M}[\![S_1]\!] \blacktriangleright T[\![S_2]\!])$$

This definition shows that the composition is only required to terminate on states in which both S_1 terminates and its meaning relation can not give rise to a state in which S_2 fails to terminate.

The meaning relation for the simple conditional construct[15] is given by:

$$\mathcal{M}[\![mk\text{-}If(B, TH, EL)]\!] \triangleq (\overline{B} \lhd \mathcal{M}[\![TH]\!]) \cup (\overline{\neg B} \lhd \mathcal{M}[\![EL]\!])$$

The termination set is given by:

$$T[\![mk\text{-}If(B, TH, EL)]\!] \triangleq (\overline{B} \cap T[\![TH]\!]) \cup (\overline{\neg B} \cap T[\![EL]\!])$$

The least fixed point operator (fix) is needed to define the semantics for *While* statements. The meaning relation is defined by:

$$\mathcal{M}[\![mk\text{-}While(B, S)]\!] \triangleq fix(\lambda r \cdot (\overline{\neg B} \lhd I) \cup (\overline{B} \lhd \mathcal{M}[\![S]\!]; r))$$

This presents the same (angelic non-determinism) problem as with sequential composition. A similar approach to its resolution can be given:

$$T[\![mk\text{-}While(B, S)]\!] \triangleq fix(\lambda s \cdot \overline{\neg B} \cup ((\overline{B} \cap T[\![S]\!]) - \text{dom}\,(\mathcal{M}[\![S]\!] \blacktriangleright s)))$$

But this definition presents some technical difficulties below since it is equivalent to:

$$fix(\lambda s \cdot \overline{\neg B} \cup \{\overleftarrow{\sigma} \in (\overline{B} \cap T[\![S]\!]) \mid \forall \sigma \cdot (\overleftarrow{\sigma}, \sigma) \in \mathcal{M}[\![S]\!] \Rightarrow \sigma \in s\})$$

because:

$$
\begin{aligned}
s_1 - \text{dom}\,(r_1 \blacktriangleright s_2) \\
&= \{\overleftarrow{\sigma} \in s_1 \mid \overleftarrow{\sigma} \notin \text{dom}\,(r_1 \blacktriangleright s_2)\} \\
&= \{\overleftarrow{\sigma} \in s_1 \mid \neg \exists \sigma \cdot (\overleftarrow{\sigma}, \sigma) \in r_1 \land \sigma \notin s_2\} \\
&= \{\overleftarrow{\sigma} \in s_1 \mid \forall \sigma \cdot (\overleftarrow{\sigma}, \sigma) \notin r_1 \lor \sigma \in s_2\} \\
&= \{\overleftarrow{\sigma} \in s_1 \mid \forall \sigma \cdot (\overleftarrow{\sigma}, \sigma) \in r_1 \Rightarrow \sigma \in s_2\}
\end{aligned}
$$

and the fixed-point equation with the embedded universal quantifier is not ω-continuous.

Fixed-point definitions sometimes appear rather abstract. In this case, it is possible to understand them quite easily from examples (whose understanding will help with the subsequent proofs). Consider:

$$WH_1 = \text{ while } i \neq 0 \text{ do } i: \in \{0, \ldots, i\text{-}1\}$$

where the $: \in$ indicates a non-deterministic assignment. For this construct the expression $\overline{\neg B} \lhd I$ is equal to[16]:

$$\{(0, 0)\}$$

Now, $\overline{B} \lhd \mathcal{M}[\![S]\!]$ is equal to:

$$\{(i, j) \mid i, j \in \mathbf{N} \land j < i\}$$

So that, the nth approximation of $\mathcal{M}[\![WH_1]\!]$ is:

$$\{(i, 0) \mid i \in \mathbf{N} \land i \leq n\}$$

---

[14] $R \blacktriangleright S \triangleq \{(\overleftarrow{\sigma}, \sigma) \in R \mid \sigma \notin S\}$

[15] The set of states satisfying the truth-valued function p is written $\overline{p}$; I is the identity relation (on Σ). Here, expression evaluation is assumed to be total; [18] shows how the more general case is handled by a (T) function which gives the states over which an expression is defined.

[16] The, single element, states are represented as a single integer.

Thus:

$$\mathcal{M}[\![WH_1]\!] = \{(i,0) \mid i \in \mathbf{N}\}$$

Similarly:

$$T[\![WH_1]\!] = \mathbf{N}$$

The problem of ω-continuity becomes apparent in the following, unboundedly, non-deterministic case:

$$WH_2 = \text{ while } i \neq 0 \text{ do } IF_2$$

$$IF_2 = \text{ if } i < 0$$
$$\quad \text{ then } i{:}\in \mathbf{N}$$
$$\quad \text{ else if } i > 0$$
$$\quad\quad \text{ then } i{:}= i - 1$$
$$\quad\quad \text{ else fail}$$

Here:

$$\mathcal{M}[\![IF_2]\!] = \{(i,j) \mid i < 0 \wedge j \geq 0\} \cup \{(i,i-1) \mid i > 0\}$$
$$T[\![IF_2]\!] = \mathbf{Z} - \{0\}$$

Clearly:

$$\mathcal{M}[\![WH_2]\!] = \{(i,0) \mid i \in \mathbf{Z}\}$$

But what of $T[\![WH_2]\!]$? Zero and all positive integers get brought into the fixed-point; a negative value, however, can only be added when all of its possible successor states have been put into the fixed-point. Thus:

$$\bigcup_{n=0}^{\infty} \mathcal{F}^n(\{\}) = \mathbf{N}$$

But another fixed-point of T is:

$$\mathcal{F}(\mathbf{Z}) = \mathbf{Z}$$

The only way of arriving at this is to move (following Park in [28]) into the transfinite and note:

$$\mathcal{F}^{\omega+1} = \mathcal{F}(\mathcal{F}^\omega(\{\})) = \mathcal{F}(\mathbf{N}) = \mathbf{Z}$$

4.3   Properties of the Semantics

The first property to be considered is the containment of the termination set within the domain of the meaning relation. This has been assumed (A1) for *Atomic* statements; it must now be shown to inherit across each of the constructions for composite statements.

The result required for *Composition* is:

Lemma (C1)

$$T[\![S_1]\!] \subseteq \text{dom } \mathcal{M}[\![S_1]\!], T[\![S_2]\!] \subseteq \text{dom } \mathcal{M}[\![S_2]\!] \vdash$$
$$T[\![mk\text{-}Composition(S_1,S_2)]\!] \subseteq \text{dom } \mathcal{M}[\![mk\text{-}Composition(S_1,S_2)]\!]$$

The proof[17] is given in Figure 7; this uses a Lemma (T1)[18] whose proof is given in Figure 6.

---

[17] In each of these proofs an appeal to $\mathcal{M}$ or T is to be read as a reference to the appropriate case of the semantic function—they are summarised in Figure 5 for ease of reference.

[18] This Lemma was suggested by Lynn Marshall. Notice that the result does not hold if the consequent of the sequent is an equality; consider:

$$s_1 = \{a\}$$
$$r_1 = \{a \mapsto m, a \mapsto n\}$$
$$s_2 = \{m\}$$

$Stmt = Atomic \mid Composition \mid If \mid While$
$Composition :: Stmt \; Stmt$
$If :: Expr \; Stmt \; Stmt$
$While :: Expr \; Stmt$

$M: Stmt \to \mathcal{P}(\Sigma \times \Sigma)$
$T: Stmt \to \mathcal{P}(\Sigma)$

$\forall s \in Atomic \cdot T[\![s]\!] \subseteq \operatorname{dom} M[\![s]\!]$

$M[\![mk\text{-}Composition(S_1, S_2)]\!] \triangleq M[\![S_1]\!]; M[\![S_2]\!]$
$T[\![mk\text{-}Composition(S_1, S_2)]\!] \triangleq T[\![S_1]\!] - \operatorname{dom}(M[\![S_1]\!] \triangleright T[\![S_2]\!])$

$M[\![mk\text{-}If(B, TH, EL)]\!] \triangleq (\overline{B} \triangleleft M[\![TH]\!]) \cup (\overline{\neg B} \triangleleft M[\![EL]\!])$
$T[\![mk\text{-}If(B, TH, EL)]\!] \triangleq (\overline{B} \cap T[\![TH]\!]) \cup (\overline{\neg B} \cap T[\![EL]\!])$

$M[\![mk\text{-}While(B, S)]\!] \triangleq fix(\lambda r \cdot (\overline{\neg B} \triangleleft I) \cup (\overline{B} \triangleleft M[\![S]\!]; r)$
$T[\![mk\text{-}While(B, S)]\!] \triangleq fix(\lambda s \cdot \overline{\neg B} \cup ((\overline{B} \cap T[\![S]\!]) - \operatorname{dom}(M[\![S]\!] \triangleright s)))$

Figure 5: Summary of Language Semantics

from $s_1 \subseteq \operatorname{dom} r_1$

1	$s - \operatorname{dom}(s \triangleleft r) = s - \operatorname{dom} r$	—
2	$\operatorname{dom} r_2 - \operatorname{dom} r_3 \subseteq \operatorname{dom}(r_2 - r_3)$	dom
3	$\operatorname{dom}(r - (r \triangleright s)) = \operatorname{dom}(r \triangleright s)$	dom, $\triangleright$
4	$s_1 - \operatorname{dom}(r_1 \triangleright s_2)$	1
	$\quad = s_1 - \operatorname{dom}(s_1 \triangleleft r_1 \triangleright s_2)$	
5	$\quad = \operatorname{dom}(s_1 \triangleleft r_1) - \operatorname{dom}(s_1 \triangleleft r_1 \triangleright s_2)$	4,h
6	$\quad \subseteq \operatorname{dom}((s_1 \triangleleft r_1) - (s_1 \triangleleft r_1 \triangleright s_2))$	5,2
infer	$s_1 - \operatorname{dom}(r_1 \triangleright s_2) \subseteq \operatorname{dom}(s_1 \triangleleft r_1 \triangleright s_2)$	6,3

Figure 6: Proof of Lemma T1

from $T[\![S_1]\!] \subseteq \operatorname{dom} M[\![S_1]\!]$, $T[\![S_2]\!] \subseteq \operatorname{dom} M[\![S_2]\!]$

1	$\operatorname{dom}(M[\![mk\text{-}Composition(S_1, S_2)]\!]) = \operatorname{dom}(M[\![S_1]\!]; M[\![S_2]\!])$	M
2	$T[\![mk\text{-}Composition(S_1, S_2)]\!]$	T
	$\quad = T[\![S_1]\!] - \operatorname{dom}(M[\![S_1]\!] \triangleright T[\![S_2]\!])$	
3	$\quad \subseteq \operatorname{dom}(T[\![S_1]\!] \triangleleft M[\![S_1]\!] \triangleright T[\![S_2]\!])$	T1(h)
4	$\quad \subseteq \operatorname{dom}(M[\![S_1]\!] \triangleright T[\![S_2]\!])$	3,$\triangleleft$,dom, h
5	$\quad \subseteq \operatorname{dom}(M[\![S_1]\!] \triangleright \operatorname{dom} M[\![S_2]\!])$	4,h
6	$\quad \subseteq \operatorname{dom}(M[\![S_1]\!]; M[\![S_2]\!])$	5,dom
infer	$T[\![mk\text{-}Composition(S_1, S_2)]\!] \subseteq \operatorname{dom}(M[\![mk\text{-}Composition(S_1, S_2)]\!])$	1,6

Figure 7: Proof of Lemma C1

The result required for *If* statements is:

Lemma (I1)

$$T[\![TH]\!] \subseteq \text{dom } \mathcal{M}[\![TH]\!], T[\![EL]\!] \subseteq \text{dom } \mathcal{M}[\![EL]\!] \vdash$$
$$T[\![mk\text{-}If(B, TH, EL)]\!] \subseteq \text{dom } \mathcal{M}[\![mk\text{-}If(B, TH, EL)]\!]$$

The proof of this is given in Figure 8.

The result required for *While* statements is:

Lemma (W1)

$$T[\![S]\!] \subseteq \text{dom } \mathcal{M}[\![S]\!] \vdash T[\![mk\text{-}While(B, S)]\!] \subseteq \text{dom } \mathcal{M}[\![mk\text{-}While(B, S)]\!]$$

A direct proof of this result is made difficult to understand because the technicalities of the need to reason about a continuous version of T are obscured by the length of the specific definitions for *While* statements. It is worth proving a more general result about such recursive semantic equations:

Lemma (R1)

$$BS \subseteq \text{dom } BR, IS \subseteq \text{dom } IR \vdash$$
$$fix(\lambda s \cdot BS \cup (IS - \text{dom } (IR \rhd s))) \subseteq \text{dom } fix(\lambda r \cdot BR \cup (IR; r))$$

A continuous version of the expression in the first term is used in the proof:

$$\mathcal{F}(s) \triangleq BS \cup \{\overleftarrow{\sigma} \in IS \mid \exists \sigma \cdot (\overleftarrow{\sigma}, \sigma) \in IR \wedge \sigma \in s\}$$
$$\subseteq BS \cup \text{dom } (IR \rhd s)$$

another expression used in the proof is:

$$\mathcal{G}(r) \triangleq BR \cup (IR; r)$$

The proof is given in Figure 9. Then, using the following identities:

$$BS = \overline{\neg B}$$
$$BR = \overline{\neg B} \lhd I$$
$$IS = \overline{B} \cap T[\![S]\!]$$
$$IR = \overline{B} \lhd \mathcal{M}[\![S]\!]$$

and noting that:

$$BS = \text{dom } BR$$
$$T[\![S]\!] \subseteq \text{dom } \mathcal{M}[\![S]\!] \vdash IS \subseteq \text{dom } IR$$

the proof of W1 is an immediate corollary of R1.

The above results (A1, C1, I1, W1) combine to give the result for the whole language:

Theorem (L1)

$$\forall s \in Stmt \cdot T[\![s]\!] \subseteq \text{dom } \mathcal{M}[\![s]\!]$$

The notion of *satisfaction* is introduced in Section 3. It can be expressed in the notation used here as:

$$S' \text{ sat } S \triangleq T[\![S]\!] \subseteq T[\![S']\!] \wedge T[\![S]\!] \lhd \mathcal{M}[\![S']\!] \subseteq \mathcal{M}[\![S]\!]$$

The reduction of a pre/post-condition specification to such pairs is also described above. The semantics for *Stmt* completes the picture: specifications and programs can be treated on a common semantic footing. There is, furthermore, no difficulty with inserting specifications as *Atomic* statements in programs. What does *compositionality* mean in terms of the sat relation? It requires that each of the ways of forming composite statements is monotone in the sat ordering. Thus, for sequential composition:

Lemma (C2)

$$S'_1 \text{ sat } S_1, S'_2 \text{ sat } S_2 \vdash mk\text{-}Composition(S'_1, S'_2) \text{ sat } mk\text{-}Composition(S_1, S_2)$$

from $\mathcal{T}[\![TH]\!] \subseteq \text{dom}\,\mathcal{M}[\![TH]\!]$, $\mathcal{T}[\![EL]\!] \subseteq \text{dom}\,\mathcal{M}[\![EL]\!]$

1	$\mathcal{T}[\![mk\text{-}If(B, TH, EL)]\!]$	$\mathcal{T}$
	$\quad = (\overline{B} \cap \mathcal{T}[\![TH]\!]) \cup (\neg\overline{B} \cap \mathcal{T}[\![EL]\!])$	
2	$\quad \subseteq (\overline{B} \cap \text{dom}\,\mathcal{M}[\![TH]\!]) \cup (\neg\overline{B} \cap \text{dom}\,\mathcal{M}[\![EL]\!])$	1,h,h
3	$\quad \subseteq \text{dom}\,(\overline{B} \lhd \mathcal{T}[\![TH]\!]) \cup \text{dom}\,(\neg\overline{B} \lhd \mathcal{M}[\![EL]\!])$	2, $\lhd$
4	$\quad \subseteq \text{dom}\,((\overline{B} \lhd \mathcal{M}[\![TH]\!]) \cup (\neg\overline{B} \lhd \mathcal{M}[\![EL]\!]))$	3, $\cup$
infer	$\quad \subseteq \text{dom}\,\mathcal{M}[\![mk\text{-}If(B, TH, EL)]\!]$	4, $\mathcal{M}$

Figure 8: Proof of Lemma I1

from $BS \subseteq \text{dom}\,BR$, $IS \subseteq \text{dom}\,IR$

1	$\mathcal{F}^o(\{\,\}) \subseteq \text{dom}\,\mathcal{G}^o(\{\,\})$	set
2	$\mathcal{F}^1(\{\,\}) \subseteq \text{dom}\,\mathcal{G}^1(\{\,\})$	$\mathcal{F},\mathcal{G},$h
3	from $\mathcal{F}^n(\{\,\}) \subseteq \text{dom}\,\mathcal{G}^n(\{\,\}), n \geq 1$	
3.1	$\quad \mathcal{F}^{n+1}(\{\,\}) \subseteq BS \cup \text{dom}\,(IR \rhd \mathcal{F}^n(\{\,\}))$	$\mathcal{F}$
3.2	$\quad\quad \subseteq BS \cup \text{dom}\,(IR \rhd \text{dom}\,\mathcal{G}^n(\{\,\}))$	3.1,h3
3.3	$\quad \mathcal{G}^{n+1}(\{\,\}) = BR \cup (IR;\mathcal{G}^n(\{\,\}))$	$\mathcal{G}$
3.4	$\quad \text{dom}\,\mathcal{G}^{n+1}(\{\,\})$	3.3,dom
	$\quad\quad = \text{dom}\,BR \cup \text{dom}\,(IR;\mathcal{G}^n(\{\,\}))$	
3.5	$\quad\quad = \text{dom}\,BR \cup \text{dom}\,(IR \rhd \text{dom}\,\mathcal{G}^n(\{\,\}))$	3.4,dom , $\rhd$
infer	$\mathcal{F}^{n+1}(\{\,\}) \subseteq \text{dom}\,\mathcal{G}^{n+1}(\{\,\})$	3.2,3.5,h
4	$\forall n \in \mathbf{N} \cdot \mathcal{F}^n(\{\,\}) \subseteq \text{dom}\,\mathcal{G}^n(\{\,\})$	N-ind(1,2,3)
5	$\bigcup_{n \leq 0} \mathcal{F}^n(\{\,\}) \subseteq \text{dom}\,\bigcup_{n \leq 0} \mathcal{G}^n(\{\,\})$	4, monotonicity
6	$\mathit{fix}(\lambda s \cdot BS \cup (IS - \text{dom}\,(IR \rhd s)))$	T1(h)
	$\quad \subseteq \mathit{fix}(\lambda s \cdot BS \cup \text{dom}\,(IS \lhd IR \rhd s))$	
7	$\quad \subseteq \mathit{fix}(\lambda s \cdot BS \cup \text{dom}\,(IR \rhd s))$	6,h
8	$\quad \subseteq \bigcup_{n \geq 0} \mathcal{F}^n(\{\,\})$	7,$\mathcal{F}$,fix
infer	$\mathit{fix}(\lambda s \cdot BS \cup (IS - \text{dom}\,(IR \rhd s))) \subseteq \text{dom}\,\mathit{fix}(\lambda r \cdot BR \cup IR; r)$	8,5,$\mathcal{G}$,fix

Figure 9: Proof of Lemma R1

The proof of this result is given in Figure 10.

The result for *If* statements:

Lemma(I2)

$$TH' \text{ sat } TH, EL' \text{ sat } EL \vdash mk\text{-}If(B, TH', EL') \text{ sat } mk\text{-}If(B, TH, EL)$$

is proved in Figure 11.

The final result of this form on the whole language (L2 below) ensures that, if a series of statements are developed so as to satisfy a specification SP, then the statements can be used in the implementation of any design which needs a component specified as SP; and that implementation is bound to satisfy its specification even though its proof used only the properties SP and not the series of statements.

But the achievement of this goal requires that the corresponding property is proved for *While* statements;

Lemma (W2)

$$S' \text{ sat } S \vdash mk\text{-}While(B, S') \text{ sat } mk\text{-}While(B, S)$$

is proved in Figure 12.

The overall result (L2) that all of the language constructs are monotone in sat follows from C2, I2 and W2.

4.4 Justification of the Proof Rules

The proof obligations for the various language constructs can now be justified with respect to the T/M semantics which is given above. The link between the triples:

$$\{P\}S\{R\}$$

where:

$$P: \Sigma \to \mathbf{B}$$
$$R: \Sigma \times \Sigma \to \mathbf{B}$$

is given by[19]:

$$\{P\}S\{R\} \triangleq \overline{P} \subseteq T[\![S]\!] \wedge \overline{P} \vartriangleleft M[\![S]\!] \subseteq \overline{R}$$

The proof obligations for sequence and conditional are justified in Figures 13 and 14 respectively.

The use of a transitive, well-founded relation R in the proof obligation for while gives rise to a (complete) induction rule:

$$R\text{-}ind \qquad \frac{s \subseteq S, \; \text{rng}(s \vartriangleleft R^+) \subseteq T \vdash s \subseteq T}{S \subseteq T}$$

This rule can be used to reason about T (where Scott induction is not applicable because of the lack of continuity). As in the complete induction rule over integers, the induction hypothesis is taken here to cover all (R^+) predecessors of the required set. To find the apparently omitted base case for the inductive proof one must consider those elements with no predecessors ($s - \text{dom } R$). It is however possible to avoid this case distinction in some proofs and the proof of Lemma W3 is given below is simpler than the corresponding proof in [18] for precisely this reason.

The result about the termination of the while is:

Lemma (W3)

$$\overline{P} \cap \overline{B} \subseteq T[\![S]\!], \; (\overline{P} \cap \overline{B}) \vartriangleleft M[\![S]\!] \subseteq \overline{R}, \; \text{rng}((\overline{P} \cap \overline{B}) \vartriangleleft M[\![S]\!]) \subseteq \overline{P} \vdash$$
$$\overline{P} \subseteq T[\![mk\text{-}While(B, S)]\!]$$

---

[19]Some care is needed in the interpretation of post-conditions which are conjunctions.

from S_1' sat S_1, S_2' sat S_2

1	$\mathcal{T}[\![S_1]\!] \subseteq \mathcal{T}[\![S_1']\!]$	h, sat
2	$\mathcal{T}[\![S_1]\!] \triangleleft \mathcal{M}[\![S_1']\!] \subseteq \mathcal{M}[\![S_1]\!]$	h, sat
3	$\mathcal{T}[\![S_2]\!] \subseteq \mathcal{T}[\![S_2']\!]$	h, sat
4	$\mathcal{T}[\![S_2]\!] \triangleleft \mathcal{M}[\![S_2']\!] \subseteq \mathcal{M}[\![S_2]\!]$	h, sat
5	$\mathcal{T}[\![mk\text{-}Composition(S_1,S_2)]\!]$	$\mathcal{T}$
	$= \mathcal{T}[\![S_1]\!] - \mathrm{dom}\,(\mathcal{M}[\![S_1]\!] \triangleright \mathcal{T}[\![S_2]\!])$	
6	$\subseteq \mathcal{T}[\![S_1]\!] - \mathrm{dom}\,(\mathcal{M}[\![S_1']\!] \triangleright \mathcal{T}[\![S_2]\!])$	5,2, −
7	$\subseteq \mathcal{T}[\![S_1]\!] - \mathrm{dom}\,(\mathcal{M}[\![S_1']\!] \triangleright \mathcal{T}[\![S_2']\!])$	6,3, $\triangleright$
8	$\subseteq \mathcal{T}[\![S_1']\!] - \mathrm{dom}\,(\mathcal{M}[\![S_1']\!] \triangleright \mathcal{T}[\![S_2']\!])$	7,1
9	$\subseteq \mathcal{T}[\![mk\text{-}Composition(S_1',S_2')]\!]$	8,$\mathcal{T}$
10	$\mathcal{T}[\![mk\text{-}Composition(S_1,S_2)]\!] \triangleleft \mathcal{M}[\![mk\text{-}Composition(S_1',S_2')]\!]$	$\mathcal{T},\mathcal{M}$
	$= (\mathcal{T}[\![S_1]\!] - \mathrm{dom}\,(\mathcal{M}[\![S_1]\!] \triangleright \mathcal{T}[\![S_2]\!])) \triangleleft (\mathcal{M}[\![S_1']\!]; \mathcal{M}[\![S_2']\!])$	
11	$\subseteq (\mathcal{T}[\![S_1]\!] - \mathrm{dom}\,(\mathcal{M}[\![S_1]\!] \triangleright \mathcal{T}[\![S_2]\!])) \triangleleft (\mathcal{M}[\![S_1]\!]; \mathcal{M}[\![S_2]\!])$	10,2,4,−, $\triangleright$
12	$\subseteq \mathcal{M}[\![S_1]\!]; \mathcal{M}[\![S_2]\!]$	11, $\triangleleft$
13	$\subseteq \mathcal{M}[\![mk\text{-}Composition(S_1,S_2)]\!]$	12, $\mathcal{M}$
infer	$mk\text{-}Composition(S_1',S_2')$ sat $mk\text{-}Composition(S_1,S_2)$	9,13, sat

Figure 10: Proof of Lemma C2

from TH' sat TH, EL' sat EL

1	$\mathcal{T}[\![TH]\!] \subseteq \mathcal{T}[\![TH']\!]$	h, sat
2	$\mathcal{T}[\![EL]\!] \subseteq \mathcal{T}[\![EL']\!]$	h, sat
3	$\mathcal{T}[\![TH]\!] \triangleleft \mathcal{M}[\![TH']\!] \subseteq \mathcal{M}[\![TH]\!]$	h, sat
4	$\mathcal{T}[\![EL]\!] \triangleleft \mathcal{M}[\![EL']\!] \subseteq \mathcal{M}[\![EL]\!]$	h, sat
5	$\mathcal{T}[\![mk\text{-}If(B, TH, EL)]\!]$	$\mathcal{T}$
	$= (\overline{B} \cap \mathcal{T}[\![TH]\!]) \cup (\overline{\neg B} \cap \mathcal{T}[\![EL]\!])$	
6	$\subseteq (\overline{B} \cap \mathcal{T}[\![TH']\!]) \cup (\overline{\neg B} \cap \mathcal{T}[\![EL']\!])$	5,1,2
7	$\subseteq \mathcal{T}[\![mk\text{-}If(B, TH', EL')]\!]$	6,$\mathcal{T}$
8	$\overline{B} \cap \overline{\neg B}$	set
9	$\mathcal{T}[\![mk\text{-}If(B, TH, EL)]\!] \triangleleft \mathcal{M}[\![mk\text{-}If(B, TH', EL')]\!]$	$\mathcal{T},\mathcal{M}$
	$= ((\overline{B} \cap \mathcal{T}[\![TH]\!]) \cup (\overline{\neg B} \cap \mathcal{T}[\![EL]\!])) \triangleleft (\overline{B} \triangleleft \mathcal{M}[\![TH']\!] \cup \overline{\neg B} \triangleleft \mathcal{M}[\![EL']\!])$	
10	$= ((\overline{B} \cap \mathcal{T}[\![TH]\!]) \triangleleft \mathcal{M}[\![TH']\!]) \cup ((\overline{\neg B} \cap \mathcal{T}[\![EL]\!]) \triangleleft \mathcal{M}[\![EL']\!])$	8,9
11	$\subseteq ((\overline{B} \cap \mathcal{T}[\![TH]\!]) \triangleleft \mathcal{M}[\![TH]\!]) \cup ((\overline{\neg B} \cap \mathcal{T}[\![EL]\!]) \triangleleft \mathcal{M}[\![EL]\!])$	10,3,4
12	$\subseteq (\overline{B} \triangleleft \mathcal{M}[\![TH]\!]) \cup (\overline{\neg B} \triangleleft \mathcal{M}[\![EL]\!])$	11
13	$\subseteq \mathcal{M}[\![mk\text{-}If(B, TH, EL)]\!]$	12, $\mathcal{M}$
infer	$mk\text{-}If(B, TH', EL')$ sat $mk\text{-}If(B, TH, EL)$	7,13, sat

Figure 11: Proof of Lemma I2

from S' sat S

1      $T[\![S]\!] \subseteq T[\![S']\!]$ h, sat

2      $T[\![S]\!] \lhd \mathcal{M}[\![S']\!] \subseteq \mathcal{M}[\![S]\!]$ h, sat

3      $T[\![mk\text{-}While(B,S)]\!]$

         $= fix(\lambda s \cdot \neg \overline{B} \cup ((\overline{B} \cap T[\![S]\!]) - \mathsf{dom}\,(\mathcal{M}[\![S]\!] \rhd s)))$ T

4      $\subseteq fix(\lambda s \cdot \neg \overline{B} \cup ((\overline{B} \cap T[\![S']\!]) - \mathsf{dom}\,(\mathcal{M}[\![S']\!] \rhd s)))$ 3,2,1,$-$

5      $\subseteq T[\![mk\text{-}While(B,S')]\!]$ 4,T

6      $T[\![mk\text{-}While(B,S)]\!] \subseteq \neg\overline{B} \cup T[\![S]\!]$ T

7      $\neg\overline{B} \lhd I \subseteq I$ $I, \lhd$

8      $(T[\![S]\!] - \neg\overline{B}) \lhd \mathcal{M}[\![S']\!] \subseteq \mathcal{M}[\![S]\!]$ 2, $\lhd$

9      $T[\![mk\text{-}While(B,S)]\!] \lhd \mathcal{M}[\![mk\text{-}While(B,S')]\!] \subseteq \mathcal{M}[\![mk\text{-}While(B,S)]\!]$ 6,7,8,fix,$\mathcal{M}$

infer $mk\text{-}While(B,S')$ sat $mk\text{-}While(B,S)$ sat ,5,9

Figure 12: Proof of Lemma W2

from $\{P_1\}S_1\{P_2 \wedge R_1\}, \{P_2\}S_2\{R_2\}$

1      $\overline{P_1} \subseteq T[\![S_1]\!]$ h, triple

2      $\overline{P_1} \lhd \mathcal{M}[\![S_1]\!] \subseteq \overline{R_1}$ h, triple

3      $\mathsf{rng}\,(\overline{P_1} \lhd \mathcal{M}[\![S_1]\!]) \subseteq \overline{P_2}$ h, triple

4      $\overline{P_2} \subseteq T[\![S_2]\!]$ h, triple

5      $\overline{P_2} \lhd \mathcal{M}[\![S_2]\!] \subseteq \overline{R_2}$ h, triple

6      $\mathsf{rng}\,(\overline{P_1} \lhd \mathcal{M}[\![S_1]\!]) \subseteq T[\![S_2]\!]$ 3,4

7      $\overline{P_1} \cap (\mathsf{dom}\,(\mathcal{M}[\![S_1]\!] \rhd T[\![S_2]\!])) = \{\,\}$ 6

8      $\overline{P_1}$ 1,7

         $\subseteq T[\![S_1]\!] - \mathsf{dom}\,(\mathcal{M}[\![S_1]\!] \rhd T[\![S_2]\!])$

9      $\subseteq T[\![mk\text{-}Composition(S_1,S_2)]\!]$ 8,T

10      $\overline{P_1} \lhd \mathcal{M}[\![mk\text{-}Composition(S_1,S_2)]\!]$ $\mathcal{M}$

         $= \overline{P_1} \lhd (\mathcal{M}[\![S_1]\!]; \mathcal{M}[\![S_2]\!])$

11      $\subseteq \overline{P_1} \lhd (\mathcal{M}[\![S_1]\!]; \overline{R_2})$ 10,3,5

12      $\subseteq \overline{P_1} \lhd (\overline{R_1}; \overline{R_2})$ 11,2

13      $\subseteq \overline{R_1}; \overline{R_2}$ 12,$\lhd$

infer $\{P_1\}S_1; S_2\{R_1 \mid R_2\}$ triple, 9, 13

Figure 13: Proof of Lemma C3

from $\{P \wedge B\} TH \{R\}$, $\{P \wedge \neg B\} EL\{R\}$

1	$\overline{P} \cap \overline{B} \subseteq T[\![TH]\!]$	h, triple
2	$(\overline{P} \cap \overline{B}) \lhd M[\![TH]\!] \subseteq \overline{R}$	h, triple
3	$\overline{P} \cap \overline{\neg B} \subseteq T[\![EL]\!]$	h, triple
4	$(\overline{P} \cap \overline{\neg B}) \lhd M[\![EL]\!] \subseteq \overline{R}$	h, triple
5	$\overline{P} \subseteq (\overline{B} \cup \overline{\neg B})$	B is total
6	$\overline{P}$	1, 3, 5
	$\subseteq (\overline{B} \cap T[\![TH]\!]) \cup (\overline{\neg B} \cap T[\![EL]\!])$	
7	$\subseteq T[\![mk\text{-}If(B, TH, EL)]\!]$	6, T
8	$\overline{P} \lhd (\overline{B} \lhd M[\![TH]\!]) \subseteq \overline{R}$	2,$\lhd$
9	$\overline{P} \lhd (\overline{\neg B} \lhd M[\![EL]\!]) \subseteq \overline{R}$	4,$\lhd$
10	$\overline{P} \lhd ((\overline{B} \lhd M[\![TH]\!]) \cup (\overline{\neg B} \lhd M[\![EL]\!])) \subseteq \overline{R}$	8,9
11	$\overline{P} \lhd M[\![mk\text{-}If(B, TH, EL)]\!] \subseteq \overline{R}$	10, M

infer $\{P\}$ if B then TH else $EL\{R\}$ triple, 7, 11

Figure 14: Proof of Lemma I3

from $\overline{P} \cap \overline{B} \subseteq T[\![S]\!]$,

$\qquad (\overline{P} \cap \overline{B}) \lhd M[\![S]\!] \subseteq \overline{R}$, rng $((\overline{P} \cap \overline{B}) \lhd M[\![S]\!]) \subseteq \overline{P}$

1	from $s \subseteq \overline{P}$, rng $(s \lhd R^+) \subseteq T[\![mk\text{-}While(B, S)]\!]$	
1.1	$s \cap \overline{\neg B} \subseteq T[\![mk\text{-}While(B, S)]\!]$	T
1.2	$s \cap \overline{B} \subseteq T[\![S]\!]$	h,h1
1.3	$(s \cap \overline{B}) \lhd M[\![S]\!] \subseteq \overline{R}$	h,h1
1.4	$((s \cap \overline{B}) \lhd M[\![S]\!]) \rhd T[\![mk\text{-}While(B, S)]\!] = \{\ \}$	1.3,h1
1.5	$s \cap \overline{B} \subseteq T[\![mk\text{-}While(B, S)]\!]$	1.4,T

infer $s \subseteq T[\![mk\text{-}While(B, S)]\!]$ 1.1,1.5

infer $\overline{P} \subseteq T[\![mk\text{-}While(B, S)]\!]$ R-ind(1)

Figure 15: Proof of Lemma W3

from $\overline{P} \cap \overline{B} \subseteq T[\![S]\!]$,
$(\overline{P} \cap \overline{B}) \lhd M[\![S]\!] \subseteq \overline{R}$, $\text{rng}((\overline{P} \cap \overline{B}) \lhd M[\![S]\!]) \subseteq \overline{P}$

1	$\overline{P} \lhd \{\} \subseteq \overline{R}^*$	set
2	$\text{rng}(\overline{P} \lhd \{\}) \subseteq \overline{P} \cup \neg \overline{B}$	set
3	from $\overline{P} \lhd r \subseteq \overline{R}^*$, $\text{rng}(\overline{P} \lhd r) \subseteq \overline{P}$, $\text{rng}(\overline{P} \lhd r) \subseteq \neg \overline{B}$	
3.1	$(\overline{P} \cap \neg \overline{B}) \lhd I \subseteq \overline{R}^*$	R^* is reflexive
3.2	$\text{rng}((\overline{P} \cap \neg \overline{B} \lhd I) \subseteq \overline{P} \cup \neg \overline{B}$	set
3.3	$(\overline{P} \cap \overline{B}) \lhd M[\![S]\!]; r \subseteq \overline{R}^*$	h3, R^* is transitive, h
3.4	$\text{rng}((\overline{P} \cap \overline{B}) \lhd M[\![S]\!]; r) \subseteq \overline{P} \cup \neg \overline{B}$	h3, R^* is transitive, h

$\quad$ infer $\overline{P} \lhd \mathcal{G}(r) \subseteq \overline{R}^* \wedge$ $\qquad\qquad\qquad\qquad$ $\mathcal{G}$, 3.1, 3.2, 3.3, 3.4
$\qquad\quad$ $\text{rng}(\overline{P} \lhd \mathcal{G}(r)) \subseteq \overline{P} \wedge \text{rng}(\overline{P} \lhd \mathcal{G}(r)) \subseteq \neg \overline{B}$

infer $\overline{P} \lhd M[\![mk\text{-}While(B,S)]\!] \subseteq \overline{R}^* \wedge$ $\qquad\qquad\qquad$ Scott-ind (1,2,3), M
$\text{rng}(\overline{P} \lhd M[\![mk\text{-}While(B,S)]\!]) \subseteq \overline{P} \wedge \text{rng}(\overline{P} \lhd M[\![mk\text{-}While(B,S)]\!]) \subseteq \neg \overline{B}$

Figure 16: Proof of Lemma W4

The proof of this is given in Figure 15.
$\quad$ The proof about the meaning function is conducted with:

$$\mathcal{G}(r) \triangleq (\neg \overline{B} \lhd I) \cup (\overline{B} \lhd M[\![S]\!]; r)$$

This is suitable for:

$$\text{Scott-ind} \quad \frac{pr(\{\}), \quad pr(r) \vdash pr(\mathcal{G}(r))}{pr(fix\ \lambda r \cdot \mathcal{G}(r))}$$

The proof of:
Lemma (W4)

$\overline{P} \cap \overline{B} \subseteq T[\![S]\!], (\overline{P} \cap \overline{B}) \lhd M[\![S]\!] \subseteq \overline{R}, \text{rng}((\overline{P} \cap \overline{B}) \lhd M[\![S]\!]) \subseteq \overline{P} \vdash$
$\quad \overline{P} \lhd M[\![mk\text{-}While(B,S)]\!] \subseteq \overline{R}^* \wedge$
$\quad \text{rng}(\overline{P} \lhd M[\![mk\text{-}While(B,S)]\!]) \subseteq \overline{P} \wedge$
$\quad \text{rng}(\overline{P} \lhd M[\![mk\text{-}While(B,S)]\!]) \subseteq \neg \overline{B}$

is given in Figure 16.
$\quad$ These two lemmas combine immediately to prove (W5) that the while rule is consistent with the T/M semantics[20].

Acknowledgements

The author gratefully acknowledges the financial support of SERC and the stimulus of the meetings of IFIP's WG 2.3.

References

[1] P. Aczel. A note on program verification. January 1982. manuscript.

[2] H. Barringer, J.H. Cheng, and C.B. Jones. A logic covering undefinedness in program proofs. *Acta Informatica*, 21:251–269, 1984.

---

[20] Peter Aczel, in [1], also proves the completeness of this rule.

[3] H. Barringer, R. Kuiper, and A. Pnueli. Now you may compose temporal logic specifications. In *Proceedings of the 16th ACM Symposium on the Theory of Computing*, Washington DC, 1984.

[4] F.L. Bauer and H. Wössner. *Algorithmic Language and Program Development*. Springer-Verlag, 1982.

[5] Dines Bjørner and Cliff B. Jones. *Formal Specification and Software Development*. Prentice Hall International, Englewood Cliffs, NJ, 1982. 501 pages.

[6] M. Broy. Partial interpretations of higher order algebraic types. In M.Broy, editor, *Logic of Programming and Calculi of Discrete Design*, Springer-Verlag, 1987.

[7] J.H. Cheng. *A Logic for Partial Functions*. PhD thesis, University of Manchester, 1986.

[8] CIP Language Group. *The Munich Project CIP—Volume 1: The Wide Spectrum Language CIP-L*. Volume 183 of *Lecture Notes in Computer Science*, Springer-Verlag, 1985.

[9] E.W. Dijkstra. *A Discipline of Programming*. Prentice-Hall, 1976. In Series in Automatic Computation.

[10] H. Ehrig and B. Mahr. *Fundamentals of Algebraic Specification 1: Equations and Initial Semantics*. EATCS Monographs on Theoretical Computer Science, Springer-Verlag, 1985.

[11] R.L. Constable et al. *Implementing Mathematics with the Nuprl Proof Development System*. Prentice-Hall, 1986.

[12] J.A. Goguen. Abstract errors for abstract data types. In E.J. Neuhold, editor, *Formal Descriptions of Programming Concepts*, North-Holland Publishing Co., 1978.

[13] D. Gries. *The Science of Computer Programming*. Springer-Verlag, 1981.

[14] I. Hayes, editor. *Specification Case Studies*. Prentice-Hall International, 1987.

[15] C.A.R. Hoare. An axiomatic basis for computer programming. *Communications of the ACM*, 12(10):576–580, October 1969.

[16] C.A.R. Hoare. Proof of correctness of data representations. *Acta Informatica*, 1:271–281, 1972.

[17] C.B. Jones. Constructing a theory of a data structure as an aid to program development. *Acta Informatica*, 11:119–137, 1979.

[18] C.B. Jones. *Development Methods for Computer Programs including a Notion of Interference*. Technical Report 25, Oxford University, Programming Research Group, June 1981.

[19] C.B. Jones. Implementation bias in constructive specification of abstract objects. September 1977. 16 pages.

[20] C.B. Jones. Program specification and verification in VDM. In M.Broy, editor, *Logic of Programming and Calculi of Discrete Design*, Springer-Verlag, 1987.

[21] C.B. Jones. *Software Development: A Rigorous Approach*. Prentice Hall International, Englewood Cliffs, NJ, 1980. 400 pages.

[22] C.B. Jones. Specification and design of (parallel) programs. In *Proceedings of IFIP '83*, pages 321–332, North-Holland, 1983.

[23] C.B. Jones. *Systematic Software Development Using VDM*. Prentice Hall International, Englewood Cliffs, NJ, 1986. 300 pages.

[24] C.B. Jones. *Teaching Notes for Systematic Software Development Using VDM*. Technical Report UMCS 86-4-2, University of Manchester, 1986.

[25] C.B. Jones. *A Technique for Showing that Two Functions Preserve a Relation Between Their Domains*. Technical Report LR 25.3.067, IBM Laboratory, Vienna, April 1970.

[26] G. Koletsos. *Sequent Calculus and Partial Logic*. Master's thesis, Manchester University, 1976.

[27] T. Nipkow. Non-deterministic data types: models and implementations. *Acta Informatica*, 22:629–661, 1986.

[28] D.M.R. Park. On the semantics of fair parallelism. In D. Bjørner, editor, *Abstract Software Specifications*, Springer-Verlag, 1980. Lecture Notes in Computer Science, Vol. 98.

MATHEMATICAL STRUCTURES AND THEIR MORPHISMS IN META-IV

Mícheál Mac an Airchinnigh
Department of Computer Science, University of Dublin,
Trinity College, Dublin, Ireland.

1. Introduction

"We wish, as we have done in the past, and as we intend to continue doing in the future, to further develop (sic.) the [VDM Meta-IV] notation and to express notions in ways for which no mechanical interpreter system can ever be provided." [Bjoerner and Jones, 1978] p.33.

The composite data types of the Vienna Development Method (VDM) metalanguage Meta-IV may be considered from the perspective of abstractions of programming language data structures. Foundational studies in VDM have established the semantics of such data types [Stoy, 1980, 1982] and they are used in the provision of model-theoretic semantics of formal specifications and in the rigorous construction of large-scale software [Bjoerner and Jones, 1982].

From a conceptual viewpoint [Mac an Airchinnigh, 1987], one may wonder why a particular class of data types and their associated operations has been chosen to form the kernel of Meta-IV. Of equal interest is the issue of data types and operations which were not included. One particular type of interest, conspicuous by its absence, is that of the relation.

The view held in this paper is that VDM Meta-IV is a mathematical notation and, therefore, its types and their operations must bear an obvious relation to algebraic structures. One may elaborate this view in either of two directions. On the one side, starting with the data types of Meta-IV, one then seeks to impose upon them some mathematical structures. An alternative approach, is to start with algebra and indicate its relevance to Meta-IV. It is this latter approach which has been adopted in the paper.

The applicative Meta-IV notation is clearly inspired by that of applicative programming languages. Whereas, an imperative style notation was also provided, a relational style was omitted. Relational Meta-IV (R-Meta-IV), an extension of Meta-IV, was developed by the author precisely to fill such a need and an implementation in Prolog provided an executable specification environment [Mac an Airchinnigh, 1987].

As well as the basic Meta-IV composite data types and their operations, the R-Meta-IV environment provides much of the functionality found in LISP, APL, SETL, and Prolog. There are data types and operations for relations, fuzzy subsets, posets, lattices, vector spaces, etc. Justification for such types and operations is based on the algebraic structures to be presented.

A note on the level of algebraic complexity or abstraction is in order. It is customary to present much of the following algebra in category theoretic terms. However, rather than speak about the categories Set, Mon, Grp, etc., specific sets, monoids, groups, etc., will be discussed. Thus the presentation will be concrete rather than abstract.

Attention will be focused exclusively on the data types Tuple, Set, and Map in that order. Familiarity with these types and their operations will be assumed [Bjoerner and Jones, 1982].

1.1 The Tuple

The tuple is both an abstraction of a sequential access structure such as the list of LISP or Prolog and a direct access structure such as the vector of APL and the array of Pascal. As well as being an actual data type used, for example, in SETL [Gotlieb and Gotlieb, 1978], it has been adopted by Hoare [1985] as the abstraction of the trace of a process in his theory of Communicating Sequential Processes (CSP). Much of his notation is similar to that of Meta-IV. Although Hoare does present his work in an algebraic setting, it is unfortunate that he did not make use of algebraic structures per se. Thus a welter of detail of algebraic laws is given, which, without accompanying mathematical structure, gives rise to conceptual difficulties for the computing science student in the sense that the student is obliged to relate the laws to structures without assistance. Of course, presentations of Meta-IV suffer from the similar defect that no algebraic laws or structures are provided. This paper proposes to remedy this deficiency in the VDM Meta-IV.

1.2 The Set

The set is an abstraction of the set data type of set processing languages such as LEAP and SETL [Gotlieb and Gotlieb, 1978] and to a lesser extent of the set data type of Pascal. It is very important to note that the concept of the data type set in Meta-IV is the counterpart of the powerset in mathematics. Towards that end, mathematical notation is employed even in those cases where the powerset is non-denumerable, viz., $\mathbb{P}$(Nat0), the powerset of the natural numbers.

1.3 The Map

The map is an abstraction of both a finite function and a direct access structure such as the array where the indexing mechanism is an enumeration type. Alternatively it may be viewed as a set of ordered pairs (d,r) such that if (d,r1) and (d,r2) are in the map, then r1 = r2. Therefore, the data type map is in reality a set of subsets of the powerset of the cartesian product of the domain and range sets.

2. Mathematical Structures

"In contemporary usage a mathematical structure consists of a set of objects S, which can be thought of as the carrier of the structure, a set of operations or relations, which are defined on the carrier, and a set of distinguished elements in the carrier ..." [Davis and Hersh, 1981] p.140.

In computer science one speaks of data structures and structured programming. Every field of computing uses structure of one form or another as a necessary tool. Perhaps this is essentially a consequence of the centrality of the concept of data structure. Modern algebra is essentially the study of mathematical structures which are distinguished from data structures in so far that mathematics is concerned with the abstract properties of structures, whereas computing focuses on the representation of structures in a machine [Gotlieb and Gotlieb, 1978].

Most of the material presented in the paper focuses on the structure of the monoid and on monoid homomorphisms. However, other algebraic structures are also applicable to Meta-IV, a brief presentation of which are given in the second part of the paper.

2.1 Monoids

<u>Definition</u>: A Semigroup (S,o) is a set S together with an associative binary operation o: S x S ⟶ S.

<u>Definition</u>: A Monoid (M,o,u) is a semigroup (M,o) with an element u which is an identity element for o. If the operation o is commutative then one speaks of a commutative monoid.

<u>Example</u> 1: The set of natural numbers Nat0 under addition is a commutative monoid, denoted (Nat0,+,0). The set of natural numbers Nat1 under multiplication is a commutative monoid, denoted (Nat1,*,1).

<u>Example</u> 2: Given any set S, then the free monoid (S*, ⌢,<>) with base S is defined to be the set of n-tuples t = <s1 s2 ... sn>, n >= 0 of elements of S. The product of two tuples

    t1 = <a1 ... an> ,t2 = <b1 ... bm>,

denoted t1 ⌢ t2, is the concatenation:

    t1 ⌢ t2 = <a1 ... an b1 ... bm>

The identity element is the empty tuple <>. Writing s for <s> and s1s2...sn for t, then t is a called a word, s a letter, and S an alphabet [Eilenberg, 1974] p.5.

Note that (S*, ⌢,<>) is a non-commutative monoid. Arbib and Manes [1975] p.53, calls S* the free monoid on the set S of generators. Thus the Meta-IV data type definition "tuple of Element", written Element*, is essentially a free monoid with base Element. Moreover, Element+ is basically a semigroup, <> being excluded. The free monoid (S*, ⌢,<>) plays a fundamental role in automata theory and formal language theory [ibid.] p.111. The Theory of Strings is also the study of the free monoid S* with base S.

<u>Example</u> 3: The Meta-IV data type set is a commutative monoid under set union, denoted (ℙ(S),U,{}), and a commutative monoid under set intersection, denoted (ℙ(S),∩,S), where ℙ(S) is the powerset of the set S of elements.

<u>Example</u> 4: The Meta-IV data type map gives rise to two commutative monoids, (M,U,[]) and (M,+,[]), where U and + denote map merge and map

override (overwrite), respectively. Note that (M,U,[]) is a submonoid
of (M,+,[]).

2.2 Homomorphisms

A homomorphism is a mapping from one mathematical structure to
another with the property that structure is preserved. The homomorphism
is mono-, epi-, or iso- if the mapping is injective, surjective, or
bijective, respectively. If the homomorphism is from a structure onto
itself, and if the mapping is bijective it is called an automorphism,
otherwise an endomorphism.

The actual definition of a homomorphism is specific to the
mathematical structure in question. Thus, one speaks of homomorphisms
of monoids, of groups, etc. Let h denote a homomorphism. A homomorphic
image of a structure S, denoted h(S), is the set of elements h(x) for
all x in S. If h is an isomorphism, then h(S) has basically the same
structure as S. If h is an epimorphism then h(S) in a sense a simpler
structure than S. The inverse homomorphic image of S, denoted inv h(S),
is the set of all elements x of S such that h(x) is in h(S). Properties
of h(S) have their counterparts in S. Proofs based on h(S) may be used
to establish results in S. This approach is used extensively, for
example, in the modern theory of formal languages [Hopcroft and Ullman,
1979].

3. Monoid Homomorphisms of Tuple

Recall that the free monoid S* with base S is the algebraic
structure which is equivalent to the tuple data type in Meta-IV. One
may seek to determine monoid homomorphisms of (S*, ⌢, <>) and examine the
relationship that these might have with operations on tuples. A
suitable starting point is the following important theorem.

Theorem: Given the free monoid (S*, ⌢, <>) with base S and a monoid
(M,o,u) and any map f from S to M viewed as a set, there is a unique
monoid homomorphism psi from (S*, ⌢, <>) to (M,o,u) which extends f
[Arbib and Manes, 1975] p.111:

1. psi(<>) = u

2. psi(<s1 s2 ... sn>) = f(s1) o f(s2) o ... o f(sn)

To illustrate the theorem, four examples are given.

1. Let S be some alphabet. Let e denote the empty word. If u and v are words in S*, then represent the concatenation o of u and v by u o v = uv. Define f: S ⟶ S to be the identity map. Then psi is just the homomorphism which establishes the equivalence of tuples of S and words over S*:

   psi(<>) = e

   psi(<s1 s2 ... sn>) = s1s2...sn

2. Define f: S ⟶ Nat0, f(s) = 1, for all s in S. Then psi is the homomorphism len: (S*, ⌢, <>) ⟶ (Nat0,+,0):

   psi(<>) = 0

   psi(<s1 s2 ... sn>) = 1 + 1 + 1 + ... + 1 = n

3. Define f: S ⟶ ℙ(S), f(s) = {s}, for all s in S. Then psi is the homomorphism elems: (S*, ⌢, <>) ⟶ (ℙ(S),U,{}):

   psi(<>) = {}

   psi(<s1 s2 ... sn>) = {s1} U {s2} U ... U {sn}

4. Define f: S ⟶ F(M) U {Fu}, f(s) = Fs, for all s in S. Define F(M) to be the set of all partial functions Fs: Q ⟶ Q, for all s in S, where M is a finite state machine (Q,S,F), Q is the set of states, S is the alphabet, F: Q x S ⟶ Q is the state transition function, and Fs(q) def= F(q,s). Then psi is the homomorphism from the free monoid S* onto the monoid of partial functions F(M) U {Fu} where F(M) is a semigroup which is isomorphic to the semigroup group of the state machine M and Fu is the identity element:

   psi(<>) = Fu

   psi(<s1 s2   sn>) = Fs1 o Fs2 o ... o Fsn

Whereas, on the one hand, the theorem states essentially all that there is to know about monoid homomorphisms of (S*, ⌢, <>), it is profitable to consider a few of these in detail and to show how they may be used to explain and develop various aspects of computing with the tuple in Meta-IV.

3.1 The Monoid Homomorphism len

The length of a tuple w, denoted len w, is an epimorphism from the monoid (S*, ⌢, <>) to the monoid (Nat0,+,0) and is defined by:

1. len(<>) = 0

2. len(w1 ⌢ w2) = len(w1) + len(w2)

Since, for distinct elements s1, s2 in S, len(<s1>) = len(<s2>), then len is surjective, i.e. an epimorphism. Thus (Nat0,+,0) is an epimorphic image of (S*,⌢,<>) and is evidently a simpler structure than (S*,⌢,<>).

Alternatively, the homomorphism property of len may be stated by saying that the following diagram commutes:

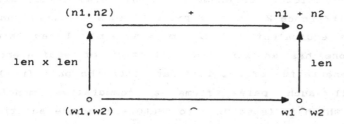

Note that on the left hand side one has the mapping:

   len x len: (w1,w2) ⟶ (n1,n2)

where len(w1) = n1 and len(w2) = n2

Rewriting line 2 of the definition of the homomorphism len in the form:

   len(<hd w>⌢tl w) = len(<hd w>) + len(tl w)
                    = 1 + len(tl w)

gives the "intuitive" recursive definition of len.

Application: Considering the monoid (Nat0,+,0), it is natural to ask if there are any operations on Nat0 which might have counterparts in the monoid of tuples (S*,⌢,<>). In other words, one wants to focus on the epimorphic image len(S*).

The difference of two natural numbers n1, n2 (i.e., the operation of subtraction) may be defined by the equation:

   n1 - n2 = n if and only if n + n2 = n1

This suggests a difference operation on (S*,⌢,<>). Define the difference of two tuples (words) w1 and w2 to be:

   w1 - w2 = w if and only if w⌢w2 = w1.

This leads to the definition of difference lists as used in Prolog [Clark and McCabe, 1984].

The difference of two natural numbers may be represented by an ordered pair of natural numbers. Consider pairs of natural numbers (n1,n2) such that there is a natural number n with $n1 = n + n2$, i.e., $n1 >= n2$. Then $(n1,n2)$ represents the difference $n1 - n2$.

Definition: Given two natural numbers $n1$, $n2$ in Nat0, such that $n1 >= n2$. Define $(n1, n2)$ to be a difference pair where $n1 - n2$ is in Nat0.

The representation is not unique. For example, $(7,5)$, $(6,4)$, etc., all represent the same difference 2. Two representations $(n1,n2)$ and $(m1,m2)$ are said to be equivalent iff $n1 + m2 = n2 + m1$. Under this equivalence relation, one has an infinite collection of equivalence classes. Choose as representative of a particular class the pair $(n,0)$. Then the set of all such pairs forms a commutative monoid $\langle$ (Nat0,Nat0),+,(0,0) $\rangle$ which is isomorphic to (Nat0,+,0) where addition in the former may be defined by:

$(n1,n2) + (m1,m2) = (n1+m1,n2+m2)$

This kind of construction provides a basis for the definition of negative numbers [Godement, 1969]. One is now in a position to give a formal definition of difference lists.

Definition: A difference list (u,v) is defined to be an ordered pair of tuples u, v such that there is a tuple w with $u = w \frown v$.

Again the representation is not unique. For example, $(<a\ b\ c>,<c>)$, $(<a\ b\ d>,<d>)$ etc., all denote the same list $<a\ b>$. Analogous to the construction in the case of natural numbers, one has an infinite collection of equivalence classes of difference lists. Choosing $(t,<>)$ as the representative of all difference lists $(t \frown u,u)$ for arbitrary u, then $\langle$ (S*,S*), $\frown$,(<>,<>) $\rangle$ is a non-commutative monoid isomorphic to (S*, $\frown$,<>) where the new law of concatenation is defined by:

$(s \frown u,u) \frown (t \frown v,v) = \langle (s \frown t) \frown (u \frown v),(u \frown v) \rangle$

By removing the restriction that $n1 >= n2$, the set of difference pairs $(n1,n2)$, with addition and the equivalence relation defined as above, gives a group which is isomorphic to the group of integers under addition.

Another operation on Nat0 is the predecessor function pred which is defined by:

$pred(n) = n - 1$ iff $n <> 0$

The counterpart in $(S^*, \frown, <>)$ is the operation tl, which returns the tail of a tuple.

3.2 The Monoid Homomorphism elems

The set of elements of tuple w, denoted elems w is an epimorphism from the monoid $(S^*, \frown, <>)$ to the monoid $(\mathbb{P}(S), \cup, \{\})$, where $\mathbb{P}(S)$ denotes the powerset of the set S, and is defined by:

    1. elems(<>) = {}

    2. elems(w1 $\frown$ w2) = elems(w1) U elems(w2)

Note that since elems(<e1 e2> = elems(<e2 e1>), for distinct elements e1, e2 in S, then elems is surjective, i.e., an epimorphism:

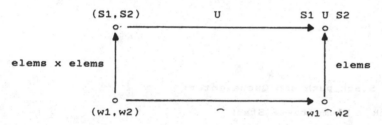

where S1 = elems(w1), S2 = elems(w2), are in $\mathbb{P}(S)$. Note that one may define an operator elems' on tuples which returns the set of elements <u>not</u> in a tuple. It is easy to show that elems' is an epimorphism from $(S^*, \frown, <>)$ to $(\mathbb{P}(S), \cap, S)$.

3.3 The Monoid anti-Homomorphism rev

The operation which reverses a tuple w, denoted rev(w), is an anti-automorphism from the monoid $(S^*, \frown, <>)$ to itself, and is defined by:

    1. rev(<>) = <>

    2. rev(w1 $\frown$ w2) = rev(w2) $\frown$ rev(w1)

That rev is not an automorphism of the monoid $(S^*, \frown, <>)$ is clear from the "reversing" of the order of the arguments in line 2 of the definition. To exhibit clearly the "anti-" nature of the homomorphism rev, define the monoid $(S^*, \&, <>)$ of tuples where the binary operation & is defined in terms of the ordinary concatenation:

  w1 & w2 def= w2 $\frown$ w1

The operator & may be called an anti-concatenation operator. Then rev is an isomorphism from $(S*, \frown, <>)$ to $(S*, \&, <>)$:

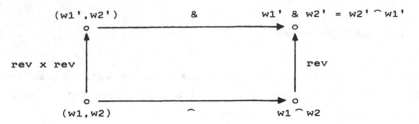

But there is basically no difference between the monoids $(S*, \frown, <>)$ and $(S*, \&, <>)$. Thus, absorbing the concept of anti-concatenation, one may describe rev as an anti-homomorphism.

<u>Application</u>: Consider the models for (unbounded) Stack and (infinite) Queue:

   Stack = Element*

   Queue = Element*

and the operations Stack_push and Queue_enter:

   Stack_push: Stack x Element $\longrightarrow$ Stack

   Stack_push(s,e) def= $<e> \frown s$

   Queue_enter: Queue x Element $\longrightarrow$ Queue

   Queue_enter(q,e) def= $q \frown <e>$

then it can be shown that rev(Stack) = Queue. In other words, Queue is the anti-automorphic image of Stack under rev, and vice-versa.

3.4 The Monoid Homomorphism map-op

The MAPCAR function of Lisp suggests a generic homomorphism, denoted map-op, on the monoid $(S*, \frown, <>)$. For example, if the domain is Nat0 and the operation is the square function, then map-square transforms $<2\ 1\ 0\ 4>$ into $<4\ 1\ 0\ 16>$. Map-square is essentially an endomorphism on $(Nat0, +, 0)$. The term generic is used here to denote a whole class of homomorphisms represented by map-op. Assuming that op is suitably defined for s in S and that op(s) = s' in S, then map-op is the generic homomorphism from $(S*, \frown, <>)$ to $(S*, \frown, <>)$ defined by:

    1. map-op($<>$) = op($<>$) = $<>$

2. map-op(<e>) = op(<e>) = <op(e)>

3. map-op(w1 ⌢ w2) = map-op(w1) ⌢ map-op(w2)

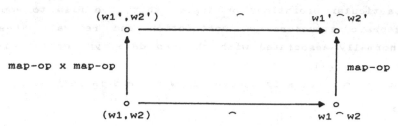

Note:

1. It has been assumed here that op is essentially a function of one argument. Of course, one may extend the definition to include functions of n arguments, n >= 2.

2. The notation map-op(w) is an abbreviation for map(op,w). Then

$$map\text{-}op(<e>) = map(op,<e>) = op(<e>) = <op(e)>$$

and

$$map\text{-}op(w1 ⌢ w2) = map(op,w1 ⌢ w2) = map(op,w1) ⌢ map(op,w2).$$

3.5 The Monoid Homomorphism op/

The reduction operator of APL [Iverson, 1980], FP [Backus, 1978], and SETL [Gotlieb and Gotlieb, 1978] suggests another generic homomorphism from (S*, ⌢,<>) to the monoid (S,op,u), where S is some set with binary operation op and unit u. For example, +/ transforms <2 1 4> to 7, the sum of all the elements. If one defines +/(<>) = 0, then +/ is an epimorphism from (Nat0*, ⌢,<>) onto (Nat0,+,0). In general, the op/ homomorphism is given by:

1. op/(<>) = u

2. op/(<e>) = e

3. op/(w1 ⌢ w2) = op/(w1) op op/(w2)

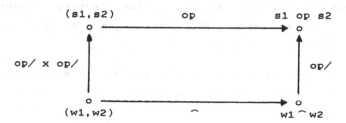

Note: ⌢/ is the distributed concatenation of tuples in Meta-IV.

4. Monoids of Endomorphisms

There are two particular operations on tuples that give rise to some
interesting algebraic structures - restriction and removal. These
operations are normally associated with the map data type of Meta-IV.
They are, of course, equally applicable to tuples. The restriction of a
tuple w with respect to a set s is denoted by w | s and is defined by:

    <> | s def= <>

    <h>^t | s def= if h in s then <h> ^ (t | s) else t | s

Note the use of the notation <h>^t to denote a non-empty tuple w
instead of the more usual <hd w>^tl w. Another variant which is
particularly useful is the bar notation: <h|t>.

The removal of a tuple w with respect to a set s is denoted by w \ s
and is defined by:

    <> \ s def= <>

    <h>^t \ s def= if h in s then t \ s else <h> ^ (t \ s)

Both of these operators are endomorphisms on the free monoid S* with
base S in the following manner. Let S be some (finite) set of elements.
Let s in P(S) be a <u>fixed</u> subset. Then |s and \s are endomorphisms on
the free monoid (S*, ^,<>):

    |s(<>) = <>

    |s(w1^w2) = |s(w1) ^ |s(w2)

and

    \s(<>) = <>

    \s(w1^w2) = \s(w1) ^ \s(w2)

Define | P(S) be to the set of endomorphisms |s on (S*, ^,<>). Define
the inner law o: | P(S) x | P(s) ⟶ | P(S) to be the binary composition
such that |s1 o |s2 = |(s1∩s2). Then |S is the identity element for o
and (| P(S),o,|S) is a commutative monoid of endomorphisms on
(S*, ^,<>).

Similarly, (\P(S),o,\{}) is a commutative monoid of endomorphisms on
(S*, ^,<>), where o: \P(S) x \P(S) ⟶ \P(S) is the inner law such
that \s1 o \s2 = \(s1 U s2).

These monoids are isomorphic to $(\mathbb{P}(S), \cap, S)$ and $(\mathbb{P}(S), \cup, \{\})$, respectively, and may be said to be induced by them.

5. Monoids with Operators

Let S be a set of elements such that for every s in S, s is an endomorphism of the monoid (M, o, u). Then S is called a set of operators for (M, o, u). Formally, this may be stated as follows.

Definition: Every monoid (M, o, u) provided with an outer law:

$$S \times M \longrightarrow M : (s, m) \mapsto sm$$

which is distributive with respect to o, is called a monoid with operators and denoted $\langle S, (M, o, u) \rangle$.

Consider the free monoid S* with base S. Then $\langle S, (S^*, \frown, <>) \rangle$ is a monoid with operators where the outer law is removal with respect to singleton sets $\{s\}$ for every s in S, defined by:

$$S \times S^* \longrightarrow S^* : (s, w) \mapsto w \setminus \{s\}$$

Writing sw for $w \setminus \{s\}$, then the distributive law:

$$(u \frown v) \setminus \{s\} = (u \setminus \{s\}) \frown (v \setminus \{s\})$$

has the more familiar form:

$$s(u \frown v) = su \frown sv$$

Application: The filter algorithm: Define filter to be an operation on $(S^*, \frown, <>)$ that removes all duplicates from a tuple. Its definition is:

```
filter: S* ──→ S*

filter(<>) def= <>

filter(<h>⌒t) def= <h> ⌒ filter(delall(t,h))
```

where delall is an algorithm that deletes all occurrences of an element e from a tuple w:

```
delall: S* x S ──→ S*

delall(<>,e) def= <>

delall(<e>⌒t,e) def= delall(t,e)

delall(<h>⌒t,e) def= <h> ⌒ delall(t,e)
```

Writing et in place of delall(t,e) gives the following version of the definition of delall:

```
e<> = <>

e(<e>^t) = e<e> ^ et
         = <> ^ et
         = et

e(<h>^t) = e<h> ^ et
```

Thus, delall is essentially an algorithmic version of an operator from the monoid with operators $(S,(S*, \char94,<>))$ described above.

The above monoid with operators may be generalised in the obvious manner to $(P(S),(S*, \char94,<>))$ where the outer law is generalised to removal with respect to elements of $P(S)$:

$$P(S) \times S* \longrightarrow S* : (s,w) \mapsto w \setminus s$$

Note the following laws:

1. $\{\}w = w$

2. $s(u \char94 v) = su \char94 sv$

3. $(s \cup t)w = s(tw)$

Thus, the set of operators $P(S)$ has its own structure - that of a commutative monoid $(P(S),\cup,\{\})$ which is isomorphic to the monoid of endomorphisms $(\setminus P(S),o,\setminus\{\})$ given above.

6. Other Monoid Homomorphisms

The previous sections have focused almost exclusively on the free monoid $(S*, \char94,<>)$ and on homomorphisms thereof. To complete this part of the paper a very brief presentation of other monoids and their morphisms is given with reference to the VDM Meta-IV data types Set and Map.

Let S denote a set, and $P(S)$ denote the powerset of S. Then $(P(S),\cup,\{\})$ and $(P(S),\cap,S)$ are commutative monoids.

It might be supposed that the cardinality of a set s, denoted card s, is an epimorphism from $(P(S),\cup,\{\})$ to $(Nat0,+,0)$, in analogy to the epimorphism len on tuples. This is, in general, not correct. For all s1, s2 in $P(S)$:

```
card(s1 U s2) <= card(s1) + card(s2)
```

with equality if and only if s1 and s2 are disjoint. The inequality may be turned into an equality by writing:

```
card(s1 U s2) = card(s1) + card(s2) - card(s1 ∩ s2)
```

However, as will be shown below, card is an epimorphism of the group $(\mathbb{P}(S), \triangle)$, where $\triangle$ is the symmetric difference of two sets.

Definition: A Group (G,o) is a monoid (G,o,u) such that every element g in G has an inverse g' in G:

```
g o g' = u = g' o g
```

Example 5: The set of integers (Intg,+) is an additive commutative group.

Example 6: The Group $(\mathbb{P}(S), \triangle)$: The symmetric difference between two sets s1, s2, denoted s1 $\triangle$ s2, may be defined in terms of set union, set intersection, and set difference:

```
s1 △ s2 = (s1 U s2) - (s1 ∩ s2)
```

An alternative definition, using set difference and set union only is:

```
s1 △ s2 = (s1 - s2) U (s2 - s1)
```

The powerset $\mathbb{P}(S)$ of a set S forms a commutative group under set difference where {} is the identity element and each element is its own inverse.

One particular property of the symmetric difference operator is worth emphasising here. The insertion, removal of an element e from a set s is usually expressed by s U {e}, s - {e}, respectively. A more succinct form is s $\triangle$ {e} where:

```
if e not in s then s △ {e} = s U {e}

if e in s then s △ {e} = s - {e}
```

6.1 The Monoid Homomorphism card

The cardinality of a set s, denoted card s, is an epimorphism from the group $(\mathbb{P}(S), \triangle)$, considered as a monoid to the commutative monoid (Nat0,+,0):

```
1. card({}) = 0
```

2. card(s1 △ s2) = card(s1) + card(s2)

with the corresponding commutative diagram given by:

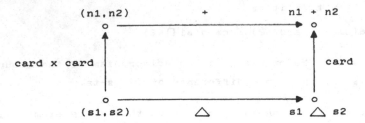

As might be expected, there are monoid homomorphisms on $(\mathbb{P}(S),U,\{\})$ and $(\mathbb{P}(S),\cap,S)$ analogous to the map-op and op/ monoid homomorphisms of Tuple for suitable domains S.

6.2 The Monoid Homomorphism dunion

Let T be some set and S = $\mathbb{P}(T)$ its powerset. Then $(S,U,\{\})$ is a commutative monoid. Now form the powerset $\mathbb{P}(S)$. Then the distributed union operator dunion is a monoid homomorphism from $(\mathbb{P}(S),U,\{\})$ to $(S,U,\{\})$:

  1. dunion({ { } }) = { }

  2. dunion(s1 U s2) = dunion(s1) U dunion(s2)

This is analogous to the distributed concatenation of tuples and is, therefore, just a reduction operator U/.

In what follows, it is convenient to consider a map in the context of some universal sets D and R from which domain and range elements are taken, respectively. In Meta-IV one writes M = D m→ R. Recalling that (M,U,[]) is a submonoid of (M,+,[]), the following homomorphisms are given in terms of the latter and are equally applicable to the former unless otherwise stated.

6.3 The Monoid Homomorphisms dom and rng

The domain of a map m, denoted dom m, is a homomorphism from (M,+,[]) to $(\mathbb{P}(D),U,\{\})$:

  1. dom([]) = { }

  2. dom(m1 + m2) = dom(m1) U dom(m2)

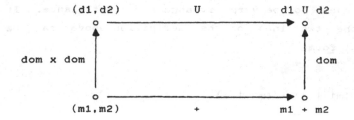

The card operator may be used to distinguish between the monoids $(M,+,[])$ and $(M,U,[])$:

   card (dom(m1 U m2)) = card (dom(m1)) + card (dom(m2))

but

   card (dom(m1 + m2)) <= card (dom(m1)) + card (dom(m2))

The range of a map m, denoted rng m, is a homomorphism from $(M,+,[])$ to $(\mathbb{P}(R),U,\{\})$:

   1. rng([]) = {}

   2. rng(m1 + m2) = rng(m1) U rng(m2)

The commuting diagram is similar to that for dom.

6.4 The Monoid Homomorphisms restrict and remove

One has already discussed the restrict and remove operators in the context of the data type Tuple above. All that material carries over without change to restrict and remove on maps. A very brief representation of the argument is repeated in this new context.

The restriction of a map m with respect to a set s in $\mathbb{P}(D)$, denoted m | s, is a generic endomorphism |s on $(M,+,[])$:

   1. |s([]) = []

   2. |s(m1 + m2) = |s(m1) + |s(m2)

This may expressed graphically by the commuting diagram:

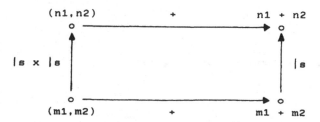

Remark: This notation seems to be very strange at first glance. It should be noted that the two lines of the definition above can be written in the more usual form:

1. [] | s = []

2. (m1 + m2) | s = (m1 | s) + (m2 | s)

The remove of a map m with respect to a set s in $\mathbb{P}(D)$, denoted m \ s, is a generic endomorphism \s on (M,+,[]):

1. \s([]) = []

2. \s(m1+m2) = \s(m1) + \s(m2)

where the corresponding commutative diagram is:

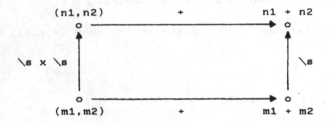

With the same binary composition o defined in section 4, the set of all endomorphisms |s of a map M = D m→ R, where s is an element of $\mathbb{P}(D)$, is a commutative monoid (|$\mathbb{P}(D)$,o,|D). Similarly, the set of all endomorphisms \s of a map M = D m→ R, where s is an element of $\mathbb{P}(D)$, is a commutative monoid (\$\mathbb{P}(D)$,o,\{}).

Let s denote an element in $\mathbb{P}(D)$ and s' denote its complement, i.e., s' = D - s, where - denotes set difference. Then, the relationship between restrict and remove may be stated in the form:

m | s = m \ s' and m \ s = m | s'

Such a relationship suggests that the structures (|$\mathbb{P}(D)$,o,|D) and (\$\mathbb{P}(D)$,o,\{}) are isomorphic. That this is indeed the case may be demonstrated by the homomorphism F: (|$\mathbb{P}(D)$,o,|D) ⟶ (\$\mathbb{P}(D)$,o,\{}) where F(|s) = \s', s' = D - s, and:

1. F(|D) = \{}

2. F(|s1 o |s2) = \s1' o \s2'

which may be summarised by the commutative diagram:

$(\backslash \mathbb{P}(D), o, \backslash \{\})$

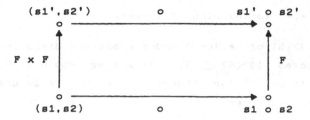

$(|\mathbb{P}(D), o, |D)$

In fact, more can be said of the relationship between the two monoids. Since

$(m \mid s1) \mid s2 = m \mid (s1 \cap s2)$

and

$(m \setminus s1) \setminus s2 = m \setminus (s1 \cup s2)$

and $\mathbb{P}(D)$ is a complete lattice (see below for definition of lattice) under intersection and union, then the two monoids are duals with respect to the underlying lattice.

Finally, one notes that restrictions and removals may be combined.

Definition: The composition of $|s$ and $\setminus s$ is defined by:

$|s1 \circ \setminus s2 = |(s1 - s2) = \setminus s2 \circ |s1$

where $-$ denotes set difference.

7. Other Algebraic Structures

Whereas this paper has for the most part concentrated on monoids and their homomorphisms with respect to the VDM Meta-IV types Tuple, Set, and Map, other operations on these types must be viewed in the context of other algebraic structures.

Definition: A Ring $(R, +, *)$ is a set with two binary operations, addition $+$ and multiplication $*$, and a unit element 1, such that:

1. $(R, +)$ is a commutative group.

2. $(R, *, 1)$ is a monoid.

3. $*$ is distributive over $+$

Example 7: The set {0} is a trivial ring.

Example 8: The set (Intg,+,*) is the ring of integers.

Example 9: The powerset $\mathbb{P}(S)$ of a set S under symmetric difference $\triangle$ and intersection $\cap$, denoted $(\mathbb{P}(S),\triangle,\cap)$, is a ring. The unit element is the empty set {}. This particular mathematical structure is used as the basis for the formal differentiation of Set Theoretic expressions in SETL [Sharir, 1982].

Example 10: The set of all non-empty tuples whose elements are real numbers (R) is a ring, called the ring of polynomials and denoted by (R+,+,*). The unit element is the tuple <1>. Addition of two polynomials p + q is defined by:

   _+_: R+ x R+ ⟶ R+

   p + <e> def= <hd p + e>⌢tl p

   p + q def= if len q > len p then q + p

   p + q def= <hd p + hd q>⌢(tl p + tl q)

Multiplication of two polynomials p * q is defined by:

   _*_: R+ x R+ ⟶ R+

   p * <e> def= <hd p * e>⌢(tl p * <e>)

   p * q def= if len q > len p then q * p

   p * q def= (p * <hd q>) + (<0>⌢p) * tl q

The tuple <0 1> is usually given the special name x.

7.1 The Polynomial Ring Homomorphism psi

Let R be a commutative ring with unit element 1. Consider the set of all functions R ⟶ R, denoted RR. Define the "pointwise" addition and multiplication of two functions f,g to be:

   (f + g)(r) = f(r) + g(r)

   (f * g)(r) = f(r) * g(r)

for all r in R. Then the set of all such functions is a ring (RR,+,*).

Definition: A homomorphism of a ring (R,+,*) to a ring (S,+,*) is a function H: R ⟶ S such that:

1. H(r1 + r2) = H(r1) + H(r2)

2. H(r1 * r2) = H(r1) * H(r2)

Consider the algorithm Eval:

Eval: R+ x R ——➤ R

Eval(<e>, r) def= e

Eval(<a b>⌒t, r) def= Eval(<a*r + b>⌒t, r)

Let p be a polynomial. Define the function psi(p): R ——➤ R by:

psi(p)(r) def= Eval(rev(p),r)

for all r in R. Then psi is a ring homomorphism from the ring of polynomials (R+,+,*) to the ring of functions (RR,+,*). The ring Im psi (i.e., the image of the ring of polynomials under the homomorphism psi) is called the ring of polynomial functions. The ring ker psi (i.e., the kernel of the homomorphism psi) is the ring of all polynomials which "vanish identically" on R, i.e., the set of all polynomials p such that psi(p)(r) = 0. Two polynomials p,q are said to determine the same function on R if and only if p - q is in ker psi.

Theorem: The algorithmic form Eval(rev(p),r) (= psi(p)(r)) correctly evaluates a polynomial p.

Proof:

Case 1: p = <e>, a constant polynomial

```
Eval(rev(p),r) = Eval(rev(<e>),r)
               = Eval(<e>,r)
               = e
```

Case 2: p = q⌒<an-1 an>, a polynomial of degree n

```
Eval(rev(p),r) = Eval(rev(q⌒<an-1 an>,r)
               = Eval(<an an-1>⌒rev(q),r)
               = Eval(<an*r + an-1>⌒rev(q),r)
               = Eval(rev(q⌒<an-1 + an*r>),r)
```

Q.E.D.

The proof will certainly appear strange to most mathematicians. It is basically just the so-called Horner's method for polynomial evaluation.

Definition: A Field is a nontrivial commutative ring in which every non-zero element a has a multiplicative inverse a'.

Example 11: The set of real numbers is a field.

Example 12: The set of complex numbers is a field.

Definition: An R-Module M is a commutative group (M,+) together with a function R x M $\longrightarrow$ M, denoted (r,m) $\longmapsto$ r*m, such that, for all r, s in R, m, m1, m2 in M:

1. r*(m1 + m2) = r*m1 + r*m2

2. (r + s)*m = r*m + s*m

3. (r*s)*m = r*(s*m)

4. 1*m = m

Definition: A Vector Space is an F-module over a Field F.

To denote that a vector space V is of dimension n, n in Nat1, one writes V(n).

Since the tuple is an abstraction of a vector in the sense of APL, then it can be used as an abstraction of an element of a vector space over the field of real numbers. Let T(n) denote a vector space of dimension n, n > 0, over the field of real numbers R and let 0 denote the tuple <0, 0, ..., 0> of length n. A tuple t = <r1, r2, ..., rn> is a vector with respect to the canonical basis <1, 0, ..., 0>, <0, 1, ..., 0>, ..., <0, 0, ..., 1>. Addition and scalar multiplication of tuples in T(n) is given by the usual rules.

7.1 The Vector Space Homomorphism [i]

The projection operator [i], 1 <= i <= n, which selects the ith component of a tuple is an epimorphism from the vector space T(n) to the field R, considered as a 1-dimensional vector space. Since the vector space is equipped with two binary operations, + and *, then the definition is in two parts:

1. [i](0) = 0

2. [i](t1 + t2) = [i](t1) + [i](t2)

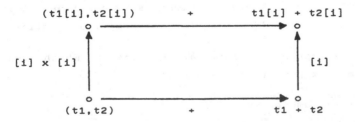

Note: The projection homomorphism [i] is just the operation of direct access of tuples in Meta-IV.

For the second part of the definition:

    [i](r*t) = r*[i](t)

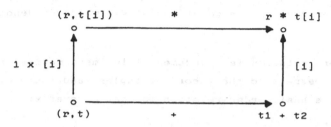

Note:

1. The tuple operator inds in Meta-IV returns the index set of a tuple. For all i in inds t, [i] is a projection homomorphism of the vector space T(card(inds t)).

2. The len operator on T gives the dimension of the vector space, i.e., len t = card(inds(t)).

8. Substructures

"Algebraic systems have [homo]morphisms and subsystems. Their [homo]morphisms can be analyzed by the use of categories; to handles their subsystems we now consider lattices." [MacLane and Birkhoff, 1979] p.143.

Definition: A binary relation <= on a set S is called a partial order on S when it is:

1. reflexive, i.e. for all s in S,

   s <= s

2. antisymmetric, i.e., for all s1, s2 in S,

   s1 <= s2 and s2 <= s1 implies s1 = s2

3. transitive, i.e., for all s1, s2, s3 in S,

   s1 <= s2 and s2 <= s3 implies s1 <= s3

A set S with a partial order <= is called a poset, denoted (S,<=).

Example 13: (Nat0,<=) is a poset where <= is the usual archimedean order.

Example 14: Let | denote the relation "divides". Then (Nat1,|) is a poset.

Example 15: A set S gives rise to the poset (P(S),<=) where <= denotes the subset relation.

The concept of an order relation is fundamental in mathematics and computer science. With respect to the theory of tuples (and therefore, formal language theory), a basic order relation is that of prefix:

  prefix: S* x S* —→ Bool

  prefix(<>,w) def= true

  prefix(<h>⌒t,w) def= if h = hd w and prefix(t,w)

Note that, by convention, it is not necessary to give a definition for the case when prefix is false. A relational form of the algorithm is much clearer:

  prefix: S* x S*

  prefix(<>,w).

  prefix(<h|t1>,<h|t2>) :- prefix(t1,t2).

where ":-" is used to denote "if". Note the use of the bar notation to separate a tuple into its head and tail. It is simple to show that (S*,<=) is a poset where <= denotes the prefix operation. In Hoare's CSP [1985] this poset is fundamental in writing specifications of processes. Other order relations for tuples are suffix and subsequence.

Definition: A homomorphism of posets H: (S,<=) —→ (S',<=') is a function H: S —→ S' such that for all x, y in S:

  x <= y implies H(x) <=' H(y)

Some of the monoid homomorphisms on Meta-IV types also feature as poset homomorphisms. A few of these are given briefly in the following subsections.

8.1 The Poset Homomorphism card

The card operator is a homomorphism of posets:

```
card: (P(S),<=) ──→ (Nat0,<=)

s1 <= s2 implies card(s1) <= card(s2)
```

Alternatively, the definition may be written in the form:

```
subset(s1,s2) implies card(s1) <= card(s2)
```

8.2 The Poset Homomorphism len

The len operator is a homomorphism of posets:

```
len: (S*,<=) ──→ (Nat0,<=)

w1 <= w2 implies len(w1) <= len(w2)
```

An alternative form is:

```
prefix(w1,w2) implies len(w1) <= len(w2)
```

8.3 The Poset Homomorphism elems

The elems operator is a homomorphism of posets:

```
elems: (S*,<=) ──→ (P(S),<=)

w1 <= w2 implies elems(w1) <= elems(w2)
```

which also may be written in the form:

```
prefix(w1,w2) implies subset(elems(w1),elems(w2))
```

8.4 The Poset Homomorphism rev

The rev operator is an isomorphism of posets:

```
rev: (S*,<=) ──→ (S*,<=')

w1 <= w2 implies rev(w1) <=' rev(w2)
```

where <=' denotes the suffix relation. Thus an algorithmic definition of the rev homomorphism is:

```
prefix(w1,w2) implies suffix(rev(w1),rev(w2))
```

Note that here rev is a poset homomorphism whereas above it was shown to be a monoid anti-homomorphism.

__Definition__: A poset (S,<-) is called a chain (or simply ordered set) if for all x,y in S, either x <= y or y <= x.

__Example__ 16: The chain of natural numbers m, m+1, ..., n, where m <= n, is usually denoted {m:n} in Meta-IV. If the restriction m <= n is removed, then {m:n} = {} for all m > n. Let w be an arbitrary tuple of elements. Then inds w = {1:len w}.

Every chain of length n is isomorphic to the chain {1:n}. An enumeration type in programming languages such as Pascal and Ada is a chain. Maps whose domains are chains model precisely the array type of Pascal and Ada. Where the domain of a map is the chain {1:n}, then one has the Meta-IV tuple.

A chain is conveniently represented by the tuple in Meta-IV. Given the order relation <=, then a tuple t of length n is called an ascending chain if t[i] <= t[j], for all i < j, i,j in {1:n}. If addition card(elems(t)) = n, then the chain is said to be reduced. A sort operation may then be provided which maps chains into ascending chains.

Further structure may be imposed on posets by introducing the concepts of upper and lower bounds.

__Definition__: Let x, y be two elements of a poset (S,<=). An element b in S is a lower bound of x and y if

  b <= x and b <= y

__Definition__: Let x, y be two elements of a poset (S,<=). An element m in S is a meet of x and y, denoted x $\wedge$ y, when it is a lower bound of x and y that contains all lower bounds:

  m <= x and m <= y

  and if b is lower bound of x and y then b <= m.

A meet of two elements x and y, when it exists, is unique. Similarly, the upper bound and join ($\vee$) of two elements x,y of a poset (S,<=) may be defined analogously.

__Definition__: A set S with a single binary operation o which is idempotent, i.e., for all s in S, s o s = s, commutative, and associative is called a semilattice.

Definition: A meet semilattice is a poset in which any two elements have a meet. A join semilattice is a poset in which any two elements have a join.

Example 17: Let G = (V,T,P,S) be a context-free grammar where V is the set of variables, T is the set of terminals, P is the set of productions, and S in V is the start symbol. Consider sentential forms t, u, v such that t derives both u and v, denoted t ==>* u, t ==>* v, respectively. Then define t to be the meet of u and v, which is denoted t = u $\wedge$ v. The set of all sentential forms of G is a meet semilattice, denoted (G,$\wedge$).

Example 18: Let S* be the free monoid with base S. Let maxp denote the maximal common prefix of two words u, v in S*. The definition of maxp is given by:

  maxp: S* x S* $\longrightarrow$ S*

  maxp(<>,w) def = <>

  maxp(w,<>) def= <>

  maxp(<h>⌒t1, <h>⌒t2) def= <h> ⌒ maxp(t1,t2)

  maxp(<h1>⌒t1, <h2>⌒t2) def= <>

Then (S*,maxp) is a meet semilattice.

A join semilattice is defined analogously.

Definition: A homomorphism of semilattices H: $(S,\wedge) \longrightarrow (S',\wedge')$ is a function H: S --> S' such that for all x, y in S:

  H(x $\wedge$ y) = H(x) $\wedge'$ H(y)

8.5 The Semilattice Homomorphism rev

Let $\wedge$ and $\wedge'$ denote maximal common prefix and suffix, respectively. Then rev is an isomorphism of semilattices:

  rev: $(S^*,\wedge) \longrightarrow (S^*,\wedge')$

  rev(w1 $\wedge$ w2) = rev(w1) $\wedge'$ rev(w2)

or in algorithmic notation:

  rev(maxprefix(w1,w2)) = maxsuffix(rev(w1),rev(w2))

The use of lattice theory in the mathematical foundations of denotational semantics (with particular reference to VDM Meta-IV) ought to be familiar to most users of Meta-IV [Stoy, 1980]. To complete this section, the definition of a lattice, together with some examples is given.

Definition: A lattice is a poset in which any two elements have both a meet and join.

Example 19: $(Nat1, \wedge, \vee)$ is a lattice where $\wedge$ denotes the greatest common divisor (gcd) and $\vee$ denotes the least common multiple (lcm) of two natural numbers m and n in Nat1.

Example 20: The powerset $\mathbb{P}(E)$ of a set E is a lattice $(\mathbb{P}(E), \cap, \cup)$, where meet is set intersection and join is set union. It is in fact a Boolean lattice. Of course, $(\mathbb{P}(E), \cap)$ and $(\mathbb{P}(E), \cup)$ are meet and join semilattices, respectively.

An alternative definition of a lattice allows one to examine the possibility of the construction of a lattice of maps.

Definition: Any set with two binary operations $\wedge$ and $\vee$ which satifies the following four laws is a lattice:

L1	$x \wedge x = x, \qquad x \vee x = x$	idempotent
L2	$x \wedge y = y \wedge x, \qquad x \vee y = y \vee x$	commutative
L3	$x \wedge (y \wedge z) = (x \wedge y) \wedge z$ $x \vee (y \vee z) = (x \vee y) \vee z$	associative
L4	$x \wedge (x \vee y) = x \vee (x \wedge y) = x$	absorption

Interpreting $\wedge$ and $\vee$ as set intersection and set union, respectively, then a map M = D m-> R might possibly be a boolean lattice $(M, \wedge, \vee)$. That it is not, is shown below. Moreover, map override (overwrite) is not a candidate binary operation:

$[A \to 0] + [A \to 1] = [A \to 1]$

$[A \to 1] + [A \to 0] = [A \to 0]$

In other words, override is not, in general, commutative. Map merge, on the other hand, is almost a suitable binary operation, corresponding to $\vee$. For all m1, m2 in M such that dom m1 $\cap$ dom m2 = {}:

m1 U m2 = m2 U m1

Unfortunately merge is undefined in the case that the argument domains overlap. Therefore, one is forced to ask the question whether set operators such as intersection, union, and symmetric difference are useful as map operations with respect to formal specifications in the VDM. At first glance, a redefinition of map merge as map symmetric difference seems to have some merit. First, m1 $\triangle$ m2 has the same semantics as m1 U m2 in the case of non-overlapping domains. Second, if the maps have a non-empty intersection, then m1 $\triangle$ m2 has the semantics of m1 \ dom m2. There is just one problem. What interpretation should be given to the expression:

$$[A \mapsto 0] \triangle [A \mapsto 1] \quad ?$$

Neither {[A $\mapsto$ 0], [A $\mapsto$ 1]} nor {[]} are justified, the first result not even being a map! A sensible solution is simply to declare the result undefined. The same sort of resolution is required for map intersection and map union. However, a choice of undefined leads to non-closure of the operations and hence, defeats the attempt at lattice construction.

The appropriate lattice structure is, of course, immediately obtained by introducing a new Meta-IV data type - the relation. It is a generalisation of the map data type and all the map operators can be generalised to relation operators in an obvious way. A relation R may be defined by the expression R = D r$\rightarrow$ C, where C denotes the codomain with the operator codom replacing the rng operator of the map. Intersection and union are now available with the usual set-theoretic meaning and one has immediately a lattice of relations.

Definition: A homomorphism of lattices H: (S,$\wedge$,$\vee$) $\longrightarrow$ (S',$\wedge$',$\vee$') is a function H: S $\longrightarrow$ S' such that for all x, y in S:

1. H(x $\wedge$ y) = H(x) $\wedge$' H(y)

2. H(x $\vee$ y) = H(x) $\vee$' H(y)

The material in this section on posets, semilattices, and lattices is, of course, of profound significance in the foundational studies of Meta-IV. However, at the time of writing, its relevance to the ordinary user of the VDM is not at all clear. It has been shown that operations such as len, card, elems, and rev are poset homomorphisms as well as monoid homomorphisms. The Set data type of Meta-IV is, of course, a complete Boolean lattice. But then that is not very surprising. An attempt to impose a lattice structure on the Map data type is fraught with difficulties. By generalising the Map data type to a Relation, oen does obtain a lattice. A full discussion of the new data type Relation, its operators and mathematical structure, as well as its application for formal specification of knowledge engineering based software is presented in [Mac an Airchinnigh, 1987].

9. Data Reification or Data Refinement

In the rigorous method of specification and development of software, espoused by the Bjoerner and Jones [1982], one starts with a very abstract model and refines it by stages into successively more concrete ones. At each concrete level, a retrieve function relates the model to that at the next higher level of abstraction above and forms the basis for data refinement proofs. Such a relationship may be expressed by the commuting diagram:

Abstract

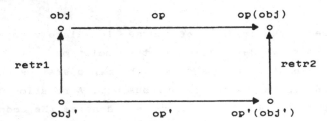

Concrete

where retr2(op'(obj')) = op(retr1(obj'))

From the analysis of the composite VDM data types given above, it is clear from the diagram that retrieve functions are essentially homomorphisms from one mathematical structure (the concrete one) to another (the abstract one). Technically, one is now dealing with homomorphisms of hetereogeneous algebras.

To illustrate this, consider a very simple example:

An unbounded Stack is specified to be a tuple of Element, i.e., the abstract model of Stack is:

    Stack-spec = Element*

where the suffix -spec denotes specification. A more concrete definition of Stack is given by the singly linked list:

```
  Stack-impl = [Cell]

  Link = [Cell]

  Cell :: s-el: Element s-nxt: Link
```

where the suffix -impl denotes implementation and [Cell] denotes
Cell or nil. Note that to obtain a "readable" specification, it is
necessary to include the "redundant" specification Link = [Cell]. This
also happens to be the case in programming languages such as Pascal
where a pointer data type is used for the implementation of a singly
linked list, for example.

Define the retrieve function:

```
  retr: Stack-impl ——> Stack-spec

retr(si) def=
            if si = nil
            then <>
            else let e = s-el(si), lnk = s-nxt(si) in
                <e> ^ retr(lnk)
```

Define the unary operations:

```
  SS.pop: Stack-spec ——> Stack-spec

  SS.pop(ss) def=
            if ss = <>
            then undefined
            else tl ss

  SI.pop: Stack-impl ——> Stack-impl

  SI.pop(si) def=
            if si = nil
            then undefined
            else let lnk = s-nxt(si) in
                lnk
```

Then one may prove that SI.pop is a correct implementation of SS.pop:

```
  retr(SI.pop(si)) = retr(SI.pop(mk-Stack-impl(si',e)))
                   = retr(si')

  SS.pop(retr(si)) = SS.pop(retr(mk-Stack-impl(si',e)))
                   = SS.pop(<e> ^ retr(si'))
                   = retr(si')
```

A more complete treatment of retrieve functions may be found in
[Bjoerner and Jones, 1982].

10. Conclusion

VDM Meta-IV was originally intended for the formal specification
of the semantics of programming languages and the development of their
processors [Boerner and Jones, 1978]. It is clear that Meta-IV was, and
still is, regarded as a mathematical notation. However, whereas much
work has been done in mathematical foundations of Meta-IV, very little
work on the relationship between Meta-IV and algebra has been reported.
This paper has taken some basic algebraic concrete structures and has
shown the relationship between these and the Meta-IV data types tuple,
set, and map. Operators on these types have been exhibited as homomorphisms of different kinds of structure.

By binding together the Meta-IV types and operations, and the
appropriate algebraic structures and their homomorphisms, a three-fold
goal has been realised:

1. <u>Extension of the range of Meta-IV</u>: VDM Meta-IV may be used
   profitably in those areas of computing theory where one is
   accustomed to manipulating algebraic structures. One of the
   most important areas is in the Theory of Formal Languages and
   State Machines where the free monoid S* with base S features
   prominently.

2. <u>Enrichment of Meta-IV</u>: Algebraic results may become more
   accessible to the users of Meta-IV. A simple example given in
   the paper was the foundation for the difference list of Prolog.

3. <u>Executable Specifications</u>: Applicative Meta-IV may be readily
   implemented in a functional (Lisp) or relational (Prolog)
   programming language [Mac an Airchinnigh, 1987]. The actual
   operations on the basic data types may be chosen according to
   criteria based on the algebraic structures.

One notable feature of a formal specification language which is
currently lacking in Meta-IV is the relation, which is particularly
important for knowledge representation. One may argue that a relation
data type is inessential in so far that it may be provided by the set
data type, but then so can the map! The relation data type defined in
[ibid.] has many operators similar to that of map and the suggested
R-Meta-IV domain expression is:

$$R = D \; r \twoheadrightarrow C$$

Such a type allows one to invert a map m where, in general, the inverse
image is a relation. It has been shown above that the relation has
mathematical structure similar to that of the set and would seem to
provide a good basis for a further study of Meta-IV maps.

In order that Software Engineering deserve that title its practitioners must build on a sound body of applicable mathematics as engineers in other disciplines are obliged to do. Acquisition of a formal specification language such as Meta-IV is but one aspect. Equally important is the acquisition of the appropriate algebra. Whereas the category theoretic approach is still beyond the reach of many in the field and since it is the norm in the specification of abstract data types as heterogeneous algebras, the material of this paper may be regarded as a bridge whereby Meta-IV practitioners may be tempted to cross.

11. References

Arbib, Michael A. and Manes, Ernest G., *Arrows, Structures, and Functors, The Categorical Imperative*, Academic Press, Inc., New York San Francisco London, 1975.

Backus, John., *Can Programming be Liberated from the von Neumann Style? A Functional Style and its Algebra of Programs*, Comm. of the ACM, Vol.21(8), 1978.

Bjoerner, D. and Jones, C.B. (eds), *The Vienna Development Method: The Meta-Language*, Lecture Notes in Computer Science, Vol.61, Springer-Verlag, Berlin Heidelberg New York, 1978.

Bjoerner, Dines and Jones, Cliff B., *Formal Specification and Software Development*, Prentice / Hall International, Englewood Cliffs, New Jersey London New Delhi Singapore Sydney Tokyo Toronto Wellington, 1982.

Clark, K.L. and McCabe, F.G., *micro-PROLOG: Programming in Logic*, Prentice / Hall International, Englewood Cliffs, New Jersey London New Delhi Rio de Janeiro Singapore Sydney Tokyo Toronto Wellington, 1984.

Davis, Philip J. and Hersh, Reuben., *The Mathematical Experience*, Birkhauser, Boston, 1981, Pelican Books, 1983.

Eilenberg, Samuel., *Automata, Languages, and Machines*, Vol.A, Academic Press, New York London, 1974.

Godemont, Roger., *Algebra*, Kershaw Publishing Company Ltd., London, 1969.

Gotlieb, C.C. and Gotlieb, Leo R., *Data Types and Structures*, Prentice-Hall, Inc., Englewood Cliffs, New Jersey, 1978.

Hoare, C.A.R., *Communicating Sequential Processes*, Prentice-Hall International, Englewood Cliffs, New Jersey London Mexico New Delhi Rio de Janiero Singapore Sydney Tokyo Toronto Wellington, 1985.

Hopcroft, John E. and Ullman, Jeffrey D., *Introduction to Automata Theory, Languages, and Computation*, Addison-Wesley Publishing Company, Reading, Masachussetts Menlo Park, California London Amsterdam Don Mills, Ontario Sydney, 1979.

Iverson, Kenneth E., *Notation as a Tool of Thought*, Comm. of the ACM, Vol.23(8), 1980.

Mac an Airchinnigh, Mícheál., *Conceptual Models and Computing - Theory and Practice*, Ph.D. Thesis, The University of Dublin, Trinity College, Dublin, 1987.

MacLane, S. and Birkhoff G., _Algebra_, Second Edition, MacMillan Publishing Co., Inc., New York, Collier MacMillan Publishers, London, 1979.

Sharir, Micha., _Some Observations Concerning Formal Differentiation of Set Theoretic Expressions_, ACM Trans. on Prog. Lang. and Systems, Vol.4 (2), 1982, pp.196-225.

Stoy, Joseph E., _Foundations of Denotational Semantics_, _in_: Bjoerner, D. (ed), _Abstract Software Specifications_, Lecture Notes in Computer Science, Vol._86_, Springer-Verlag, Berlin Heidelberg New York, 1980, pp.43-99.

Stoy, Joseph E., _Mathematical Foundations_, in: Bjoerner, Dines and Jones, Cliff B., _Formal Specification and Software Development_, Prentice/Hall International, Englewood Cliffs, New Jersey London New Delhi Singapore Sydney Tokyo Toronto Wellington, 1982, pp.47-81.

Objectives of the British Standardisation of a language to support
the Vienna Development Method

The BSI VDM Specification Language Standardisation Panel
United Kingdom
D. Sen,
STC Technology Ltd.,
London Road,
HARLOW,
Essex CM17 9NA,
United Kingdom

1   INTRODUCTION

The introduction of VDM as an industrial software engineering tool
has been made more difficult by the lack of a consistant language to
support the method. In order to ease this situation a project has been
started to develop a standard language to support VDM. This short paper
gives the overall objectives of this project.

2   BACKGROUND

VDM has been used to support two broad classes of software
development which has resulted in two different styles in its use. The
support for the development of programming language processors has
resulted in an operational style , whereas the support for abstract
system specification has given rise to the model-oriented style.

This has resulted in the existence of two closely related
languages to support each style of development. The standardisation
project will as its starting point take these two language definitions
and harmonise them to produce a single language definition. This
language will be called VDM Specification Language or VDM-SL. The
first draft for public comment will be available by the end of 1987 and
it is expected that a British Standard will be available by Autumn
1988.

The standardisation project is being run under the auspices of the
British Standards Institute. The technical work is being undertaken by
a panel of experts from Denmark, West Germany and the United Kingdom.
The panel has established close links with the VDM Europe group. The
project has also been publicised at the International Standards
Organisation by BSI and it is hoped that links with other member
countries of ISO will develop during the lifetime of the project.

The panel has set up two working parties, one working on the
concept of state and the type model for VDM-SL, and the other is
working on the problem of structuring (modularisation) of large
specifications. The work is being done by generating working papers
which covering the major topics that will be included in the standard.
In addition a skeletal standard document has been produced which is
being used as a framework for integrating the contributions from
members of the panel.

The following sections give a brief description of the of the
topics that are expected to be included in the final standard document.

3   CONCRETE AND ABSTRACT SYNTAXES

The standard will define one or more concrete (or information
exchange) syntaxes. The exact number has not been finalised yet. It
will most probably be two, one covering the special symbols commanly

used in most VDM texts and another giving an ASCII equivalent. The concrete syntax defines the acceptable symbols and strings used to express specifications written in VDM-SL. It is actually not necessary for a concrete syntax to be definitive but this is desirable form a user's point of view. All concrete syntaxes for a language must follow an underlying structure, a representation of this underlying structure is known as the abstract syntax.

Although the concrete syntax may vary, its underlying structure does not change and this can be represented by a grammar which omits the concrete symbols. This is the abstract grammar of the language, sometimes called the abstract syntax. The abstract grammar is the definitive grammar for the language; any concrete syntax which obeys the grammar and allows a specification to be parsed according to the grammar is acceptable.

4   SEMANTICS

In contrast to Abstract and Concrete Syntax(es) which define the acceptable form of specifications in VDM-SL, the Semantics defines its meaning. It is intended that the proposed standard will define, in addition to the Abstract and Concrete syntax(es), a definition of the Semantics. The definition of the semantics is expected to fall into three parts: the Context Conditions, the Type Model, and the Semantic Mappings.

4.1   Context Conditions

The techniques used for defining grammars used for the Concrete and Abstract Syntax definitions cannot express all the constraints needed for defining all the rules pertaining to well-formed specifications in the VDM-SL. This is a general property true of the vast majority of programming languages also. It is convenient to express these further constraints on the Abstract Syntax, which are all dependent on the context of individual constructs, with some of the same techniques as are used for expressing the semantics. Thus, while perhaps not strictly a semantic issue, these language rules are classified with the semantics, and indeed are sometimes known as 'Static Semantics'.

4.2   Type Model

This is a mathematical model of the types of information which form the 'universe of discourse' of the language. The type model of a language is sometimes known as its 'Semantic Domains' or 'Semantic Universe'.

Hence if VDM-SL dealt only with numbers, the type model need contain only a mathematical definition of the conventional number system. As it is, VDM-SL deals with many more complex notions and so the Type Model is both fairly extensive and necessary for a full definition of the semantics of the language.

4.3   Semantic Mappings

The Semantic Mappings fill the remaining gap in the semantics definition by relating the Abstract Syntax to the Type Model (universe of discourse). Thus for each construct in the Abstract Syntax, the Semantic Mappings define a construction in the Type Model which it denotes. For this reason the Semantic Mappings are sometimes called the 'Meaning Functions'.

5.   PROOF THEORY

In order to support the process of reasoning about formal specifications in VDM-SL and to provide a firm basis for computer based support of this process it is thought appropriate to supply proof theory for VDM-SL in the standard.

This standard proof theory will define what is a formal proof. We do not propose to offer any guidance on what level of detail should be presented in informal proofs, whatever their degree of rigour.

The particular proof rules will serve primarily to give a definition of what theorems should be provable. They will form an example of a proof system which is sound, and reasonably complete in respect of the standard VDM-SL semantics. Developers of tools intended to support proofs in VDM-SL need not adopt the axioms and inference rules provided in the standard, but insofar as they deviate they take upon themselves the obligation to demonstrate the soundness of their proof rules. This might be done by reference to (or relative to) the proof rules in the standard.

The aspects of proof theory which will be addressed are:

(i)   Syntax of Proofs
        An abstract syntax will be supplied for formal proofs in
        VDM-SL. This will encompass formal specification of a
        decidable set of axioms, and a formal specification of
        what is a valid inference step. A soundness proof will
        be sought, but need not be published in the standard.

(ii)   Verification Conditions

        The documented "context conditions" for VDM indicate at
        various points that certain "verification conditions"
        need proof to establish the type correctness of the
        specification. If the type system of standard VDM-SL is
        not effectively decidable then these points at which
        proof is required will be fully documented in the
        standard.

(iii)   Proof Obligations

        The literature on VDM provides details of "proof
        obligations". Some of the information documented under
        this heading properly belongs under the heading "syntax
        of proofs" and as such will form part of the standard.
        Such material as genuinely constitues advice about what
        should be proven rather than definitions of what
        constitutes a proof will be reproduced in the standard
        but will be clearly shown to be advisory.

6   FURTHER INFORMATION

If you would like to work on the standardisation panel or are interested in receiving further information , please contact:

        D. Sen,
        STC Technology Ltd.,
        London Road,
        HARLOW,
        Essex CM17 9NA,
        United Kingdom
        +44 279 29531 ext. 2291
        sen@uk.co.stc.stl

USE OF VDM WITHIN CCITT

Peter Haff

Dansk Datamatik Center

Lundtoftevej 1C

DK–2800 Lyngby

Anders Olsen

Telecom Research Lab

Borups Alle 43

DK–2200 Copenhagen N

Two CCITT Recommendations are accompanied by formal definitions expressed in MetaIV. Their background and modelling techniques are described.

1   CCITT

CCITT is the *Comité Consultatif International Téléphonique et Télégraphique.* It is a body under the International Telecommunication Union (ITU) which is again under the auspices of the United Nations.

CCITT deals with all standardization issues within its indicated areas and therefore covers a rather diverse set of topics. These are split among about 15 Study Groups that work in Study Periods of four years. At the end of a Study Period there is a Plenary Assembly that passes Recommendations — as standards are called — and assigns new topics for study (Questions). CCITT works by consensus.

Interest within CCITT in artificial languages started around 1968 and the first significant result came in 1976 when it was decided that three new languages were to be developed within CCITT: SDL (Specification and Description Language), CHILL (CCITT High Level Language) and MML (Man-Machine Language). Individual Recommendations containing descriptions of these languages appeared in 1980. Extended — and debugged — versions of the language descriptions came in 1984 and a further set is expected in 1988.

The 1980 Recommendation of CHILL was in 1981 supplemented by a VDM formal definition. The 1984 version of SDL contained elements of a VDM formal definition and the 1988 version is expected to be accompanied by a full-fledged formal definition.

2   The Formal Definition of CHILL

2.1   Background

The programming language CHILL was conceived in 1976 with the decision to establish a group that were to attempt to provide an initial definition of the new language. CHILL is designed primarily for programming SPC telephone exchanges; among its requirements were: to allow extensive compile-time checking, to permit efficient code generation for various kinds of hardware, and to encourage modular and structured program development. CHILL is now a general-purpose language suited for programming embedded systems.

CHILL was born in 1977 with the appearance of the first version of the language description. The remaining part of the Study Period until 1980 was to be devoted to gaining insight into the language and its problems by trial implementations.

CHILL fell into the hands of the VDM community in Denmark during 1978 when it was decided to attempt to establish a formal definition in collaboration between the Telecoms Research Lab and the Department of Computer Science at the Technical University of Denmark (ID/DtH). Ultimately, the formal definition that was the result of this collaboration was made the official CCITT Formal Definition of CHILL ([1]).

Work on the formal definition produced a large amount of input to the language definition group in the forms of comments, questions and suggestions. This group received input from actual compiler implementations and the work on another mathematical definition ([2]) as well, and based on the combined effort the Recommendation Z.200 appeared in 1980. [3] is the revised language definition from 1984.

2.2   Modelling Techniques

CHILL had properties and posed problems that had not been tackled by MetaIV: The visibility rules were significantly extended from the usual Algol style; it had notions that were of compile-time interest only; it included a notion of processes and concurrency; and it was (or became) quite a large language.

2.2.1 Visibility Aspects

The notion of modules with explicit visibility control across their boundaries called for new dictionary modelling techniques as compared with the more traditional block-inheritance scheme of Algol. In the latter, the visibility of names in a scope depends on the local declarations and the names in the surrounding scope. In the module scheme also names from nested scopes may contribute.

These problems were considered in a research environment and gave rise to a rather more recursive model of visibility than previously seen.

2.2.2 Static Semantics

The traditional MetaIV model of a programming language consisted of four parts: The Syntactic domains expressing the structure of the sentences of the language; the Well-formedness predicates constraining these sentences further; the Semantic domains giving models of the objects of the language; and the Elaboration functions expressing the semantics of sentences over the Syntactic domains in terms of the Semantic domains.

It was gradually experienced that a number of features in CHILL were only of interest for stating the Well-formedness predicates of the language. Examples of such are modules, the properties of which almost exclusively relates to visibility; aspects of modes (novelty, read-onlyness); and literal expressions (such that a compiler is forced to evaluate at compile-time). It was felt that in having to deal with these features, the Elaboration functions became unnecessarily complicated. It was therefore decided to introduce a second set of Syntactic domains, covering only statically correct sentences of the language and including only features relevant to the Elaboration functions, and to introduce Transformation functions that would transform sentences over the first set of Syntactic domains — known as AS_1 — to corresponding sentences over the second set of Syntactic domains (AS_2), providing that they were statically correct. For this to be worthwhile, AS_2 should evidently be significantly simpler that AS_1.

Logically, the formal definition of CHILL now have seven parts: Syntactic domains AS_1 and AS_2, two sets of Semantic domains, Well-formedness predicates, Transformation functions and Elaboration functions. In practice, the Well-formedness predicates and the Transformation functions are combined into one set of functions, together with the first set of Semantic domains referred to as the Static Semantics. They express a part of the meaning of sentences of the language which is not apparent in the Elaboration functions — now called the Dynamic Semantics.

2.2.3 Concurrency Aspects

In order to be able to model the CHILL notion of concurrency, MetaIV had to be extended. The choice was made to incorporate Hoare's original notion of CSP ([4]) into the notation. An operational semantics was provided for this MetaIV extension ([5]).

This extension provides a fairly satisfactory way of writing MetaIV programs; when used in the area of specifications, the concrete level of expression often leads to overspecification.

2.3 Summary and a few Facts

The development of the Formal Definition of CHILL gave rise to extensions to MetaIV so as to be able to model concurrency, as well as some new modelling techniques, notably the separation of Static and Dynamic Semantics and a highly recursive description of the visibility of names in the language.

Efforts were made that the use of MetaIV should be economic and consistent, and the Formal Definition includes a Meta Notation Summary, which documents the notation used. This summary has later been widely circulated.

The following effort was involved: 30 months effort by graduate students, 4 months research effort, 24 month professional effort and a years struggle with a text-formatting system for phototypesetting. The result is published in two volumes [1], the first containing 90 pages of text and annotations, the second 186 pages of MetaIV.

3 The formal definition of SDL

In the CCITT study period 1972–1976, it was decided to standardize a specification and description language suitable for specifying and describing the behavior of telephone exchanges. As many people already were using some state-oriented flow chart technique, it was natural to base the SDL language definition on a graphical representation. In the beginning, SDL was a rather informal language. The 1976 Recommendation (3 pages) defined only the main ideas and how the various graphical symbols should be written, due to the attitude that the users should have maximum freedom in the choice of abilities. However, in the next study period (1976–1980) SDL was extended with a considerable amount of new concepts due to the call for a more powerful language. This evolution continued in the next study period where also demands for the ability to cope with

SDL in a machine readable form came up resulting in the introduction of an alternative textual representation of SDL. Instead of defining the semantics of SDL twice in the 1984 Recommendation (i.e. defining it for the graphical and for the textual representation) it was decided to introduce an "abstract syntax" for SDL defined in plain text, which the semantics could be defined in terms of, and which the concrete syntaxes could be related to.

At the Danish Telecom Research Lab, it was in 1984 decided to develop an SDL tool to be used by the Danish teleadministrations. As the SDL language had become a language of a considerable size, it was decided to develop and base the work on a formal VDM definition of SDL. Concurrently, it was decided in CCITT that SDL should be suitable for use by other Study Groups in the area of standardization of protocol specifications which meant that SDL had to get the status of being a formal language. Therefore it was decided that the next Recommendation (1988) should define the language as formally as it is possible when using plain text and that a formal VDM definition should be provided. As a formal definition was already under development at the Danish Telecom Research Lab, it was assigned the job to provide the complete definition.

The work on the formal definition has influenced the SDL language definition considerably. About 50 contributions have been submitted to CCITT pointing out inconsistences in the SDL–84 Recommendation and it has been agreed to use a common MetaIV abstract syntax in the new SDL–88 Recommendation and in the formal definition. The MetaIV domain definition notation will be documented in the new Recommendation.

3.1 Modelling Techniques

For the sake of unification, it was decided to use the same MetaIV notation as used in [1]. No documentation of the MetaIV notation is present in the formal definition of SDL, instead there is a reference to the Meta Notation Summary included in [1].

Like in the formal definition of CHILL, objects in the Syntactic domains (called AS_0) are first transformed into another set of Syntactic domains (called AS_1) before Elaboration takes place. The AS_1 domains are identical to the abstract syntax also found in the 1988 Recommendation. The transformation part (also called the Static Semantics) also defines the Well-formedness conditions for SDL. It is not suitable to split these two tasks into different parts as the Well-formedness conditions are easily derivable during the transformation. Almost identical Semantic Domains should otherwise be constructed in both cases.

The AS_0 domains reflect the textual representation and it is self-contained (as opposed to the graphical representation which uses the textual representation inside the graphical symbols). It is easy to derive a textual representation from a graphical as the same BNF non-terminal symbols in the Recommendation is used for productions in both representations.

3.2   Summary

Since the MetaIV domain notation has been introduced in the SDL–88 Recommendation (the Recommendation is already prepared for publishing by CCITT because the other groups are going to use SDL in their 1988 Recommendations), MetaIV will be known to a wider forum.

In january 1987 the formal definition is presented to CCITT and it is decided whether the formal definition of SDL should become an additional SDL Recommendation or whether it should be a CCITT manual as is the case for the formal definition of CHILL. If it becomes a Recommendation, precedence rules must be settled, covering the case of inconsistencies between the two Recommendations.

In the spring and summer 1987 the definition is going to be reviewed by delegates in CCITT and will hopefully be ready for final approval in october 1987.

About 2 man-years of effort has so far been involved in the work on the formal definition. The result will be published in two volumes : The Static Semantics (about 240 pages including annotations) and the Dynamic Semantics (about 80 pages including annotations).

References

[1] The Formal Definition of CHILL
    CCITT Manual
    ITU, Geneva 1981

[2] P. Branquart, G. Louis, P. Wodon
    An Analytical Description of CHILL
    LNCS Vol. 128, 1982

[3] CCITT High Level Language (CHILL)
    Recommendation Z.200
    Red Book Fascicle VI.12
    ITU, Geneva 1985

[4] C.A.R. Hoare
    Communicating Sequential Processes
    CACM Vol. 21, No. 8, aug.1978

[5] P. Folkjær and D. Bjørner
    A formal model of a Generalised CSP-like Language,
    in: IFIP 8th Wold Computer Conference Preceedings,
    North-Holland Publ. 1980

A Formal Semantics for a DataFlow Machine — using VDM

Kevin D. Jones
Department of Computer Science
The University
Manchester
England
kevin@uk.ac.man.cs.ux, mcvax!ukc!man.cs.ux!kevin

Abstract

This paper presents a formal description of a non-conventional machine architecture (The Manchester DataFlow Machine) in the denotational style, using an extension of the traditional VDM methods.

The semantics is defined in terms of two fixed-point expressions over a relational domain. Some general and specific properties of such a semantics are presented.

1 Introduction

This paper presents an outline of a semantic description of the Manchester Dataflow Machine (MDFM) written in VDM [Jon86]. The full description can be found in [KDJ85], which includes the design of a non-determinate applicative programming language and the development of an associated compiler.

This work can be taken as illustrative of the extension of "traditional" VDM methods to parallel — or more generally, non-determinate — environments. Dataflow Machines would seem to serve as a good example in this situation since they are inherently non-deterministic and seem likely to be of importance in the future due to commercial interest.

1.1 Dataflow Machines

All dataflow machines are based on the theoretical concept of a dataflow graph, derived originally from [KM66]. Such a graph is a structure consisting of nodes and arcs. These represent operations and data paths, respectively. Graphs are represented pictorially as shown in Fig. 1.

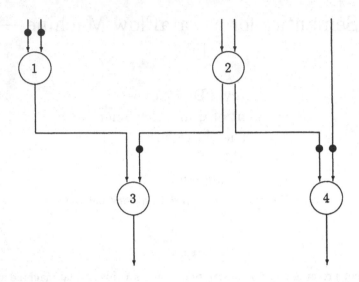

Figure 1: An example of a dataflow graph

Since all input tokens to some nodes are present, action can occur. In the above graph, nodes 1 and 4 are in a position to fire (i.e. consume their input tokens and produce output).

More formally, dataflow graphs are considered to be 2-dimensional descriptions of a partial ordering on computational events. They are structured by data dependency. Nodes represent indivisible atomic actions. Arcs connect dependent nodes unidirectionally, showing the direction of dependency. They are connected to the input/output points of nodes. Tokens are items of data passed along arcs. The condition for a node to execute is that all of its inputs are available. This is referred to as the *firing rule*. When all inputs are available, the node is permitted to fire. It will, at some time in the future, consume the tokens on the input arcs. Later, a result token is produced on the output arc. This is the only constraint on execution, so it can be seen that all sequencing is implicit in the model. This means that a central controller, such as the program counter of the von Neumann Model, is unnecessary. Variations on the model exist which affect the exact definition of the firing rule, but all follow the above description to some extent.

The concept of a dataflow machine arose from considering direct execution of these graphs. Data is represented as tokens actually moving along arcs. An architecture that uses (a representation of) these graphs as its basic programs forms the basis of a dataflow machine. The graph showing data dependencies does not enforce a linear ordering. It can be seen how this partial order leads naturally to a parallel architecture. At any point in time, more than one node may be in a position to fire. Any (or all) ready nodes may be activated in parallel (since they are independent) provided there are sufficient processors available.

The major difference between various implementations of the dataflow model can be found in the way code re-usability is dealt with. Re-usable code causes a problem, since it is necessary to preserve the context of tokens in order to ensure correct tokens are matched together. The first approach, illustrated in [DFL74], is to make all arcs first in first out queues. In the extreme case, these queues are limited to a maximum length of one. This gives the static approach to dataflow (using the terminology of [GW83]). This is capable of handling re-usability in an iterative sense but does not naturally extend to recursion, since multiple re-entry would cause difficulties.

Alternatives have been proposed, usually in an attempt to increase asyncronicity. One approach, the code-copying model [Dav78], achieves this by dynamically planting private copies of re-entrant code as required. An alternative, used in the Manchester DataFlow Machine (MDFM) [GW80], is to allow code to be truly re-entrant and to force tokens to carry tagging information, to preserve matchings. From a pragmatic point of view, the dynamic tagged approach seems to give certain advantages in terms of available parallelism and quantity of code held. There is no proliferation of program code by copying, and reuse is limited only by the number of "colours" available.

1.2   The Manchester DataFlow Machine

For a complete description of the MDFM, the reader is referred to the various papers published by the Manchester DataFlow Group (e.g. [GW80]). The following is intended to be a general introduction sufficient to enable the reader to understand the intention of the formal semantics presented in the next section.

The MDFM is an example of a strongly-typed, tagged token architecture with multiple processors. It permits re-entrant code and allows dynamic generation of graphs (i.e. dynamic arcs). The theoretical concept of a dataflow graph has been described above, so here we examine the way in which the machine implements such graphs.

A graph is represented by storing its nodes, and sufficient information (at each node) to define the arcs. Just as for the abstract graphs, nodes are considered to be the basic entities. They are taken as basic operations of the machine and are represented by a structure of the form

> *Node* ::   *Operator*
> *Destination*

An *operator* is a primitive operation of the machine e.g. DUP, BRA [1]. A *destination* is the "arc" of the dataflow graph, i.e. it defines where output is to go.

The data items (*tokens*) within the machine are represented as

---

[1] See [Kir81] for a complete list

Token ::   *Data*
                  Label
            Destination

The meaning of these fields is

data gives the value (and type) of the token e.g. an integer, a character, etc. See [Kir81] for full list of types and values.

label is the tag used to identify the token uniquely. This actually consists of 3 subfields. These are used as:

1. *activation_name* - separates instantiations of re-entrant code in the case of functions;
2. *iteration_level* - used for iterative code;[2]
3. *index* - used for data structuring.

destination is used to identify the node to which the token is being sent i.e. implicitly defines the data arcs. This field also includes other information which is described below.

The machine is physically based on a ring structure. This is composed of a number of independent units around which the data tokens (and composite structures) circulate. The ring has the configuration shown in Fig. 2. [3]

Specific details such as number of bits in a token, catalogue number of processing elements, length of wire between units and other information vital to engineers will not be given. Anyone interested to this level should consult [Gur82]. Looking at each of the units on the ring in more detail:

1. The Switch.
   This routes information from, and to, the host machine. It can be ignored if input is taken to be present in the ring and that output remains there. It is also used to load the graph into the node store, using special instructions that identify tokens as node store data, but this is not considered further.

2. The Token Queue.
   This unit is present for purely pragmatic reasons. It is used to buffer tokens. The actual representation strategy has no effect and both a FIFO queue and a stack are used interchangeably. This has no effect beyond some difference in processing speed for particular sorts of programs. [4]

---

[2] Fields 1 and 2 are grouped together under the name *colour*

[3] The current version of the MDFM also has a *structure store* [Sar85] on the ring. As this was a research topic being undertaken at the same time as the work reported here, it is not considered further.

[4] That is not completely true. Changing the queue/stack switch could sometimes have an interesting effect, since some local "wizards" have been known to depend on properties of the queue to make "unsafe" programs execute!

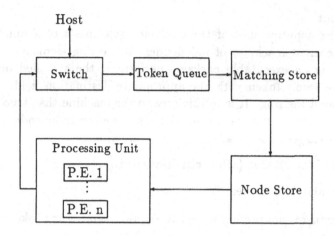

Figure 2: The Configuration of the Manchester DataFlow Machine

3. Matching Store

This is a unique feature of the MDFM and gives the architecture a flexibility that would not be found in a "pure" dataflow machine. Assuming all nodes are binary, a simplified description of the function of the Matching Store can be given as:

When a token enters the matching store, a search is made within the store for the matching token. A Token matches if it has the same destination (i.e. is going to the same node) and the labels are identical. If such a match is made, the pair are packaged together into a *group package* and passed along the ring to the Node Store. If no match is found then the incoming token is placed in the store to await the arrival of its matching token. More complex matching facilities are available and these are described later.

4. The Node Store

This unit holds the representation of the dataflow graph and can be taken to be equivalent to the program store of a conventional machine. Each node of the graph is stored, according to the representation described above, in a uniquely addressed location. This representation, actually consisting of an operator code and a node store address representing the arc to the next node, is loaded into the store from the host. This is similar to the loading of a program in a conventional machine. When a group package arrives from the Token Store, the relevant node is selected according to the destination field of the incoming tokens. A copy of the operator and the result destination are added to the package. This is known as an *executable package*. It is then sent to the Processing Unit.

5. The Processing Unit

This is the actual computing unit of the machine. It consists of a number (up to twenty in the current machine) of independent processing elements. Each is capable of accepting an executable package, performing the specified operation and producing the result token with the appropriate destination field. This is then passed on round the ring. It is in this area of the machine that true parallel processing is found. Since the processing elements operate independently, they accept incoming packages on an availability basis, in parallel.

In summary, the action of the MDFM (after initialisation) is:

- a token enters the Matching Store;

- if the matching partner is not present within the store, the incoming token is placed in the store to wait;

- if the matching token is found, then all inputs to a particular node are present and that node is eligible to fire. The tokens are grouped together and sent to the Node Store;

- the relevant operator and the result destination are picked up;

- this package goes to the Processing Unit where it is executed by one of the processing elements, producing a result. This is sent back around the ring to continue the process.

The termination of a program, executed on this machine can occur in one of two ways. The first way is *clean termination*. In this case, all tokens have left the ring (i.e. have been given destinations in the host and so are switched out). Termination occurs when there are no tokens left anywhere in the ring and the host machine has received all expected output. In the second case, output is handled as above but the difference is that tokens are still present in the ring. As will be seen below, use of special matching functions can cause tokens to be left in the Matching Store with no possibility of a matching token ever arriving. In this case, the program is said to terminate when all tokens left in the ring are stored in the Matching Store (i.e. there is no chance of a match, and so no possibility of any further action). It is intended that good examples of dataflow programs leave the store empty. A dataflow program which does so is said to be well-formed.

As was mentioned earlier, one interesting feature of the MDFM is the fact that dataflow arcs can be generated dynamically i.e. during execution. The mechanism for handling this is the provision of primitive operations to extract and set the destination fields of tokens. In fact, destinations, colours etc. can generally be handled as data values. (For precise details, see [Kir81].)

The above description of the operation and structure of the MDFM is sufficient for a general understanding of the machine. However, it does contain one major simplification. In reality, the Matching Store may be used in a more complex manner.

1.2.1 Matching

The matching process described above is the default action of the store. This is known as Extract Wait (*EW*) since its function is to extract a token if there is a match and to cause a token to wait otherwise. This is sufficient for almost all "normal" programming and represents pure dataflow. However there are cases, such as explicit non-determinate programming [Cat81], where other actions may be desirable. To facilitate this, the action of the Matching Store can be controlled explicitly by use of a *matching function* carried by the incoming token. This matching function specifies the action to be taken by the Matching Store, both in the case of a match and a failure to match. These are usually denoted by a two letter code, the first denoting the match action and the second denotes the fail action (as in *EW* above). This code is carried in the token's destination field, along with the (previously described) node address.

Before going into the detail of matching, it is necessary to give a more complete description of a token. In fact, the destination field contains a further sub-field known as the *input point*. This specifies whether the token is the right or left operand of the node to which it is sent. This also explains the many-one matching situation mentioned in Defer, below, in that two tokens with the same input point could arrive before the matching token with the opposite input point. The situation where two tokens with identical destination fields are both present in the store is forbidden in the MDFM (since a true matching token would have the opposite input point) and is known as a *Matching Store Clash*. The matching function Defer exists to avoid such a clash. In dataflow terminology, a program is said to be *unsafe* if there is the possibility of Store clashes and *safe* if there is no such possibility.

In the current implementation, there are four possible match actions and four possible fail actions. These are:

Match Action

1. Extract
   The matching token is removed from the store, combined with the incoming token to form a group package and passed on to the Node Store.

2. Preserve
   A copy of the matching token (present in the store) is taken to form the group package but the stored token is not removed from the store.

3. Increment
   As preserve, except the token in store has its value field increased by one.

4. Decrement
   As increment, except the field is decreased as opposed to being increased.

Fail Action

1. Wait

   The incoming token is placed in the store to wait for a match. This is the normal way of placing a token in the Matching Store.

2. Defer

   The incoming token is not stored but is passed back to the Token Queue (via the rest of the ring but in transparent fashion) to be re-submitted. This is used to avoid store clashes when many tokens could match. See [Bow81] for examples.

3. Abort

   The incoming token is not stored but it is grouped with a special EMPTY token and passed on. This is usually used to control explicit non-determinacy [Cat81].

4. Generate

   The action of generate is identical to Abort except that a copy of the incoming token with its input point is stored. This means future tokens with identical destinations to the original incoming token will find a match. This again finds its main usage in situations involving non-determinacy.

There is also a further matching function, Bypass (BY), which simply allows the token to pass through the store unaffected. This is used for input to unary nodes where no matching is required.

Not all possible combinations of available matching functions are implemented. The currently available combinations are:

1. Extract Wait (EW)

2. Bypass (BY)

3. Extract Defer (ED)

4. Preserve Defer (PD)

5. Increment Defer (ID)

6. Decrement Defer (DD)

7. Extract Abort (EA)

8. Preserve Generate (PG)

For a more complete description of the function and usage of matching functions on the MDFM, the reader is referred to [Bus83].

By the use of special matching functions, it is possible to deviate considerably from the model of pure dataflow. As Section 3 illustrates this causes increased complexity in the formal semantics of the architecture.

2 The Development of a Denotational Semantics for the MDFM

Formal semantics for various aspects of dataflow have been written in a number of forms. The early work in [KM66] subsumes dataflow in a more general framework. This, and much other work, is at an operational level being based on execution sequences. Later, [DFL74] looked at a restricted version of dataflow, in terms of states defined over the flowgraphs. This work was limited to a deterministic model. More recently, steps have been made to present a semantics of a more general model specifically involving non-determinism and to do so in a denotational style. [Kos78] and [BA81] are some contributions to this approach. In [Fau82], the equivalence between an operational semantics given using automata and "hiaton streams" and a denotational semantics in the LUCID [AW77] notation, is shown. All of the above are concerned with the static model of dataflow. Much less work has been done on the dynamic model. In work inspired by the MDFM, [Vee81] presents a very general model covering dynamic dataflow. This uses markings of execution sequences to provide the semantics. All of the above work considers dataflow at the graphical level. Very little work has been done dealing with a specific architecture designed to represent dataflow. Some relevant work, being pursued largely concurrently with the work described here, has been done at Manchester. This work is concerned with the use of FP [Bac78] to provide a semantic basis for reasoning about programs in the MDFM environment. This work, reported in [VBO83] and [Oli84] has, to date, largely been concerned with deterministic situations.

One of the goals of the work reported here is to produce a denotational semantics of the MDFM at a sufficiently low level to capture all the relevant detail of the machine, including matching functions, etc.

2.1 The Semantics of a Simple DataFlow Machine

The most suitable approach was deemed to be the production of a denotational semantics, giving meaning at the level of a program within the machine (i.e. a *Node_store*).

It is necessary to decide on a suitable denotation, since the non-determinism inherent in the machine means the usual denotation of continuous functions cannot be used. It was decided that the extension to powerdomains [Plo76] was unnecessary in this case. An adequate semantics could be given using relations as denotations, following [Par80]. So the basic approach is to define the semantics of the machine in terms of a fixed point over a relation on a set of tokens, characterising the state of the machine.

In order to facilitate the understanding of the formal semantics, a greatly simplified version of the machine is taken as a starting point. Additional complexity is added in stages, eventually leading to the complete MDFM. The presentation below follows that development.[5]

---

[5]The formalisms are presented in a standard VDM notation, as in [Jon86]. The set constructor is

The first machine is greatly simplified. Its programs[6] consist of pure, loop-free dataflow graphs with all nodes being binary input/unary output.

The basic computation is performed by a *Node* — representing the basic program elements of the machine. Each *Node* consists of an *Operator*, which is a function describing the computation, and a *Destination* specifying to where the result should be sent:

$Node$ :: O : $Operator$
$\quad\quad\quad\quad D$: $Destination$

$Operator$ = Value $\times$ Value $\rightarrow$ Value

A *Destination* contains the *Node_address* to which the value is to be sent plus an *Input_point*. [7]

$Destination$ :: NA : $Node\_address$
$\quad\quad\quad\quad\quad\quad IP$: $Input\_point$

The meaning of an individual *Node* is defined (by the function $\mathcal{M}_N$) in terms of the application of its operator to the values in a set of appropriate input *Tokens* and the creation of a new *Token* containing the result sent to the given *Destination*.

$\mathcal{M}_N$: $Node$ $\rightarrow$ set of $Token$ $\rightarrow$ $Token$

$\mathcal{M}_N \llbracket mk\text{-}Node(o, d) \rrbracket \{ mk\text{-}Token(v_1, d_1), mk\text{-}Token(v_2, d_2) \} \quad \triangle$
$\quad\quad mk\text{-}Token(o(v_1, v_2), d)$

A program is represented by a *Node_store*, which is a collection of *Nodes* indexed by their addresses.

$Node\_store$ = map $Node\_address$ to $Node$

A subsidiary function *ips* is used to identify the *Tokens* destined for a particular *Node*.

ips : $Node\_address$ $\times$ set of $Token$ $\rightarrow$ set of $Token$

$ips(d, ts) \quad \triangle \quad \{ t \in ts \mid NA(D(t)) = d \}$

---

taken to denote the powerset and is not restricted to the finite cases. Any extra notation used to deal with relational concepts, generally follows [Jon81]. To avoid confusion due to the use of μ as both a fixed point operator and record update operator in previous VDM related work, the former is represented as $\underline{\mu}$.

[6] for convenience, the term program will be used to refer to the graph representation held in the Node Store

[7] At this level of simplicity, input points are not checked. However, if they were not included, two tokens with identical values input to a node would be coalesced by the set construction, preventing valid firings occurring. Since the set construction is required in later definitions, it does not seem appropriate to use (say) a pair construct here.

The meaning of a "program" is defined as the fixed point of a relation over token sets. The basis of this expression are those sets of *Tokens* in which no further computation is possible. [8] Any *Node* which has two input *Tokens* can be "fired" i.e. the $\mathcal{M}_N$ function can apply. To allow for the parallelism in the machine (which is "side effect" free), all such *Nodes* can fire at once. This is modelled by use of a distributed union.

$\mathcal{M}_P : Node\_store \rightarrow \text{set of}\,(\text{set of } Token \times \text{set of } Token)$

$\mathcal{M}_P\,[\![ns]\!] \quad \triangle$
$\qquad \mu \mathcal{R} \cdot (\{(ts, ts) \mid \nexists d \in \text{dom } ns \cdot \text{card } ips(d, ts) = 2\} \cup$
$\qquad \bigcup\{\{(ts, ts') \mid (ts - fs \cup \mathcal{M}_N\,[\![ns(d)]\!](fs), ts') \in \mathcal{R}\}$
$\qquad\qquad \mid d \in \text{dom } ns \wedge fs = ips(d, ts) \wedge \text{card } fs = 2\})$

The above formulae can be interpreted as follows. A meaning function ($\mathcal{M}_P$) is given from a program to a relation on token sets. The meaning of a program is found by building a fixed point, backwards from terminated states. The basis for the construction is the set of states that don't change (i.e. have no nodes that could possibly fire). States that can be arrived at by an eligible node firing are added at each step. This is done for all eligible nodes and the distributed union is taken.

The firing of a node is represented by the removing of its input tokens from, and adding its result tokens to, the state. The result of a particular node firing is given by the meaning function $\mathcal{M}_N$ on given node address. This is defined to be the construction of a result token which has the result destination and a value given by the node operator being applied to the input values.

The input set (*ips*) of the node is generated, giving the candidates for firing.

This gives the general idea of the way in which the semantics is developed. In order to gain a better grasp of the formalism, and the way it "works" on a data flow program, it is worth examining a small example.

Considering the graph to calculate $(a + b) * (c + d)$, as shown in Fig. 3.

If we look how this graph would be represented, we get to following node store [9]:

$$ns = \{1 \mapsto (+, 3), 2 \mapsto (+, 3), 3 \mapsto (*, out)\}$$

where 1,2 and 3 are destinations (representing the node store addresses). *out* is just meant to represent a destination that is not within the graph being considered.

Assume the initial token set is:

$$ts_0 = \{(val_a, 1), (val_b, 1), (val_c, 2), (val_d, 2)\}$$

The construction of the relation is based on the "final" states (i.e. those which will not transform further). It can be seen that the relation must allow the following actions:

---

[8] in this simple case, that means there are no *Nodes* which have two input *Tokens*
[9] dropping constructors and input points for simplicity

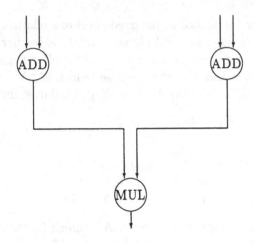

Figure 3: A simple example

At the first step, either node 1 or node 2 could fire giving

$$R^1 = \{(ts_0, ts_1), (ts_o, ts_2)\}$$

where ts_1 results from node 1 firing i.e

$$ts_1 = \{(val_{a+b}, 3), (val_c, 2), (val_d, 2)\}$$

and ts_2 results from node 2 firing i.e.

$$ts_2 = \{(val_a, 1), (val_b, 1), (val_{c+d}, 3)\}$$

derived from the $\mathcal{M}_N$ function on the + operator in each case.

At the next step only 1 or 2, depending on which has not already fired, is eligible to fire, and so on.

So, it can be seen why the meaning is given as a distributed union within a fixed-point construction. The fixed point builds the sequences of token sets produced as each action takes place in time. Each future action is enabled by the tokens produced at the current step. The starting point for the construction is the set of tokens for which no action takes place. This undergoes the identity transformation. Each step in the construction represents a firing action taking place. The union operation allows for many non-deterministic choices of which of the eligible nodes actually fires at any particular step. In other words, all possible computation paths are included in the expression.

This should enable an intuitive grasp of the semantics. More complex examples are not presented in detail as they become tedious very quickly.

2.2 The Semantics of a More General Dataflow Machine

For this version of the machine, some of the restrictions are removed. Specifically, labels are added to tokens and nodes are generalised to n-input, n-output.

The major modification needed is a more complex means of checking if a node is eligible to fire. It is now possible to have more than one set of inputs to a node. There needs to be a means of keeping these sets distinct. To deal with this, a label field is added to tokens.

$$Token :: \quad V \; : \; Value$$
$$D \; : \; Destination$$
$$L \; : \; Label$$

A *Node* is extended to contain information about the number of expected inputs and the output *Destination* is generalised to a set.

$$Node :: \quad O \; : \; Operator$$
$$D \; : \; \text{set of } Destination$$

Operators now contain details of their arity in addition to the *Function*.

$$Operator :: \quad F \; : \; Function$$
$$NIP \; : \; N$$

Function : set of Token × set of Destination → set of Token

Since the definitions are seen to be becoming longer, a slightly different style of definition is used for $\mathcal{M}_P$. The identity relation over the set s is written as $\mathcal{E}_s$, following [Jon81]. The relation is now defined in terms of relational composition (;) over $\mathcal{R}$. This combinator has type

set of (set of *Token* × set of *Token*) × set of (set of *Token* × set of *Token*)
→ set of (set of *Token* × set of *Token*)

and has the usual meaning for composition.

Using these operators:

$$\mathcal{M}_P : Node\_store \to \text{set of (set of } Token \times \text{set of } Token)$$

$$\mathcal{M}_P \, [\![ns]\!] \quad \triangleq \quad \mu \mathcal{R} \cdot \mathcal{E}_s \cup \bigcup \{ \mathcal{M}_N \, [\![ns(d), d]\!] ; \mathcal{R} \mid d \in \text{dom } ns \}$$

where
let $n = NIP(o)$ in
$s = \{ ts \in \text{set of } Token \mid \forall d \in \text{dom } ns \cdot rdys(d, ts, n) = \{ \} \}$

The meaning of a single node firing is extended to the relational type to allow use of composition.

$$\mathcal{M}_N : Node \times Node\_address \to \text{set of (set of } Token \times \text{set of } Token)$$

$$\mathcal{M}_N \llbracket mk\text{-}Node(o, nd), d \rrbracket \triangleq$$
$$\text{let } f = F(o)$$
$$\text{and}$$
$$n = NIP(o) \text{ in}$$
$$\mathcal{E}_s \cup \bigcup\{\{(ts, (ts - rs) \cup f(rs, nd)) \mid rs \in rdys(d, ts, n)\} \mid ts \in \text{set of } Token\}$$
$$\text{where}$$
$$s = \{ts \in \text{set of } Token \mid rdys(d, ts, n) = \{\}\}$$

The function $rdys$ extracts those sets of $Tokens$ which constitute complete input sets to the given $Node$.

$$rdys : Nodeaddress \times \text{set of } Token \times \mathbb{N} \rightarrow \text{set of (set of } Token)$$

$$rdys(d, ts, nip) \triangleq$$
$$\{rts \subseteq ts \mid \forall t_1, t_2 \in rts \cdot (L(t_1) = L(t_2) \wedge NA(D(t_1)) = d) \wedge \text{card } rts = nip\}$$

Most of this definition should be easily understood since it does not differ very much from the earlier definition above. The noticeable additions are the checking for a given cardinality on a nodes input set as opposed to the default of two in a binary case and the multiple level of choice on the $rdys$ function. This is due to the fact that it is necessary, in the first instance, to select all possible ready sets to the given node and to take the distributed union of the result of any of these being used. This gives the desired result at the $\mathcal{M}_N$ level.

The use of $\mathcal{M}_N$ and ;(relational composition) within the definition of $\mathcal{M}_P$ make it easier to see how the composition is used to build fixed point. This notation is maintained for the later definitions.

2.2.1 Termination

Before increasing the complexity of the machine any further, a significant technical difficulty needs to be considered. It is well known that problems are encountered when using relations as a denotation [Jon73], particularly due to relational composition. This is most easily illustrated by the case of distinguishing between $\{(a, b)\}$ and $\{(a, b), (a, \perp)\}$, when non-termination is a possible result. (The symbol bottom $\perp$ is used in its traditional sense to represent non-termination i.e. undefined result.) To solve this problem, the approach of [Par80] is followed. That is the denotation of a program is a pair of functions:

1. the meaning function as before

2. an additional function giving the set of inputs over which termination is guaranteed.

The termination function appropriate to the previous definition[10] is

---

[10] The following conventions simplify considerations of input/output:

1. Tokens which are addressed to a destination not within the Node Store (i.e. $NA(D(t)) \notin \text{dom } ns$) are assumed to be output;

$\mathcal{T}_{P} : Node\_store \rightarrow \text{set of (set of } Token)$

$\mathcal{T}_{P} \llbracket ns \rrbracket \quad \triangle \quad \mu\mathcal{S} \cdot termset(ns) \cup$
$\qquad \{ts \mid \forall na \in \text{dom } ns \cdot \forall ts' \cdot ts\,\mathcal{M}_{N} \llbracket ns(na), na \rrbracket ts' \;\Rightarrow\; ts' \in \mathcal{S}\}$

The function $termset$ generates sets of $Tokens$ which are all terminated.

$termset : Node\_store \rightarrow \text{set of (set of } Token)$

$termset(ns) \quad \triangle \quad \{ts \mid \forall t \in ts \cdot D(t) \notin \text{dom } ns\}$

The termination function ($\mathcal{T}_{P}$) is also defined in terms of a fixed point. This is built over the possible token sets. An informal explanation of the derivation of this function can be given as follows. The starting point is given by the function $termset$ (i.e. those states containing only tokens that can not be modified further since they have destinations that do not apply to any nodes in the node store). The fixed point is then built by adding all states which must yield one of these states whichever node fires, and so on.

This definition is as far as it is reasonable to progress using an abstract machine. Further steps are necessary to consider the precise details found in the MDFM.

3 The Formal Semantics of the MDFM

To give the semantics of the complete machine, it is necessary to work at a slightly less abstract level. Some of the abstractions used previously need to be removed as they hide information important at this level. For example, previous definitions used a function from set of $Token$ to set of $Token$ to represent primitive operators. This is not sufficiently detailed to characterise the machine precisely and so is replaced by enumeration of available operators. These operators do not conform precisely to those present in the Manchester hardware but represent a somewhat idealized representation of them. This decision is justified on the grounds of simplicity. [11] Most of the modifications made are of this nature.

As before, the new definition is built by expanding the previous definition where possible. However, due to the increasing length, a slightly different style of definition, making use of more subsidiary functions is adopted making it necessary to modify some of the earlier work.

More significantly, matching functions and associated matching actions are introduced. As can be seen below, this causes some increase in the complexity of the definition. This is caused by the fact that it is no longer possible to represent non-matching as the identity relation. Previously, non-matching was equivalent to nothing happening

---

2. it is assumed that any program which has a state composed entirely of output tokens has terminated.

---

[11] Given that the actual instruction set is micro-codable, this is reasonable even from a practical point of view.

and firing meant tokens were consumed. Special matching may introduce extra tokens, both for success and fail cases. This means further checking of the state and additional processes for firing have to be added.

However a simplification is also possible. Since the MDFM is restricted to either unary or binary nodes, it is no longer necessary for nodes to hold information about the number of expected inputs as this is deducible from inspection of the matching function of the incoming token (unary if BY; binary otherwise).

A list of differences from the previous definition is given below along with an indication of the reason for the modification.

1. Type checking and error detail are added — these use the extra information carried by tokens to perform some error checking.

2. Tokens carry type information — this is necessary to reflect the "strong typing" present in the machine.

3. Labels are expanded — this is to allow labels to be used both to separate tokens in multiple instantiations of a piece of graph and to separate elements of a data structure. [12]

4. Matching functions are included in destinations to enable matching actions to be considered.

5. Operators are made explicit — This is done to allow a more precise characterisation of the actual machine. Not all implemented operators are included.

6. Alternative result destinations are included — This addition is necessary to deal with branching and switching nodes. In fact, the hardware only gives a restricted version of this facility but it can be achieved using DUP nodes.

7. Literals are added to nodes. That is, constant values could be attached to one input of a binary node removing the need to pass in fixed constants.

8. The identity relation used in previous definitions to represent "no firing" is replaced by an operator allowing for Deferred failures — this is forced by the fact that defer and wait have a slightly different action. The matching functions of waiting tokens are not considered again (they are within the store). On the other hand, a deferred token is represented as if the defer had not occurred.

9. The test of a node's readiness to fire is more complex. It is no longer enough to simply test if the cardinality of the ready set is equal to the number of expected inputs since action is also required in the case of some failures involving special matching functions.

---

[12] only 2 fields are given since the 3rd field is used in practice to separate a special case of multiple instantiation.

10. The meaning function for nodes ($\mathcal{M}_N$) is rewritten — This is again made necessary by the possibility of failure actions.

11. An additional meaning function is included ($\mathcal{M}_{OP}$) — this is used in conjunction with the enumerated set to define the available primitive operations.

12. Test and special action functions are added — to deal with matching functions.

13. One further complexity is introduced by the use of the *GCL* node. This node returns a unique identifier (colour) each time it fires. In the machine, this is possible by the use of a global variable containing a set of unused colours. Given the applicative style of the definition, this is difficult to reflect here without the extra complexity of passing an extra parameter through all levels of the definition. In order to avoid this, the notation is abused and an external variable is used, following the operation definition style of VDM.

As can be seen most of the above present no particular difficulties. The exception is the treatment of matching functions, which is explained in detail below.

It is not feasible to present the full definition here, it can be found in [KDJ85]. The following is a skeleton of the complete definition which serves to illustrate the structure.

3.1 The Complete Definition

The basic types are extended to contain complete information.

$Token$ :: $\quad V$: $Value$
$\qquad TY$: $Type$
$\qquad L$: $Label$
$\qquad D$: $Destination$

$Type$ = **Machine types e.g.** INT,COLOUR

$Label$ :: C : $Colour$
$\qquad I$: $Index$

$Destination$ :: NA : $Node\_address$
$\qquad\qquad MF$: $Matching\_function$
$\qquad\qquad IP$: $Input\_point$

Matching_function = {EW,...,EA}

$$\vdots$$

$Node$ :: $\quad O$: $Operator$
$\qquad\quad D$: $Nextdestinations$
$\qquad LIT$: $Literal$

Operator = **Primitive Machine Operations**

$$\vdots$$

The meaning of a program is largely as before. The extension is to allow a more general test for an action occurring, to allow for special matching functions.

$\mathcal{M}_P$: $Node\_store \rightarrow$ set of (set of $Token \times$ set of $Token$)

$\mathcal{M}_P \llbracket ns \rrbracket \;\triangleq\; \mu \mathcal{R} \cdot nfail(s) \cup \bigcup \{\mathcal{M}_N \llbracket ns(na), na \rrbracket; \mathcal{R} \mid na \in \text{dom } ns\}$
    where
      $s = \{ts \in \text{set of } Token \mid \nexists na \in \text{dom } ns \cdot is\_action(ts, na)\}$

The termination function is also similar to the previous definition.

$\mathcal{T}_P$: $Node\_store \rightarrow$ set of (set of $Token$)

$\mathcal{T}_P \llbracket ns \rrbracket \;\triangleq\; \mu \mathcal{S} \cdot baseset(ns) \cup$
    $\bigcup\{\{ts \in \text{dom } \mathcal{M}_N \llbracket ns(na), na \rrbracket \mid \forall ts' \cdot ts \mathcal{M}_N \llbracket ns(na), na \rrbracket ts'$
       $\Rightarrow\; ts' \in \mathcal{S}\} \mid na \in \text{dom } ns\}$

The $\mathcal{M}_N$ function now has to allow for special failures as well as normal firing.

$\mathcal{M}_N$: $Node \times Node\_address \rightarrow$ set of (set of $Token \times$ set of $Token$)

$\mathcal{M}_N \llbracket mk\text{-}Node(op, nd, l), na \rrbracket \;\triangleq\;$
    $ident(na) \cup fireaction(na, op, nd, l) \cup failaction(na, op, nd)$

The meaning of an *Operator* is given by $\mathcal{M}_{OP}$. This function also generates any extra tokens caused by special success matching.

  $\mathcal{M}_{OP}$: $Operator \times$ set of $Token \times Nextdestinations \times Literal \rightarrow$ set of $Token$

  $\mathcal{M}_{OP} \llbracket op, ts, ds, l \rrbracket \;\triangleq\;$
    the result of performing the operation plus extra match tokens

The rest of the definition consists of subsidiary functions handing the details of this scheme.

As was mentioned above, most of the extra complexity in this definition is caused by the mechanisms added to handle matching functions. To facilitate the understanding of this, an informal explanation of the way in which matching is modelled is given below.

In the previous definitions, matching was implicitly Extract Wait i.e. pure dataflow. This resulted in the simple mechanism of removing tokens from the state when finding matches, and performing an identity transformation in the case of waiting. In the complete definition, the matching functions are divided into 3 general cases:

1. successful matching actions;

2. normal failing actions i.e. Wait and Defer;

3. special fail actions.

The first case, that of successful matching, is dealt with by an extra section to the $\mathcal{M}_{OP}$ function. (In some sense, successful matching and firing could legitimately be regarded as closely linked since all tokens succeeding in matching immediately proceed to fire.) Extra tokens are generated and added to the state to represent the effect of special matchings. In the case of Extract, no extra tokens are generated. (Firing tokens are consumed in the *fireaction* function.) Preserve causes a copy of the waiting token (identified by the *NIL* matching function) to be added to the state. Increment and decrement cause a token with the appropriately adjusted value to be generated.

Normal failing, i.e. failures that do not "change" the state, is handled by the *nfail* operator. The reason for the quotes in the previous sentence is the fact that Wait does require a slight modification to the state. It is necessary to identify the token as having undergone a failed matching, i.e. being resident in the store, for subsequent successful matchings. To enable this, the matching function of the waiting token is replaced with *NIL*. This is necessary to avoid the selection of the wrong token's succeed function, on subsequent matches. The defer action leaves the state completely unchanged. This would be expected since it is primarily an "engineering" solution to a problem and could be imagined to have the meaning "forget that ever happened and try again later".

The final case, that the fail matching functions requiring special action is a little more complex. this condition is detected by the test function *failaction*. This uses the function *specialfail* to examine the state for incomplete input sets containing a token which has a matching function that is a member of the *Failmf* set. The function *failres* uses the subsidiary function *ft* to generate the appropriate new token i.e. an *EMPTY* token for abort and an inverted token for generate.

This completes the record of the derivation of the formal semantics for the MDFM. The full definition contains some simplifications of the actual machine but these were simply to reduce the length of the definitions to a manageable size. All of the important characteristics have been described and the complete detail could be included at the cost of increased bulk. It should be noted that the definition is, in some sense, parameterised on certain features to the level of the $\mathcal{M}_{OP}$ function. To give a semantics for a different version of the same machine, e.g. with different matching functions, the same general definition could be used. To make this definition fully parameterised on these sets, it would be necessary to add another level of function below *MOP* to deal with matching separately.

4   Some comments on Relational Semantics

The approach taken above is not the most common. Most work dealing with parallelism has followed the powerdomain approach or used other complex domain structures. For example, [Bro82] uses multiple domains. This is because powerdomains offer greater generality but at the cost of increased complexity. Powerdomains are generalizations of

Scott Domains [Sto77]. As such, they are able to handle all the constructs for which Domains are suitable, such as reflexive objects. Being extended to a "powerset" basis, they can also express non-determinism. The price paid for this is a(n even) more complex mathematical basis. Domains are considered to be complete lattices on continuous functions, and extending this approach is not obvious. For example, the ordering required is more complex e.g. the Egli-Milner ordering [Bro82]. The increase in mathematical complexity can be seen from examination of the papers by [Plo76] and [Smy78].

It was felt that mathematical complexity should be avoided, where possible. The step from functions to relations, as denotations is easier to comprehend than the powerdomain approach. This makes relations useful in practice despite the fact that certain features (e.g. self-application) cannot be handled.

Since the current work was inherently first order, the relational approach is used here. Previous work along these lines can be found in [Hit74], [HP72], [Par80] and [Jon81]. A similar approach is currently being examined in [Bli83].

4.1 General Properties

It is worthwhile looking at some properties that would be expected to hold in a semantics given in this style. First of all, a general theorem is proven. This is then instantiated for the MDFM semantics and some further properties of this definition are illustrated.

Since this style of semantics involves two functions — a meaning function ($\mathcal{M}$) and a termination set function ($\mathcal{T}$) — an obvious property to examine is the relationship between these functions. Since $\mathcal{T}$ delivers the set of input states for which termination is guaranteed under $\mathcal{M}$, a desired property would be that $\mathcal{M}$ is applicable to $\mathcal{T}$. Formally, $\mathcal{T} \subseteq \text{dom } \mathcal{M}$. In earlier work [Jon81][Jon87], this property was shown for the specific semantics involved. Since it seemed likely that this would have to be repeated for any definition done in this style, it was decided to attempt to prove this property as a general theorem.

In the general case, a function $\mathcal{M}$ is constructed as a fixed point from a basis br. A termination set, given by $\mathcal{T}$, is constructed as a fixed point from bs. It is assumed the property holds for the base cases.

Theorem

For a meaning function $\mathcal{M}$ and a termination set $\mathcal{T}$, given the basis of br and bs respectively

$$bs \subseteq br \vdash \mathcal{T} \subseteq \text{dom } \mathcal{M}$$

where

$$\mathcal{T} \triangleq \mu \mathcal{S} \cdot bs \cup \{s \in \text{dom } \mathcal{R} \mid \forall s' \cdot s \mathcal{R} s' \Rightarrow s \in \mathcal{S}\}$$

and

$$\mathcal{M} \triangleq \mu \mathcal{R} \cdot br \cup \mathcal{R}_1 ; \mathcal{R}$$

Proof

(Following [Jon81])

Since the function generating $\mathcal{T}$ is non-continuous and we wish to use fix point induction, we define a continuous expression, which contains the set generated by $\mathcal{T}$. If the containment holds for this set then it must hold for $\mathcal{T}$. (Informally, this is the set of inputs that may terminate.)

1. let $\mathcal{F}(\mathcal{S}) \triangleq bs \cup \{s \in \operatorname{dom} \mathcal{R}_1 \mid \exists s' \cdot s \mathcal{R}_1 s' \wedge s' \in \mathcal{S}\}$

2. $\mathcal{F}(\{\}) = bs$ 1

3. $\mathcal{F}^{n+1}(\{\}) = \{s \in \operatorname{dom} \mathcal{R}_1 \mid \exists s' \cdot s \mathcal{R}_1 s' \wedge s' \in \mathcal{F}^n(\{\})\}$ 1

4. let $\mathcal{G}(\mathcal{R}) \triangleq br \cup \mathcal{R}_1 ; \mathcal{R}$

5. $\mathcal{G}(\{\}) = br$ 4

6. $\mathcal{G}^{n+1}(\{\}) = \mathcal{R}_1 ; \mathcal{G}^n(\{\})$ 4

7. $\mathcal{F}(\{\}) \subseteq \operatorname{dom} \mathcal{G}(\{\})$ hyp,2,4

8. assume $\mathcal{F}^n(\{\}) \subseteq \operatorname{dom} \mathcal{G}^n(\{\})$

9. $\{s \in \operatorname{dom} \mathcal{R}_1 \mid \exists s' \cdot s \mathcal{R}_1 s' \wedge s' \in \mathcal{F}^n(\{\})\} \subseteq \operatorname{dom} \mathcal{R}_1 ; \mathcal{G}^n(\{\})$ monotonicity

10. $\mathcal{F}^{n+1}(\{\}) \subseteq \operatorname{dom} \mathcal{G}^{n+1}(\{\})$ 3,6,9

11. $\bigcup \mathcal{F}^n(\{\}) \subseteq \operatorname{dom} \bigcup \mathcal{G}^n(\{\})$ induction,7,8,10

12. $\{x \in \operatorname{dom} \mathcal{R} \mid \forall y \cdot x \mathcal{R} y \Rightarrow y \in Y\} \subseteq \{x \in \operatorname{dom} \mathcal{R} \mid \exists y \cdot x \mathcal{R} y \wedge y \in Y\}$ $\operatorname{dom} \mathcal{R} \neq \{\}$

13. $\mathcal{T} \subseteq \mu \mathcal{S} \cdot \mathcal{F}(\mathcal{S})$ 12

14. $\mathcal{T} \subseteq \bigcup \mathcal{F}^n(\{\})$ continuity,4,15

15. $\mathcal{T} \subseteq \operatorname{dom} \bigcup \mathcal{G}^n(\{\})$ 11,14

16. $\mathcal{T} \subseteq \operatorname{dom} \mu \mathcal{R} \cdot \mathcal{G}(\mathcal{R})$ continuity,5,14

17. $\mathcal{T} \subseteq \operatorname{dom} \mathcal{M}$ 16

This gives a general theorem which could be instantiated for any specific semantics. Following this for the specific case of the MDFM semantics, we arrive at the following proof.

Theorem

For the definition of the MDFM given above, it holds that:

$$\mathcal{T}_{\mathrm{P}} [\![ns]\!] \subseteq \operatorname{dom} \mathcal{M}_{\mathrm{P}} [\![ns]\!]$$

Proof

The proof is sketched by:

1. $T_P \triangleq \mu S \cdot baseset \cup \{s \in \operatorname{dom} r_1 \mid \forall s' \cdot s r_1 s' \Rightarrow s' \in S \wedge r_1 \in \mathcal{R}_1\}$
2. $M_P \triangleq \mu \mathcal{R} \cdot baserel \cup \bigcup\{r_1 \mathrel{;} \mathcal{R} \mid r_1 \in \mathcal{R}_1\}$
3. let $\mathcal{R}^u \triangleq \bigcup\{r_1 \in \mathcal{R}_1\}$
4. let $M \triangleq \mu \mathcal{R} \cdot baserel \cup \mathcal{R}^u \mathrel{;} \mathcal{R}$
5. $\operatorname{dom} r_1 \in \mathcal{R}_1 \subseteq \operatorname{dom} \bigcup\{r_1 \in \mathcal{R}_1\}$
6. $baseset \subseteq \operatorname{dom} baserel$ **def. of nfail, baseset**
7. $T_P \subseteq \operatorname{dom} M$ **theorem,1,4,6**
8. $\operatorname{dom} \mu \mathcal{R} \cdot baserel \cup \bigcup\{r_1 \in \mathcal{R}_1\} \mathrel{;} \mathcal{R} \subseteq \operatorname{dom} \mu \mathcal{R} \cdot baserel \cup \bigcup\{r_1 \mathrel{;} \mathcal{R} \mid r_1 \in \mathcal{R}_1\}$
9. $\operatorname{dom} M \subseteq \operatorname{dom} M_P$ **1,7,8**
10. $T_P \subseteq \operatorname{dom} M_P$ **7,9**

So, this gives the proof of the essential theorem on the MDFM definition. To illustrate the semantics further, some example programs are analysed.

The first case looked at is the meaning of the empty program. This turns out as:

$ns = \{\}$

1. $M_P[\![\{\}]\!] = \mu \mathcal{R} \cdot nfail(s) \cup \bigcup\{M_N[\![ns(na), na]\!] \mathrel{;} \mathcal{R} \mid na \in \operatorname{dom}\{\}\}$
2. $M_P[\![\{\}]\!] = nfail(s)$ **def of $ns, \bigcup, \mu$**
3. $s = \{ts \mid \not\exists na \in \operatorname{dom}\{\} \cdot is\_action(ts, na)\}$ **def of M_P**
4. $s = \mathcal{P}(ts)$ **$ns = \{\},3$**
5. $M_P[\![\{\}]\!] = nfail(\mathcal{P}(ts))$ **2,4**
6. $M_P[\![\{\}]\!] \approx \mathcal{E}_{ts}$

The symbol $\approx$ is used here to mean essentially equal (i.e. values are unchanged but matching functions are altered). This is irrelevant since there will be no matching.

This is as would be hoped, since the only thing that would be altered by the submission of any input tokens to an empty program are the matching functions of the waiting tokens. So, the identity relation is a reassuring result.

As a final example, the termination set of a non-terminating program is examined. A simple non-terminating program is a single DUP node recycling its input as in Fig. 4. The termination set of graph is given by [13]:

---

[13] In the following, constructor functions are dropped for the sake of compactness.

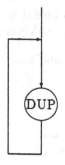

Figure 4: A Simple Non-terminating Graph

1. $ns \triangleq \{1 \mapsto (DUP, (\{1\}, \{\,\}), NIL)\}$

2. let $\mathcal{R} \triangleq \mathcal{M}_N [\![ns(1), 1]\!]$

3. $\mathcal{T}_P [\![ns]\!] \triangleq \mu S \cdot baseset(ns) \cup \{ts \in \text{dom } \mathcal{R} \mid \forall ts' \cdot ts \mathcal{R} ts' \Rightarrow ts' \in S\}$

4. $baseset(ns) = \{ts \in \text{dom } \mathcal{R} \mid \forall ts' \cdot ts \mathcal{R} ts' \Rightarrow \forall t \in ts' \cdot NA(D(t)) \notin \text{dom } ns\}$

5. $\forall ts' \in \text{rng } \mathcal{R} \cdot \forall t \in ts' \cdot NA(D(t)) = 1$ 1

6. $\forall ts' \in \text{rng } \mathcal{R} \cdot \forall t \in ts' \cdot NA(D(t)) \in \text{dom } ns$ 1,5

7. $baseset(ns) = \{\,\}$ 6,4

8. $\mathcal{T}_P [\![ns]\!] = \{\,\}$ **prop of μ,3,7**

Again the result is reassuring, since we find the guaranteed termination set for a non-terminating program is empty.

The above section gives an indication of the way the previous semantic definition could be used to formally prove properties of dataflow programs.

5 Acknowledgements

Thanks are due to : Cliff Jones, who supervised this work; the DataFlow group at Manchester, for providing necessary information; the SERC, for providing financial support.

References

[AW77] E.A. Ashcroft and W. Wadge. LUCID — a non-procedural language with iteration. *CACM*, 20(7), 1977.

[BA81]   Brock and Ackerman. Scenarios — a model for non-determinate computation. In *LNCS 107*, pages 252 – 259, Springer-Verlag, 1981.

[Bac78]   J. Backus. Can programming be liberated form the von neumann style? *CACM*, 21(8), 1978.

[Bli83]   A. Blikle. Concurrent distributed processes. 1983.

[Bow81]   D.L. Bowen. *The Implementation of Data Structures in a Dataflow Computer.* PhD thesis, University of Manchester, 1981.

[Bro82]   M. Broy. Fixed point theory for communication and concurrency. In *Proc of TC2 Working Conference on Formal Description of Programming Concepts II*, IFIP, 1982.

[Bus83]   V.J. Bush. A survey of the use of matching functions. 1983.

[Cat81]   A.J. Catto. *Non-Deterministic Programming in a Dataflow Environment.* PhD thesis, University of Manchester, 1981.

[Dav78]   A.L. Davies. The architecture and system method of DDM1. In *Proc. 5th Annual Symposium on Computer Architecture*, pages 210 – 215, 1978.

[DFL74]   J.B. Dennis, J.B. Fossen, and J.P. Linderman. Dataflow schemas. In *LNCS 5*, Springer-Verlag, 1974.

[Fau82]   A. Faustini. *The Equivalence of an Operational and a Denotational Semantics for Pure Dataflow Programs.* PhD thesis, University of Warwick, 1982.

[Gur82]   J.R. Gurd. Manchester prototype dataflow system description. 1982.

[GW80]   J.R. Gurd and I. Watson. A data driven system for high speed parallel computing. *Computer Design*, 19(6 – 7), 1980.

[GW83]   J.R. Gurd and I. Watson. Priliminary evaluation of a prototype dataflow computer. In *Proc. IFIP 83*, North Holland, 1983.

[Hit74]   P. Hitchcock. *An Approach to Formal Reasoning about Programs.* PhD thesis, University of Warwick, 1974.

[HP72]   P. Hitchcock and D. Park. Induction rules and termination proofs. In *IRIA Proc.*, 1972.

[Jon73]   C.B. Jones. *Formal Development of Programs.* Technical Report TR12.117, IBM Hursley, 1973.

[Jon81]   C.B. Jones. *Development Methods for Computer Programs — including a Notion of Interference.* PhD thesis, University of Oxford, 1981.

[Jon86] Cliff B. Jones. *Systematic Software Development using VDM*. Prentice Hall International, 1986.

[Jon87] C.B. Jones. VDM proof obligations and their justification. In *this volume*, 1987.

[KDJ85] K.D.Jones. *The Application of a Formal Development Method to a Parallel Machine Environment*. PhD thesis, The University of Manchester, 1985.

[Kir81] C.C. Kirkham. The basic programmers manual. 1981.

[KM66] R.M. Karp and R.E. Miller. Properties of a model for parallel computing. *SIAM. Journal of Applied Maths*, 14:1390 – 1417, 1966.

[Kos78] P.R. Kosinski. A straightforward non-deterministic semantics for dataflow programs. In *Proc. 5th Annual Symposium on Principles of Programming Languages*, 1978.

[Oli84] J. Oliveira. *A Semantics for Deterministic Dataflow Programs*. PhD thesis, University of Manchester, 1984.

[Par80] D. Park. On the semantics of fair parallelism. In *LNCS 86*, Springer-Verlag, 1980.

[Plo76] G.D. Plotkin. A powerdomain construction. *SIAM Journal of Computing*, 5(3), 1976.

[Sar85] J. Sargeant. *Efficient Stored Data Structures for Dataflow Computing*. PhD thesis, University of Manchester, 1985.

[Smy78] M.B. Smyth. Powerdomains. *Journal of Computer System Sciences*, 16:23 – 26, 1978.

[Sto77] J.E. Stoy. *Denotational Semantics*. MIT Press, 1977.

[VBO83] J.R. Gurd V.J. Bush and J. Oliviera. FP as a basis for dataflow program transformation. 1983.

[Vee81] A.H. Veen. *A Formal Model for Dataflow Programs with Token Colouring*. Technical Report IW 179/81, Mathematisch Centrum, 1981.

INTRODUCTION TO THE VDM TUTORIAL

Mícheál Mac an Airchinnigh
Department of Computer Science, University of Dublin,
Trinity Cóllege, Dublin, Ireland.

1. Introduction

The Vienna Development Method (VDM) is a formal software development method, a brief history of which is given in the foreword to these proceedings. The specification language (metalanguage) of the VDM has been traditionally known as Meta-IV. Although this tutorial is primarily an elementary introduction to the VDM, it should be borne in mind that much of the basic mathematical concepts and notation underlying Meta-IV is to be found elsewhere. For example, in Hoare's recent work on Communicating Sequential Processes (CSP) [1985], his theory rests on the theory of sequences (i.e., tuples in VDM, traces in CSP) and much of his notation is similar to that of Meta-IV. Thus, a knowledge of the VDM Meta-IV is a good foundation for the study of CSP. The theory of sequences also forms the basis for the Theory of Formal Languages.

The Tutorial is primarily intended for those attendees of the VDM Symposium 87 who are unfamiliar with or do not frequently use the VDM. Moreover it forms an integral part of the Symposium itself unlike the kind of tutorials which usually accompany Conferences in Information Technology. The tutorial speakers do not intend to teach the VDM. For such a task is impossible in one day. Rather the goal is to give a flavour of the methodology and to present an overview of the Meta-IV notation. As well as being able to follow the papers at the Symposium, participants will be in a position to continue their study of the VDM using a textbook such as that of Cliff B. Jones [1976].

Some effort has been made to contribute examples of VDM specifications not found elsewhere. Where duplication occurs, an appropriate reference is given.

2. VDM Reference Works

There are exactly four VDM reference works currently available in English:

1. "The Vienna Development Method: The Meta-Language", [Bjoerner and Jones, 1978].

2. "Software Development - A Rigorous Approach", [Jones 1980].

3. "Formal Specification & Software Development", [Bjoerner and Jones, 1982].

4. "Systematic Software Development Using VDM", [Jones, 1986].

Of these four, the two by Jones [1980, 1986] may be regarded as "textbooks". However, one ought to note that the 1986 work supercedes that of 1980. The original work on the VDM [Bjoerner and Jones, 1978], although superceded by that of 1982, is still of some practical use but can not be regarded as a textbook. The 1982 work is still the standard reference book for the VDM. A six volume work will be appearing in 1987/88, entitled "Software Architectures and Programming Systems Design", of which Dines Bjoerner will be the (principal) author.

In addition to the reference books cited above, there are numerous papers published on all aspects of the VDM, a list of which will be available at the VDM Symposium.

3. Notation and Style of Use

Notation and style of use of the VDM is somewhat controversial. One may distinguish two principal schools of thought - the English school (associated with Cliff B. Jones) and the Danish school (associated with Dines Bjoerner). Both schools use the model-theoretic approach towards semantics and formal specification. There is no difference in philosophy; rather the two schools must be seen to be complementary to each other.

That there are differences in notation and style of use is a direct result of several factors:

1. Originally a "pencil and paper" method, VDM users were limited only by their own ingenuity with regard to notation.

2. Differences in notation in published works has been dictated largely by the quality of the printing technology available at the time.

3. As efforts were made to teach the VDM to a wider audience, and in particular to practitioners in the Software Industry, certain notational variants were introduced to facilitate the learning process.

4. Application of the VDM to different kinds of problem domains has resulted in the development of notation and styles peculiar to each.

The VDM, and its associated metalanguage Meta-IV, is never static. The concrete notation and terminology used has evolved continuously and will continue to do so. Although there is an effort being made in formulating a "standard" for the VDM, it is clear that use of the VDM itself can not and should not be "standardised". Consequently, one may identify another partition of VDM practitioners - those who wish to provide support tools for specifications in the VDM and therefore demand a standard concrete syntax, and those who consider the VDM Meta-IV to be a mathematical notation and therefore insist on inventing new notations in extending the scope of VDM specifications. Both groups have right on their side. Such a tension is a healthy sign that the VDM will not stagnate, but continue to grow in expressive power and range of applicability. At various stages of development one may expect to find a consolidation phase where an agreed compromise between opposing factions will lead to the production of further tool support.

The English school has diverged considerably from the notation of the 1978 work, which is basically that still in use by the Danish school. Even within the English school, changes have taken place. For example, there are considerable differences between the notation of [Jones, 1980] and that of its successor [Jones, 1986]. One may characterise the distinction between the two schools by noting that the notation of the Danish school is more terse and mathematical-like whereas that of the English school approaches that of a conventional programming language form:

"The first line of this specification defines the signature of the function. The syntax used is slightly different from that used in Chapter 1: here, the style is intentionally closer to that of programming languages like Pascal." [Jones, 1986] p.53.

While there are divergences in notation, there are also common features. However, the existence of significant notational differences between two large groups of VDM practitioners has inevitably posed a major challenge to the organisation and presentation of an

international VDM tutorial such as this. There can be no question of
siding with one school or the other. The author who is responsible for
the tutorial has tried to strike a balance in organising the material.

4. The Structure

The structure of the tutorial is similar to that of [Jones, 1986]. It
consists of three sections:

1. Specification by pre- and post-conditions - Roger Shaw;

2. Specification by Data Types - Micheal Mac an Airchinnigh;

3. Data Reification or Refinement - Derek Andrews.

Each section logically follows from the one preceding it.

5. Glossary

To facilitate tutorial participants in furthering their knowledge of
the VDM, a very brief glossary of notation is presented in this
section. The material is organised as follows. First, for each kind of
VDM Meta-IV expression, the nearest mathematical equivalent is
presented. Where none exists, then Computer Science itself has been
used as a source. Second, some of the more common Meta-IV "variants"
are given and the appropriate reference cited. For convenience, the
latter is abbreviated in an obvious manner.

The Set Data Type

A set in VDM is in reality an element of a powerset. The Meta-IV
notation for sets is generally that of mathematics.

```
{1,2,3,4}                a set of four elements

P(S)                     powerset of S
S-set                    [B&J,78,82], [J,80]
set of S                 [J,86]

U/ss                     distributed union of set of sets
union ss                 [B&J,78,82], [J,80]
Uss                      [J,86]
```

The Map Data Type

The Map data type of the VDM is basically an abstraction of a finite mathematical function. A map is, therefore, simply an element of a powerset of a cartesian product.

{(1,1),(2,4),(3,9)}	a map of three elements
[1→1,2→4,3→9]	[B&J,78,82], [J,80]
{1↦1,2↦4,3↦9}	[J,86]
F: D ⟶ R	map (function) from domain D to range R
M = D m→ R	[B&J,78,82]
M = D → R	[J,80]
M = map D to R	[J,86]
m1 + m2	override (overwrite) of m1 with m2
	[B&J,78,82]
m1 † m2	[J,80,86]
m | s	restriction of map m to set s
	[B&J,78,82], [J,80]
s ◁ m	[J,86]
m \ s	removal of map m with respect to set s
	[B&J,78,82]
s ◁ m	[J,86]
U/ms	distributed merge of set of maps
merge ms	[B&J,78,82]

The Tuple Data Type

Other terms for tuple [B&J,78] are list [J,80] and sequence [J,86].

<1,2,3,4>	a sequence of 4 elements
	[B&J,78,82], [J,80]
[1,2,3,4]	[J,86]
S*	a (possibly empty) tuple of elements
	[B&J,78,82]
S-list	[J,80]
seq of S	[J,86]
<x>^y	a tuple with head x and tail y
	[B&J,78,82]
<x>||y	[J,80]
[x]^y	[J,86]
<x|y>	a relational form
^/tt	distributed concatenation
conc tt	[B&J,78,82], [J,80,86]

The Tree Data Type

The VDM tree [B&J,78,82] is called a (composite) object in [J,80,86].

```
O ::  s-d1: D1              a tree with n components
      s-d2: D1              [B&J,78,82]
      ...
      s-dn: Dn
O ::  d1: D1                [J,80,86]
      d2: D2
      ...
      dn: Dn
```

6. References

Bjoerner, D. and Jones, C.B. (eds), The Vienna Development Method: The Meta-Language, Lecture Notes in Computer Science, Vol.61, Springer-Verlag, Berlin Heidelberg New York, 1978.

Bjoerner, Dines and Jones, Cliff B., Formal Specification and Software Development, Prentice / Hall International, Englewood Cliffs, New Jersey London New Delhi Singapore Sydney Tokyo Toronto Wellington, 1982.

Bjoerner, Dines., Software Architectures and Programming Systems Design, to be published in 6 volumes, 1987/88.

Hoare, C.A.R., Communicating Sequential Processes, Prentice-Hall International, Englewood Cliffs, New Jersey London Mexico New Delhi Rio de Janiero Singapore Sydney Tokyo Toronto Wellington, 1985.

Jones, Cliff B., Software Development, A Rigorous Approach, Prentice/Hall International, Englewood Cliffs, New Jersey London New Delhi Singapore Sydney Tokyo Toronto Wellington, 1980.

Jones, Cliff B., Systematic Software Development Using VDM, Prentice/Hall International, Englewood Cliffs, New Jersey London Mexico New Delhi Rio de Janiero Singapore Sydney Tokyo Toronto Wellington, 1986.

SPECIFICATION BY DATA TYPES

Micheal Mac an Airchinnigh
Department of Computer Science, University of Dublin,
Trinity College, Dublin, Ireland

1. Introduction

An abstract data type is to be regarded as a non-empty collection of sorts, one of which is distinguished and may be called <u>the</u> (abstract) data type, together with operations on those sorts.

- A data type in the VDM is characterised by its behaviour [Jones, 1986] p.140;

- A data type is specified in the VDM by providing a model [Jones, 1986] p.141;

- The basic set of VDM models is {tuple, set, map, tree};

Strictly speaking the mathematical function (of the lambda calculus) is a fifth basic model. The qualifier "basic" is used to distinguish that set of models which is accepted as part of the VDM in general. The user of the VDM is permitted (nay encouraged) to introduce other models as needed. For example, the relation finds an important role in specification of knowledge representations. However, a note of caution is in order. The basic set of models have at least a sound mathematical foundation. Other models are introduced at the users' own risk.

The notation used in this paper is generally that of the Bjoerner School [Bjoerner and Jones, 1978, 1982].

The user of the VDM, faced with a particular problem to be solved in a given application domain, is required to identify the objects of interest and operations on those objects. Choosing an appropriate VDM data type (i.e., model) for each object, the user then provides the corresponding semantics for the operations using the inbuilt data type operations. This is the so-called model theoretic semantics approach. In this paper attention will be focused on the VDM metalanguage as a formal specification language. The VDM is itself a complete formal software development method and this aspect shall be addressed in the paper by Derek Andrews on "Data Reification and Operation Decomposition" (in these proceedings).

Each of the four basic models - tuple, set, map, and tree, are considered in that order in the following sections. Some basic operations on each model are provided. For a complete list of such operations the reader is referred to the VDM reference works given in the introductory paper to this Tutorial. Associated with each model are a number of simple examples which are used to illustrate the method of specification. To show the applicability of the VDM Meta-IV to areas not normally associated with it, some special application subsections are provided.

The reader must actively work at the formal material presented here. The VDM is akin to mathematics in this respect. One does not read a paper in mathematics passively. One works through the mathematics presented. So it is with the VDM. In following the examples, the reader is urged to have paper and pencil (and eraser!) at hand. The author has tried to be as careful as possible to ensure that the specifications are correct(?) Even so, it would not be surprising to find errors, if any there are.

2. The Tuple

The tuple is the appropriate abstraction for the list of LISP or Prolog and the array of Pascal or Ada. (N.B. Ada is a registered trademark of the U.S. Department of Defense, Ada Joint Programme Office). Alternative names for tuple [Bjoerner and Jones, 1978, 1982] are sequence [Jones, 1986] and (homogeneous) list [Jones, 1980].

Let D denote some domain, i.e., set of entities. Then D* and D+ denotes a tuple of zero or more, and one or more, elements of D, respectively.

- The empty tuple is denoted by <>.

- The first (head) element of a non-empty tuple t is denoted hd t.

- The rest (tail) of a non-empty tuple t is denoted tl t.

- The concatenation of two tuples t1 and t2 is denoted t1 ⌢ t2.

For example, let S denote the set of all lower case English letters. Then S* denotes the set of all tuples of S. Typical elements of S* are <>, <c a t>, <d o g>, and <m o u s e>.

Let w1 = <m o u s e> and w2 = <t r a p>

Then <u>hd</u> w1 = m

<u>tl</u> w1 = <o u s e>

<h>⌢ <u>tl</u> w1 = <h o u s e>

w1 ⌢ w2 = <m o u s e t r a p>

The structure of a tuple may be exhibited by using the bar (|) notation. Let w = <x|y>. Then <u>hd</u> w = x and <u>tl</u> w = y. Such a notation provides an alternative form to the use of the <u>hd</u> and <u>tl</u> operators on tuples.

Let <u|v> = <m o u s e> and <x|y> = <t r a p>

Then u = m and x = t

v = <o u s e> and y = <r a p>

<h|v> = <h o u s e>

<u|v> ⌢ <x|y> = <m o u s e t r a p>

One must be careful to distinguish between x used as a variable and t used as a letter. If there is danger of confusion, then the latter may be written "t". Alternatively, Greek letters may be used for variables. One further convention on the use of the bar notation is to be noted. Tuples t1 and t2, whose first elements are identical, are denoted by t1 = <x|y> and t2 = <x|z>. Tuples t1 and t2, whose tails are identical are denoted t1 = <u|w> and t2 = <v|w>. Such a convention permits abbreviated specifications which depend on the notions of pattern matching and unification.

2.1 Basic Operations on Tuples

The number of elements in a tuple is given by the operator <u>len</u>. For example, <u>len</u> <m o u s e> = 5. Its formal definition is:

<u>len</u>: S* ⟶ Nat0

<u>len</u>(w) def= <u>if</u> w = <> <u>then</u> 0 <u>else</u> 1 + <u>len</u>(<u>tl</u> w)

Alternatively, the specification of operators such as <u>len</u> may be given by mutually independent clauses:

len: S* $\longrightarrow$ Nat0

len(<>) def= 0

len(<x|y>) def= 1 + len(y)

The set of elements in a tuple is given by the operator elems. For example, elems <m a d a m> = {m,a,d}. Its formal definition is:

elems: S* $\longrightarrow$ $\mathbb{P}$(S)

elems(<>) def= {}

elems(<x|y>) def= {x} U elems(y)

Let w be the word <p a r t>. Then the reversal of w, denoted rev w, is the word <t r a p>. The formal definition is:

rev: S* $\longrightarrow$ S*

rev(<>) def= <>

rev(<x|y>) def= rev(y) $^\frown$ <x>

2.2 Specification by the Data Type Tuple

To introduce the tuple as a data abstraction mechanism two familiar computer science data structures are chosen as illustration - the stack and the queue.

Example 2.1: A Stack of Natural Numbers: The data type Stack may be formally defined as a tuple of natural numbers:

Stack = Nat0*

Typical Stacks are:

<> -- the empty stack

<6> -- a stack of one element

<3 1 2 5 1 2 2 6 0> -- a stack whose top element is 3

Operations on a Stack may be specified in terms of operations on tuples. Thus, for example:

1. Operation: Creation of a new Stack

new: $\longrightarrow$ Stack

new def= <>

2. Operation: Top of a Stack

top: Stack ⟶ Nat0

top(<e|s>) def= e   -- alternatively top(<e>^s) def= e

3. Operation: Pop a Stack

pop: Stack ⟶ Stack

pop(<e|s>) def= s   -- alternatively pop(<e>^s) def= s

4. Operation: Push a Stack

push: Stack x Nat0 ⟶ Stack

push(s,n) def= <n|s>   -- alternatively push(s,n) def= <n>^s

5. Operation: Depth of a Stack

depth: Stack ⟶ Nat0

depth(s) def= len s

6. Operation: Test if a Stack is empty

is-empty: Stack ⟶ Bool

is-empty(s) def= s = <>

end of example 2.1.

Stack, as formally specified in example 2.1, is an abstract data type (ADT) with sorts {Stack, Nat0, Bool}, and operations {new, top, pop, push, depth, is-empty}. The semantics of Stack are given by the model Stack = Nat0* and the semantics of the operations by corresponding tuple operations. This is the model-theoretic approach.

A more general specification of Stack is given by

    Stack = Element*

with every occurrence of Nat0 replaced by Element. Such a specification forces one to focus on the structure of Stack, independently of the type of elements of which it may be composed. In such a case, one may speak about a generic specification of Stack.

Example 2.2: A Queue of Natural Numbers: The data type Queue may be formally specified as a tuple of natural numbers:

    Queue = Nat0*

Recalling that Stack is defined by

  Stack = Nat0*

it is clear that there is no distinction between the two at the basic model level. The distinction can only be made at operations level.

Typical instances of Queue are:

  <> -- the empty queue

  <7> -- a queue of one element

  <3 1 6 3 2 1 7> -- a queue with front element 3

Operations on a queue are formally specified in terms of tuple operations:

  1. Operation: Creation of a new Queue

  new: $\longrightarrow$ Queue

  new def= <>

  2. Operation: The front of a Queue

  front: Queue $\longrightarrow$ Nat0

  front(<e|q>) def= e   -- alternatively front(<e>$^\frown$q) def= e

  3. Operation: Remove the first entry of a Queue

  remove: Queue $\longrightarrow$ Queue

  remove(<e|q>) def= q   -- alternatively remove(<e>$^\frown$q) def= q

  4. Operation: Enter a new element into the Queue

  enter: Queue x Nat0 $\longrightarrow$ Queue

  enter(q,n) def= q$^\frown$<n>

Note that one can not use the bar notation in the specification of the semantics of the enter operation.

  5. Operation: The length of a queue

  length: Queue $\longrightarrow$ Nat0

  length(q) def= <u>len</u>(q)

Operation: Test if the Queue is empty

is-empty: Queue $\longrightarrow$ Bool

is-empty(q) def= q = <>

<u>end of example 2.2</u>.

Wherever VDM Meta-IV is used for the formal specification of abstract data types, the distinction between pre- and post-conditions (i.e., implicit semantics), and explicit semantics is only of a cosmetic nature in general. Thus, the operation enter for a Queue, in pre- and post-condition style is:

enter: Queue x Nat0 $\longrightarrow$ Queue

pre-enter: Queue x Nat0 $\longrightarrow$ Bool

pre-enter(q,n) def= true

post-enter: Queue x Nat0 x Queue $\longrightarrow$ Bool

post-enter(q,n,q') def= q' = q $\frown$ <n>

Such a specification is succinctly given in relational form as

enter: Queue x Nat0 x Queue

enter(q,n,q') :- pre-enter(q,n), post-enter(q,n,q').

where ":-" denotes "if", "," denotes "and", and

pre-enter: Queue x Nat0

pre-enter(q,n).

and pre-enter is always true and

post-enter: Queue x Nat0 x Queue

post-enter(q,n,q $\frown$ <n>).

The next example has been chosen to illustrate the style of algorithmic specification of operations on a data type.

<u>Example 2.3</u>: Strings: A string may be formally specified as a tuple of characters taken from some domain S. Technically one speaks of S as an alphabet and of S* as the set of words over S:

String = S*

Let   alph be an operation which gives the set of characters in a string.
Thus, alph(<m a d a m>) = {m,a,d}:

   alph: String ⟶ ℙ(S)

   alph(s) def= <u>elems</u>(s)

where   <u>elems</u> is the tuple operation which gives the set of elements in a
tuple.

Let   is-prefix be   an operation   to test   if a   string p   is a prefix of
string s:

   1. The empty string <> is a prefix of every string s.

   2. The   string p = <h|pt>   is a   prefix of the string s = <h|st> if
      the string pt is a prefix of the string st.

Formally,

   is-prefix: String x String ⟶ Bool

   1. is-prefix(<>,s) def= true

   2. is-prefix(<h|pt>,<h|st>) def= is-prefix(pt,st)

Note   that in   such algorithms   where the   result type   is Bool,   it   is
customary   to provide only those clauses which evaluate to true. Instead
of such a functional notation, a relational notation may be preferred:

   is-prefix: String x String

   1. is-prefix(<>,s).

   2. is-prefix(<h|pt>,<h|st>) :- is-prefix(pt,st)

where ":-" may be read as "if".

There   are a   large number of useful operations that may be provided for
Strings,   some of   which are   given in   the exercises below. To conclude
this   elementary introduction,   let us consider the problem of computing
the   maximal common   prefix (maxprefix)   of   two   strings   u and v.   For
instance,

   maxprefix(<m o u s e>,<h o u s e>) = <>

   maxprefix(<p r o g r a m>,<p r o c e d u r e>) = <p r o>

The algorithm is:

   1. The maxprefix of the empty string <> and every string v is <>.

   2. The maxprefix of every string u and the empty string <> is <>.

3. The maxprefix of every string u and u is u.

4. The maxprefix of string u = <h|ut> and string v = <h|vt> is the string <h|t> where t is the maxprefix of strings ut and vt.

5. The maxprefix of strings u and v which differ in their first letter is <>.

Formally, maxprefix may be specified as:

  maxprefix: String x String $\longrightarrow$ String

1. maxprefix(<>,v) def= <>

2. maxprefix(u,<>) def= <>

3. maxprefix(u,u) def= u

4. maxprefix(<h|ut>,<h|vt>) def= <h|maxprefix(ut,vt)>

5. maxprefix(<uh|ut>,<vh|vt>) def= <>

end of example 2.3.

2.3 Exercises:

1. A Dequeue is a computer science data structure that behaves like a double ended queue. Elements may be entered at either the front or the rear, and the front or rear elements may be examined or removed. Give a formal specification for a Dequeue.

2. Design an algorithm (del) to delete the first occurrence of a character from a string. Assume del(<>,c) = <>.

3. Design an algorithm (delall) to delete all occurrences of a character from a string. Assume delall(<>,c) = <>.

4. Design an algorithm (filter) to delete all duplicates of characters from a string. For example,

    filter(<m a d a m>) = <m a d>

5. Design an algorithm (eqelems) to test if two strings contain the same characters. For example,

    eqelems(<m a d a m>, <d a m>) = true

Other interesting operations and exercises on tuples (i.e., lists and sequences) may be found in [Jones, 1980, 1986].

2.4 The World of Tuples

The tuple (sequence or list) is not unique to the VDM. Two applications of the Theory of Sequences are given. The intention is to expose the similarity between the place of the tuple in VDM Meta-IV and corresponding entities in other fields.

Application 2.1: Traces in Hoare's CSP [1985]: "A <u>trace</u> of the behaviour of a process is a finite sequence of symbols recording the events in which the process has engaged up to some moment in time ... A trace will be denoted as a sequence of symbols, separated by commas and enclosed in angular brackets

$<x,y>$ consists of two events, x followed by y.

$<x>$ is a sequence containing only the event x.

$<>$ is the empty sequence containing no events."

The trace of CSP is equivalent to the tuple of VDM Meta-IV. Therefore, expertise in the use of tuples permits immediate access to the concept and use of traces in CSP.

Consider the following specification of the process STACK in CSP [Hoare, 1985] p.138:

$$STACK = P_{<>}$$

$$\text{where } P_{<>} = (empty \longrightarrow P_{<>} \mid left?x \longrightarrow P_{<x>})$$

$$\text{and } P_{<x>^\frown s} = (right!x \longrightarrow P_s \mid left?y \longrightarrow P_{<y>^\frown <x>^\frown s})$$

When empty, STACK participates in the <u>empty</u> event or may input x on the left channel. In general, STACK may output its top element x on the right channel or may input an element y on the left channel.

The process BUFFER [ibid.] is similar to the queue data type:

$$BUFFER = P_{<>}$$

$$\text{where } P_{<>} = left?x \longrightarrow P_{<x>}$$

$$\text{and } P_{<x>^\frown s} = (left?y \longrightarrow P_{<x>^\frown s^\frown <y>}$$

$$\mid right!x \longrightarrow P_s)$$

<u>end of application 2.1</u>.

Application 2.2: Alphabets, Words, Grammars, Parsers: Let S be some alphabet. A word w is a sequence of letters $s_1 s_2 \ldots s_n$, s_i in S,

1 <= i <= n. The set of all words over the alphabet S is denoted S*.
Let u = a1...am and v = b1...bn be two words. Then the concatenation of
u and v, denoted uv is the word a1...amb1...bn.

Representing the word w = s1...sn by the tuple <s1 ... sn>, and
concatenation uv of words u and v by u⌢v, it is clear that expertise in
tuples gives immediate access to the theory of formal languages.

__Theorem__: Let w be an arbitrary word in S*. Then w⌢rev(w) is a
palindrome.

__Proof__: Since

  REV 1: rev(u⌢v) = rev(v)⌢rev(u)

  REV 2: rev(rev(w)) = w

  then

  rev(w⌢rev(w)) = rev(rev(w))⌢rev(w)   -- by law REV 1

                     = w⌢rev(w)   -- by law REV 2

Q.E.D.

__end of application 2.2.__

__3. The Set__

Let S denote an arbitrary set of elements and $\mathbb{P}(S)$ denote the powerset
of S.

The empty set is denoted by {}.

The union, intersection, and difference of two sets s1 and s2 is denoted by s1 U s2, s1∩s2, and s1 - s2, respectively.

For example, let Nat0 denote the set of natural numbers, i.e.,

  Nat0 = {0,1,2,...}

Then $\mathbb{P}$(Nat0) denotes the powerset of Nat0, i.e.,

```
   P(Nat0) = { {},
               {0}, {1}, {2}, ...,
               {0,1}, {0,2}, ..., {1,2}, {1,3} ..., {2,3}, ...
               {0,1,2}, {0,1,3}, ...,
               ...}
```

$\mathbb{P}$(Nat0) is non-denumerable. It is customary in the VDM to use the notation Nat0-set [Bjoerner and Jones, 1978, 1982], or set of Nat0 [Jones, 1986], to emphasise that only finite sets are intended.

3.1 Basic Operations on Sets

The number of elements in a set is given by the operator card. Thus, for example, card {2,1,4,3} = 4. The formal definition of card is given by:

card: $\mathbb{P}$(S) $\longrightarrow$ Nat0

card({}) def= 0

card(s) def= let e memb s in 1 + card(s - {e})

Note that card(s1 U s2) = card(s1) + card(s2) - card(s1 $\cap$ s2).

Define the symmetric difference of two sets s1,s2 in $\mathbb{P}$(S), denoted s1 $\triangle$ s2, to be:

s1 $\triangle$ s2 = (s1 U s2) - (s1 $\cap$ s2)

or, alternatively

s1 $\triangle$ s2 = (s1 - s2) U (s2 - s1)

For example, {1,3,5,7} $\triangle$ {1,2,3} = {2,5,7}

3.2 Specification by Set

Example 3.1: Sets of Natural Numbers: The set of all even numbers is a subset of Nat0. It may be specified formally by

Even = {n|n memb Nat0 $\wedge$ n mod 2 = 0}

The set of odd numbers is also a subset of Nat0 specified by:

Odd = {n|n memb Nat0 $\wedge$ n mod 2 = 1}

To indicate the fact that the set Nat0 is partitioned into Even and Odd, one may write

Nat0 = Even $\triangle$ Odd

The set of all natural numbers in the range m to n where m <= n, including m and n, may be denoted by {m:n}. If m > n then one may define {m:n} to be the empty set {}. To generate such a set one may use the following algorithm:

chain: Nat0 x Nat0 $\longrightarrow$ $\mathbb{P}$(Nat0)

1. chain(m,n) def= <u>if</u> m > n <u>then</u> {}

2. chain(m,n) def= <u>if</u> m <= n <u>then</u> {m} U chain(m+1,n)

<u>end of example 3.1</u>.

Example 3.2: Students in a Classroom [Jones, 1980]: Let Student-name denote the set of all possible students in a particular school. Naturally one assumes that students are uniquely identified by their names. If one worries that students with the same name might exist, say Cliff Jones and Cliff Jones, then they may be considered to have the names "Cliff Jones 1" and "Cliff Jones 2". A class of students may be specified by

Class = $\mathbb{P}$(Student-name)

Some obvious operations on the data type class are:

1. Operation: Create a new class of students

new: $\longrightarrow$ Class

new def= {}

2. Operation: Enter a student into the class

enter: Class x Student-name $\longrightarrow$ Class

enter(c,sn) def= c U {sn}

3. Operation: Checking if a student is already in a class

is-present: Class x Student-name $\longrightarrow$ Bool

is-present(c,sn) def= sn <u>memb</u> c

4. Operation: Removing a student from a class

remove: Class x Student-name $\longrightarrow$ Class

remove(c,sn) def= c - {sn}

<u>end of example 3.2</u>.

Note that in the specification of the enter and remove operations one may replace union and difference with symmetric difference:

enter(c,sn) def= <u>if</u> <u>not</u> sn <u>memb</u> c <u>then</u> c $\triangle$ {sn} remove(c,sn) def= **if** sn **memn** c **then** c △ {sn}

3.3 Exercises

1. A multiset (or bag) is similar to a set except that it may contain duplicates. Specify operations such as union, intersection, and difference for multisets.

2. Design an algorithm that converts a multiset into a set by removing all duplicates.

3. Design an algorithm that takes a multiset and an element as arguments and returns the count of the element in the multiset.

3.4 The World of Sets

The concept of set is all pervasive. It is a trivial matter to pick up its use in almost any branch of computer science. As with tuple, the two application areas chosen are CSP and the Theory of Formal Languages.

Application 3.1: Deterministic Processes in Hoare's CSP [1985]: A **deterministic process** is a pair (A,S) where A is any set of symbols and S is any subset of A* which satisfies the two conditions:

    C0   <> **memb** S

    C1   As,t such that s ⌒ t **memb** S, then s **memb** S

Simple examples of deterministic processes are

  A process which does nothing

  STOP   = (A, {<>})
     A

  A process which will do anything at any time

  RUN   = (A, A*)
    A

If B is a subset of A then

  (x:B ⟶ (A, S(x)) =

      (A, {<>} U {<x> ⌒ s | x **memb** B ∧ s **memb** S(x)}

If s **memb** S then

  (A,S)/s = (A, {t | (s ⌒ t) **memb** S}

Application 3.2:   Languages: Let S be a finite set of symbols, called an alphabet, and let l1,l2 be sets of words from S*. The concatenation of L1 and L2, denoted L1L2, is the set {xy | x <u>memb</u> L1 $\wedge$ y <u>memb</u> L2}. If $\in$ denotes the empty word, define L0 = { $\in$ } and Li = LLi-1 for i >= 1. The Kleene closure of L, denoted L*, is the set

   L* = L0 U L1 U L2 U ... U Li U ...

The positive Kleene closure of L, denoted L+, is defined by

   L+ = L* - L0

Let S be an alphabet.

   1. O is a regular expression and denotes the empty set.

   2. $\in$ is a regular expression and denotes the set { $\in$ }.

   3. For each a in S, a is a regular expression and denotes the set {a}.

   4. If r and s are regular expressions denoting the languages R and S, respectively, then (r + s), (rs), and (r*) are regular expressions that denote the sets R U S, RS and R*, respect-vely.

There are some basic theorems associated with regular sets. Let S be an alphabet. Then:

   1. Complementation: If L is a regular set, then S* - L is a regular set

   2. Intersection: If L1, L2 are regular sets, L1 $\cap$ L2 is a regular set.

4. The Map

The map is an abstraction for a finite function. It may also be regarded as an abstraction of an array in Pascal or Ada where the indexing mechanism is an enumeration type.

Let D and R denote some domains. Then D m$\rightarrow$ R denotes the set M of all ordered pairs (d,r) such that M is a finite function. Specifically, if (d1,r1) and (d2,r2) are elements of M and r1 = r2, then d1 = d2.

Consider $\mathbb{P}$(DxR), the powerset of the set DxR. Then M = D m$\rightarrow$ R is a subset of $\mathbb{P}$(DxR).

The empty map is denoted [].

The set of all elements in the domain of a map is given by the operator dom.

The set of all elements in the range (codomain) of a map is given by the operator rng.

For example, let A denote the set of all ASCII characters. Then, the map from ASCII characters onto their numerical codes is:

M = A m→ {0:255}

A typical map m has the form:

m = [A → 65, B → 66, C → 67, ..., Z → 90]

and dom m = {A,B,C,...,Z}

rng m = {65,66,...90}

There are two operators which "construct" maps, the merge operator, denoted U, and the overwrite (or override) operator, denoted +.

The merge of two maps m1 and m2, denoted m1 U m2, is defined if and only if dom m1 ∩ dom m2 = {}.

Let m = [2 → 1, 3 → 2, 5 → 3] be a map.

Then m U [7 → 4] is the new map

[2 → 1, 3 → 2, 5 → 3, 7 → 4].

The overwrite of a map m1 with respect to a map m2, denoted m1 + m2, is defined if and only if dom m2 is a subset of dom m1.

Let m = [2 → 1, 3 → 2, 5 → 3] be a map.

Then m + [3 → 4] is the new map

[2 → 1, 3 → 4, 5 → 3].

Let m be a map and d memb D, then m(d) is the image of d under m. For example, if m = [A → 65, B → 66, ...], then m(Z) = 90.

Since a map is just a set of ordered pairs, then one may speak of the cardinality of a map. Let m be a map. Then by definition of a map,

card m = card dom m

The map m is bijective if card rng m = card dom m, surjective if card rng m < card dom m. A map is always injective. Why?

4.1 Basic Operations on a Map

A map may be restricted to a subset of its domain. Let m be a map and s memb $\mathbb{P}(D)$, then the map m restricted to s is denoted m | s. A formal definition of restriction is:

_|_: (D m$\twoheadrightarrow$ R) x $\mathbb{P}(D)$ $\longrightarrow$ (D m$\twoheadrightarrow$ R)

_|_([],s) def= []

_|_(m,{}) def = []

_|_(m,s) def= let d memb s in
$\qquad$ [d $\longrightarrow$ m(d)] U (m \ {d} | s - {d})

where _|_ signifies that the operator is an infix one and m \ {d} denotes the removal of m with respect to {d} defined below.

Restrictions may be combined. As1,s2 memb $\mathbb{P}(D)$:

(m | s1) | s2 = m | (s1 $\bigcap$ s2)

A map may be restricted to a complement of its domain (removal). Let m be a map and s memb $\mathbb{P}(D)$, then the removal of m with respect to s is denoted by m \ s. A formal definition of removal is:

__: (D m$\twoheadrightarrow$ R) x $\mathbb{P}(D)$ $\longrightarrow$ (D m$\twoheadrightarrow$ R)

__([],s) def= []

__(m,{}) def= m

__(m,s) def= let d memb s in
$\qquad$ (m - { $\langle$ d,m(d) $\rangle$ }) \ (s - {d})

where m - { $\langle$ d,m(d) $\rangle$ } is difference of the two sets m and { $\langle$ m,m(d) $\rangle$ }.

Removals may be combined. As1,s2 memb $\mathbb{P}(D)$:

(m \ s1) \ s2 = m \ (s1 U s2)

The relationship between restriction and removal may be expressed in the form m \ s = m | (D - s).

The composition of two maps m1 and m2, denoted m1 o m2 (m1 after m2), is defined if and only if dom m1 = rng m2:

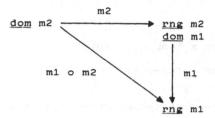

4.2 Specification by Map

Example 4.1: Temperature Chart: During the week of January 12, 1987,
Europe was in the grip of a particularly severe cold spell. One is
required to model a temperature chart giving the temperature in degrees
celsius for a particular set of European cities. Using the map data
type one writes:

   TempChart = City m→ Temp

where

   City = DUBLIN | LONDON | BRUSSELS | ...

and

   Temp = Intg

Note that this specification permits "absurd" entries such as:

   [DUBLIN → -1000]

Moreover, the fact that temperatures are expressed in degrees Celsius
is not captured in the model. Other relevant aspects omitted are date
and time of recorded temperatures. Some moot operations on a temperature chart are:

   1. Operation: Creation of a new temperature chart:

   new: ⟶ TempChart

   new def= []

   2. Operation: Addition of a new (City,Temp) pair:

   add: TempChart x City x Temp ⟶ TempChart

   add(tch,c,t) def= tch U [c → t]

3. Operation: Updating the temp of a city:

update: TempChart x City x Temp ⟶ TempChart

update(tch,c,t) def= tch + [c → t]

4. Operation: Determining the temperature of a given city:

inq-temp: TempChart x City ⟶ Temp

inq-temp(tch,c) def= tch(c)

5. Operation: Determining if the temperature of a given city is recorded in the chart:

is-recorded: TempChart x City ⟶ Bool

is-recorded(tch,c) def= c memb dom tch

Pre-conditions are essential to specify the validity of the add, update, and inq-temp operations:

2.1 pre-add: TempChart x City x Temp ⟶ Bool

pre-add(tch,c,t) def= c not memb dom tch

3.1 pre-update: TempChart x City x Temp ⟶ Bool

pre-update(tch,c,t) def= c memb dom tch

4.1 pre-inq-temp: TempChart x City ⟶ Bool

pre-inq-temp(tch,c) def= c memb dom tch

end of example 4.1.

Example 4.2: A Bill of Materials (BOM) [Jones, 1986], [Bjoerner, 1983]: Consider a bicycle. It consists of (among other things) a frame, two wheels, a handlebars, and a seat. Each wheel consists of a rim, a tyre, and 40 spokes, say. The bicycle structure may be described by the following indented bill of materials:

```
bicycle (1)
    frame (1)
    wheel (2)
        rim (1)
        tyre (1)
        spoke (40)
    handlebars (1)
    seat (1)
```

The bicycle is an assembly or product. The frame, rim, tyre, spoke, handlebars, and seat are basic parts or components. The wheel is a subassembly. A particular bicycle map be modelled as a map of maps:

```
[bicycle  → [frame → 1,
             wheel → 2,
             handlebars → 1,
             seat → 1],

 wheel    → [rim → 1,
             tyre → 1,
             spoke → 40],

 frame       → [],
 handlebars  → [],
 seat        → [],
 rim         → [],
 type        → [],
 spoke       → []]
```

The formal specification is:

Product = Part-name m→ PartRec

where

Part-name = BICYCLE | WHEEL | FRAME | ...

and

PartRec = Part-name m-> Nat1

An arbitrary map of maps does not necessarily constitute a product. Some constraints must be specified. For example, (1) all parts of a (sub-)assembly must be recorded, and (2) no (sub-)assembly is recursively defined:

is-wf-Product: Product ⟶ Bool

is-wf-Product(p) def=

$$(\mathsf{A}pnm \ \underline{memb} \ \underline{rng} \ p) \ (\underline{dom} \ pnm \ \underline{psubset} \ \underline{dom} \ p)$$
$$\wedge \ (\mathsf{A}pn \ \underline{memb} \ \underline{dom} \ p) \ (pn \ \underline{not} \ \underline{memb} \ Parts(p,pn))$$

where

Parts: Product x Part-name ⟶ ℙ(Part-name)

Parts(p,pn,pns) def=
```
pns = { pm | pm memb dom p(pn)
             ∨ ( Epn' memb pns ) ( pm memb dom p(pn') ) }
```

where

pre-Parts: Product x Part-name ⟶ Bool

pre-Parts(p,pn) def= pn memb dom p

Some typical operations on such a product are as follows. In this particular model, operations on Product are given entirely in terms of pre- and post-conditions:

1. Operation: Creation of a new product:

new: $\longrightarrow$ Product

new def= []

2. Operation: Addition of a basic part or a (sub-)assembly:

enter: Product x Part-name $\longrightarrow$ Product

pre-enter: Product x Part-name $\longrightarrow$ Bool

pre-enter(p,pn,pr) def= pn <u>not</u> <u>memb</u> <u>dom</u> p $\wedge$ <u>dom</u> pr <u>psubset</u> <u>dom</u> p

post-enter: Product x Part-name x Product $\longrightarrow$ Bool

enter(p,pn,p') def= p' = p U [pn $\rightarrow$ pr]

3. Operation: Deletion of a part:

del: Product x Part-name $\longrightarrow$ Product

pre-del: Product x Part-name $\longrightarrow$ Bool

pre-del(p,pn) def= pn <u>memb</u> <u>dom</u> p $\wedge$ is-wf-Product(p \ {pn})

post-del: Product x Part-name x Product $\longrightarrow$ Bool

post-del(p,pn,p') def= p' = p \ {pn}

Note the use of the predicate is-wf-Product (defined above). This is essential to prevent deletion of a part pm in the case that there exists a (sub-)assembly pn such that pn $\rightarrow$ [..., pm $\rightarrow$ n, ...].

4. Operation: Extending a (sub-)assembly:

add: Product x Part-name x Part-name x Nat1 $\longrightarrow$ Product

pre-add: Product x Part-name x Part-name x Nat1 $\longrightarrow$ Bool

pre-add(p,pn,pm,n) def=
$\qquad$ pn <u>memb</u> <u>dom</u> p $\wedge$
$\qquad$ pm <u>memb</u> <u>dom</u> p $\wedge$
$\qquad$ pm <u>not</u> <u>memb</u> p(pn)

post-add: Product x Part-name x Part-name x Nat1 x Product $\longrightarrow$ Bool

post-add(p,pn,pm,n,p') def=
$\qquad$ <u>let</u> p' = p + [pn $\rightarrow$ p(pn) U [pm $\rightarrow$ n]] <u>in</u>
$\qquad$ is-wf-Product(p')

5. Operation: Erasing a component of a (sub-)assembly:

erase: Product x Part-name x Part-name $\longrightarrow$ Product

pre-erase: Product x Part-name x Part-name $\longrightarrow$ Bool

pre-erase(p,pn,pm) def=

$$\text{pn } \underline{\text{memb}} \ \underline{\text{dom}} \ p \ \bigwedge$$
$$\text{pm } \underline{\text{memb}} \ \underline{\text{dom}} \ p \ \bigwedge$$
$$\text{pm } \underline{\text{memb}} \ \underline{\text{dom}} \ p(pn)$$

post-erase: Product x Part-name x Part-name x Product $\longrightarrow$ Bool

post-erase(p,pn,pm,p') def= p' = p + [pn $\rightarrow$ p(pn) $\setminus$ {pm}]

<u>end of example 4.2</u>.

The set of operations for the Product given above are essentially those which permit one to construct the bill of materials for the product.

4.3 Exercises

1. Give English descriptions for each of the following operations on the TempChart:

    op1: TempChart x Temp $\longrightarrow$ $\mathbb{P}$(City)

    op1(tch,t) def= {c $|$ tch(c) = t}

    op2: TempChart x $\mathbb{P}$(City) $\longrightarrow$ TempChart

    op2(tch,cs) def= tch $|$ cs

    op3: TempChart x $\mathbb{P}$(City) $\longrightarrow$ TempChart

    op3(tch,cs) def= tch $\setminus$ cs

2. Give the required pre-conditions for each of the operations in question 1 above.

3. Each student in a particular university is assigned, upon completion of registration, a unique numerical identifier called a student number. Use the map data type to specify a model for student registration (StudentReg). Suggest a set of appropriate operations and give their semantics.

4.4 The World of Maps

<u>Application 4.1</u>: Finite State Machines: A finite state machine (FSM) is a triple M = (Q,S,F) where Q is a set of states, S is the input alphabet, and F is a (partial) function F: Q x S $\longrightarrow$ Q. An FSM is completely determined either by its state transition diagram or by its state

transition table. The latter is of course just a map in the sense of VDM Meta-IV. A formal specification of an FSM in Meta-IV is

$$F = Q \times S \ m\rightarrow Q$$

where

  is-wf-F: F $\longrightarrow$ Bool

  is-wf-F(f) def= <u>proj1</u> <u>dom</u> f = Q $\bigwedge$ <u>proj2</u> <u>dom</u> f = S

For example, if Q = {q} and S = {0,1}, then

  f = [(q,0) $\rightarrow$ q, (q,1) $\rightarrow$ q]

is a FSM.

The transition of a machine f in state q on input s is given by:

  transition: F x Q x S $\longrightarrow$ Q

  transition(f,q,s) def= f(q,s)

The transition function may be extended to words over S. Algorithmically it is defined by:

  transition: F x Q x S* $\longrightarrow$ Q

  transition(f,q,<e>) def= f(q,e)

  transition(f,q,<h|t>) def=
              <u>let</u> q' = f(q,h) <u>in</u>
                  transition(f,q',t)

<u>end of application 4.1</u>.

5. The Tree

The Tree data type of Meta-IV is basically an abstraction of both the record data type of Pascal or Ada, and recursively defined types. In [Jones, 1986] a tree is called a composite object.

For example, a rational number which is defined to be an ordered pair of integers (p,q), q <> 0, may be specified by:

  RatNum :: s-num: Intg   s-den: Intg

and a binary tree may be specified by:

```
BinTree = [Node]

   Node :: s-l: BinTree     s-v: Value     s-r: Bintree
```

where [Node] denotes Node | nil and Value = NatO, say.

5.1 Basic Operations on the Tree

There are essentially only three basic operations on trees - constructor functions (mk-), selector functions (s-), and test for equality. In general, every tree data type usually requires a well-formedness constraint (is-wf-). Thus, for the rational number example given above, it is necessary to specify:

```
   is-wf-RatNum: RatNum ⟶ Bool
   is-wf-RatNum(mk-RatNum(p,q)) def= q <> 0
```

5.2 Specification by Tree

Example 5.1: A Point: A point will be considered to be an ordered pair (x,y) of real numbers. Formally, we define Point as:

```
   Point :: s-x: Real     s-y: Real
```

Addition of points and multiplication of points by a real number are defined by:

```
   _+_: Point x Point ⟶ Point

   _+_(p1,p2) def= let x1 = s-x(p1), y1 = s-y(p1),
                       x2 = s-x(p2), y2 = s-y(p2) in
                       mk-Point(x1+y1, x2+y2)

   _*_: Real x Point ⟶ Point

   _*_(k,p) def= let x = s-x(p), y = s-y(p) in mk-Point(k*x, k*y)

   end of example 5.1.
```

Example 5.2: Abstract Syntax: The VDM has been traditionally associated with the formal specification of the semantics of programming languages. Given a concrete syntax for a programming language such as Pascal, then an abstract syntax gives the essential grammatical structure of the language. Consider the following concrete syntax given in BNF:

```
   program ::= program-heading block "."
```

```
program-heading ::= "program" identifier "(" file-identifier
                             {"," file-identifier} ")" ";"
```

A possible abstract syntax is:

```
Prog :: s-id:  Ident
        s-ids: P(Ident)
        s-b:   Block
```

and a possible well-formedness constraint given by:

```
is-wf-Prog: Prog ——→ Bool

is-wf-Prog(mk-Prog(nm,ids,b) def= card ids > 0
                              ∧ nm not memb ids
                              ∧ ...
```

end of example 5.2.

Example 5.3: TempChart Revisited: A slightly improved model of a temperature chart is one which includes a specification of the temperature scale (say Celsius or Fahrenheit), and the date and time of the recorded temperatures. The basic model is still given by a map:

```
TempChart = City m→ TempRec
```

where City is unchanged and TempRec is given by the model

```
TempRec :: s-tp: Temp    s-t: Time    s-d: Date

Temp :: s-deg: Intg    s-sc: Scale

Time :: s-h: {0:23}    s-m: {0:59}

Date :: s-d: {1:31}    s-m: Month    s-y: {1950:2050}
```

and

```
Scale = CELSIUS | FAHRENHEIT

Month = JANUARY | FEBRUARY | MARCH | ...
```

Some well-formedness constraints are:

```
is-wf-Temp: Temp ——→ Bool

is-wf-Temp(mk-Temp(deg,CELSIUS)) def= -273 <= deg <= 273
```

Remark: The lower bound -273 is well determined since it is absolute zero in degrees Celsius. However, the upper bound will depend completely on the domain of application for which Temp is being used. For example, a model for Temp in the metal industry will have a much higher bound than one for weather records.

```
is-wf-Date: Date  ⟶  Bool

is-wf-Date(mk-Date(d,m,y)) def=
    cases m:
        FEBRUARY  →  if is-leap-yr(y) then d <= 29 else d <= 28,
        APRIL, JUNE, SEPTEMBER, NOVEMBER  →  d <= 30,
        T  →  d <= 31
```

Each of the objects Temp, Time, and Date may be furnished with appropriate operations. A typical operation on Temp is conversion from degrees Celsius to degrees Fahrenheit and vice versa.

```
convert: Temp  ⟶  Temp

convert(mk-Temp(deg,sc)) def=
    sc = CELSIUS     →  mk-Temp(deg/5*9 + 32, FAHRENHEIT),
    sc = FAHRENHEIT  →  mk-Temp((deg - 32)/9*5, CELSIUS)
```

end of example 5.3.

5.3 Exercises

1. A Window is defined to be an ordered pair of points (p,q) such that p is the left bottom point and q is the right top point of the window. Give a tree data type specification for window. Specify operations to determine (1) if a point is inside a window, and (2) if two windows overlap.

2. A complex number is an ordered pair of real numbers (x,y). Give a tree data type specification and provide the semantics for the addition and multiplication of complex numbers.

3. Provide operators to increment Time by 1 minute and Date by 1 day.

6. Summary and Future Directions

This paper has focused on the use of the basic VDM Meta-IV data types tuple, set, map, and tree for the specification of objects and their operations. Derek Andrews' paper which follows focuses specifically on the software development aspects of the VDM.

Specification using the VDM Meta-IV is an activity much akin to mathematical exposition. The formal material in papers on the VDM is definitely not to be read but to be performed. In other words, an active reading of the text is essential. By doing so, the reader will acquire skill in the understanding and use of the formal notation.

A user should adopt a single notation that is to his/her taste. In reading specifications in another notation one should then transcribe them into the adopted one. A similar recommendation applies to other formal notations and methods. For example, a good learning exercise is to work through Hoare's book on CSP [1985], using Meta-IV notation wherever possible.

7. Glossary

p1 $\wedge$ p2	logical and of p1 and p2
p1 $\vee$ p2	logical or of p1 and p2
not p	logical not of p
$\forall$	for all
$\exists$	there exists
$\mathbb{P}$(S)	powerset of S
e memb S	element e is a member of set S
s1 subset s2	s1 is a subset of s2
s1 psubset s2	s1 is a proper subset of s2

8. References

Bjoerner, D. and Jones, C.B. (eds), The Vienna Development Method: The Meta-Language, Lecture Notes in Computer Science, Vol.61, Springer-Verlag, Berlin Heidelberg New York, 1978.

Bjoerner, Dines and Jones, Cliff B., Formal Specification and Software Development, Prentice / Hall International, Englewood Cliffs, New Jersey London New Delhi Singapore Sydney Tokyo Toronto Wellington, 1982.

Bjoerner, Dines., Software Architectures and Programming Systems Design, to be published in 6 volumes, 1987/88., manuscript 1983.

Hoare, C.A.R., Communicating Sequential Processes, Prentice/Hall International, Englewood Cliffs, New Jersey London Mexico New Delhi Rio de Janiero Singapore Sydney Tokyo Toronto Wellington, 1985.

Jones, Cliff B., Software Development, A Rigorous Approach, Prentice/Hall International, Englewood Cliffs, New Jersey London New Delhi Singapore Sydney Tokyo Toronto Wellington, 1980.

Jones, Cliff B., Systematic Software Development Using VDM, Prentice/Hall International, Englewood Cliffs, New Jersey London Mexico New Delhi Rio de Janiero Singapore Sydney Tokyo Toronto Wellington, 1986.

Data Reification and Program Decomposition

Derek Andrews
University of Leicester

Introduction

The formal specification of a computer system needs to be translated into a form that can be executed on a computer. The gap between the specification and the implementation is closed by adding detail to the specifications: moving from the abstract to the concrete. A specification is, to use a phrase which has crept back into use, "economical with the truth" – minor details, such as how the system will be implemented, have been left out. The specification of a computer system defines what the operations are in terms of abstract data types and truth valued functions that describe the properties of the answers which are required. The code of the final system must supply the missing details and also satisfy the specification. One possible way of developing the code is to just go away and write it and then prove that it satisfies the specification, but this is unsatisfactory; if no systematic method is followed there are possibilities of bugs being introduced during this development process.

A current approach to program writing is to develop the code and its proof of correctness in parallel, with the proof driving the development. This technique will certainly work in going from the predicates in the specification down to executable code, but there is still the problem of abstract data types. There are no supports for sets, lists, and mappings in most programming languages, or certainly not support that gives adequate performance for large amounts of information. Thus, as well as deriving code from the specifications we also need to develop code and data structures to represent the abstract data types. Techniques are needed that will allow the representation of abstract data and specifications to be turned into code together with a proof of correctness.

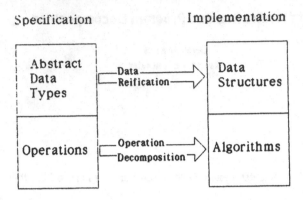

The process of translating abstract data types into data structures which can be implemented in a programming language is called Data Reification, and the process of translating pre- and post-conditions into executable code is called Program Decomposition. Both of these techniques will be illustrated with a simple problem.

Data Reification

The basic abstract data types of the specification language are sets, sequences (lists), and mappings. In most programming languages, such as Pascal or PL/I, data can be represented using scalars, arrays, structures (records), and pointers. With these basic building blocks a variety of data-structures can be constructed that are implementations of abstract data types.

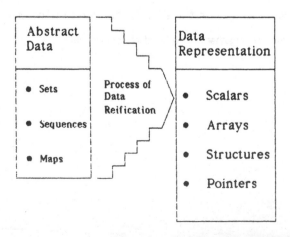

To see how this could work, consider the problem of supplying a security system to the Acme Widget Company:

The company requires a program that records the names of employees who enter and leave the main building. Each door into the building is controlled by an electronic lock and can be opened under computer control. The doors have badge-readers connected to the computer which can read a magnetic stripe on identification badges issued to all staff. Thus the system can detect when anyone wishes to leave or enter the building and can open the doors as necessary.

The basic operations that are needed for the system are:

```
init()
```

This operation initialises the system at the start of the day; it can be assumed that the building is empty as nobody has yet arrived.

```
enter(nm : Name)
```

An operation to record an employee entering the building, their name will be read from the badge lock when their security badge is inserted into the badge-reader.

```
exit(nm : Name)
```

An operation to record an employee leaving the building; their name will be read from a security card.

```
is-present(nm : Name) r : Bool
```

An operation to check the presence of a particular employee.

The state for the system must model the employees who are currently at work, and the data type which will do this is a set. The employees who are at work can be represented by a set containing their names so the situation of "Dormann", "Thievent", and "Fischer" being the only employees at work is represented by a set containing just those elements.

(Dormann, Thievent, Fischer)

The state for the system is thus a set of employee's names.

```
Work-force = set of Name
Name = (* to be defined *)
```

When the system is initialised there is nobody at work; this situation is modelled by the empty set, so the specification for the operation to intialise the system is

```
init()
ext wr  nms : Work-force
post nms = {}
```

When an employee arrives and enters the building, their name must be added to the set of employee names that represent those currently at work. The pre-condition will specify that the operation need only work if the employee is not already registered as being in the building. The specification for enter is:

enter(nm : Name)

ext wr nms : Work-force

pre nm∉nms

post nms = nm̃s ∪ {nm}

When an employee leaves, all that is necessary is to remove their name from the set of names that represents the employees currently in the building. The operation need only work if the employee is currently thought to be in the building (that is where the model thinks the employee is).

exit(nm : Name)

ext wr nms : Work-force

pre nm∈nms

post nms = nm̃s - {nm}

To check if a particular employee is present at work, the is-present operator just checks if his/her name is in the set that represents the employees currently at work:

is-present(nm : Name) r : Bool

ext rd nms : Work-force

post r ⟺ nm∈nms

As an enhancement, the senior manager requests some additional functions; one to select a list of "volunteers" to do some overtime, and one to enquire how many employees are present. The latter function can also be used to check there are sufficient number of employees available for any overtime work.

The properties that need to be satisfied for the get-volunteers operation that chooses people for the (well-paid) overtime are:

1. That they are currently at work.

2. That there are the right number of them.

Both of these properties are specified in the post-condition.

get-volunteers(n : N) r : Work-force

ext rd nms : Work-force

pre cardnms≥n

post r⊆nms ∧ cardr=n

Notice that the implementor of this operation has complete freedom to choose any employee who is at work that day to do the well-paid overtime. The developer could even arrange that he was always chosen, or was always left out depending on how keen or short of money he was. The implementor could choose those who had arrived late, those who had arrived early, or some random selection. Who is chosen for overtime has been left undefined, only that a sufficient number of people are selected.

Finally an operation to find out how many people are at work at a particular instant (prior to running the get-volunteers operation) can be specified:

at-work() r : N

ext rd nms : Work-force

post r=cardnms

In the above specification, the event of an employee arriving at work is modelled by adding their name to the set; an employee leaving the building is modelled by removing his name from the set; and the answer to the question "Is an employee present?" is modelled by set membership.

The specification can be checked against the understanding of the problem. To be fully convinced on the correctness of this specification, properties (theorems) can be written down and proved from the specification. Once satisfied that it is "correct", the high-level design can be started. The representation of data in the implementation language (Pascal in this example) suggests a representation in terms of ordered objects, so it should not come as too much of a surprise that the initial step for the data reification is to respecify the problem in terms of sequences. From this representation, either an array or a link-list implementation in terms of structures and pointers can be chosen to implement sequences.

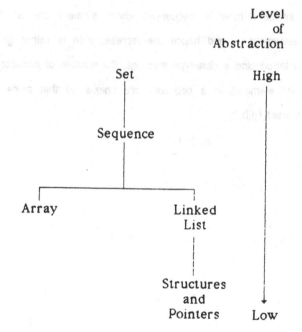

The development of a new specification in terms of sequences will be carried out in two stages. The first stage will be to choose a more concrete representation of a set, one that contains some implementation detail. This will be done by representing a set by a sequence; the implementation detail is the order in which the elements of the set are to be held in the final implementation. It will be necessary to show that this new data representation is equivalent to the old one. When this step has been completed, the operations which have been specified in terms of operators on sets will have to be modelled by new operations which are described in terms of operators on sequences. In the subsequent text, rather than referring to the new data-type and its corresponding operations as "less abstract", the term "concrete" will be used. It should be realized that this concrete specification will later become the abstract specification for the next development step.

One of the things that has to be checked in a data reification is that the new representation is adequate: every abstract state is represented by at least one concrete state. This is done in the following manner; a retrieve function is defined which relates a sequence of employee names to a set of employee names. The new model is such that a set of employee names will be modelled by a sequence containing just those names; thus the set containing the employee's names "a", "b", and "c" can be represented by an infinite number of sequences whose element are "a", "b", and "c" (repetitions are allowed in sequences) - and hence the representation is rather generous. This freedom can be restricted by introducing a data-type invariant; the number of possible elements is restricted by requiring that the elements in a sequence are unique so that there are only six possibilities for representing the set {a,b,c}.

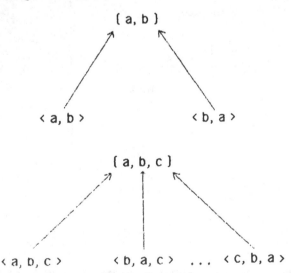

An alternative would be to ask that the names in the sequence be both unique and in alphabetical order. In this case there is only one representative sequence for each set of names. In this example the former invariant is chosen - that the elements in the sequence be unique. Having chosen the representation of the set of names, it is now necessary to show that the model is adequate in the sense that every set that can occur in the original specification can be represented by a sequence that satisfies the data-type invariant.

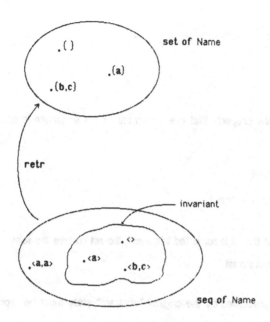

The retrieve function relates the representation of the employees in the building as a sequence to the representation as a set. The data-type invariant restricts the sequences to have no duplicate elements.

Work-force = set of Name

Work-force1 = seq of Name
where
inv-Work-force1(l)▲is-unique1(l)

retr-Work-force : Work-force1 → Work-force

retr-Work-force(l) ≙ elems l

The elems operator converts a sequence into a set containing only those elements in the sequence.

elems : seq of X → set of X

elems(l) ≙ { l(i) | i∈inds l }

The is-uniquel operator checks the property that every element of the sequence is different.

is-uniquel : seq of X → Bool

is-uniquel(l) ≙ card elems l = len l

The list l contains no duplicates if the list is converted into a set, the set contains the same number of elements as the length of the list.

All possible values that can be represented by the original "abstract" state must be represented in the reification, otherwise an obvious problem will occur. Given this requirement, a proof rule can be written down that say "for every abstract state (in the specification) there must exist a concrete state (in the data reification), that is mapped by the retrieve function to the abstract state". Introducing invariants makes the problem a little more difficult but roughly speaking what is needed to be said is that for all states in the abstract state that are "interesting", i.e. that satisfy the abstract invariant, there is a concrete state which satisfies the concrete invariant and is retrieved correctly.

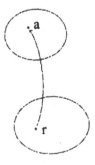

∀a∈Abs . ∃r∈Rep . a=retr(r)

The concrete representation must be capable of representing every valid value of the abstract state. The adequacy proof is fairly straightforward. It is necessary to show that for every element in the set of employee names there exists a sequence with unique elements that is retrieved to the set.

An informal proof goes as follows: given a set, construct a sequence from that set by removing the elements one by one and placing them in a sequence. Hence, the elements in the sequence are identical to those in the set and the sequence does not contain any duplicates. It is easy to see that this satisfies the adequacy rule. A more rigorous proof is possible.

The proof rule also checks two further points that need to be fulfilled by the concrete states and the data-type invariant:

1. The retrieve function must be defined everywhere on those states that satisfy the concrete invariant.

2. Any retrieved states should satisfy the abstract invariant.

The second of these two requirements is about the concrete representation being "small-enough" i.e. not too adequate; if the concrete invariant is not strong enough, there could be a state in the concrete representation which did not correspond to a state in the abstract specification. This would seem to indicate that there is a missing component in the concrete invariant that would otherwise disallow the state. If there is an abstract data-type invariant, the rule also checks that its equivalent is "captured" in the concrete data-type invariant.

A Diversion - Data Type Invariants

The concept of a data type invariant is used in the security problem described above. Although introduced as part of a design decision during the development of that system, it has a much wider application. Consider the problem of describing an abstract version of the date. If only dates of this century were of interest this would be fairly straightforward. A date consists of three fields: the year - a value between 0 and 99; the month - a value between 1 and 12; and the day - a value between 1 and 31.

```
Date :: year  : {0,...,99}
        month : {1,...,12}
        day   : {1,...,31}
```

Unfortunately this mathematical model is not quite correct: it allows dates such as the 31st November or even the 29th February '83. An additional property is needed, the mathematical equivalent of the old rhyme "30 days hath September, April, June, and November ..."

```
inv-Date : Date → Bool
inv-Date(d) ≙ (m∈{9,4,6,11} ∧ d∈{1,...,30}) ∨
                (m∈{1,3,5,7,8,10,12} ∧ d∈{1,...,31}) ∨
                (m=2 ∧ is-leap-year(y) ∧ d∈{1,...,29}) ∨
                (m=2 ∧ ¬is-leap-year(y) ∧ d∈{1,...,28})
```

This property describes a valid date and any operations on dates, such as tomorrow, or yesterday, or create-date, should preserve (or in the case of create-date establish) the property. The system should not be allowed to produce any invalid dates. The data type invariant documents some property of the real world which the system should model. The invariant can be put together with the state description to give:

Date :: year : {0,...,99}

        month : {1,...,12}

        day : {1,...,31}

where

inv-Date(mk-Date(y,m,d)) $\triangle$

  (m$\in${9,4,6,11} $\wedge$ d$\in${1,...,30}) $\vee$

  (m$\in${1,3,5,7,8,10,12} $\wedge$ d$\in${1,...,31}) $\vee$

  (m=2 $\wedge$ is-leap-year(y) $\wedge$ d$\in${1,...,29}) $\vee$

  (m=2 $\wedge$ $\neg$is-leap-year(y) $\wedge$ d$\in${1,...,28})

The proof rule that must be satisfied by all operations is:

$$\forall \hat{s} \in State \,.\, inv(\hat{s}) \wedge pre\text{-}OP(\hat{s}) \wedge post\text{-}OP(\hat{s},s) \Rightarrow inv(s)$$

The rule expresses the following - if a value satisfied the invariant and is acceptable to the operation (i.e. satisfied the pre-condition), then the corresponding output value must satisfy the invariant too. (Remember that decorated variables represent values before the operation is executed.)

There is a second type of data type invariant of which the example in the security problem above is one. These data type invariants document design decisions which are made during the development process. This also models some fixed property of the world, but the one involved is the computer system rather than the real world. Once a data type invariant exists it must be preserved by all operations and so one of the proof obligations of a developer is to show that the data-type invariants are preserved by any operations which are included in the system.

Those invariants which are introduced by design decisions document those very decisions and thus act as signposts through the development process. Once the invariants have been shown to be preserved by all operations, then, when it is necessary to add new operations to the system (due to changing or new requirements) it is fairly easy to check that the invariants are still preserved by these additions. If not, there is a major problem and thus the cost of changing requirements can be calculated. New operations that involve a change in the data-type invariant are likely to be expensive.

Acme Security System - Second Version

Work-force1 = seq of Name
where
inv-Work-force1(l) ≙ is-unique1(l)

init1()
ext wr room : Work-force1
post nms = []

There is nobody at work yet, so the list of employees is set to the empty sequence.

enter1(nm : Name)
ext wr nms : Work-force1
pre ¬is-there(nm,nms)
post nms = nm$\overleftarrow{s}$ ^ [nm]

An employee has arrived in the building, so his name is added to the list of those employees who are in the building.

exit1(nm : Name)
ext wr nms : Work-force1
pre is-there(nm,nms)
post ∃i∈inds nm$\overleftarrow{s}$. nm$\overleftarrow{s}$(i)=nm ∧
        is-permutation(nms,del(nm$\overleftarrow{s}$,i))

An employee has left work, so his name is removed from the list of employees in the building. The is-permutation truth valued function is to allow the implementor to re-order the sequence.

> is-present1(nm : Name) r : Bool
>
> ext rd nms : Work-force1
>
> post r ⟺ is-there(nm,nms)

The operation just checks to see if the employee's name is in the list of those at work.

> get-volunteers1(n : N) r : Work-force1
>
> ext rd nms : Work-force1
>
> pre len nms≥n
>
> post r=nms(1,...,n)

The specification for this operation just returns the first n names in the sequence that represents the people currently at work when the operation is used. This design decision might be postponed to a later development step, the specification could be written:

> get-volunteers1(n : N) r : Work-force1
>
> ext rd nms : Work-force1
>
> pre len nms≥n
>
> post let i∈{1,...,(lennms-n)+1} in r=nms(i,...,i+n-1)

In this version, the result of the operation is any list of consecutive employees from those recorded at work. Even this might be too specific, since the order in which the employees arrive (and leave) gives the order of the names in the sequence; it might still be a good idea not to define the way in which the employees are selected.

get-volunteers1(n : N) r : Work-force1

ext rd nms : Work-force1

pre len nms≥n

post let sel ⊆ inds nms be s.t. card sel = n in

r = restrict(nms,sel)

The restrict operation constructs a new sequence containing those elements whose indices are in the set.

restrict : seq of X × set of N → seq of X

restrict(l,s) ≜ if s={} then l

else let i = mins(s) in [l(i)] ⁀ restrict(l,s-{i})

pre-restrict(l,s) ≜ s⊆inds l

mins(s : set of N) r : N

pre s≠{}

post r∈s ∧ ∀i∈s . r≤i

In this version the employees are picked at random from the sequence representing those who are currently at work. When developing the code of a system through several development steps, it is useful to be able to make implementation decisions, or postpone them, as necessary.

at-work() r : N

ext rd nms : Work-force1

post r = len nms

The at-work operation returns the length of the list. The auxiliary functions used above are defined below.

$$\text{is-there} : \text{Name} \times \text{Work-force1} \to \text{Bool}$$

$$\text{is-there}(nm, nms) \triangleq \exists i \in \text{inds } nms \ . \ nms(i) = nm$$

$$\text{del} : \text{Work-force1} \times N \to \text{Work-force1}$$

$$\text{del}(l, i) \triangleq \text{if } i = 1 \text{ then } tl \ l \text{ else } [hd \ l] \ \widehat{} \ \text{del}(tl \ l, i-1)$$

The initial state, that of an empty building, is modelled by an empty sequence. A employee entering the building is modelled by appending the employee's name to the sequence that represents who is currently in the building. A employee leaving the building is modelled by deleting the employee's name from the sequence, and a employee's presence or absence is found by checking the sequence for the employee's name Each of the operations has been (re)specified in terms of the sequence model: set-union is modelled with sequence concatenation, set-difference by deleting elements from the sequence, and membership by finding the element in the sequence.

There is a proof obligation, that of showing that the data-type invariant is preserved. The pre-condition on enter1 states that the employee's name cannot be found in the sequence, so appending his name will not cause any duplicates to occur. For the exit1 operation, deleting a employee's name from the sequence will not cause any duplicates. The operation is-present1 only needs read-access to the state. For the operation init1, the empty sequence has no duplicates, hence the invariant is established Thus the data type invariant is preserved by all the operations.

The next step is to prove that the operations of init1, enter1, exit1, and is-present1 model the operations of the original specification. For each operation there are two things to prove. First, the domains work: any value that is acceptable to an operation (OPA) of the abstract specification, then the concrete equivalent of the value should also be acceptable to the equivalent concrete operation (OPR). The domain rule is

$$\forall r \in Rep . \ pre\text{-}OPA(retr(r)) \Rightarrow pre\text{-}OPR(r)$$

The proof obligation for domains roughly states that if the retrieve of a concrete value is acceptable to the abstract operation, then the value must be acceptable to the concrete operation.

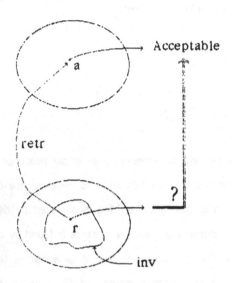

For the results of an operation, things are a little more complicated. Before looking at the actual proof rule, let us look at a particular example. To prove that enter1 models enter can be done by chasing round the diagram. The sequence containing the names "Dormann" and "Thievent", represents the state of the building at a particular instant in time. If "Fischer" enters the building, the sequence containing "Dormann", "Thievent", and "Fischer" models the new situation. In terms of the abstract specification, the set containing "Dormann" and "Thievent" models the building before Fischer has entered; after he has entered, the set containing "Dormann", "Thievent", and "Fischer" represents the new situation. If enter1 is modelling enter, then the retrieve function should work in the obvious way. The general proof rule for this is fairly straightforward. We can indicate where the rule comes from as follows: if a state is valid input to the concrete operation and satisfies the (concrete) invariant, then the result of the operation should satisfy the abstract specification.

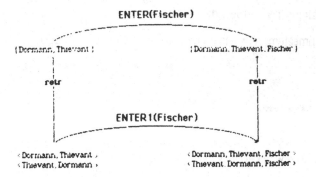

ENTER(Fischer)

{Dormann, Thievent }   {Dormann, Thievent, Fischer }

retr   retr

ENTER1(Fischer)

⟨ Dormann, Thievant ⟩   ⟨ Dormann, Thievant, Fischer ⟩
⟨ Thievant, Dormann ⟩   ⟨ Thievant, Dormann, Fischer ⟩

The actual rule is:

$$\forall \bar{r}, r \in Rep \, . \, pre\text{-}OPA(retr(\bar{r})) \wedge post\text{-}OPR(\bar{r}, r) \Rightarrow post\text{-}OPR(retr(\bar{r}), retr(r))$$

Rigorous proofs of the enter and exit operations are given below.

The enter Operation

The domain rule

$$\forall r \in Work\text{-}force1 \, . \, pre\text{-}enter(retr\text{-}Work\text{-}force(r)) \Rightarrow pre\text{-}enter1(r)$$

Using the fact that the rule can be rewritten as

$$\forall r \in seq \; of \; Name \, . \, inv\text{-}Work\text{-}force1(r) \wedge pre\text{-}enter(retr\text{-}Work\text{-}force(r))$$
$$\Rightarrow pre\text{-}enter1(r)$$

and substitute the definitions gives, for any $r \in seq$ of Name:

$$is\text{-}unique1(r) \wedge nm \notin retr\text{-}Work\text{-}force(r) \Rightarrow \neg is\text{-}there(nm, r)$$

408

is-uniquel(r) ∧ nm∉elems r ⇒' ¬(∃i∈inds r . r(i)=nm)

∃i∈inds r . r[i]=nm ⇒ nm∈elems r ∧ ¬is-uniquel(r)   QED

The result rule can also be reorganised:

$$\forall \tilde{r},r \in \text{Work-force1} \ . \ \text{inv-Work-force1}(\tilde{r}) \land$$

$$\text{pre-enter1}(\text{retr}(\tilde{r})) \land$$

$$\text{post-enter1}(\tilde{r},r)$$

$$\Rightarrow \text{post-enter}(\text{retr-Work-force}(\tilde{r}),\text{retr-Work-force}(\tilde{r}))$$

Again for any reseq of Name **it must be shown:**

$$\text{is-uniquel}(\tilde{r}) \land nm \notin \text{retr-Work-force}(r) \land r = \tilde{r} \ \hat{} \ [nm]$$

$$\Rightarrow \text{retr-Work-force}(r) = \text{retr-Work-force}(\tilde{r}) \cup \{nm\}$$

Taking the right-hand-side of the implication, and using the equalities on the left-hand side as necessary, the proof is fairly straightforward.

$$\text{retr-Work-force}(r) = \text{elems } r$$

$$= \text{elems}(\tilde{r} \ \hat{} \ [nm])$$

$$= \text{elems}(\tilde{r}) \cup \text{elems}([nm])$$

$$= \text{elems}(\tilde{r}) \cup \{nm\}$$

$$= \text{retr-Work-force}(\tilde{r}) \cup \{nm\}$$

QED

The exit Operation

Domain Rule

∀reseq of Name . inv-Work-force1(r) ∧ pre-exit(retr-Work-force(r))

⇒ pre-exit1(r)

is-unique1(r) ∧ nm∈elems(r) ⇒ is-there(nm,r)   TRIVIAL

Results Rule

∀reseq of Name . inv-Work-force1(r̄) ∧

pre-exit(retr(r̄)) ∧

post-exit1(r̄,r)

⇒ post-exit(retr-Work-force(r̄),retr-Work-force(r))

is-unique1(r̄) ∧ nm∈retr-Work-force(r̄) ∧

is-permutation(r,del(r̄,i)) ∧ ∃i∈inds r̄ . r̄(i) = nm

⇒ retr-Work-force(r) = retr-Work-force(r̄) - {nm}

As before,take the right-hand-side of the implication, and substituting the equalities on the left-hand side as necessary. The following three lemmas are also needed.

unique1(r̄) ⇒ ∃i∈inds r̄ . r̄(i) = nm

r̄(i) = nm ∧ unique1(r) ⇒ nm∉del(r̄,i)

is-permutation(r,del(r̄,i)) ⇒ elems(r) = elems(del(r̄,i))

$$\text{retr-Work-force}(r) = \text{elems}(r)$$

$$= \text{elems}(\text{del}(\bar{r},i))$$

$$= \text{elems}(\bar{r}) - \{\bar{r}(i)\}$$

$$= \text{elems}(\bar{r}) - \{nm\}$$

$$= \text{retr-Work-force}(\bar{r}) - \{nm\}$$

The reification can be continued with the specification in terms of sequence becoming the abstract specification and a new data reification attempted. This time the building will be modelled as an array with a counter for the number of employees in the room.

```
const M = card Name,
. . .

type
 . Work-force3 = record
                   C : 0..M,
                   N : array [1..M] of Name
                 end;
```

We proceed as before, find the retrieve function; prove that the reification is both adequate and defined properly; rewrite the operations in terms of the new data representation; show that the data-type invariant (if any) is preserved by the new operations; and finally prove that the new operations correctly model the old.

```
const M = card Name;

type Work-force2 = record

                pnt   : 0 .. M;

                nms : array [1 .. M] of Name

         end


init2()

ext wr pnt : 0 .. M,  nms : array [1 .. M] of Name

post pnt = 0


enter2(nm : Name)

ext wr pnt : 0 .. M,  nms : array [1 .. M] of Name

pre   ¬is-therea(nm,pnt,nms)

post  ∀i∈{1,...,pnt̄} . nms[i]=nms̄[i] ∧

      pnt =pnt̄+1 ∧

      nms[pnt]=nm


exit2(nm : Name)

ext wr pnt : 0 .. M,  nms : array [1 .. M] of Name

pre   is-therea(nm,pnt,nms)

post  ∃i∈{1,...,pnt̄} . nm=nms̄[i] ∧

                pnt=pnt̄-1 ∧

                nms[i]=nms̄[pnt̄]
```

is-present2(nm: Name) r : Bool

ext wr pnt : 0 .. M, nms : array [1 .. M] of Name

post r ⟺ is-therea(nm,pnt,nms)

is-therea(nm : Name,

        pnt : 0 .. M,

        nms : array [1 .. M] of Name) r : Bool

post r ⟺ ∃i∈{1,...,pnt} . nms[i]=nm

The retrieve function is straightfoward, and hence the rules for data reification are easily shown to be correct.

Summary of Data Reification

The stepwise reification of data can be summaries as follows:

1. Choose a new data representation, a "more concrete" representation Rep.

2. Discover the retrieve function that relates the abstract representation Astate, to the concrete representation Rep.

    retr : Rep → Abs

3. Prove adequacy

    ∀sa∈Abs . ∃sr∈Rep . sa=retr(sr)

4. Rewrite the operations in terms of the new concrete data representation.

5 Show that the new operations preserve the data-type invariant of the concrete syntax.

6. Show that the new operations model those of the specification.

Domain Rule:

$$\forall sr \epsilon Rep \, . \, pre\text{-}OPA(retr(sr)) \Rightarrow pre\text{-}OPR(sr)$$

Operation Modelling Rule:

$$\forall \widetilde{sr} \, . \, sr \epsilon Rep \, . \, pre\text{-}OPA(retr(\widetilde{sr})) \wedge post\text{-}OPR(\widetilde{sr}, sr)$$

$$\Rightarrow post\text{-}OPA(retr(\widetilde{sr}), retr(sr))$$

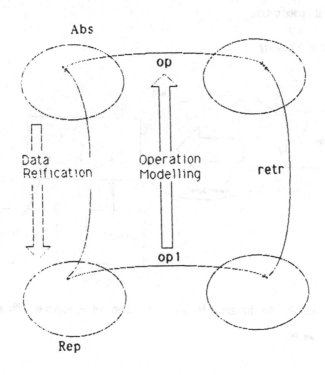

From Specifications to Code

To illustrate how code can be developed from a formal specification, the next step will be to develop Pascal code from the specification given above. Experience suggests that the specification for the enter2 operation can be broken down into two operations; one to set up the value of pnt, the other to add the new name to the array.

The strategy is to take the original specification, and create two sub-specifications, SpecA and SpecB. A proof rule will guarantee that if code is written to satisfy SpecA and code is written to satisfy SpecB then if the two pieces of code are joined together by "semicolon", then the resulting code will satisfy the original specification.

Decomposition Strategy

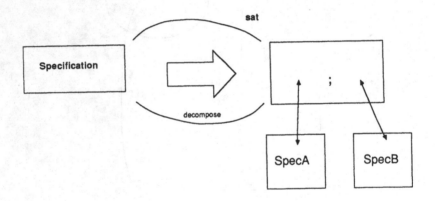

The proof rule for the "semicolon" glue for assembling text is shown below, together with a flow chart hinting on how it might be derived.

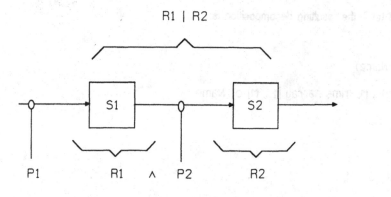

$$\frac{\{\,P1\,\}\,S1\,\{\,R1 \wedge P2\,\}\,,\,\{\,P2\,\}\,S2\,\{\,R2\,\}}{\{\,P1\,\}\ S1\,;\,S2\ \{\,R1|R2\,\}}$$

where $R1\,|\,R2$ is defined as $\exists si\,.\,R1(\bar{s},si) \wedge R2(si,s)$

For the operation enter2 **the resulting decomposition is:**

enter2(nm : Name)

ext wr pnt : 0 .. M, nms : array [1 .. M] of Name

pre   ¬is-therea(nm,pnt,nms)

  enter2a

  ext wr pnt : 0 .. M,

     rd nms : array [1 .. M] of Name,

       nm : Name

  pre   ¬is-therea(nm,pnt,nms)

  post $pnt = \overleftarrow{pnt} + 1$

  enter2b

  ext rd pnt : 0 .. M,

     wr nms : array [1 .. M] of Name,

     rd nm : Name

  pre   ¬is-therea(nm,pnt-1,nms)

  post $\forall i \in \{1,...,\overleftarrow{pnt}-1\} \, . \, nms[i] = \overleftarrow{nms}[i] \wedge$

     $nms[pnt] = nm$

post $\forall i \in \{1,...,\overleftarrow{pnt}\} \, . \, nms[i] = \overleftarrow{nms}[i] \wedge$

    $pnt = \overleftarrow{pnt} + 1 \wedge$

    $nms[pnt] = nm$

There is a proof obligation is to show that

enter2a;

enter2b

is equivalent to the original specification. The proof just consists of substituting in the decomposition rule and simplifying.

$\{ \neg\text{is-therea}(nm,pnt,nms) \}$ S1 $\{ pnt=\widetilde{pnt}+1 \}$

$\{ \neg\text{is-therea}(nm,pnt-1,nms) \}$ S2 $\{ \forall i\in\{1,...,\widetilde{pnt}-1\} . nms[i]=\widetilde{nms}[i] \wedge$

$nms[pnt]=nm \}$

post-enter2a | post-enter2b =

$\exists pnt', nms' . pnt'=\widetilde{pnt}+1 \wedge \widetilde{nms}=nms' \wedge \forall i\in\{1,...,pnt'-1\} . nms[i]=nms'[i] \wedge$

$nms[pnt]=nm \wedge pnt'=pnt$ (rd information added)

=

$pnt'=\widetilde{pnt}+1 \wedge \widetilde{nms}=nms' \wedge \forall i\in\{1,..., \widetilde{pnt}+1 -1\} . nms[i]=nms'[i] \wedge nms[pnt]=nm \wedge$

$\widetilde{pnt}+1 =pnt$

=

$\forall i\in\{1,...,\widetilde{pnt}\} . nms[i]=\widetilde{nms}[i] \wedge nms[pnt]=nm \wedge \widetilde{pnt}+1=pnt$

= post-enter2

Once the proof obligation has been fulfilled and provided the implementor of enter2a does his job correctly and similarly the implementor of enter2b, then the results combined with a "semicolon" will satisfy the original specification. Thus, the two components can be developed independently of each other, and each developer can further refine (decompose) his particular specification until the result can easily be translated into Pascal.

The operation enter2a can easily be satisfied by the following code fragment:

```
pnt := pnt+1
```

and enter2b can be satisfied by:

```
name[pnt] := nm
```

The exit2 operation can also be decomposed into two sub-specifications joined by a semi-colon.

```
exit2(nm : Name)
ext wr pnt : 0 .. M,  nms : array [1 .. M] of Name
pre    is-therea(nm, pnt,nms )
  exit2a
  ext rd  pnt : 0 .. M,
             nms : array [1 .. M] of Name,
        wr pos : N,
        rd nm : Name
    pre    is-therea(nm,pnt,nms)
  post nm=nms~[pos]
  ;
  exit2b
  ext wr pnt : 0 .. M,
             nms : array [1 .. M] of Name,
        rd pos : N,
             nm : Name
    pre  nm=nms[pos]
    post nms[pos]=nms~[pnt~] ∧ pnt=pnt~-1
  post   ∃i∈{1,...,pnt~} . nm=nms~[i] ∧
                    pnt=pnt~-1 ∧
                    nms[i]=nms~[pnt~]
```

The proof of the above is left for the reader! One of the truth valued functions in the specification above postulates the existence of a value which has a certain property ($nm=nm\bar{s}[pos]$). A function can be specified which will find that value:

```
find( nm : Name,
         pnt : 0 .. M,
         nms : array [1 .. M] of Name ) r : Bool
pre    true
post (r∈{1,...,pnt} ∧ nms[r]=nm) ∨
        (∀i∉{1,...,pnt} . nms[i]≠nm ∧ r=0)
```

The operation is-therea can be implemented in terms of it.

```
is-therea(nm : Name,
            pnt : 0 .. M,
            nms : array [1 .. M] of Name ) r : Bool
    r:=not find(nm,pnt,nms)=0
post r ⟺ ∃i∈{1,...,pnt} . nms[i]=nm
```

It may be that a specification needs to be satisfied by an iteration, the specification for find is a good example of one. In these cases a subspecification, Spec, will need to be discovered; if the implementor of Spec satisfies his specification, and the code is made the body of a while-loop, then the resultant code will satisfy the original specification.

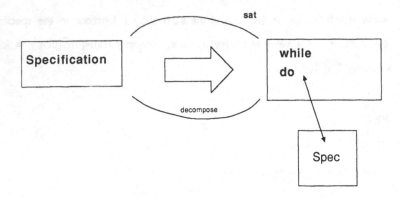

The proof obligation together with a flow chart for its derivation, as before, is:

$$\frac{\{\,P \wedge B\,\}\, S\, \{\,P \wedge R\,\}}{\{\,P\,\}\ \text{while } B \text{ do } S\ \{\,P \wedge R \wedge \neg B\,\}}$$

The writer of the new specification must find an invariant P and a transitive relation R.

There is a proof rule for the remaining "standard" construct of programming languages: if-then-else; The strategy is to find two subspecifications SpecA and SpecB that, when put together using if-then-else, will satisfy the original specification.

Decomposition Strategy

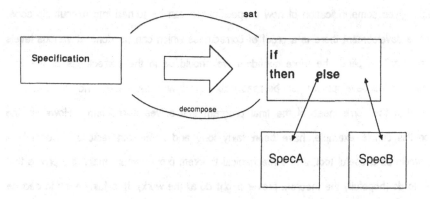

The proof rule for this case and its flow chart are:

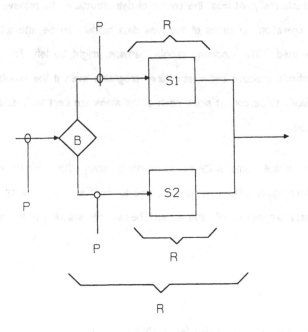

$$\frac{\{\,P \wedge B\,\}\,S1\,\{\,R\,\}, \{\,P \wedge \neg B\,\}\,S2\,\{\,R\,\}}{\{\,P\,\}\ \text{if}\ B\ \text{then}\ S1\ \text{else}\ S2\ \{\,R\,\}}$$

For an excellent introduction to proofs of correctness in general the reader is refered to [1]; and for an introduction to proves done in the style outlined above, refer to [2].

Postscript

The above example gives some indication of how a specification can be turned into executable code. For each step of the development there is a proof of correctness which can be done at various levels of detail; the more detail supplied, the more confident we should be in the correctness of the final program. Each step in the development can be reasonably small and checkable, and we should be reasonably confident in the correctness of the final program that solves a problem. However, the proofs, even for this simple example, have been fairly long and somewhat tedious. Certainly a theorem checker would be a useful tool, and a mechanical theorem prover would make the proofs that much more easier to do (hopefully the theorem prover might do all the work). It is fairly easy to deduce that for large examples "hand" proofs are going to be almost impossible. Should this be a reason for rejecting this technique? The answer is no. Certainly given a specification for a large program, it is possible do the data reifications informally. At least the choice of data structure, the retrieve function, and the re-definition of all the operations in terms of the new data model can be attempted. The adequacy proof should also be tried. The modelling proofs, perhaps, might be left. The discipline encouraged by this technique should produce better structured programs even if the proofs are not done; and programs are more likely to be correct since each of the steps are kept fairly small by the discipline enforced by the method.

It is certainly necessary to undertake some software development using these ideas, if only to understand the type of proof techniques which are needed, and to aid the developments of proper software tools. Adoption of these techniques will give a much better understanding of the science of program development.

References

[1] D. Gries, "The Science of Programming", Springer-Verlag 1981.

[2] C. B. Jones, "Systematic Software Development Using VDM", Prentice Hall International 1986.